SCHAUM'S OUTLINE OF

THEORY AND PROBLEMS

of

BUSINESS MATHEMATICS

•

by

JOEL J. LERNER, M.S., P.D.
Chairman, Faculty of Business
Sullivan County Community College

and

PETR ZIMA, M.B.A.
Professor of Business Administration
Conestoga College of Applied Arts and Technology

•

SCHAUM'S OUTLINE SERIES

McGRAW-HILL BOOK COMPANY

New York   St. Louis   San Francisco   Auckland   Bogotá   Guatemala   Hamburg   Johannesburg
Lisbon   London   Madrid   Mexico   Montreal   New Delhi   Panama   Paris
San Juan   São Paulo   Singapore   Sydney   Tokyo   Toronto

JOEL J. LERNER is Professor and Chairman of the Business Division at Sullivan County Community College, Loch Sheldrake, New York. He received his B.S. from New York University and his M.S. and P.D. from Columbia University. Professor Lerner has published a booklet for *The New York Times* on teaching college business courses and has acted as editor for both *Readings in Business Organization and Management* and *Introduction to Business: A Contemporary Reader*. He is the author of *Schaum's Outline of Bookkeeping and Accounting* and has coauthored *Schaum's Outlines of Accounting I, Accounting II*, and *Intermediate Accounting*. He is also the publisher of *The Middle/Fixed Income Advisor*, a monthly financial newsletter.

PETER ZIMA was awarded the M.Sc. by Charles University of Prague and the M.B.A. by the Prague School of Economics. He presently serves on the busines faculties of two Canadian institutions—Conestoga College and Wilfrid Laurier University—and is the author of several works in financial mathematics and operations research. He is co-author of *Schaum's Outline of Contemporary Mathematics of Finance*.

Schaum's Outline of Theory and Problems of
BUSINESS MATHEMATICS

1 2 3 4 5 6 7 8 9 10 11 12 13 14 15 16 17 18 19 20 SHP SHP 8 9 8 7 6 5 4

ISBN 0-07-037212-8

Sponsoring Editor, Elizabeth Zayatz
Editing Supervisor, Marthe Grice
Production Manager, Nick Monti

Library of Congress Cataloging in Publication Data

Lerner, Joel J.
    Schaum's outline of theory and problems of business mathematics.

    (Schaum's outline series)
    Includes index.
    1. Business mathematics.   I. Zima, Petr.   II. Title.
HF5691.L46   1984   513'.93   84-10078
ISBN 0-07-037212-8

Preface

This book brings to the study of business mathematics the same solved-problems approach which has proved so successful in other volumes of the Schaum's Outline Series. *Schaum's Outline of Business Mathematics* is organized around the practical application of mathematical concepts used in the financial world. The work that is presented in the following pages will provide students with

1. concise definitions and explanations in easily understood terms with illustrative examples

2. fully worked-out solutions to a large range of problems (against which students can check their own solutions)

3. supplementary problems

The primary purpose of this book is to increase the student's competency in the mathematical computation of practical business problems. However, the student need not fear the mathematics involved. It is presented here in an easy-to-understand, readable way, and if the student is willing to expend a little time and effort, he or she will be rewarded with basic knowledge of the field of business mathematics.

JOEL J. LERNER
PETR ZIMA

Contents

CONTENTS

Chapter 1

Review of Arithmetic

1.1 OPERATIONS WITH WHOLE NUMBERS AND DECIMAL FRACTIONS

Addition is the process of combining two or more numbers into a single number called the *sum*. When adding numbers, proper alignment of the digits is important. Whole numbers are aligned on the rightmost digit. Decimal fractions are aligned on the decimal point. Addition may be checked by adding the numbers in reverse order.

EXAMPLE 1

What is the sum of 234, 4,978, 15, and 369?

Note the numbers carried over

```
           1 12      ⟵ Note alignment
           234
         4,978
            15
           369        To check, add from the bottom up
         ───────
         5,596
```
thousands hundreds tens ones

The numbers printed in small type at the top have been carried over from the previous column. If we add the rightmost column, we have

$$4 + 8 + 5 + 9 = 26$$

The two 10s in 26 are carried over to and written on top of the tens column so that we remember to add them. Likewise, we carry over to the hundreds column any hundreds from the addition of the tens column, and so on.

To check the addition, add the numbers in each column in reverse order, that is, from the bottom (above the line) up. If we do this for the rightmost column, we have

$$9 + 5 + 8 + 4 = 26$$

The addition of decimal fractions is carried out in the same manner as for whole numbers, except that we first line up the numbers on the decimal point.

```
              Line up on decimal point
                        ↓
Carried over ⟶  2 1
                      .21
                     7.05
                    28.70
                     9.11       Check
                   ────────
                   45.07
```

Subtraction is the process of finding the *difference* between two numbers. Since subtraction is the opposite operation of addition, the answer may be checked by adding the answer to the number subtracted.

1

2

EXAMPLE 2

What is the difference between 279.15 and 161.03?

Note alignment

$$\begin{array}{r} 279.15 \\ -161.03 \\ \hline 118.12 \end{array}$$ To check, add these two numbers; their sum should equal the top number

$$\begin{array}{r} 161.03 \\ +118.12 \\ \hline 279.15 \end{array}$$

Multiplication is a shortened form of repetitive addition. The numbers multiplied are called the *factors*, and the result of multiplication is called the *product*. Multiplication may be checked by changing the order of the factors.

When multiplying decimal fractions, we insert the decimal point in the product according to the following rule:

> A product has as many decimal places as the sum of decimal places in the factors.

EXAMPLE 3

(*a*) 7 times 5 is the same as adding five 7s (or seven 5s).

$$\begin{array}{r} 7 \\ \times 5 \\ \hline 35 \end{array}$$ Factors
Product → 35

$$\begin{array}{r} 7 \\ 7 \\ 7 \\ 7 \\ 7 \\ \hline 35 \end{array} \quad or \quad \begin{array}{r} 5 \\ 5 \\ 5 \\ 5 \\ 5 \\ 5 \\ 5 \\ \hline 35 \end{array}$$

To check the multiplication, reverse the factors:

$$\begin{array}{r} 5 \\ \times 7 \\ \hline 35 \end{array}$$

(*b*)

$$\begin{array}{r} 18.7 \\ \times 2.15 \\ \hline 9\,35 \\ 1\,87 \\ 37\,4 \\ \hline 40.2\,05 \end{array}$$

The sum of decimal places is 3

9 35 ← 187 × 5
1 87 ← 187 × 1
37 4 ← 187 × 2

Count off three places from the right and insert decimal point

To check the multiplication, reverse the factors and multiply:

$$\begin{array}{r} 2.1\,5 \\ \times 1\,8.7 \\ \hline 1\,5\,0\,5 \\ 17\,2\,0 \\ 21\,5 \\ \hline 40.2\,0\,5 \end{array}$$

1 5 0 5 ← 215 × 7
17 2 0 ← 215 × 8
21 5 ← 215 × 1

When multiplying by 10, 100, 1,000, etc., add as many zeros after a whole number as there are zeros in the multiplier. If the number being multiplied is a decimal fraction, move the decimal point to the *right* by the number of zeros in the multiplier. When multiplying by 0.1, 0.01, 0.001, etc., count the number of places that the 1 is from the decimal point and then move the decimal point in the number being multiplied that many places to the *left*.

EXAMPLE 4

Multiplier has two 0s

$$25 \times 100 = 2{,}500$$

Add two 0s to number being multiplied

Multiplier has one 0

$$1.358 \times 10 = 13.58$$

Move decimal point one place to the right

The numeral 1 is three places to the right of the decimal point

$$1{,}836 \times 0.001 = 1.836$$

Move decimal point three places to the left

The numeral 1 is two places to the right of the decimal point

$$72.01 \times 0.01 = 0.7201$$

Move decimal point two places to the left

Division is the inverse process of multiplication and as such, it is a form of repetitive subtraction. The number to be divided is the *dividend*, the number divided by is the *divisor*, and the result of division is the *quotient*. If the divisor does not divide evenly into the dividend, the part left over is the *remainder*. The remainder may be shown as part of the quotient either as a common fraction or as a decimal fraction. Division may be checked by multiplying the quotient by the divisor and adding any remainder to obtain the dividend.

When dividing by 10, 100, 1,000, etc., move the decimal point in the dividend to the *left* by as many places as there are zeros in the divisor. When dividing by 0.1, 0.01, 0.001, etc., move the decimal point in the dividend to the *right* by the number of places the digit "1" is from the decimal point. Example 5 illustrates division of whole numbers and decimal fractions.

EXAMPLE 5

(*a*) Divide 5,129 by 14.

$$
\begin{array}{r}
366 \quad \leftarrow \text{Quotient} \\
\text{Divisor} \rightarrow 14) \overline{5{,}129} \quad \leftarrow \text{Dividend} \\
-42 \quad \leftarrow 14 \times 3 \\
\overline{92} \\
-84 \quad \leftarrow 14 \times 6 \\
\overline{89} \\
-84 \quad \leftarrow 14 \times 6 \\
\overline{5} \quad \leftarrow \text{Remainder}
\end{array}
$$

The answer may be written as $366\frac{5}{14}$. To check your answer, multiply the quotient by the divisor and add any remainder. The result should equal the dividend.

$$
\begin{array}{r}
366 \quad \leftarrow\text{Quotient} \\
\times 14 \quad \leftarrow\text{Divisor} \\
\hline
1{,}464 \\
3\ 66 \\
\hline
5{,}124 \\
+5 \quad \leftarrow\text{Remainder} \\
\hline
5{,}129 \quad \leftarrow\text{Dividend}
\end{array}
$$

(b) Divide 1.44 by 12.

   The dividend is a decimal fraction, so you must align the decimal point in the quotient with the decimal point of the dividend.

Insert and align decimal point

$$
\begin{array}{r}
0.12 \\
12\overline{)\,1.44} \\
-1\ 2 \\
\hline
24 \\
-24 \\
\hline
0
\end{array}
$$

Check:

$$
\begin{array}{r}
0.12 \\
\times 12 \\
\hline
24 \\
1\ 2 \\
\hline
1.44
\end{array}
$$

(c) Divide 144 by 0.12.

   To divide a whole number by a decimal fraction, make the divisor a whole number by moving the decimal point to the right. To keep the value of the dividend proportionately equal, move its decimal point to the right the same number of places by adding zeros.

$$
\begin{array}{r}
12\ 00. \\
0.12\overline{)\,144.00} \\
-12 \\
\hline
24 \\
-24 \\
\hline
0
\end{array}
$$

In divisor and dividend, move decimal point the same number of places to the right, until divisor is a whole number

Check:

$$
\begin{array}{r}
1{,}2\ 00 \\
\times 0.12 \\
\hline
2\ 4\ 00 \\
1\ 2\ 0\ 0 \\
\hline
1\ 4\ 4.00
\end{array}
$$

(d) Divide 1.44 by 1.2.

Insert and align decimal point

Make divisor a whole number by moving decimal point to the right

$$
\begin{array}{r}
1.2 \\
1.2\overline{)\,1.4\,4} \\
-1\ 2 \\
\hline
2\ 4 \\
-2\ 4 \\
\hline
0
\end{array}
$$

Move the decimal point in the dividend the same number of places to the right as was done in the divisor

Check:

$$
\begin{array}{r}
1.2 \\
\times 1.2 \\
\hline
2\ 4 \\
1\ 2 \\
\hline
1.4\ 4
\end{array}
$$

SOLVED PROBLEMS

1.1   Add 548, 3,217, 85, 317.

   SOLUTION

   Numbers carried over → ₁₁₂

```
          548  ↑
        3,217  |
           85  |
          317  |   Check by adding from bottom to top
        ------
        4,167
```

1.2   A deposit slip has the following entries: currency, $284.00; coins, $12.83; and checks for $182.51, $1,803.37, and $47.18. Find the total deposit.

   SOLUTION

   Numbers carried over → 1 2 11 1

```
        $  284.00  ↑
            12.83  |
           182.51  |
         1,803.37  |
            47.18  |   Check
        ---------
        $2,329.89
```

1.3   Subtract $218.87 from $756.25.

   SOLUTION

```
        $  756.25        Check:  $  537.38
         - 218.87                + 218.87
        ---------                ---------
        $  537.38                $  756.25
```

1.4   The owner of an apartment building received cash rentals totaling $7,825.75. During the same period she had the following cash expenses: taxes, $818.21; utilities, $1,675.83; repairs, $389.17; insurance, $217.50; interest, $3,815.35; and miscellaneous, $183.74. Find the owner's net cash flow from rentals.

   SOLUTION

```
Add expenses:  $  818.21      Subtract:
                1,675.83      Rentals        $  7,825.75
                  389.17      Less expenses   - 7,099.80
                  217.50      Net cash flow  $     725.95
                3,815.35
                  183.74
               ---------
               $7,099.80
```

1.5   Find the product of 213 and 52 and check the answer.

   SOLUTION

```
                                    Check:        52
           213                                  × 213
          × 52                                  -----
          ----                                    156  ← 52 × 3
           426  ← 213 × 2                          52  ← 52 × 1
         1 0 65  ← 213 × 5                       10 4   ← 52 × 2
        -------                                -------
        1 1,076  ← Product                     11,076  ← Product
```

1.6   Multiply 31.3 by 2.18.

SOLUTION

$$
\begin{array}{r}
3\,1.3 \quad \leftarrow \text{one decimal place} \\
\times 2.1\,8 \quad \leftarrow \text{two decimal places} \\
\hline
2\,5\,0\,4 \quad \leftarrow 313 \times 8 \\
3\,1\,3 \quad\;\; \leftarrow 313 \times 1 \\
62\,6 \quad\quad \leftarrow 313 \times 2 \\
\hline
68.2\,3\,4
\end{array}
$$

$\}$ three decimal places total

Count off three decimal places from the right and insert decimal point

1.7   Multiply 26.48 by (*a*) 100, (*b*) 1,000, (*c*) 0.01, (*d*) 0.0001.

SOLUTION

(*a*) $26.48 \times 100 = 26.48$ Move the decimal point two places to the right

(*b*) $26.48 \times 1{,}000 = 26.480$ Move the decimal point three places to the right

(*c*) $26.48 \times 0.01 = 0\,26.48$ Move the decimal point two places to the left

(*d*) $26.48 \times 0.0001 = 0\,0026.48$ Move the decimal point four places to the left

1.8   Divide 381 by 21, and check your answer.

SOLUTION

$$
\begin{array}{r}
18 \quad \leftarrow \text{Quotient} \\
\text{Divisor} \rightarrow 21\overline{)381} \quad \leftarrow \text{Dividend} \\
21 \quad\quad \\
\hline
171 \\
168 \\
\hline
3 \quad \leftarrow \text{Remainder}
\end{array}
$$

Check:
$$
\begin{array}{r}
18 \quad \leftarrow \text{Quotient} \\
\times 21 \quad \leftarrow \text{Divisor} \\
\hline
18 \\
36 \quad\; \\
\hline
378 \\
+\,3 \quad \leftarrow \text{Remainder} \\
\hline
381 \quad \leftarrow \text{Dividend}
\end{array}
$$

Thus $\dfrac{381}{21} = 18\dfrac{3}{21} = 18\dfrac{1}{7}$

1.9   Divide (*a*) 21.84 by 14 and (*b*) 2.184 by 3.12.

SOLUTION

(*a*)
$$
\begin{array}{r}
1.56 \\
14\overline{)21.84} \\
14 \quad\quad \\
\hline
78 \\
70 \\
\hline
84 \\
84 \\
\hline
0
\end{array}
$$

If the divisor is a whole number, the decimal point in the quotient is located directly over the decimal point in the dividend

(*b*)
$$
\begin{array}{r}
0.7 \\
3.12\overline{)2.18\,4} \\
2\,18\,4 \\
\hline
0
\end{array}
$$

If the divisor has decimals, move the decimal point in both divisor and dividend as many places to the right as needed to change the divisor into a whole number (two places in this problem)

1.10	Divide 4.82 by (*a*) 100, (*b*) 10,000, (*c*) 0.1, (*d*) 0.001.

> **SOLUTION**
>
> (*a*)	$4.82 \div 100 = 0.04.82$	Move the decimal point two places to the left
>
> (*b*)	$4.82 \div 10,000 = 0.0004.82$	Move the decimal point four places to the left
>
> (*c*)	$4.82 \div 0.1 = 4.8.2$	Move the decimal point one place to the right
>
> (*d*)	$4.82 \div 0.001 = 4.820.$	Move the decimal point three places to the right

1.2 OPERATIONS WITH COMMON FRACTIONS AND MIXED NUMBERS

Division of two whole numbers may be written in fractional form. The dividend, called the *numerator*, is written above the fraction line and the divisor, called the *denominator*, is written below the fraction line.

Fractions other than decimal fractions are known as *common fractions*. A *proper fraction* is one in which the numerator is less than the denominator, such as $\frac{4}{7}$. An *improper fraction* is one in which the numerator is equal to or greater than the denominator, such as $\frac{9}{9}$, $\frac{11}{8}$. A *complex fraction* is a fraction in which the numerator or denominator, or both, are fractions, such as $\frac{1}{3}/(\frac{1}{2} - \frac{1}{5})$. A *mixed number* is a whole number and a fraction, such as $8\frac{3}{4}$.

Multiplying or dividing both numerator and denominator by the same number does not change the value of the fraction and results in an *equivalent fraction*. Thus $\frac{1}{3} = \frac{2}{6}$ or $\frac{3}{9}$ or $\frac{4}{12}$ (the multipliers are 2, 3, and 4, respectively) and $\frac{24}{32} = \frac{12}{16}$ or $\frac{6}{8}$ or $\frac{3}{4}$ (the divisors are 2, 4, and 8, respectively). A fraction is in lowest terms when there is no number other than 1 that will divide evenly into both the numerator and the denominator. For example, $\frac{24}{32}$ in lowest terms is $\frac{3}{4}$.

To add or subtract common fractions that have the same denominator, we add or subtract the numerators of the various fractions and retain the common denominator. To add or subtract fractions that do not have the same denominator, we must change the fractions to equivalent fractions that have a common denominator.

EXAMPLE 6

(*a*)

$$\underbrace{\frac{3}{18} + \frac{11}{18} + \frac{1}{18}}_{\text{Add numerators}} = \frac{15}{18} \left(= \frac{5}{6} \right) \xleftarrow{\frac{15 \div 3}{18 \div 3}}$$

Retain common denominator

(*b*)

$$\frac{2}{5} + \frac{1}{4} =$$

1.	Find the least common denominator. The lowest number that can be evenly divided by both 4 and 5 is 20.

2.	Change the fractions into equivalent fractions with a common denominator by multiplying the numerator and denominator of both by 20 as follows:

$$20 \div 4 = 5 \longrightarrow \quad \frac{2 \times \frac{4}{20}}{\frac{5}{1} \times 20} + \frac{1 \times \frac{5}{20}}{\frac{4}{1} \times 20} = \frac{8}{20} + \frac{5}{20}$$

Equivalent to $\frac{2}{5}$

Equivalent to $\frac{1}{4}$

$$20 \div 5 = 4$$

3.	Add the numerators and retain the common denominator:

$$\frac{8}{20} + \frac{5}{20} = \frac{13}{20}$$

Therefore
$$\frac{2}{5} + \frac{1}{4} = \frac{13}{20}$$

To multiply two or more common fractions, multiply the numerators to obtain the numerator of the product and multiply the denominators to obtain the denominator of the product.

To divide one common fraction by another one, multiply the dividend by the reciprocal (formed by reversing numerator and denominator) of the divisor.

EXAMPLE 7

(a)
$$\frac{7}{9} \times \frac{4}{5} = \frac{7 \times 4}{9 \times 5} = \frac{28}{45}$$

(b)
$$\frac{7}{9} \div \frac{4}{5} = \frac{7}{9} \times \frac{5}{4} = \frac{7 \times 5}{9 \times 4} = \frac{35}{36}$$

One way to add, subtract, multiply, or divide mixed numbers is to first convert them into improper fractions. Addition or subtraction of mixed numbers may also be performed by combining the whole number parts and the fractional parts separately.

EXAMPLE 8

(a) To convert a mixed number into an improper fraction
1. Write the mixed number as a sum:
$$4\frac{1}{2} = 4 + \frac{1}{2}$$

2. Write the whole number as an improper fraction with a denominator of 1:
$$\frac{4}{1} + \frac{1}{2}$$

3. Change the improper fraction to an equivalent fraction with the same denominator as the original fractional part of the mixed number:
$$\frac{4}{1} + \frac{1}{2} = \frac{4}{1}\left(\frac{2}{2}\right) + \frac{1}{2} = \frac{8}{2} + \frac{1}{2}$$

4. Add the two fractions:
$$\frac{8}{2} + \frac{1}{2} = \frac{9}{2}$$

Therefore
$$4\frac{1}{2} = \frac{9}{2}$$

A shortcut to this procedure is to multiply the whole number by the denominator and add it to the numerator:
$$4\frac{1}{2} = \frac{(4 \times 2) + 1}{2} = \frac{8 + 1}{2} = \frac{9}{2}$$

(b) Add $4\frac{1}{2}$ and $3\frac{5}{8}$

    1. Convert the mixed numbers into improper fractions:

$$4\frac{1}{2} + 3\frac{5}{8} = \frac{9}{2} + \frac{29}{8}$$

    2. Change the improper fractions to equivalent fractions with a common denominator:

$$\frac{9}{2} + \frac{29}{8} = \frac{9}{2}\left(\frac{4}{4}\right) + \frac{29}{8} = \frac{36}{8} + \frac{29}{8}$$

    3. Add the fractions by adding the numerators and retaining the common denominator:

$$\frac{36}{8} + \frac{39}{8} = \frac{65}{8}$$

    4. Convert the improper fraction to a mixed number by dividing the denominator into the numerator and expressing the remainder as a fraction:

$$\frac{65}{8} = 8\frac{1}{8}$$

$$\begin{array}{r} 8 \\ 8)\overline{65} \\ -64 \\ \hline 1 \end{array}$$

Alternative solution:

The addition may also be carried out by adding the whole and fractional parts separately.

$$\begin{array}{r} 4\dfrac{1}{2} \\ +3\dfrac{5}{8} \end{array}$$ ← Change fractional parts to equivalent fractions with a common denominator

$$\begin{array}{r} 4\dfrac{4}{8} \\ +3\dfrac{5}{8} \\ \hline 7\dfrac{9}{8} \end{array} = 7 + \frac{9}{8} = 7 + 1\frac{1}{8} = 8\frac{1}{8}$$

Convert improper fraction to mixed number and add

SOLVED PROBLEMS

1.11 Reduce (a) $\dfrac{36}{48}$, (b) $\dfrac{33}{120}$, (c) $\dfrac{75}{625}$, and (d) $\dfrac{105}{126}$ to lowest terms.

    SOLUTION

    (a) $\dfrac{36}{48} = \dfrac{36 \div 12}{48 \div 12} = \dfrac{3}{4}$ Highest common factor of 36 and 48 is 12

    (b) $\dfrac{33}{120} = \dfrac{33 \div 3}{120 \div 3} = \dfrac{11}{40}$ Highest common factor of 33 and 120 is 3

    (c) $\dfrac{75}{625} = \dfrac{75 \div 25}{625 \div 25} = \dfrac{3}{25}$ Highest common factor of 75 and 625 is 25

    (d) $\dfrac{105}{126} = \dfrac{105 \div 21}{126 \div 21} = \dfrac{5}{6}$ Highest common factor of 105 and 126 is 21

1.12 Simplify (a) $\dfrac{4}{25}+\dfrac{13}{25}+\dfrac{2}{25}$, (b) $\dfrac{7}{13}-\dfrac{4}{13}$, and (c) $\dfrac{9}{5}-\dfrac{3}{5}+\dfrac{2}{5}-\dfrac{4}{5}$.

SOLUTION

(a)
$$\frac{4}{25}+\frac{13}{25}+\frac{2}{25}=\frac{4+13+2}{25}=\frac{19}{25}\ \leftarrow\text{Add the numerators}$$
$$\phantom{\frac{4}{25}+\frac{13}{25}+\frac{2}{25}=\frac{4+13+2}{25}=\frac{19}{25}}\ \leftarrow\text{Retain the common denominator}$$

(b)
$$\frac{7}{13}-\frac{4}{13}=\frac{7-4}{13}=\frac{3}{13}\ \leftarrow\text{Subtract the numerators}$$
$$\phantom{\frac{7}{13}-\frac{4}{13}=\frac{7-4}{13}=\frac{3}{13}}\ \leftarrow\text{Retain the common denominator}$$

(c)
$$\frac{9}{5}-\frac{3}{5}+\frac{2}{5}-\frac{4}{5}=\frac{9-3+2-4}{5}=\frac{4}{5}\ \leftarrow\text{Combine the numerators}$$
$$\phantom{\frac{9}{5}-\frac{3}{5}+\frac{2}{5}-\frac{4}{5}=\frac{9-3+2-4}{5}=\frac{4}{5}}\ \leftarrow\text{Retain the common denominator}$$

1.13 Simplify (a) $\dfrac{2}{3}+\dfrac{3}{2}$, (b) $\dfrac{3}{4}-\dfrac{1}{3}$, and (c) $\dfrac{1}{2}-\dfrac{2}{5}+\dfrac{3}{4}-\dfrac{4}{12}$.

SOLUTION

(a)
$$\frac{2}{3}+\frac{3}{2}=\frac{4}{6}+\frac{9}{6}\ \leftarrow\text{Change to equivalent fractions}$$
$$\phantom{\frac{2}{3}+\frac{3}{2}=\frac{4}{6}+\frac{9}{6}}\ \ \text{with the least common denominator}$$
$$=\frac{4+9}{6}=\frac{13}{6}\ \leftarrow\text{Add the numerators}$$
$$\phantom{=\frac{4+9}{6}=\frac{13}{6}}\ \leftarrow\text{Retain the common denominator}$$

(b)
$$\frac{3}{4}-\frac{1}{3}=\frac{9}{12}-\frac{4}{12}\ \leftarrow\text{Change to equivalent fractions}$$
$$\phantom{\frac{3}{4}-\frac{1}{3}=\frac{9}{12}-\frac{4}{12}}\ \ \text{with the least common denominator}$$
$$=\frac{9-4}{12}=\frac{5}{12}\ \leftarrow\text{Subtract the numerators}$$
$$\phantom{=\frac{9-4}{12}=\frac{5}{12}}\ \leftarrow\text{Retain the common denominator}$$

(c)
$$\frac{1}{2}-\frac{2}{5}+\frac{3}{4}-\frac{4}{12}=\frac{30}{60}-\frac{24}{60}+\frac{45}{60}-\frac{20}{60}\ \leftarrow\text{Change to equivalent}$$
$$\phantom{\frac{1}{2}-\frac{2}{5}+\frac{3}{4}-\frac{4}{12}=\frac{30}{60}-\frac{24}{60}+\frac{45}{60}-\frac{20}{60}}\ \ \text{fractions with the}$$
$$\phantom{\frac{1}{2}-\frac{2}{5}+\frac{3}{4}-\frac{4}{12}=\frac{30}{60}-\frac{24}{60}+\frac{45}{60}-\frac{20}{60}}\ \ \text{least common denominator}$$
$$=\frac{30-24+45-20}{60}=\frac{31}{60}\ \leftarrow\text{Combine the numerators}$$
$$\phantom{=\frac{30-24+45-20}{60}=\frac{31}{60}}\ \leftarrow\text{Retain the common}$$
$$\phantom{=\frac{30-24+45-20}{60}=\frac{31}{60}}\ \ \text{denominator}$$

1.14 Multiply (a) $\dfrac{3}{4}\times\dfrac{3}{2}$, (b) $\dfrac{2}{3}\times\dfrac{5}{6}\times\dfrac{3}{4}$, and (c) $\dfrac{4}{9}\times\dfrac{3}{8}\times\dfrac{27}{18}$.

SOLUTION

(a)
$$\frac{3}{4}\times\frac{3}{2}=\frac{3\times 3}{4\times 2}=\frac{9}{8}$$

(b)
$$\frac{2}{3}\times\frac{5}{6}\times\frac{3}{4}=\frac{\overset{1}{\cancel{2}}\times 5\times\overset{1}{\cancel{3}}}{\underset{1}{\cancel{3}}\times 6\times\underset{2}{\cancel{4}}}\ \leftarrow\text{Reduce the numerator and}$$
$$\phantom{\frac{2}{3}\times\frac{5}{6}\times\frac{3}{4}=\frac{2\times 5\times 3}{3\times 6\times 4}}\ \ \text{the denominator to keep}$$
$$\phantom{\frac{2}{3}\times\frac{5}{6}\times\frac{3}{4}=\frac{2\times 5\times 3}{3\times 6\times 4}}\ \ \text{the numbers low}$$
$$=\frac{1\times 5\times 1}{1\times 6\times 2}=\frac{5}{12}$$

(c)
$$\frac{4}{9}\times\frac{3}{8}\times\frac{27}{18}=\frac{\overset{1}{\cancel{4}}\times\overset{1}{\cancel{3}}\times\overset{3}{\cancel{27}}}{\underset{1}{\cancel{9}}\times\underset{2}{\cancel{8}}\times\underset{6}{\cancel{18}}}\ \leftarrow\text{Reduce the numerator}$$
$$\phantom{\frac{4}{9}\times\frac{3}{8}\times\frac{27}{18}=\frac{4\times 3\times 27}{9\times 8\times 18}}\ \ \text{and the denominator}$$
$$=\frac{1\times 1\times 3}{1\times 2\times 6}=\frac{3}{12}=\frac{1}{4}\ \leftarrow\text{Reduce to lowest terms}$$

1.15 Simplify (a) $\dfrac{9}{12}\div\dfrac{30}{24}$, (b) $\dfrac{6}{15}\div\dfrac{2}{10}$, and (c) $\dfrac{7}{12}\times\dfrac{8}{3}\div\dfrac{35}{20}$.

SOLUTION

(a)
$$\frac{9}{12} \div \frac{30}{24} = \frac{\overset{3}{\cancel{9}}}{\underset{1}{\cancel{12}}} \times \frac{\overset{2}{\cancel{24}}}{\underset{10}{\cancel{30}}} = \frac{3 \times \overset{1}{\cancel{2}}}{1 \times \underset{5}{\cancel{10}}} = \frac{3 \times 1}{1 \times 5} = \frac{3}{5}$$

(b)
$$\frac{6}{15} \div \frac{2}{10} = \frac{\overset{2}{\cancel{6}}}{\underset{5}{\cancel{15}}} \times \frac{\overset{5}{\cancel{10}}}{\underset{1}{\cancel{2}}} = \frac{2 \times \overset{1}{\cancel{5}}}{\cancel{5} \times 1} = \frac{2 \times 1}{1 \times 1} = 2$$

(c)
$$\frac{7}{12} \times \frac{8}{3} \div \frac{35}{20} = \frac{7}{12} \times \frac{8}{3} \times \frac{\overset{4}{\cancel{20}}}{\underset{7}{\cancel{35}}} = \frac{\overset{1}{\cancel{7}} \times 8 \times \overset{1}{\cancel{4}}}{\underset{3}{\cancel{12}} \times 3 \times \underset{1}{\cancel{7}}} = \frac{1 \times 8 \times 1}{3 \times 3 \times 1} = \frac{8}{9}$$

1.16 Convert (a) $3\frac{1}{8}$ and (b) $5\frac{2}{3}$ to common fractions.

SOLUTION

(a)
$$3\frac{1}{8} = 3 + \frac{1}{8} \leftarrow \text{Write the mixed number as a sum}$$
$$= \frac{3}{1} + \frac{1}{8} \leftarrow \text{Write the whole number as an improper}$$
$$\qquad\qquad\quad \text{fraction with denominator 1 and}$$
$$= \frac{24}{8} + \frac{1}{8} \quad \text{change to equivalent fractions with}$$
$$\qquad\qquad\quad \text{the least common denominator}$$
$$= \frac{25}{8}$$

(b)
$$5\frac{2}{3} = 5 + \frac{2}{3} = \frac{5}{1} + \frac{2}{3} = \frac{15}{3} + \frac{2}{3} = \frac{17}{3}$$

1.17 Simplify (a) $3\frac{2}{3} + 2\frac{1}{8}$ and (b) $6\frac{4}{5} - 2\frac{3}{10} + 4\frac{5}{6}$; show your answer as a mixed number.

SOLUTION

(a)
$$3\frac{2}{3} + 2\frac{1}{8} = \frac{11}{3} + \frac{17}{8} \leftarrow \text{Convert the mixed numbers}$$
$$\qquad\qquad\qquad\qquad \text{into improper fractions and}$$
$$\qquad\qquad = \frac{88}{24} + \frac{51}{24} \quad \text{change to equivalent fractions}$$
$$\qquad\qquad\qquad\qquad \text{with the least common denominator}$$
$$\qquad\qquad = \frac{139}{24} = 5\frac{19}{24} \leftarrow \text{Convert the improper fraction}$$
$$\qquad\qquad\qquad\qquad\qquad \text{into a mixed number}$$

Alternative solution:

$$\begin{array}{r} 3\dfrac{2}{3} \\ +\,2\dfrac{1}{8} \end{array} \leftarrow \text{Convert to equivalent fractions with common denominator}$$

$$\begin{array}{r} 3\dfrac{16}{24} \\[4pt] +\,2\dfrac{3}{24} \\[4pt] \hline 5\dfrac{19}{24} \end{array}$$

(b)
$$6\frac{4}{5} - 2\frac{3}{10} + 4\frac{5}{6} = \frac{34}{5} - \frac{23}{10} + \frac{29}{6} = \frac{204}{30} - \frac{69}{30} + \frac{145}{30} = \frac{280}{30} = \frac{28}{3} = 9\frac{1}{3}$$

Alternative solution:

$$
\begin{array}{r}
6\ \dfrac{4}{5} \\[4pt]
-2\ \dfrac{3}{10} \\[4pt]
+4\ \dfrac{5}{6}
\end{array}
\quad\leftarrow\text{Convert to equivalent fractions with common denominator}
$$

$$
\text{Subtract}\left\{
\begin{array}{r}
6\ \dfrac{24}{30} \\[4pt]
-2\ \dfrac{9}{30} \\[4pt]
+4\ \dfrac{25}{30}
\end{array}
\right\}
\quad
\left.
\begin{array}{r}
4\ \dfrac{15}{30}
\end{array}
\right\}\text{Add}
$$

$$
8\ \dfrac{4\!\!\!/\,0}{3\!\!\!/\,0}\;=8+1\dfrac{1}{3}=9\dfrac{1}{3}
$$

Reduce to lowest
terms and convert
to mixed number

1.18   Simplify (a) $2\frac{1}{4}\times 3\frac{2}{3}$, (b) $15\frac{3}{4}\div 5\frac{1}{8}$, and (c) $3\frac{1}{5}\times 2\frac{1}{4}\div 5$; show your answer as a mixed number.

SOLUTION

(a)
$$2\frac{1}{4}\times 3\frac{2}{3}=\frac{9}{4}\times\frac{11}{3}\quad\leftarrow\text{Convert the mixed numbers into}$$
$$\text{improper fractions and find the product}$$
$$=\frac{99}{12}\quad\leftarrow\text{Convert the improper fraction}$$
$$\text{into a mixed number}$$
$$=8\frac{3}{12}=8\frac{1}{4}$$

(b)
$$15\frac{3}{4}\div 5\frac{1}{8}=\frac{63}{4}\div\frac{41}{8}\quad\leftarrow\text{Convert the mixed numbers}$$
$$\text{into improper fractions}$$
$$=\frac{63}{\overset{}{\underset{1}{4}}}\times\frac{\overset{2}{8}}{41}\quad\leftarrow\text{Convert the division into}$$
$$\text{a multiplication and reduce}$$
$$=\frac{63}{1}\times\frac{2}{41}\quad\leftarrow\text{Find the product}$$
$$=\frac{126}{41}\quad\leftarrow\text{Convert the improper fraction}$$
$$\text{into a mixed number}$$
$$=3\frac{3}{41}$$

(c)
$$3\frac{1}{5}\times 2\frac{1}{4}\div 5=\frac{16}{5}\times\frac{9}{\overset{}{\underset{1}{4}}}\times\frac{1}{5}=\frac{4\times 9\times 1}{5\times 1\times 5}=\frac{36}{25}=1\frac{11}{25}$$

1.19   A man left one-third of his estate to his widow, one-fifth to each of his three children, and the remainder to his church. What fraction of the estate did his church receive?

SOLUTION

Widow: $\dfrac{1}{3}$

Three children:

$$3\times\frac{1}{5}=\frac{3}{5}\left.\right\}
\quad
\begin{array}{r}\dfrac{1}{3}\\[4pt]+\dfrac{3}{5}\end{array}
\quad\rightarrow\quad
\begin{array}{r}\dfrac{5}{15}\\[4pt]+\dfrac{9}{15}\\[2pt]\hline \dfrac{14}{15}\end{array}$$

Total estate: $1 = \dfrac{15}{15}$

Amount to church:

$$\dfrac{15}{15} \quad \leftarrow \text{Total estate}$$

$$-\dfrac{14}{15} \quad \leftarrow \text{Amount to widow and children}$$

$$\dfrac{1}{15}$$

1.20 The opening price of a stock was $28\frac{3}{8}$ and the closing price was $35\frac{1}{4}$. Find the net gain in price.

SOLUTION

$$\begin{array}{c} 35\frac{1}{4} \\ -28\frac{3}{8} \\ \hline \end{array} \rightarrow \begin{array}{c} 35\frac{2}{8} \\ -28\frac{3}{8} \\ \hline \end{array} \rightarrow \begin{array}{c} 34 + 1 + \frac{2}{8} \\ -28\frac{3}{8} \\ \hline \end{array} \rightarrow$$

$$\begin{array}{c} 34 + \frac{8}{8} + \frac{2}{8} \\ -28\frac{3}{8} \\ \hline \end{array} \rightarrow \begin{array}{c} 34 + \frac{10}{8} \\ -28\frac{3}{8} \\ \hline \end{array} \rightarrow \begin{array}{c} 34\frac{10}{8} \\ -28\frac{3}{8} \\ \hline 6\frac{7}{8} \end{array}$$

1.21 Find the total dollar value of 22 shares of stock at $27\frac{3}{8}$ per share and 16 shares of stock at $39\frac{5}{8}$.

SOLUTION

$$22 \times 27\frac{3}{8} + 16 \times 39\frac{5}{8} = \overset{11}{\cancel{22}} \times \dfrac{219}{\underset{4}{\cancel{8}}} + \overset{2}{\cancel{16}} \times \dfrac{317}{\underset{1}{\cancel{8}}}$$

$$= \dfrac{2{,}409}{4} + 634 = 602\frac{1}{4} + 634$$

$$= \$1{,}236\frac{1}{4} \quad \text{or} \quad \$1{,}236.25$$

1.3   COMMON FRACTIONS AND DECIMAL FRACTIONS

To convert a common fraction into a decimal fraction divide the numerator by the denominator to the desired number of decimal places (or until the decimal terminates). When expressed as decimals, some common fractions do not terminate but continue repeating and are referred to as *repeating decimals*. Repeating decimals are designated by a dot or short bar over the repeating numeral(s) ($1.333\ldots = 1.\dot{3}$ and $0.242424\ldots = .\overline{24}$).

To convert a mixed number to a decimal fraction, change the fractional part of the mixed number to its decimal equivalent and then add this equivalent to the whole number part of the mixed number.

To convert a decimal fraction to a common fraction write the decimal in fraction form with denominator of 10, 100, 1,000, etc., as required by the number of decimal digits, and reduce the fraction to lowest term.

EXAMPLE 9

(*a*) Convert to decimal fractions.

$$\dfrac{17}{53} = 17 \div 53 \cong 0.3207547 \qquad \qquad \dfrac{430}{8} = 430 \div 8 = 53.75$$

Convert to decimal ($5 \div 9 = 0.555\ldots$) and add to whole number

$$7\underset{\downarrow}{\left(\tfrac{5}{9}\right)} = 7.555\ldots = 7.\dot{5}$$

(b)   Convert to a common fraction.

$$\overset{\text{Two decimal places}}{0.\overset{\displaystyle\frown}{48}} = 48 \text{ hundredths} = 0.48 \times \frac{100}{100} = \frac{48}{100} = \frac{12}{25}$$

$$\underset{\text{Two 0s}}{\underbrace{}} \qquad \underset{\text{Reduce } \frac{48 \div 4}{100 \div 4} = \frac{12}{25}}{}$$

SOLVED PROBLEMS

1.22   Convert (a) 3/8, (b) 11/20, and (c) 5/6 into decimal fractions. Work to the nearest thousandth.

SOLUTION

(a)
$$\frac{3}{8} = 3 \div 8 = 0.375$$

(b)
$$\frac{11}{20} = 11 \div 20 = 0.550$$

(c)
$$\frac{5}{6} = 5 \div 6 = 0.8333\ldots = 0.8\dot{3}$$

1.23   Convert (a) 112/25, (b) 4/3, and (c) 237/110 into decimal fractions. Work to the nearest ten-thousandth.

SOLUTION

(a)
$$\frac{112}{25} = 112 \div 25 = 4.4800$$

(b)
$$\frac{4}{3} = 4 \div 3 = 1.333\ldots = 1.\dot{3}$$

(c)
$$\frac{237}{110} = 237 \div 110 = 2.1545454\ldots = 2.1\overline{54}$$

1.24   Convert (a) $4\frac{3}{16}$, (b) $5\frac{10}{31}$, and (c) $7\frac{7}{9}$ into decimal fractions. Work to the nearest ten-thousandth.

SOLUTION

(a) $4\frac{3}{16}$
$$\frac{3}{16} = 3 \div 16 = 0.1875 \; \leftarrow \text{Change the fractional part to its decimal equivalent}$$

$$4\frac{3}{16} = 4 + 0.1875 = 4.1875 \; \leftarrow \text{Add the whole number part of the mixed number}$$

(b) $5\frac{10}{31}$
$$\frac{10}{31} = 10 \div 31 = 0.3225806\ldots \cong 0.3226$$

$$5\frac{10}{31} = 5 + 0.3226 = 5.3226$$

(c) $7\frac{7}{9}$
$$\frac{7}{9} = 7 \div 9 = 0.7777\ldots = 0.\dot{7}$$

$$7\frac{7}{9} = 7 + 0.\dot{7} = 7.\dot{7}$$

1.25   Convert (a) 0.0125, (b) 0.66, and (c) 3.015 to common fractions.

SOLUTION

(a)
$$0.0125 = 125 \text{ ten-thousandths} = \frac{125}{10,000} = \frac{1}{80}$$

Four decimal places · Four 0s

(b)
$$0.66 = 66 \text{ hundredths} = \frac{66}{100} = \frac{33}{50}$$

(c)
$$3.015 = 3\tfrac{15}{1,000} = 3\tfrac{3}{200} \quad \text{or} \quad \frac{603}{200}$$

Reduce $\dfrac{15 \div 5}{1,000 \div 5} = \dfrac{3}{200}$

1.4 ORDER OF OPERATIONS AND COMPLEX FRACTIONS

In an arithmetic expression that contains parentheses, powers, multiplication, division, addition, and subtraction, we must adhere to the following *order of operations*:

1.   Perform the operations inside parentheses in proper order
2.   Perform powers (e.g., $10^2 = 10 \times 10 = 100$; $2^3 = 2 \times 2 \times 2 = 8$)
3.   Perform multiplications and/or divisions
4.   Perform addition and/or subtraction.

A *complex fraction* is a fraction in which the numerator or denominator or both contain fractions. To simplify complex fractions we must use the order of operations.

EXAMPLE 10

Simplify by carrying out the correct order of operations above and below the fraction bar first.

$$\frac{712 + 4 \times \frac{1}{2}}{1 + 2.5 \times \frac{7}{8}} = \frac{712 + \frac{\overset{2}{\cancel{4}}}{1} \times \frac{1}{\cancel{2}_1}}{1 + 2\frac{\cancel{5}^1}{\underset{2}{\cancel{10}}} \times \frac{7}{8}} = \frac{712 + 2}{1 + \frac{5}{2} \times \frac{7}{8}}$$

Multiply · Add

Change to common fraction · Change to improper fraction and reduce to lowest terms · Multiply

$$= \frac{714}{1 + \frac{35}{16}} = \frac{714}{\frac{16}{16} + \frac{35}{16}} = \frac{714}{\frac{51}{16}}$$

Change to equivalent fraction · Add · Invert to reciprocal

$$= \overset{14}{\cancel{714}} \times \frac{16}{\cancel{51}} = 224$$

Multiply

SOLVED PROBLEMS

1.26 Simplify (a) $15 + 8 \div 2$, (b) $2(12 - 6) \div 4 - 2$, (c) $3 \times 4 + 12 \div 6$, (d) $(12 - 5)/(3 + 11)$, and (e) $3 \times 4^2 - 5$.

SOLUTION

(a)
$$15 + 8 \div 2 = 15 + 4 = 19 \qquad \text{Do division before addition}$$

(b)
$$2(12 - 6) \div 4 - 2 = 2(6) \div 4 - 2 \qquad \text{Work inside parentheses first}$$
$$= 12 \div 4 - 2 \qquad \text{Then do multiplication and division}$$
$$= 3 - 2 = 1 \qquad \text{Followed by subtraction}$$

(c)
$$3 \times 4 + 12 \div 6 = 12 + 2 = 14 \qquad \text{Do multiplication and division before addition}$$

(d)
$$\frac{12 - 5}{3 + 11} = (12 - 5) \div (3 + 11) \qquad \text{The fraction line indicates parentheses as well as division}$$
$$= 7 \div 14 = 0.5$$

(e)
$$3 \times 4^2 - 5 = 3 \times (4 \times 4) - 5 \qquad \text{Do the power first}$$
$$= 3 \times 16 - 5 \qquad \text{Then do the multiplication}$$
$$= 48 - 5 \qquad \text{Followed by subtraction}$$
$$= 43$$

1.27 Simplify (a) $800[1 + 0.06 \times (150/360)]$, (b) $300[1 - 0.1 \times (9/12)]$, (c) $1,000(1 - 0.3)^2$.

SOLUTION

(a)
$$800\left(1 + 0.06 \times \frac{150}{360}\right) = 800\left(1 + 0.06 \times \frac{5}{12}\right) \qquad \text{Reduce common fraction to lowest terms and multiply inside the parentheses}$$

$$= 800\left(1 + \frac{0.3}{12}\right) \qquad \text{Divide 0.3 by 12}$$

$$= 800(1 + 0.025) \qquad \text{Add inside parentheses}$$
$$= 800(1.025)$$
$$= 820 \qquad \text{Multiply}$$

(b)
$$300\left(1 - 0.1 \times \frac{9}{12}\right) = 300\left(1 - 0.1 \times \frac{3}{4}\right) = 300\left(1 - \frac{0.3}{4}\right)$$
$$= 300(1 - 0.075) = 300(0.925) = 277.5$$

(c)
$$1,000(1 - 0.3)^2 = 1,000(0.7)^2 = 1,000(0.7 \times 0.7) = 1,000 \times 0.49 = 490$$

1.28 Simplify (a) $\dfrac{\frac{3}{4} - \frac{2}{3}}{\frac{1}{2} + \frac{5}{6}}$, (b) $\dfrac{20}{800 \times \frac{15}{360}}$, and (c) $\dfrac{605}{1 + 0.1 \times \frac{1}{12}}$.

SOLUTION

(a) Perform the operations above and below the main fraction bar first.

$$\frac{\frac{3}{4} - \frac{2}{3}}{\frac{1}{2} + \frac{5}{6}} = \frac{\frac{9}{12} - \frac{8}{12}}{\frac{3}{6} + \frac{5}{6}} = \frac{\frac{1}{12}}{\frac{8}{6}} = \frac{1}{12} \times \frac{6}{8} = \frac{1}{2} \times \frac{1}{8} = \frac{1}{16} = 0.0625$$

Change to equivalent fractions   Reciprocal

(b)
$$\frac{20}{800 \times \frac{15}{360}} = \frac{20}{800 \times \frac{1}{24}} = \frac{20}{\frac{800}{24}} = \overset{1}{20} \times \frac{24}{800} = \frac{\overset{6}{24}}{\underset{10}{40}} = \frac{6}{10} = 0.6$$

$$\underbrace{\quad}_{\text{Reduce}} \quad \underbrace{\quad}_{\text{Multiply}} \quad \underbrace{\quad}_{\text{Reciprocal}} \quad \text{Reduce}$$

(c)
$$\frac{605}{1 + 0.1 \times \frac{1}{12}} = \frac{605}{1 + \frac{1}{10} \times \frac{1}{12}} = \frac{605}{1 + \frac{1}{120}} = \frac{605}{\frac{121}{120}} = \overset{5}{605} \times \frac{120}{\underset{1}{121}} = 5 \times 120 = 600$$

$$\underbrace{\quad}_{\text{Convert to fraction}} \quad \underbrace{\quad}_{\text{Multiply}} \quad \underbrace{\quad}_{\text{Add}} \quad \underbrace{\quad}_{\text{Reciprocal}}$$

Supplementary Problems

1.29   Find the sum of each of the following and check your answers:

(a)   732, 192, 17, 1,385

(b)   9,815, 306, 14, 5,835, 217

(c)   3.82, 715.11, 0.98, 81.47

(d) $356, $81.23, $3.08, $965.75

1.30   Find the difference as indicated and check your answers:

(a)   Subtract 381 from 1,870

(b)   Subtract 14,821 from 17,008

(c)   Subtract 105.9 from 382.7

(d)   Subtract $1,305.83 from $2,385.75

1.31   The outside diameter of a copper tubing is 1.625 in. If the wall thickness is 0.185 in, what is the inside diameter?

1.32   Betty's checkbook showed a balance of $917.28. She then wrote checks for $12.78, $260, $115.83, and $32.25. Find her new balance.

1.33   Find the product of the following and check your answers:

(a)   356 and 27   (c)   121.83 and 10.8

(b)   41.3 and 2.8   (d)   64 and 218.3

1.34   If the regular wage rate is $8 per hour and for work in excess of 40 h per standard week the rate is 1.5 times the regular rate, what will be the gross pay for an employee who worked 56 hours during the week?

1.35   Find the quotient and the remainder, if any, for each of the following and check your answers:

(a)   918 ÷ 35   (c)   31.5 ÷ 105

(b)   7,875 ÷ 83   (d)   62.5 ÷ 0.025

1.36   A taxi driver used 520 gal (gallons) of gasoline in a month and drove 11,245 mi (miles). How many miles per gallon did the driver average?

1.37   Find the product of each of the following:

(a) $34.08 \times 1,000$ (e) 18.7×0.01

(b) 0.873×100 (f) 208×0.0001

(c) $1.0783 \times 100,000$ (g) $55,815 \times 0.001$

(d) $2.35 \times 10,000$ (h) 855.7×0.1

1.38   Find the quotient for each of the following:

(a) $9.86 \div 100$ (e) $81.93 \div 0.1$

(b) $18 \div 10$ (f) $7.5 \div 0.001$

(c) $17.88 \div 1,000$ (g) $55 \div 0.01$

(d) $500.1 \div 10,000$ (h) $235.78 \div 0.0001$

1.39   Reduce each of the following fractions to lowest terms:

(a) $\dfrac{135}{360}$ (b) $\dfrac{210}{315}$ (c) $\dfrac{75}{180}$ (d) $\dfrac{219}{365}$

1.40   Simplify each of the following and reduce the answer to lowest terms:

(a) $\dfrac{5}{11}+\dfrac{3}{11}+\dfrac{2}{11}$ (c) $\dfrac{7}{15}-\dfrac{2}{15}+\dfrac{11}{15}-\dfrac{13}{15}$

(b) $\dfrac{9}{16}-\dfrac{3}{16}$ (d) $\dfrac{13}{7}-\dfrac{6}{7}+\dfrac{12}{7}-\dfrac{5}{7}$

1.41   Simplify each of the following:

(a) $\dfrac{11}{8}+\dfrac{5}{12}$ (c) $\dfrac{2}{3}+\dfrac{3}{4}+\dfrac{4}{5}+\dfrac{5}{6}$

(b) $\dfrac{7}{6}-\dfrac{3}{5}$ (d) $\dfrac{8}{15}-\dfrac{7}{6}+\dfrac{4}{5}-\dfrac{1}{10}$

1.42   Multiply each of the following and reduce the answer to lowest terms:

(a) $\dfrac{7}{6}\times\dfrac{12}{35}$ (c) $\dfrac{7}{36}\times\dfrac{9}{15}\times\dfrac{60}{21}$

(b) $\dfrac{9}{10}\times\dfrac{160}{360}$ (d) $\dfrac{1}{2}\times\dfrac{2}{3}\times\dfrac{3}{4}\times\dfrac{4}{5}$

1.43   Simplify each of the following:

(a) $\dfrac{4}{5}\div\dfrac{8}{9}$ (c) $\dfrac{8}{3}\times\dfrac{7}{12}\div\dfrac{28}{15}$

(b) $\dfrac{30}{8}\div\dfrac{5}{12}$ (d) $\dfrac{5}{8}\div\dfrac{9}{15}\times\dfrac{16}{5}$

1.44   Convert each of the following mixed numbers to a common fraction:

(a) $8\frac{1}{6}$ (b) $3\frac{2}{7}$ (c) $2\frac{3}{5}$ (d) $5\frac{2}{9}$

1.45   Convert each of the following improper fractions to a mixed number:

(a) $\dfrac{28}{5}$ (b) $\dfrac{182}{9}$ (c) $\dfrac{19}{4}$ (d) $\dfrac{382}{15}$

1.46 Simplify each of the following and show your answer as a mixed number:

(a) $5\frac{1}{4} + 3\frac{2}{3}$ (c) $3\frac{1}{4} + 5\frac{3}{8} - 2\frac{5}{16}$

(b) $17\frac{3}{8} - 13\frac{1}{4}$ (d) $3 + 2\frac{1}{5} + 5\frac{8}{15} - 4\frac{3}{10}$

1.47 Simplify each of the following and show your answer as a mixed number:

(a) $4\frac{3}{8} \times 3\frac{1}{5}$ (c) $2\frac{1}{4} \times 1\frac{1}{5} \div 2\frac{1}{3}$

(b) $3\frac{1}{3} \div 2\frac{1}{12}$ (d) $4 \div \frac{6}{5} \times \frac{12}{25}$

1.48 How many cubic feet of sand will fill a lot $5\frac{1}{2} \times 8\frac{1}{4} \times 3\frac{1}{3}$ ft?

1.49 Fahrenheit temperature is found by dividing the degrees Celsius by $\frac{5}{9}$ and then adding 32 to the quotient. Find the Fahrenheit temperature if the degrees Celsius is 40.

1.50 Five electricians worked at a construction site $12\frac{1}{2}$, $14\frac{3}{4}$, $16\frac{1}{4}$, $18\frac{3}{4}$, and $20\frac{1}{4}$ hours, respectively. What was the total cost of labor if the electricians were paid \$14.50 each per hour?

1.51 Convert each of the following fractions into a decimal fraction. Work to the nearest hundred-thousandth:

(a) $\dfrac{5}{9}$ (b) $\dfrac{11}{7}$ (c) $\dfrac{218}{125}$ (d) $\dfrac{89}{45}$

1.52 Convert each of the following mixed numbers into a decimal fraction. Work to the nearest thousandth:

(a) $11\frac{1}{11}$ (b) $4\frac{1}{14}$ (c) $20\frac{5}{8}$ (d) $13\frac{3}{1,000}$

1.53 Convert each of the following decimal fractions to a common fraction:

(a) 0.875   (b) 1.056   (c) 19.025   (d) $21.\overset{.}{3}$

1.54 Simplify each of the following:

(a) $18 - 30 \div 6$ (d) $(2 \times 5 - 3) \times (8 - 9 \div 3)$

(b) $(12 + 6) \div 3 - 3$ (e) $500\left(1 - 0.02 \times \frac{1}{2}\right)$

(c) $3 \times 2^2 - 5$ (f) $750\left(1 + 0.15 \times \frac{8}{12}\right)$

1.55 Simplify each of the following:

(a) $\dfrac{3(5 - 2) - 12 \div 4}{3 \times \frac{2}{3} - 1}$ (c) $\dfrac{436}{1 + 0.12 \times \frac{3}{4}}$

(b) $\dfrac{\frac{2}{3} + \frac{3}{5} - 1}{\frac{2}{5} - \frac{1}{3}}$ (d) $\dfrac{570}{1 - 0.15 \times \frac{4}{12}}$

Answers to Supplementary Problems

1.29   (*a*) 2,326, (*b*) 16,187, (*c*) 801.38, (*d*) $1,406.06

1.30   (*a*) 1,489, (*b*) 2,187, (*c*) 276.8, (*d*) $1,079.92

1.31   1.255 in

1.32 $496.42

1.33   (*a*) 9,612, (*b*) 115.64, (*c*) 1,315.764, (*d*) 13,971.2

1.34 $512

1.35   (*a*) $26\frac{8}{35}$, (*b*) $94\frac{73}{63}$, (*c*) 0.3, (*d*) 2,500

1.36   21.625 mi

1.37   (*a*) 34,080, (*b*) 87.3, (*c*) 107,830, (*d*) 23,500, (*e*) 0.187, (*f*) 0.0208, (*g*) 55.815, (*h*) 85.57

1.38   (*a*) 0.0986, (*b*) 1.8, (*c*) 0.01788, (*d*) 0.05001, (*e*) 819.3, (*f*) 7,500, (*g*) 5,500, (*h*) 2,357,800

1.39   (*a*) 3/8, (*b*) 2/3, (*c*) 5/12, (*d*) 3/5

1.40   (*a*) 10/11, (*b*) 3/8, (*c*) 1/5, (*d*) 2/1 = 2

1.41   (*a*) 43/24 = $1\frac{19}{24}$, (*b*) 17/30, (*c*) 61/20 = $3\frac{1}{20}$, (*d*) 1/15

1.42   (*a*) 2/5, (*b*) 2/5, (*c*) 1/3, (*d*) 1/5

1.43   (*a*) 9/10, (*b*) 9, (*c*) 5/6, (*d*) 10/3 = $3\frac{1}{3}$

1.44   (*a*) 49/6, (*b*) 23/7, (*c*) 13/5, (*d*) 47/9

1.45   (*a*) $5\frac{3}{5}$, (*b*) $20\frac{2}{9}$, (*c*) $4\frac{3}{4}$, (*d*) $25\frac{7}{15}$

1.46   (*a*) $8\frac{11}{12}$, (*b*) $4\frac{1}{8}$, (*c*) $6\frac{5}{16}$, (*d*) $6\frac{13}{30}$

1.47   (*a*) 14, (*b*) $1\frac{3}{5}$, (*c*) $1\frac{11}{70}$, (*d*) $1\frac{3}{5}$

1.48 $151\frac{1}{4}$ ft^3

1.49   104°F

1.50 $1,196.25

1.51   (*a*) 0.55555 . . . = $0.\dot{5}$, (*b*) 1.571428 = 1.57143, (*c*) 1.744, (*d*) 1.97777 . . . = $1.9\dot{7}$

1.52   (*a*) 11.0909 . . . = $11.\overline{09}$, (*b*) 4.071, (*c*) 20.625, (*d*) 13.003

1.53   (*a*) 7/8, (*b*) 132/125, (*c*) 761/40, (*d*) 64/3

1.54   (*a*) 13, (*b*) 3, (*c*) 7, (*d*) 35, (*e*) 495, (*f*) 825

1.55   (*a*) 30, (*b*) 4, (*c*) 400, (*d*) 600

Chapter 2

Ratio, Proportion, and Percent

2.1 RATIO AND PROPORTION

A *ratio* is a comparison of two or more quantities. Ratios can be written using fractions or colons. When comparing 60 minutes to 40 minutes, the comparison may be expressed as $\frac{60}{40}$ or $60:40$. In either case, the ratio is read "sixty to forty." The numbers can be simplified to $\frac{3}{2}$ or $3:2$ or $1.5:1$. Since a ratio is considered to be a common fraction, problems involving ratios may be solved using the same methods as for fractions (see Chap. 1).

When comparing more than two quantities, the use of colons is preferred and any accompanying unit of measurement is dropped. A comparison of 8 kilograms (kg), 5 kg, and 3 kg may be expressed as the ratio $8:5:3$. The numbers appearing in a ratio are called the *terms* of the ratio. Before the units can be dropped, the terms of the ratio must be expressed in the same unit of measurement.

EXAMPLE 1

Gini, Matt, and Sandy work at the same office. Gini's traveling time to work is $\frac{1}{2}$ hour (h), Matt's is 23 minutes (min), and Sandy's is 18 min. Express their comparative traveling time as a ratio.

$$\tfrac{1}{2}\,\text{h}:23\,\text{min}:18\,\text{min}$$

Convert all traveling time to the same unit of measurement and drop the units from the ratio.

$$\tfrac{1}{2}\,\text{h} = 30\,\text{min}$$

$$30\,\text{min}:23\,\text{min}:18\,\text{min} = 30:23:18$$

We can also convert all traveling time into hours (by dividing the minutes by 60).

$$\tfrac{1}{2}\,\text{h}:\tfrac{23}{60}\,\text{h}:\tfrac{18}{60}\,\text{h} = 0.5:0.38\dot{3}:0.3$$

Partnership profits, estates, departmental overhead costs, etc. are allocated according to a ratio. The total amount to be allocated is the sum of the terms of the ratio. If the terms of the ratio are fractions, they must be converted into equivalent fractions with the same denominator, and the whole amount is then allocated in the ratio of the numerators.

EXAMPLE 2

(*a*) Allocate \$1,500 in the ratio $6:4:2$. Determine the total number of parts to be allocated:

$$6 + 4 + 2 = 12$$

Determine the value of a single part:

$$\$1,500 \div 12\,\text{parts} = \$125/\text{part}$$

To allocate, multiply each term of the ratio by the value of a single part.

First term:	$6 \times \$125 = \$750$	
Second term:	$4 \times \$125 = \$500$	
Third term:	$2 \times \$125 = \$250$	

Thus the allocation will be in the amounts of \$750, \$500, and \$250.

(*b*) Note that we could have reduced the ratio:

$$6:4:2 = 3:2:1$$

Total parts to be allocated:

$$3 + 2 + 1 = 6$$

Value of a single part:

$$\$1,500 \div 6 \text{ parts} = \$250/\text{part}$$

Allocation:

First term:	$3 \times \$250 = \$750$
Second term:	$2 \times \$250 = \$500$
Third term:	$1 \times \$250 = \$250$

EXAMPLE 3

A profit of $438,500 from the sale of a business is to be allocated among the four partners in the ratio of $3/5 : 1/4 : 2/3 : 4/7$. Determine the amount of the profit for each partner.

$$\frac{3}{5} : \frac{1}{4} : \frac{2}{3} : \frac{4}{7} = \frac{252}{420} : \frac{105}{420} : \frac{280}{420} : \frac{240}{420}$$

Multiply the
denominators to
find the common
denominator and
convert to equiva-
lent fractions

Determine the total parts to be allocated by adding the numerators:

$$252 + 105 + 280 + 240 = 877$$

Determine the value of a single part:

$$\$438,500 \div 877 \text{ parts} = \$500/\text{part}$$

Allocate according to the ratio of the numerators:

First term:	$252 \times \$500 = \$126,000$
Second term:	$105 \times \$500 = \$\ 52,500$
Third term:	$280 \times \$500 = \$140,000$
Fourth term:	$240 \times \$500 = \$120,000$

The allocation among the partners will be $126,000, $52,500, $140,000, and $120,000.

When two ratios are equal, they form a *proportion*. For example, $3 : 5 = 6 : 10$ or $a/2 = 3/5$. Each proportion consists of four terms. The first and last terms are called the *extremes*; the second and third terms are called the *means*.

$$\overset{\lceil\text{Means}\rceil}{4 : 5 \ = \ 5.6 : 7}$$

$$\lfloor\text{Extremes}\rfloor$$

When one of the terms is unknown, cross multiplication is used to find it.

$$x : 5 = 7 : 12$$

$$\frac{x}{5} = \frac{7}{12}$$

$$12x = 5(7)$$

$$12x = 35$$

$$x = \frac{35}{12} = 2.916$$

The principles governing statements of proportion are

1. The product of the means equals the product of the extremes.

    If $4:5 = 5.6:7$

    Then $4 \times 7 = 5 \times 5.6$

                                                $28 = 28$

    Note that this is the same as cross multiplying when the proportion is written using fractions.

    $$\frac{4}{5} \diagdown \frac{5.6}{7}$$

    $$4 \times 7 = 5 \times 5.6$$

    $$28 = 28$$

2. The product of the extremes divided by either mean gives the other mean.
    For the preceding proportion we have:

    $$4 \times 7 \div 5 = 5.6$$

    $$4 \times 7 \div 5.6 = 5$$

3. The product of the means divided by either extreme gives the other extreme.

    $$5 \times 5.6 \div 4 = 7$$

    $$5 \times 5.6 \div 7 = 4$$

Proportions may be direct or inverse. In *direct proportions*, as one ratio increases (or decreases) so does the other. In *inverse proportions*, as one ratio increases, the other decreases and vice versa.
Proportions may be set up in various ways. The following method may serve as a guide.

Direct proportions:

1. Write a ratio using the like units or items (miles, gallons, dollars, profits, etc.).

2. Write the second ratio in the same order, so that its *numerator* is the term that pertains to the *numerator* of the first ratio.

Inverse proportions:

1. Write a ratio using the like units (or items).

2. Write the second ratio in *inverse* order, so that its *numerator* is the term that pertains to the *denominator* of the first ratio.

EXAMPLE 4

(a) $x:3 = 75:4$ read "x is to 3 as 75 is to 4"

To solve for x rewrite the proportion using fractions:

$$\frac{x}{3} = \frac{75}{4}$$

Cross multiply and solve for x:

$$\frac{x}{3} \diagup \frac{75}{4}$$

$$4x = 3(75) \leftarrow \text{Divide both sides of the equation by 4}$$

$$x = \frac{3(75)}{4} = \frac{225}{4} = 56.25$$

(*b*) Danny and Estelle invested in the same stock. Danny earned $1,700 on an investment of $7,500. Find the return on Estelle's investment of $10,500.

To find the solution, we need to set up a proportion. We know that as the investment increases, so should the earnings on that investment. We therefore want to set up a *direct* proportion. Let x = Estelle's investment.

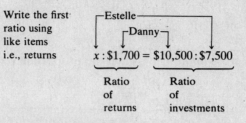

| Write the first ratio using like items i.e., returns | | Write the second ratio in the same order as the first |

$$x : \$1,700 = \$10,500 : \$7,500$$

Ratio of returns Ratio of investments

Rewrite the proportion using fractions.

$$\frac{x}{\$1,700} = \frac{\$10,500}{\$7,500}$$

Note that the numerator of the first ratio pertains to the numerator of the second (Estelle) and the denominator of the first ratio pertains to the denominator of the second (Danny)

Cross multiply and solve for x.

$$\frac{x}{\$1,700} \diagdown \frac{\$10,500}{\$7,500}$$

$$\$7,500x = \$1,700(\$10,500)$$

$$x = \frac{\$1,700(\$10,500)}{\$7,500} = \frac{\$178,500}{\$75} = \$2,380$$

Estelle's return on her investment of $10,500 was $2,380.

To check the answer, apply rule 1: The product of the means equals the product of the extremes.

Means

$$\$2,380 : \$1,700 = \$10,500 : \$7,500$$

Extremes

$$1,700 \times 10,500 = 2,380 \times 7,500$$

$$17,850,000 = 17,850,000$$

(*c*) An emergency supply of food will last 14 days when shared among four people. How long will the same supply last if it has to be shared among six people?

Logically, we know that the food will last a *shorter* length of time as the number of people *increases*. We therefore want to write an *inverse* proportion.

| Write the first ratio using like items, i.e., people | | Write the second ratio in *inverse* order to the first, so that the numerator pertains to the denominator or the first ratio |

$$\frac{6 \text{ people}}{4 \text{ people}} = \frac{14 \text{ days}}{x}$$

inverse relationship of terms

Solve for x:

$$\frac{6 \text{ people}}{4 \text{ people}} \diagdown \frac{14 \text{ days}}{x}$$

$$6 \text{ people } x = 14 \text{ days } (4 \text{ people})$$

$$x = \frac{14 \text{ days } (4 \text{ people})}{6 \text{ people}} = \frac{56 \text{ days}}{6} = 9.\dot{3} = 9\tfrac{1}{3} \text{ days}$$

When shared among 6 people the supply of food will last $9\tfrac{1}{3}$ days.

Check:

The product of the means equals the product of the extremes.

$$\text{6 people : 4 people} = \text{14 days : } 9\tfrac{1}{3}$$

with "Means" labeled above (4 people and 14 days) and "Extremes" labeled below (6 people and $9\tfrac{1}{3}$).

$$6 \times 9\tfrac{1}{3} = 4 \times 14$$

$$6 \times \frac{28}{3} = 56$$

$$\frac{168}{3} = 56$$

$$56 = 56$$

SOLVED PROBLEMS

2.1 Reduce the ratios (*a*) 240 to 72, (*b*) 18 to 30, (*c*) 9 to 15 to 21, (*d*) 5/6 to 10/9, (*e*) 1.25 to 5.5.

SOLUTION

(*a*)
$$240 \text{ to } 72 = \frac{240}{72} = \frac{10 \times 24}{3 \times 24} = \frac{10}{3} = 10:3$$

(*b*)
$$18 \text{ to } 30 = \frac{18}{30} = \frac{3 \times 6}{5 \times 6} = \frac{3}{5} = 3:5$$

(*c*)
$$9 \text{ to } 15 \text{ to } 21 = (3 \times 3):(5 \times 3):(7 \times 3) = 3:5:7$$

(*d*)
$$\frac{5}{6} \text{ to } \frac{10}{9} = \frac{5}{6} \div \frac{10}{9} = \frac{5}{6} \times \frac{9}{10} = \frac{45}{60} = \frac{3 \times 15}{4 \times 15} = \frac{3}{4} = 3:4$$

(*e*)
$$1.25 \text{ to } 5.5 = \frac{1.25}{5.5} = \frac{125}{550} = \frac{5 \times 25}{22 \times 25} = \frac{5}{22} = 5:22$$

2.2 Set up a ratio for (*a*) 3 hours to 2 days and (*b*) 2 dimes to 3 quarters to 1 dollar, and reduce to lowest terms.

SOLUTION

(*a*)
$$\text{3 h to 2 days} = \text{3 h : 48 h} = 3:48 = 1:16$$

with labels above: "Convert to hours", "Drop units", "Reduce".

or

$$\text{3 h to 2 days} = \frac{3}{24} \text{ days : 2 days} = 0.125:2$$

with "Convert to days" labeled below.

Note that

$$1:16 = 0.125:2$$

$$\frac{1}{16} = \frac{0.125}{2}$$

$$0.0625 = 0.0625$$

(*b*)
$$\text{2 dimes : 3 quarters : \$1} = 20\cent : 75\cent : 100\cent$$

$$= 20:75:100 = 4:15:20$$

2.3   Advertising expenses amounted to \$3,600 while sales volume amounted to \$84,000 for the last quarter. What is the ratio of advertising expenses to sales volume?

SOLUTION
$$3,600:84,000 = 36:840 = 9:210 = 3:70$$

2.4   A couple spent \$850 on accommodations, \$600 on meals, and \$425 on transportation during their vacation. What is the ratio between the three types of expenses?

SOLUTION
$$850:600:425 = (34 \times 25):(24 \times 25):(17 \times 25) = 34:24:17$$

2.5   In the business department there are 20 faculty members and 755 students, whereas in the technology department there are 16 faculty members and 580 students. Which department has a higher student/faculty ratio?

SOLUTION

In the business department:

$$755:20 = (151 \times 5):(4 \times 5) = 151:4$$

In the technology department:

$$580:16 = (145 \times 4):(4 \times 4) = 145:4$$

The business department has a higher student/faculty ratio.

2.6   Allocate \$900 in the ratio of (*a*) 7:3 and (*b*) 7:6:5.

SOLUTION

(*a*)   Determine the total number of parts to be allocated:

$$7 + 3 = 10 \text{ parts}$$

Determine the value of a single part:

$$\$900 \div 10 \text{ parts} = \$90/\text{part}$$

To allocate, multiply each term of the ratio by the value of a single part.

First term:	$7 \times \$90 = \$630$	To check your calculations,
Second term:	$3 \times \$90 = \underline{\$270}$	add these amounts. The sum
	Total = \$900	should equal the total amount
		to be allocated

Thus, \$900 is to be allocated in the amounts of \$630 and \$270.

(*b*)   Total number of parts to be allocated:

$$7 + 6 + 5 = 18 \text{ parts}$$

The value of each part:

$$\$900 \div 18 \text{ parts} = \$50/\text{part}$$

Allocation:

First term:	$7 \times \$50 = \$350$
Second term:	$6 \times \$50 = \$300$
Third term:	$5 \times \$50 = \underline{\$250}$
	Total = \$900

Thus, \$900 is to be allocated in the amounts of \$350, \$300, and \$250.

2.7   A profit of $8,721 is to be divided among three partners in the ratio $5:3:1$. How much should each receive?

SOLUTION

Total number of parts to be allocated:

$$5 + 3 + 1 = 9 \text{ parts}$$

The value of each part:

$$8,721 \div 9 \text{ parts} = \$969/\text{part}$$

Allocation:

First partner receives:	$5 \times \$969 = \$4,845$
Second partner receives:	$3 \times \$969 = \$2,907$
Third partner receives:	$1 \times \$969 = \$\underline{\ \ 969}$
	Total $= \$8,721$

2.8   An estate of $71,925 is to be divided among four heirs in the ratio $1/4:1/3:2/5:5/12$. What inheritance should each receive?

SOLUTION

Convert the fractions into equivalent fractions with a common denominator. (Since 4 and 3 are multiples of 12, you need to multiply only 5 and 12 to find the common denominator.)

$$\frac{1}{4}:\frac{1}{3}:\frac{2}{5}:\frac{5}{12} = \frac{15}{60}:\frac{20}{60}:\frac{24}{60}:\frac{25}{60}$$

Allocate according to the ratio formed by the numerators.

$$15:20:24:25$$

Total number of parts to be allocated:

$$15 + 20 + 24 + 25 = 84 \text{ parts}$$

The value of each part:

$$\$71,925 \div 84 \text{ parts} = \$856.25/\text{part}$$

Allocation:

First heir's inheritance:	$15 \times \$856.25 = \$12,843.75$
Second heir's inheritance:	$20 \times \$856.25 = \$17,125.00$
Third heir's inheritance:	$24 \times \$856.25 = \$20,550.00$
Fourth heir's inheritance:	$25 \times \$856.25 = \$\underline{21,406.25}$
	Total $= \$71,925.00$

2.9   In the proportions (*a*) $x:5 = 100:125$ and (*b*) $28:x = 72:125$, find the value of x.

SOLUTION

(*a*) $x:5 = 100:125$ ←Rewrite proportion using fractions

$$\frac{x}{5} \diagdown\!\!\!\!\diagup \frac{100}{125}$$ ←Cross multiply

$$125(x) = 5(100)$$

$$125x = 500$$ ←Divide both sides of the equation by 125

$$x = \frac{500}{125} = 4$$

(b)
$$28 : x = 72 : 125$$

$$\frac{28}{x} \diagdown \frac{72}{125}$$

$$125(28) = x(72)$$

$$3{,}500 = 72x$$

$$x = \frac{3{,}500}{72} = 48.6\dot{1}$$

2.10 If an investment of \$5,000 yields Mr. Smith a return of \$1,100, find the return on an investment of \$8,000 by Ms. Jones, at the same rate of return.

SOLUTION

Let x denote Ms. Jones's return. As the investment increases, the return on the investment should increase. Thus we obtain a *direct* proportion.

$$\frac{x}{\$1{,}100} = \frac{\$8{,}000}{\$5{,}000}$$

$$\frac{x}{\$1{,}100} = \frac{\$8}{\$5}$$

$$\$5(x) = \$8(\$1{,}100)$$

$$\$5x = \$8{,}800$$

$$x = \$1{,}760$$

2.11 What should Mr. Brown have invested in Prob. 2.10 to obtain a return of \$1,980?

SOLUTION

Let y denote Mr. Brown's investment. We have a direct proportion

$$\frac{y}{\$5{,}000} = \frac{\$1{,}980}{\$1{,}100}$$

$$\$1{,}100(y) = \$5{,}000(\$1{,}980)$$

$$\$1{,}100y = \$9{,}900{,}000$$

$$y = \$9{,}000$$

2.12 A construction job requires the labor of 15 workers for 28 days. How many workers are needed to complete the job in 8 days' less time?

SOLUTION

Let x be the required number of workers. As the number of days decreases, the number of people increases. Thus we obtain an *inverse* proportion.

$$\frac{x}{15 \text{ workers}} = \frac{28 \text{ days}}{20 \text{ days}}$$

$$20(x) = 15 \text{ workers}(28)$$

$$20x = 420 \text{ workers}$$

$$x = 21 \text{ workers}$$

2.13   How many days will it take to complete the job in Prob. 2.12 if only 10 workers are used?

SOLUTION

Let y be the required number of days. We again have an inverse proportion.

$$\frac{y}{28 \text{ days}} = \frac{15 \text{ workers}}{10 \text{ workers}}$$

$$10(y) = 28 \text{ days}(15)$$

$$10y = 420 \text{ days}$$

$$y = 42 \text{ days}$$

2.14   John invests \$2,500 and Kevin \$3,200 in a partnership. If profits are to be shared in the ratio of their investments, what should John receive if Kevin's share of the profits is \$800?

SOLUTION

Let x denote John's share of the profits. The ratio of the profits should equal the ratio of the investments; that is,

$$\frac{x}{\$800} = \frac{\$2,500}{\$3,200}$$

$$\frac{x}{\$800} = \frac{\$25}{\$32}$$

$$32(x) = \$800(25)$$

$$32x = \$20,000$$

$$x = \$625$$

2.2   PERCENT AND THE BASIC PERCENTAGE PROBLEM

The term *percent*, denoted by the symbol %, means per one hundred. Thus 75% is another way of expressing 75/100 (or 3/4 or 0.75).

When computing with percents, the corresponding decimal fraction is usually used. To express a percent as a decimal fraction, drop the percent sign and move the decimal point two places to the left. To convert a percent into a common fraction, drop the percent sign and multiply the number by 1/100; then reduce the resulting fraction to lowest terms.

EXAMPLE 5

(*a*)   Change 48.5% to a decimal.

$$48.5\% = 0.48.5$$

Drop   Move decimal point two places to the left

(*b*)   Change 48.5% to a common fraction.

To get rid of decimal, multiply numerator and denominator by 10

$$48.5\% = 48.5 \times \frac{1}{100} = \frac{48.5}{100} = \frac{485}{1,000} = \frac{97}{200}$$

Drop   Reduce

To change a decimal into a percent, move the decimal point two places to the right and add the percent sign. To change a fraction to a percent, first convert the fraction to a decimal and then change the decimal to a percent.

EXAMPLE 6

(*a*) Change 0.1782 into a percent.

$$0.1782 = 0.17{,}82\%$$

Add

Move decimal point two places to the right

(*b*) Change 17/25 into a percent.

$$\frac{17}{25} = 0.68 = 0.68{,}\%$$

Add

Convert to decimal   Move decimal point two places to the right

Percentage is formed by multiplying a number, called the *base* by a percent, called the *rate*. For example 20% of $120 = 0.20 \times 120 = 24$. Thus we have a formula

$$\text{Percentage} = \text{rate} \times \text{base}$$

Since three variables are involved in the above relationship, given any two, we may solve to find the third.

1. Given rate and base, we can find the percentage

$$\text{Percentage} = \text{rate} \times \text{base}$$

2. Given percentage and base, we can find the rate

$$\text{Rate} = \frac{\text{percentage}}{\text{base}}$$

3. Given percentage and rate, we can find the base

$$\text{Base} = \frac{\text{percentage}}{\text{rate}}$$

EXAMPLE 7

(*a*) What percentage is 3% of 20?

$$\text{Rate} = 3\%$$

$$\text{Base} = 20$$

$$\text{Percentage} = \text{rate} \times \text{base}$$
$$= 3\% \times 20 \qquad \leftarrow \text{Change percent to decimal}$$
$$= 0.3 \times 20 = 0.6$$

(b) What was Josie's income last year if she was in the 40% tax bracket and paid $18,350 in taxes?

$$\text{Base} = \text{income for the year}$$

$$\text{Rate} = 40\%$$

$$\text{Percentage} = \$18,350$$

$$\text{Base} = \frac{\text{percentage}}{\text{rate}}$$

$$= \frac{\$18,350}{40\%} \leftarrow \text{Change to decimal}$$

$$= \frac{\$18,350}{0.40} = \$45,875$$

Josie earned $45,875 last year.

SOLVED PROBLEMS

2.15 Change (a) 23%, (b) 115%, (c) $\frac{3}{4}\%$, (d) $12\frac{2}{3}\%$, and (e) $98\frac{3}{8}\%$ into decimals.

SOLUTION

(a) $23\% = 0.23 \leftarrow$ Drop the % sign and move the decimal
                            point two places to the left

(b) $115\% = 1.15$

(c) $\frac{3}{4}\% = 0.75\% \leftarrow$ Change the fraction to a decimal

    $= 0.0075 \leftarrow$ Drop the % sign and move the decimal point two places to the left

(d) $12\frac{2}{3}\% = 12.\dot{6}\% = 0.12\dot{6}$

(e) $98\frac{3}{8}\% = 98.375\% = 0.98375$

2.16 Change (a) 80%, (b) 18.75% (c) 325%, (d) $66\frac{2}{3}\%$, and (e) $10\frac{1}{8}\%$ into fractions.

SOLUTION

(a) $80\% = 80 \times \frac{1}{100} \leftarrow$ Drop % sign and multiply by $\frac{1}{100}$

                $= \frac{80}{100} \qquad \leftarrow$ Reduce

                $= \frac{4}{5}$

(b) $18.75\% = 18.75 \times \frac{1}{100} \leftarrow$ Drop % sign and multiply by $\frac{1}{100}$

            $= \frac{18.75}{100} \qquad \leftarrow$ Multiply numerator and denominator by 100

            $= \frac{1875}{10,000} \qquad \leftarrow$ Reduce

            $= \frac{75}{400} = \frac{3}{16}$

(c) $325\% = \frac{325}{100} = \frac{13}{4}$

(d)
$$66\tfrac{2}{3}\% = \frac{66\tfrac{2}{3}}{100} = \frac{\frac{200}{3}}{100} = \frac{200}{3} \times \frac{1}{100} = \frac{2}{3}$$

(e)
$$10\tfrac{1}{8}\% = \frac{10\tfrac{1}{8}}{100} = \frac{\frac{81}{8}}{100} = \frac{81}{8} \times \frac{1}{100} = \frac{81}{800}$$

2.17 Write (a) 15%, (b) 2%, (c) $5\tfrac{1}{2}\%$, (d) $108\tfrac{7}{8}\%$, and (e) $66\tfrac{2}{3}\%$ as decimals and equivalent common fractions.

SOLUTION

(a)
$$15\% = 0.15 = \frac{15}{100} = \frac{3}{20}$$

(b)
$$2\% = 0.02 = \frac{2}{100} = \frac{1}{50}$$

(c)
$$5\tfrac{1}{2}\% = 5.5\% = 0.055 = \frac{55}{1,000} = \frac{11}{200}$$

(d)
$$108\tfrac{7}{8}\% = 108.875\% = 1.08875 = \frac{108,875}{100,000} = \frac{871}{800}$$

(e)
$$66\tfrac{2}{3}\% = 66.\dot{6}\% = 0.66\dot{6} = \frac{200}{300} = \frac{2}{3}$$

2.18 Express (a) 0.325, (b) 1.05, (c) 0.0025, (d) $0.02\dot{6}$, and (e) 0.0002 as percents.

SOLUTION

(a)
$$0.325 = 32.5\% \quad \leftarrow \text{Move the decimal point two places}$$
$$\text{to the right and add \% sign}$$

(b)
$$1.05 = 105\%$$

(c)
$$0.0025 = 0.25\% = \tfrac{1}{4}\%$$

(d)
$$0.02\dot{6} = 2.\dot{6}\% = 2\tfrac{2}{3}\%$$

(e)
$$0.0002 = 0.02\% = \frac{2}{100}\% = \frac{1}{50}\%$$

2.19 Express (a) 3/5, (b) $1\tfrac{5}{8}$, 1/20, (d) 19/400, and (e) 3/800 as percents.

SOLUTION

(a)
$$\frac{3}{5} = 0.6 \quad \leftarrow \text{Change the fraction to a decimal}$$
$$= 60\% \quad \leftarrow \text{Change the decimal to a percent}$$

(b)
$$1\tfrac{5}{8} = \frac{13}{8} = 1.625 = 162.5\%$$

(c)
$$\frac{1}{20} = 0.05 = 5\%$$

(d)
$$\frac{19}{400} = 0.0475 = 4.75\%$$

(e)
$$\frac{3}{800} = 0.00375 = 0.375\%$$

2.20 What percentage is (*a*) 8% of 300, (*b*) $11\frac{1}{4}$% of 280, (*c*) 152.5% of 1,200, (*d*) $\frac{5}{8}$% of 8,000, and (*e*) $66\frac{2}{3}$% of 39.60?

SOLUTION

(*a*)
$$8\% \text{ of } 300 = 0.08 \times 300 = 24$$

(*b*)
$$11\tfrac{1}{4}\% \text{ of } 280 = 0.1125 \times 280 = 31.50$$

(*c*)
$$152.5\% \text{ of } 1,200 = 1.525 \times 1,200 = 1,830$$

(*d*)
$$\tfrac{5}{8}\% \text{ of } 8,000 = 0.625\% \text{ of } 8,000 = 0.00625 \times 8,000 = 50$$

(*e*)
$$66\tfrac{2}{3}\% \text{ of } 39.60 = \tfrac{2}{3} \times 39.60 = 26.4$$

2.21 What percent of (*a*) 90 is 22.5, (*b*) 8,000 is 5, (*c*) 120 is 3.36, (*d*) 180 is 390, and (*e*) $23,000 is $1,265?

SOLUTION

(*a*) Base = 90
Percentage = 22.5
$$\text{Rate} = \frac{\text{percentage}}{\text{base}} = \frac{22.50}{90} = 0.25 = 25\%$$

(*b*) Base = 8,000
Percentage = 5
$$\text{Rate} = \frac{5}{8,000} = 0.000625 = 0.0625\%$$

(*c*) Base = 120
Percentage = 3.36
$$\text{Rate} = \frac{3.36}{120} = 0.028 = 2.8\%$$

(*d*) Base = 180
Percentage = 390
$$\text{Rate} = \frac{390}{180} = 2.16\dot{6} = 216\tfrac{2}{3}\%$$

(*e*) Base = $23,000
Percentage = $1,265
$$\text{Rate} = \frac{\$1,265}{\$23,000} = 0.055 = 5\tfrac{1}{2}\%$$

2.22 Find the base given the following percentages and rates:

SOLUTION

(*a*) 120% of what number is 200?

$$\text{Percentage} = 200$$
$$\text{Rate} = 120\%$$

$$\text{Base} = \frac{\text{percentage}}{\text{rate}} = \frac{200}{1.2} = 166.6\dot{6} = 166\tfrac{2}{3}$$

(*b*) $16.80 is $10\frac{1}{2}$% of what amount?

$$\text{Percentage} = \$16.80$$
$$\text{Rate} = 10\tfrac{1}{2}\%$$

$$\text{Base} = \frac{16.8}{0.105} = \$160$$

(*c*) $57.75 is 7% tax on what amount?

$$\text{Percentage} = \$57.75$$
$$\text{Rate} = 7\%$$

$$\text{Base} = \frac{\$57.75}{0.07} = \$825$$

(d) $8\frac{1}{4}\%$ of what number is 206.25?

$$\text{Percentage} = 206.25$$
$$\text{Rate} = 8\tfrac{1}{4}\%$$

$$\text{Base} = \frac{206.25}{0.0825} = 2{,}500$$

(e) 95% of what amount is 304?

$$\text{Percentage} = 304$$
$$\text{Rate} = 95\%$$

$$\text{Base} = \frac{304}{0.95} = 320$$

2.23 What is $1\frac{1}{2}\%$ of 800?

SOLUTION

$$\text{Rate} = 1\tfrac{1}{2}\%$$
$$\text{Base} = 800$$

$$\text{Percentage} = \text{rate} \times \text{base}$$
$$= 1\tfrac{1}{2}\% \times 800 = 1.5\% \times 800 = 0.015 \times 800 = 12$$

2.24 \$18 is 5% of what amount?

SOLUTION

$$\text{Percentage} = \$18$$
$$\text{Rate} = 5\%$$

$$\text{Base} = \frac{\text{percentage}}{\text{rate}}$$

$$= \frac{\$18}{5\%} = \frac{\$18}{0.05} = \$360$$

2.25 $12\frac{1}{2}\%$ of what number is 90?

SOLUTION

$$\text{Rate} = 12\tfrac{1}{2}\%$$
$$\text{Percentage} = 90$$

$$\text{Base} = \frac{\text{percentage}}{\text{rate}}$$

$$= \frac{90}{12\tfrac{1}{2}\%} = \frac{90}{12.5\%} = \frac{90}{0.125} = 720$$

2.26 $\frac{1}{4}\%$ of \$15,000 is what amount?

SOLUTION

$$\text{Rate} = \tfrac{1}{4}\%$$
$$\text{Base} = \$15{,}000$$

$$\text{Percentage} = \text{rate} \times \text{base}$$
$$= \tfrac{1}{4}\% \times \$15{,}000 = 0.25\% \times \$15{,}000 = 0.0025 \times \$15{,}000 = \$37.50$$

2.27 What percent of $80 is $100?

SOLUTION

$$Base = \$80$$
$$Percentage = \$100$$

$$Rate = \frac{percentage}{base}$$

$$= \frac{\$100}{\$80} = 1.25 = 125\%$$

2.28 If the state sales tax is 5%, find the tax on (*a*) a car listed at $8,500 and (*b*) a TV selling for $320.

SOLUTION

(*a*)
$$Rate = 5\%$$
$$Base = \$8,500$$

$$Percentage = rate \times base$$
$$= 5\% \times \$8,500 = 0.05 \times \$8,500 = \$425$$

The sales tax on the car is $425.

(*b*)
$$Rate = 5\%$$
$$Base = \$320$$

$$Percentage = rate \times base$$
$$= 5\% \times \$320 = 0.05 \times \$320 = \$16$$

The sales tax on the TV is $16.

2.29 A jewelry store advertises "25% off price marked." Find the discount on (*a*) a ring marked $199 and (*b*) a bracelet marked $429.

SOLUTION

(*a*)
$$Rate = 25\%$$
$$Base = \$199$$

$$Percentage = rate \times base$$
$$= 25\% \times \$199 = 0.25 \times \$199 = \$49.75$$

The discount on the ring is $49.75.

(*b*)
$$Rate = 25\%$$
$$Base = \$429$$

$$Percentage = rate \times base$$
$$= 25\% \times \$429 = 0.25 \times \$429 = \$107.25$$

The discount on the bracelet is $107.25.

2.30 A merchant buys an article for $50 and sells it for $75. Express her profit as a percent of the (*a*) cost and (*b*) selling price.

SOLUTION

$$Profit = selling\ price - cost$$
$$= \$75 - \$50 = \$25$$

(*a*)
$$\text{Percentage} = \$25$$
$$\text{Base} = \$50$$

Note that we can restate the question here as "What percent of $50 is $25?"

$$\text{Rate} = \frac{\text{percentage}}{\text{base}}$$

$$= \frac{\$25}{\$50} = 0.5 = 50\%$$

The merchant made a profit of 50% on the cost of the item.

(*b*)
$$\text{Percentage} = \$25$$
$$\text{Base} = \$75$$

Here we can restate the question as "What percent of $75 is $25?"

$$\text{Rate} = \frac{\text{percentage}}{\text{base}}$$

$$= \frac{\$25}{\$75} = 0.33\dot{3} = 33\tfrac{1}{3}\%$$

The merchant made a profit of $33\tfrac{1}{3}\%$ based on the selling price of the item.

2.31 Volume of sales of a company increased from $150,000 to $321,000 in 1 year. (*a*) What percent of $150,000 is $321,000? (*b*) What will the estimated volume of sales be next year if the rate of increase remains the same?

SOLUTION

(*a*)
$$\text{Base} = \$150,000$$
$$\text{Percentage} = \$321,000$$

$$\text{Rate} = \frac{\text{percentage}}{\text{base}}$$

$$= \frac{\$321,000}{\$150,000} = 2.14 = 214\%$$

(*b*)
$$\text{Rate} = 214\%$$
$$\text{Base} = \$321,000$$

$$\text{Percentage} = \text{rate} \times \text{base}$$

$$= 214\% \times \$321,000 = 2.14 \times \$321,000 = 2.14 \times \$321,000 = \$686,940$$

2.3 PERCENTAGE PROBLEMS OF INCREASE OR DECREASE

Problems involving *change*, increase or decrease, are very common in business applications. In the case of an *increase* the amount of change is added to the original quantity; that is,

$$\text{Original quantity} + \text{increase} = \text{new quantity}$$

In the case of *decrease* the amount of change is subtracted from the original quantity; that is,

$$\text{Original quantity} - \text{decrease} = \text{new quantity}$$

The amount of increase or decrease is usually stated as a percent of the original quantity.

EXAMPLE 8

(a)   L&B's inventory for March was 1,760 items. In April, the inventory increased by 15%. April's inventory consisted of how many items?

$$\text{April's inventory (new quantity)} = x$$
$$\text{Original quantity} = 1{,}760$$
$$\text{Increase} = 15\% \text{ of } 1{,}760$$

$$\text{Original quantity} + \text{increase} = \text{new quantity}$$

$$1{,}760 + 15\% \times 1{,}760 = x$$

$$1{,}760 + 0.15 \times 1{,}760 = x$$

$$1{,}760 + 264 = x$$

$$2{,}024 = x$$

April's inventory consisted of 2,024 items.

(b)   L&B's inventory declined by 25% in May due to sales. What was May's inventory?

$$\text{May's inventory (new quantity)} = y$$
$$\text{Original quantity} = 2{,}024$$
$$\text{Decrease} = 25\% \text{ of } 2{,}024$$

$$\text{Original quantity} - \text{decrease} = \text{new quantity}$$

$$2{,}024 - 25\% \times 2{,}024 = y$$

$$2{,}024 - 0.25 \times 2{,}024 = y$$

$$2{,}024 - 506 = y$$

$$1{,}518 = y$$

May's inventory was 1,518 items.

If any two of the three variables in the preceding formulas are known, the third can be calculated.

EXAMPLE 9

The price of a car, including a 6% sales tax, was $15,443.14. (a) What was the marked price of the car and (b) how much was the sales tax?

(a)   Let x = marked price of the car.

$$\text{Original quantity} = x$$
$$\text{Increase} = 6\% \times x$$
$$\text{New quantity} = \$15{,}443.14$$

$$\text{Original quantity} + \text{increase} = \text{new quantity}$$
$$x + 6\% x = \$15{,}443.14$$
$$x + 0.06x = \$15{,}443.14$$
$$1.06x = \$15{,}443.14$$
$$x = \$14{,}569$$

The marked price of the car was $14,569.

(b)   Let y = amount of sales tax

$$\text{Original quantity} = \$14{,}569$$
$$\text{Increase} = y$$
$$\text{New quantity} = \$15{,}443.14$$

$$\text{Original quantity} + \text{increase} = \text{new quantity}$$
$$\$14{,}569 + y = \$15{,}443.14$$
$$y = \$15{,}443.14 - \$14{,}569 = \$874.14$$

The sales tax on the car was $874.14.

The *rate* of change may be found by using the following formula:

$$\text{Rate of change} = \frac{\text{amount of change}}{\text{original quantity}}$$

EXAMPLE 10

A business grew in assets from $120,000 to $580,000. What was the rate of growth?

$$\text{Original quantity} = \$120{,}000$$
$$\text{New quantity} = \$580{,}000$$

$$\text{Amount of change (increase)} = \text{difference between original quantity and new quantity}$$
$$= \$580{,}000 - \$120{,}000 = \$460{,}000$$

$$\text{Rate of change} = \frac{\text{amount of change}}{\text{original quantity}}$$
$$= \frac{\$460{,}000}{\$120{,}000} = 3.83 \times 3.83\tfrac{1}{3} = 383\tfrac{1}{3}\%$$

SOLVED PROBLEMS

2.32 What number is 20% more than $900?

SOLUTION

$$\text{Let } x = \text{new quantity}$$
$$\text{Original quantity} = \$900$$
$$\text{Increase} = 20\% \text{ of } \$900$$

$$\text{Original quantity} + \text{increase} = \text{new quantity}$$
$$\$900 + 20\% \times \$900 = x$$
$$\$900 + 0.20 \times \$900 = x$$
$$\$900 + \$180 = x$$
$$\$1{,}080 = x$$

2.33 How much is 115 increased by 120%?

SOLUTION

$$\text{Let } x = \text{new quantity}$$
$$\text{Original quantity} = 115$$
$$\text{Increase} = 120\% \text{ of } 115$$

$$\text{Original quantity} + \text{increase} = \text{new quantity}$$
$$115 + 120\% \times 115 = x$$
$$115 + 1.20 \times 115 = x$$
$$115 + 138 = x$$
$$253 = x$$

2.34   What number is 60% less than 90?

SOLUTION

$$\text{Let } x = \text{new quantity}$$
$$\text{Original quantity} = 90$$
$$\text{Decrease} = 60\% \text{ of } 90$$

$$\text{Original quantity} - \text{decrease} = \text{new quantity}$$
$$90 - 60\% \times 90 = x$$
$$90 - 0.60 \times 90 = x$$
$$90 - 54 = x$$
$$36 = x$$

2.35   What is $22,000 decreased by 12%?

SOLUTION

$$\text{Let } x = \text{new quantity}$$
$$\text{Original quantity} = \$22,000$$
$$\text{Decrease} = 12\% \text{ of } \$22,000$$

$$\text{Original quantity} - \text{decrease} = \text{new quantity}$$
$$\$22,000 - 12\% \times \$22,000 = x$$
$$\$22,000 - 0.12 \times \$22,000 = x$$
$$\$22,000 - \$2,640 = x$$
$$\$19,360 = x$$

2.36   What amount increased by 20% will equal $60?

SOLUTION

$$\text{Let } x = \text{original quantity}$$
$$\text{Increase} = 20\% \text{ of } x$$
$$\text{New quantity} = \$60$$

$$\text{Original quantity} + \text{increase} = \text{new quantity}$$
$$x + 20\% \times x = \$60$$
$$x + 0.2x = \$60$$
$$1.2x = \$60$$
$$x = \frac{\$60}{1.2} = \$50$$

2.37   150 is 60% less than what number?

SOLUTION

$$\text{Let } x = \text{original quantity}$$
$$\text{Decrease} = 60\% \text{ of } x$$
$$\text{New quantity} = 150$$

$$\text{Original quantity} - \text{decrease} = \text{new quantity}$$
$$x - 60\% \times x = 150$$
$$x - 0.6x = 150$$
$$0.4x = 150$$
$$x = \frac{150}{0.4} = 375$$

2.38 The price of a calculator, including the sales tax of 5%, was $23.52. (*a*) What was the marked price of the calculator and (*b*) how much was the sales tax?

SOLUTION

(*a*) Let x = marked price

$$\text{Original quantity} = x$$
$$\text{Increase} = 5\% \text{ of } x$$
$$\text{New quantity} = \$23.52$$

$$\text{Original quantity} + \text{increase} = \text{new quantity}$$
$$x + 5\% \times x = \$23.52$$
$$x + 0.05x = \$23.52$$
$$1.05x = \$23.52$$
$$x = \frac{\$23.52}{1.05} = \$22.40$$

(*b*) Let y = amount of sales tax

$$\text{Original quantity} = \$22.40$$
$$\text{Increase} = y$$
$$\text{New quantity} = \$23.52$$

$$\text{Original quantity} + \text{increase} = \text{new quantity}$$
$$\$22.40 + y = \$23.52$$
$$y = \$23.52 - \$22.40 = \$1.12$$

Alternative solution:

We also know that increase = 5% of original quantity. Since increase = y,

$$y = 5\% \text{ of original quantity}$$
$$= 5\% \times \$22.40 = 0.05 \times \$22.40 = \$1.12$$

2.39 After a discount of 25%, a sale price of a suitcase is $84.60. (*a*) What was the regular price and (*b*) how much was the discount?

SOLUTION

(*a*) Let x = regular price

$$\text{Original quantity} = x$$
$$\text{Decrease} = 25\% \text{ of } x$$
$$\text{New quantity} = \$84.60$$

$$\text{Original quantity} - \text{decrease} = \text{new quantity}$$
$$x - 25\% \times x = \$84.60$$
$$x - 0.25x = \$84.60$$
$$0.75x = \$84.60$$
$$x = \frac{\$84.60}{0.75} = \$112.80$$

(*b*) Let y = amount of discount

$$\text{Original quantity} = \$112.80$$
$$\text{Decrease} = y$$
$$\text{New quantity} = \$84.60$$

$$\text{Original quantity} - \text{decrease} = \text{new quantity}$$
$$\$112.80 - y = \$84.60$$
$$- y = \$84.60 - \$112.80$$
$$y = -\$84.60 + \$112.80 = \$28.20$$

Alternative solution:

$$\text{Decrease} = 25\% \text{ of original quantity} = y$$

Therefore
$$y = 25\% \text{ of } \$112.80$$
$$= 0.25 \times \$112.80 = \$28.20$$

2.40 What percent more than 80 is 124?

SOLUTION

$$\text{Original quantity} = 80$$
$$\text{New quantity} = 124$$

$$\text{Amount of change (increase)} = \text{difference between original quantity and new quantity}$$
$$= 124 - 80 = 44$$

$$\text{Rate of change (increase)} = \frac{\text{amount of change}}{\text{original quantity}}$$
$$= \frac{44}{80} = 0.55 = 55\%$$

2.41 $120 is what percent less than $150?

SOLUTION

$$\text{Original quantity} = \$150$$
$$\text{New quantity} = \$120$$

$$\text{Amount of change (decrease)} = \text{difference between original quantity and new quantity}$$
$$= \$150 - \$210 = \$30$$

$$\text{Rate of change (decrease)} = \frac{\text{amount of change}}{\text{original quantity}}$$
$$= \frac{\$30}{\$150} = 0.2 = 20\%$$

2.42 If the consumer price index changes from 180 to 195 in a year, what was the annual rate of increase?

SOLUTION

$$\text{Original quantity} = 180$$
$$\text{New quantity} = 195$$

$$\text{Amount of change (increase)} = \text{difference between original quantity and new quantity}$$
$$= 195 - 180 = 15$$

$$\text{Rate of change (increase)} = \frac{\text{amount of change}}{\text{original quantity}}$$
$$= \frac{15}{180} = 0.08\dot{3} = 8\tfrac{1}{3}\%$$

2.43 The price of a stock dropped from $62.50 per share to $52.50 per share in a week. What was the percent change in price?

SOLUTION

$$\text{Original quantity} = \$62.50$$
$$\text{New quantity} = \$52.50$$

$$\text{Amount of change} = \text{difference between original quantity and new quantity}$$
$$= \$62.50 - \$52.50 = \$10.00$$

$$\text{Rate of change (decrease)} = \frac{\text{amount of change}}{\text{original quantity}}$$

$$= \frac{10}{62.50} = 0.16 = 16\%$$

2.44 A deposit of \$2,000 has accumulated to \$2,185 in 1 year. Find the annual rate of interest.

SOLUTION

$$\text{Original quantity} = \$2,000$$
$$\text{New quantity} = \$2,185$$

$$\text{Amount of change (interest)} = \text{difference between original quantity and new quantity}$$
$$= \$2,185 - \$2,000 = \$185$$

$$\text{Rate of change (interest)} = \frac{\text{amount of change}}{\text{original quantity}}$$

$$= \frac{\$185}{\$2,000} = 0.0925 = 9\tfrac{1}{4}\%$$

2.45 A car bought new for \$7,200 has a resale value of \$5,040 after 1 year of operation. (*a*) What was the rate of depreciation? (*b*) What will be the resale value of the car after 2 years at the same rate of depreciation?

SOLUTION

(*a*) $$\text{First-year depreciation} = \text{amount of change} = \$7,200 - \$5,040 = \$2,160$$

$$\text{Rate of change (depreciation)} = \frac{\text{amount of change}}{\text{original quantity}}$$

$$= \frac{\$2,160}{\$7,200} = 0.3 = 30\%$$

(*b*) At the end of the first year, the car is valued at \$5,040. Therefore, second-year depreciation = 30% of \$5,040 = 0.3 × \$5,040 = \$1,512. Resale value after 2 years is therefore:

$$\text{Original quantity} - \text{decrease} = \text{new quantity}$$
$$\$5,040 - \$1,512 = \$3,528$$

2.46 Paul spent \$21.60 for gas selling at 45¢ per liter (45¢/L). Find the cost of the same gas at 54¢/L.

SOLUTION

$$\text{Cost of gas at 54¢/L} = x$$

$$\text{Amount of increase in price per liter} = 54¢ - 45¢ = 9¢$$

$$\text{Rate of change (increase)} = \frac{\text{amount of change}}{\text{original quantity}} = \frac{9¢}{45¢} = 0.20 = 20\%$$

$$\text{Original quantity} + \text{increase} = \text{new quantity}$$
$$\$21.60 + 20\% \times \$21.60 = x$$
$$\$21.60 + 0.2 \times \$21.60 = x$$
$$\$21.60 + \$4.32 = x$$
$$\$25.92 = x$$

Alternative solutions:

1. Cost of the gas at

2. Number of liters

Cost of gas at 5

Supplem

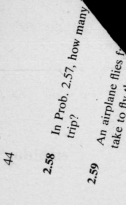

2.58 In Prob. 2.57, how many trip?

2.59 An airplane flies fi take to fly the s

2.60 A property of $990 is

2.61 How $6

2.62

2.47 Express the following ratios in lowest ter

    (a)   168 to 24   (c) $\frac{5}{3}$ to $\frac{4}{3}$

    (b)   35 to 21 to 91   (d)   1.2 to 0.48

2.48 Set up a ratio for each of the following and reduce to low

    (a)   5 min to 35 sec

    (b) $3.50 to 3 quarters

    (c)   30 in to $5\frac{1}{2}$ ft to 6 yd

2.49 The cost of a unit consists of three parts: $6.75 materials cost, $11.25 labor cost, and $2.25 overhead cost. What is the ratio between the three types of costs?

2.50 A family spent 30% of their income on food, 35% on housing, 20% on taxes, and 5% on entertainment.

    (a)   What is the ratio of food expenses to housing expenses?

    (b)   What is the ratio of taxes to food *and* housing expenses?

    (c)   What is the ratio of entertainment expenses to housing expenses to food expenses?

2.51 Allocate $6,000 in the ratio of (a) $5:7$ and (b) $11:9$.

2.52 A dividend of $8,920 is to be distributed among four shareholders in the ratio of shares held. If the shareholders have 5, 9, 11, and 15 shares, respectively, how much does each receive?

2.53 Three partners invested $12,500, $9,000, and $7,500, respectively, and the total profits of the partnership were $5,800. How much did each partner receive if the profits were divided in the ratio of the investments?

2.54 A condominium consists of three units. The monthly common area expenses are to be divided among the owners in the ratio $\frac{1}{2}:\frac{2}{3}:\frac{3}{4}$. Divide the July expenses of $437 among the owners.

2.55 Solve each of the following proportions for the unknown quantity:

    (a) $\dfrac{240}{30} = \dfrac{600}{x}$ (b) $\dfrac{x}{6.3} = \dfrac{1.4}{1.8}$ (c) $\dfrac{3}{4}:x = \dfrac{5}{8}:\dfrac{4}{9}$

2.56 If $500 is received as the profit on an investment of $6,000, what return might be expected on an investment of

    (a) $8,400   (b) $3,600   (c) $6,150

2.57 A car requires 7.5 L of gasoline for 100 kilometers (km). At the same rate of gasoline consumption, how far can the car travel if the gas tank holds 42 L?

liters of gasoline will the same car consume on (a) a 320-km trip, (b) a 54-km

om one city to another in 2 h 10 min at the average speed 540 mi/h. How long will it me route at an average speed of (a) 600 mi/h, (b) 450 mi/h?

tax is assessed at a tax rate of $18 per $1,000 assessed value. What is the assessment if a tax paid on a property?

much property tax is paid in Prob. 2.60 on a property with an assessed value of (a) $47,800, (b) 2,320?

Express each of the following as a decimal fraction:

(a) 7%   (e) 0.75%

(b) 21½%   (f) 18.35%

(c) 110%   (g) 210.5%

(d) 1⅛%   (h) ¼%

2.63 Express each of the percents in Prob. 2.62 as a common fraction.

2.64 Express each of the following decimals as a percent:

(a) 0.03   (e) 0.06̇6̇

(b) 0.125   (f) 0.18735

(c) 1.02   (g) 2.3872

(d) 0.098   (h) 0.0202

2.65 Express each of the following common fractions as a percent:

(a) $\dfrac{1}{2}$ (e) $\dfrac{7}{8}$

(b) $\dfrac{1}{4}$ (f) $\dfrac{9}{200}$

(c) $\dfrac{1}{5}$ (g) $\dfrac{11}{2,000}$

(d) $\dfrac{1}{6}$ (h) $\dfrac{17}{800}$

2.66 Find:

(a) 6% of 830   (e) 101% of 920

(b) 3½% of 1,200   (f) 95% of $7,000

(c) 11% of $5,000   (g) 7.89% of $200

(d) 12⅛% of $25,000   (h) 33⅓% of 21

2.67 What percent of

(a) 15 is 20?   (e) $4,800 is $672?

(b) 20 is 15?   (f) $152 is $167.20?

(c) 0.56 is 0.0028?   (g) $52 is $3.12?

(d) 600 is 54?   (h) $80 is $13?

2.68 (a) 12% of what number is 21.6?

(b) $8\frac{1}{2}$% of what number is 170?

(c) 125% of what number is 60?

(d) $\frac{1}{2}$% of what number is 3?

(e) 20% of what amount is $32.50?

(f) $13\frac{1}{8}$% of what amount is $105?

(g) 8.35% of what amount is $18.37?

(h) $15\frac{1}{4}$% of what amount is $884.50?

2.69 Find the missing quantities in each of the following:

	Base	Percent	Percentage
(a)	450	11	?
(b)	2,100	?	147
(c)	?	15	13.2
(d)	108	?	162
(e)	1,800	14.88	?
(f)	?	$7\frac{1}{4}$	0.85405
(g)	800	$1\frac{1}{2}$	?
(h)	?	0.05	6.4

2.70 If the state sales tax is 6%, find the tax on

(a) A sofa listed at $459

(b) A refrigerator selling for $1,289

(c) A car sold for $15,800

2.71 A furniture store is selling its entire stock at 40% off marked price. What is the discount on

(a) A dining room set marked $958

(b) A living room set marked $2,495

(c) A bedroom set marked $1,785

2.72 A real estate broker receives a commission of 7% of the sale price of a house. What is the commission on a house which sold for $62,900?

2.73 A mortgage payment of $291 is due on the first day of each month. If paid after the first of the month, a late penalty of $14.55 is charged. What is the percent penalty?

2.74 The semiannual interest on a bond is $5\frac{1}{2}$% of its face value and amounts to $110. What is the face value of the bond?

2.75 The 6% sales tax on a pair of skis amounted to $11.10. What was the price before the sales tax?

2.76 The discount of 15% off the regular price of a watch amounted to $7.20. What was the regular price?

2.77 (a) What is 160 increased by 15%?

(b) How much is $96 increased by 8%?

(c) What number is 24% more than 1,200?

2.78   (a)   What is 160 decreased by 15%?

(b)   How much is $96 decreased by 8%?

(c)   What number is 24% less than 1,200?

2.79   A clothing store advertises sale "20% off regular price." What will be the sale price of

(a)   A coat with the regular price $119

(b)   A dress with the regular price $69

2.80   What will be the total price of (a) the coat and (b) the dress in Prob. 2.79 if a 5% state sales tax is applied?

2.81   (a)   675 is 35% more than what number?

(b)   What deposit increased by 12% will equal $280?

2.82   (a)   72 is 40% less than what number?

(b)   What amount decreased by 15% will equal $13,600?

2.83   The trading price of a stock dropped 35% to $42.90. What was the trading price before the drop?

2.84   Property taxes on a house increased by 11% to $1,332. Find the property taxes before the increase.

2.85   After a cash discount of 4%, a storekeeper settled an invoice by paying $787.20. How much was the amount of discount?

2.86   The 5% state sales tax on a refrigerator amounted to $42.45. What was the total amount paid?

2.87   Sales in October decreased 14% over September sales. If October sales amounted to $13,072, what were the September sales?

2.88   A used car sold for $3,445 including 6% sales tax. How much was the sales tax on the car?

2.89   After real estate fees of 7% had been deducted from the proceeds of the sale of a property, the vendor received $26,505. What was the amount of the real estate fee?

2.90   A bank increased its prime lending rate from $12\frac{1}{2}$% to 13%. What is the percent increase in the lending rate?

2.91   Quarterly profits of a company decreased from $78,000 to $70,200. What was the quarterly rate of decrease in profits?

2.92   Enrollment in the business programs of a college increased from 580 students last year to 609 students this year. What was the rate of increase in the enrollment?

2.93   If an average hourly wage was increased from $9.60 to $12 in 3 years, what was the rate of increase?

2.94   The Dow Jones industrials index dropped from 1,048.50 to 1,006.56 in 1 day. What was the rate of decrease in the index?

2.95   If you paid $80.22 for the electric power at 6¢ per kilowatthour (kWh), how much would you pay for the same amount of electric power at 7¢/kWh?

2.96   An investment has increased in value from $1,200 to $1,363.20 in 1 year. What is the annual rate of return on this investment?

2.97   A taxpayer pays income tax at the rate of 30% of his taxable income. If he wants to reduce his income taxes by $2,100, by how much will he have to reduce his taxable income?

2.98   The cash operating expenses of a commercial rental were 40% of the total rent. If the only other cash outflow was the mortgage payment of $580 per month, what should be the monthly rent to obtain a net cash inflow before taxes of $380 per month?

Answers to Supplementary Problems

2.47   (a) $7:1$, (b) $5:3:13$, (c) $25:12$, (d) $5:2$

2.48   (a) $60:7$, (b) $14:3$, (c) $5:11:36$

2.49 $3:5:1$

2.50   (a) $6:7$, (b) $4:13$, (c) $1:7:6$

2.51   (a) $2,500, $3,500; (b) $3,300, $2,700

2.52 $1,115, $2,007, $2,453, $3,345

2.53 $2,500, $1,800, $1,500

2.54 $114, $152, $171

2.55   (a) 75, (b) 4.9, (c) $\frac{8}{15}$

2.56   (a) $700, (b) $300, (c) $512.50

2.57   560 km

2.58   (a) 24 L, (b) 4.05 L

2.59   (a) 1 h 57 min, (b) 2 h 36 min

2.60 $55,000

2.61   (a) $860.40, (b) $1,121.76

2.62   (a) 0.07, (b) 0.215, (c) 1.1, (d) 0.01125, (e) 0.0075, (f) 0.1835, (g) 2.105, (h) 0.0025

2.63   (a) $\frac{7}{100}$, (b) $\frac{43}{200}$, (c) $\frac{11}{10}$, (d) $\frac{9}{800}$, (e) $\frac{3}{400}$, (f) $\frac{367}{2,000}$, (g) $\frac{421}{200}$, (h) $\frac{1}{400}$

2.64   (a) 3%, (b) 12.5%, (c) 102%, (d) 9.8%, (e) $6\frac{2}{3}$%, (f) 18.735%, (g) 238.72%, (h) 2.02%

2.65   (a) 50%, (b) 25%, (c) 20%, (d) $16\frac{2}{3}$%, (e) $87\frac{1}{2}$%, (f) $4\frac{1}{2}$%, (g) 0.55%, (h) $2\frac{1}{8}$%

2.66   (a) 49.8, (b) 42, (c) $550, (d) $3,031.25, (e) 929.2, (f) $6,650, (g) $15.78, (h) 7

2.67   (a) $133\frac{1}{3}$%, (b) 75%, (c) $\frac{1}{2}$%, (d) 9%, (e) 14%, (f) 110%, (g) 6%, (h) $16\frac{1}{4}$%

2.68 (*a*) 180, (*b*) 2,000, (*c*) 48, (*d*) 600, (*e*) $162.50, (*f*) $800, (*g*) $220, (*h*) $5,800

2.69 (*a*) 49.5, (*b*) 7%, (*c*) 88, (*d*) 150%, (*e*) 267.84, (*f*) 11.78, (*g*) 12, (*h*) 12,800

2.70 (*a*) $27.54, (*b*) $77.34, (*c*) $948   **2.85** $32.80

2.71 (*a*) $383.20, (*b*) $998, (*c*) $714   **2.86** $891.45

2.72 $4,403   **2.87** $15,200

2.73 5%   **2.88** $195

2.74 $2,000   **2.89** $1,995

2.75 $185   **2.90** 4%

2.76 $48   **2.91** 10%

2.77 (*a*) 184, (*b*) $103.68, (*c*) 1,488   **2.92** 5%

2.78 (*a*) 136, (*b*) $88.32, (*c*) 912   **2.93** 25%

2.79 (*a*) $95.20, (*b*) $55.20   **2.94** 4%

2.80 (*a*) $99.96, (*b*) $57.96   **2.95** $93.59

2.81 (*a*) 500, (*b*) $250   **2.96** 13.6%

2.82 (*a*) 120, (*b*) $16,000   **2.97** $7,000

2.83 $66   **2.98** $1,600

2.84 $1,200

Chapter 3

Using an Electronic Pocket Calculator

By using an electronic pocket calculator, we can solve complex mathematical problems with efficiency and speed. Students using this book should have access to an inexpensive "electronic slide rule" or "scientific" calculator because the calculator's power function is needed to solve financial problems involving compound interest.

3.1 BASIC OPERATIONS

Addition, subtraction, multiplication, and division are performed on the calculator as shown in the following examples.*

EXAMPLE 1

Be sure to press the "clear" key on your calculator before calculating the answer to a new problem. Otherwise, any number or operation entered previously will be included in your current calculation.

(*a*)   Add 20.15 + 1,203.67:

Enter	Press	Display
20.15	+	20.15
1203.67	=	1223.82 ← Answer

(*b*)   Subtract 8,975.87 − 3,679.91:

Enter	Press	Display
8975.87	−	8975.87
3679.91	=	5295.96 ← Answer

(*c*)   Multiply 2,500 × 0.12:

Enter	Press	Display
2500	×	2500.
0.12	=	300. ← Answer

(*d*)   Divide 1,800 ÷ 0.12:

Enter	Press	Display
1800	÷	1800.
0.12	=	15000. ← Answer

At the end of any single operation, the number displayed as the answer is available for further calculations. We may add to it, subtract from it, multiply, or divide it. Thus we may perform chain calculations.

---

* Consult the owner's manual that came with your calculator for details about your calculator's features and operations.

EXAMPLE 2

(a) Find the sum of $3,520.25 + 583.19 + 1,871.05 - 2,482.15$:

Enter	Press	Display	
3520.25	+	3520.25	
583.19	+	4103.44	←Sum of the first two terms
1871.05	−	5974.49	←Sum of the first three terms
2482.15	=	3492.34	←Answer

(b) Multiply $15,000 \times 0.125 \times 1.75$:

Enter	Press	Display	
15000	×	15000.	
0.125	×	1875.	←Product of the first two terms
1.75	=	3281.25	←Answer

(c) Calculate $825 \div 15 \times 1.08$:

Enter	Press	Display	
825	÷	825.	
15	×	55.	←Quotient of the first two terms
1.08	=	59.4	←Answer

In calculations involving parentheses and brackets we may use the parentheses keys $\boxed{(}\ \boxed{)}$, if available, or perform the operations in the brackets or parentheses first and then perform the other operations.

EXAMPLE 3

(a) Calculate $S = 2,000[1 + (0.12)(60/360)]$:

Enter	Press	Display	
2000	×	2000.	
	(	2000.	
1	+	1.	
0.12	×	0.12	
60	÷	7.2	
360	)	1.02	←Value of $[1 + (0.12)(60/360)]$
	=	2040.	←Answer

Alternative solution:

Enter	Press	Display	
1	+	1.	
0.12	×	0.12	
60	÷	7.2	
360	=	1.02	←Value of $[1 + (0.12)(60/360)]$
	×	1.02	
2000	=	2040.	←Answer

(b)   Calculate $P = \dfrac{3{,}022.50}{1 + (0.09)(30/360)}$.

Enter	Press	Display	
3022.50	÷	3022.5	
	(	3022.5	
1	+	1.	
0.09	×	0.09	
30	÷	2.7	
360	)	1.0075	←Value of [1 + (0.09)(30/360)]
	=	3000.	←Answer

Alternative solution:

Enter	Press	Display	
1	+	1.	
0.09	×	0.09	
30	÷	2.7	
360	=	1.0075	←Value of [1 + (0.09)(30/360)]
	$\frac{1}{x}$	0.99255583	←Value of $\dfrac{1}{1 + (0.09)(30/360)}$
	×	0.99255583	
3022.50	=	3000.	←Answer

SOLVED PROBLEMS

3.1   Find the sum of $512.83 - 32.17 - 110.70 + 18.88$:

SOLUTION

Enter	Press	Display	
512.83	−	512.83	
32.17	−	480.66	
110.70	+	369.96	
18.88	=	388.84	←Answer

3.2   Calculate $(23.8 + 12.4) \div 9.05 \times 46.8$:

SOLUTION

Enter	Press	Display	
23.8	+	23.8	
12.4	=	36.2	
	÷	36.2	
9.05	×	4.0	
46.8	=	187.2	←Answer

3.3   Calculate $I = 180 \times 0.0725 \times \dfrac{72}{360}$:

SOLUTION

Enter	Press	Display	
180	$\times$	180.	
0.0725	$\times$	13.05	
72	$\div$	939.6	
360	$=$	2.61	← Answer

3.4   Calculate $r = \dfrac{15}{500(90/360)}$:

SOLUTION

Enter	Press	Display	
15	$\div$	15.	
	(	15.	
500	$\times$	500.	
90	$\div$	45000.	
360	)	125.	← Value of [500(90/360)]
	$=$	0.12	← Answer

Alternative solution:

Enter	Press	Display	
500	$\times$	500.	
90	$\div$	45000.	
360	$=$	125.	← Value of [500(90/360)]
	$\dfrac{1}{x}$	0.008	← Value of $\dfrac{1}{500(90/360)}$
	$\times$	0.008	
15	$=$	0.12	← Answer

3.5   Calculate $P = 500[1 - (0.15)(90/360)]$:

SOLUTION

Enter	Press	Display	
500	$\times$	500.	
	(	500.	
1	$-$	1.	
0.15	$\times$	0.15	
90	$\div$	13.5	
360	)	0.9625	← Value of [1 − (0.15)(90/360)]
	$=$	481.25	← Answer

Alternative solution:

Enter	Press	Display	
1	−	1.	
0.15	×	0.15	
90	÷	13.5	
360	=	0.9625	← Value of [1 − (0.15)(90/360)]
	×	0.9625	
500	=	481.25	← Answer

3.6 Calculate $S = \dfrac{752}{1 - (0.12)(180/360)}$:

SOLUTION

Enter	Press	Display	
752	÷	752.	
	(	752.	
1	−	1.	
0.12	×	0.12	
180	÷	21.6	
360	)	0.94	← Value of [1 − (0.12)(180/360)]
	=	800.	← Answer

Alternative solution:

Enter	Press	Display	
1	−	1.	
0.12	×	0.12	
180	÷	21.6	
360	=	0.94	← Value of [1 − (0.12)(180/360)]
	$\dfrac{1}{x}$	1.0638298	← Value of $\dfrac{1}{-(0.12)(180/360)}$
	×	1.0638298	
752	=	800.	← Answer

3.2 ROUNDING

Answers obtained with the help of a calculator may need to be rounded to a desired number of decimal places. In most business problems involving dollar values, the rounding is done to the nearest cent, that is, to two decimal places. Use the following rules for rounding:

1. If the first digit in the group of decimal digits to be dropped is greater than or equal to 5, the last digit retained is *increased* by 1. (This is known as *rounding up*.)

2. If the first digit in the group of decimal digits to be dropped is less than 5, the last digit retained is left *unchanged*. (This is known as *rounding down*.)

EXAMPLE 4

(*a*) Round the following numbers to the nearest hundredth.

                                   ┌────── First digit to be dropped is 5, so round up
            15.48**5**7 ≅ 15.49

                                  ┌────── First digit to be dropped is less than 5, so round down
            12.56**4**6 ≅ 12.56

                               ┌────── First digit to be dropped is greater than 5, so round up
          125.09**6**5 ≅ 125.10
         2309.9974 ≅ 2310.00
         250.02403 ≅ 250.02

(*b*) Round the numbers in part (*a*) to the nearest thousandth.

                                 ┌────── First digit to be dropped is greater than 5, so round up
            15.485**7** ≅ 15.486
            12.564**6** ≅ 12.565

                               ┌────── First digit to be dropped is 5, so round up
          125.096**5** ≅ 125.097

                               ┌────── First digit to be dropped is less than 5, so round down
        2309.997**4** ≅ 2309.997
        250.024**0**3 ≅ 250.024

(*c*) Round the numbers in part (*a*) to the nearest whole number.

                               ┌────── First digit to be dropped is less than 5, so round down
            15.**4**857 ≅ 15

                               ┌────── First digit to be dropped is 5, so round up
            12.**5**646 ≅ 13
          125.0965 ≅ 125

                               ┌────── First digit to be dropped is greater than 5, so round up
        2309.**9**974 ≅ 2310
        250.020403 ≅ 250

SOLVED PROBLEMS

3.7 Calculate $r = 11.21/385.75$, round to four decimal places, and express in percent.

    SOLUTION

Enter	Press	Display
11.21	÷	11.21
385.75	=	0.02906027

$$r = 0.0291 = 2.91\%$$

3.8 Calculate and round to the nearest cent.

$$S = \frac{\$800}{1 - (0.11)(55/360)}$$

SOLUTION

Enter	Press	Display
800	÷	800.
	(	800.
1	−	1.
0.11	×	0.11
55	÷	6.05
360	)	0.98319444
	=	813.67425

$$S = \$813.67$$

3.9   Calculate and round to the nearest cent.

$$D = \$905.38 \times 0.18 \times \frac{41}{360}$$

SOLUTION

Enter	Press	Display
905.38	×	905.38
0.18	×	162.9684
41	÷	6681.7044
360	=	18.56029

$$D = \$18.56$$

3.10   Calculate and round to the nearest dollar.

$$S = \$12,000[1 + (0.0125)(125/360)]$$

SOLUTION

Enter	Press	Display
12000	×	12000.
	(	12000.
1	+	1.
0.0125	×	0.0125
125	÷	1.5625
360	)	1.0043403
	=	12052.083

$$S = \$12,052$$

3.3   OTHER OPERATIONS

Using the Percent Key   %

In solving percentage problems (see Chap. 2, Secs. 2.2 and 2.3), we may use the "%" key of a calculator.

EXAMPLE 5

Find 5% of 820.

Enter	Press	Display	
5	%	0.05	
	×	0.05	
820	=	41.	← Answer

Alternative solution:

Enter	Press	Display	
820	$\times$	820.	
5	%	0.05	
	=	41.	← Answer

EXAMPLE 6

How much is 115 increased by 20%?

Let x be the new quantity, so that $x = 115 + (20\% \times 115)$. Note that this is the same as the formula: New quantity = original quantity + increase (see Chap. 2, Sec. 2.3).

Enter	Press	Display	
115	+	115.	
20	%	23.	
	=	138.	← Answer

Alternative solution:

$$x = 115 \times 120\%$$

Enter	Press	Display	
115	$\times$	115.	
120	%	1.2	
	=	138.	← Answer

Using the Power Key $\boxed{y^x}$

Powers or *exponents* are used to simplify multiplication when the factors are the same. Thus we may write

$$2 \times 2 \times 2 \times 2 = 2^4 \quad \text{Fourth power of 2 because there are} \\ \text{four 2s being multiplied}$$

$$(1.03)(1.03)(1.03)(1.03)(1.03)(1.03) = 1.03^6 \quad \text{Sixth power of 1.03}$$

This repeated multiplication of the same factor may be performed on a calculator by using the power key $\boxed{y^x}$.

EXAMPLE 7

(*a*)   Find the third power of 18, that is, 18^3.

Enter	Press	Display	
18	y^x	18.	
3	=	5832.	← Answer

(*b*)   Calculate $(1.0125)^{300}$.

Enter	Press	Display	
1.0125	y^x	1.0125	
300	=	41.544119	← Answer

In solving financial problems involving compound interest, we use the power key $\boxed{y^x}$ to calculate $(1 + i)^n$ for different values of i and n.

EXAMPLE 8

(a) Calculate $(1 + i)^n$ when $i = 0.083/12$ and $n = 112$.

Enter	Press	Display	
1	+	1.	
0.083	÷	0.083	
12	=	1.0069167	←Value of $(1 + i)$
	y^x	1.0069167	
112	=	2.1640899	← Answer

(b) Calculate $1/(1 + i)^n$ when $i = 0.1025/4$ and $n = 20$.

Enter	Press	Display	
1	+	1.	
0.1025	÷	0.1025	
4	=	1.025625	←Value of $(1 + i)$
	y^x	1.025625	
20	=	1.6587158	
	$\frac{1}{x}$	0.60287605	←Answer

SOLVED PROBLEMS

3.11 What is 15% of 356?

SOLUTION

Enter	Press	Display	
15	%	0.15	
	×	0.15	
356	=	53.4	←Answer

3.12 What number is 30% more than 88?

SOLUTION

Let x be the new quantity, so that $x = 88 + (30\% \times 88)$.

Enter	Press	Display	
88	+	88.	
30	%	26.4	
	=	114.4	← Answer

Alternative solution:

$$x = 88 \times 130\%$$

Enter	Press	Display
88	×	88.
130	%	1.3
	=	114.4

3.13 How much is 99 decreased by 15%?

SOLUTION

Let x be the new quantity, so that $x = 99 - (15\% \times 99)$.

Enter	Press	Display	
99	−	99.	
15	%	14.85	
	=	84.15	←Answer

Alternative solution:

$$x = 99 \times (100\% - 15\%) = 99 \times 85\%$$

Enter	Press	Display
99	×	99.
85	%	0.85
	=	84.15

3.14 A store advertises a sale of "35% off regular price." Find the sale price of a radio with a regular price of $159.

SOLUTION

$$x = \$159 - (35\% \times \$159)$$

Enter	Press	Display
159	−	159.
35	%	55.65
	=	103.35

The sale price is $103.35.

3.15 What will be the total price of the radio in Prob. 3.15, if there is a 6% state sales tax?

SOLUTION

$$x = \$103.35 + (6\% \times \$103.35)$$

Enter	Press	Display
103.35	+	103.35
6	%	6.201
	=	109.551

The total price is $109.55.

3.16 A federal tax of 12% and a 5% state sales tax are applied to the marked price. Find the total price of an item with a marked price of $48.

SOLUTION

Enter	Press	Display	
48	$\times$	48.	
12	%	0.12	
	=	5.76	←Federal tax paid
	+	5.76	
48	$\times$	48.	
5	%	0.05	
	=	8.16	←Total tax paid (federal plus state)
	+	8.16	
48	=	56.16	←Answer (item price plus taxes paid)

Alternative solution:

Enter	Press	Display	
12	+	12.	
5	=	17.	←Sum of tax rates
	%	0.17	
	$\times$	0.17	
48	=	8.16	←Total tax paid (federal and state)
	+	8.16	
48	=	56.16	←Answer

3.17 Find the tenth power of 3 (i.e., 3^{10}).

SOLUTION

Enter	Press	Display	
3	y^x	3.	
10	=	59049.	←Answer

3.18 Calculate $800(1.01)^{24}$.

SOLUTION

Enter	Press	Display	
1.01	y^x	1.01	
24	=	1.2697346	
	$\times$	1.2697346	
800	=	1015.7877	←Answer

3.19   Calculate $1,500/(1.03)^{50}$.

      SOLUTION

Enter	Press	Display
1.03	y^x	1.03
50	=	4.383906
	$\dfrac{1}{x}$	0.22810708
	×	0.22810708
1500	=	342.16062 ← Answer

Supplementary Problems

3.20   Add the following:

      (a) $82.51 + $125.68 + $1,200.07 + $7.58

      (b)   5,000 + 35.387 + 0.043 + 105.3

      (c)   1.00567 + 3.87076 + 4.73023 + 11.00841

3.21   Find the sum of the following:

      (a)   1,286 − 755 − 305 + 106 − 59

      (b) $22.71 + $1,583.70 − $287.15 − $487.55

      (c)   13.8735 − 0.7381 + 1.7776 − 10.0051

3.22   Multiply the following (round to two decimal places):

      (a) $82 \times 0.05 \times 321.7 \times 0.1$

      (b) $1.00725 \times 1,800 \times 22.3$

      (c) $1.2076576 \times 5.358 \times 215.35$

3.23   Divide the following (round to one decimal place):

      (a) $17,825 \div 62.7 \div 15$

      (b) $0.976 \div 0.0082 \div 0.195$

      (c) $10.12 \div 12,1378 \div 0.128$

3.24   Multiply and divide the following (round to nearest whole number):

      (a) $18 \times 21.07 \div 17.85$

      (b) $99.753 \div 12.8 \times 1.2378$

      (c) $14.5 \times 26.83 \div 73 \times 0.185$

3.25   Calculate and round to two decimal places:

      (a) $I = 850 \times 0.115 \times (38/360)$

      (b) $S = 4,200[1 + (0.1475)(120/360)]$

      (c) $P = 2,850[1 - (0.1325)(88/360)]$

3.26   Calculate and round to two decimal places:

(a) $P = \dfrac{2,800}{1 + (0.08)(69/365)}$

(b) $S = \dfrac{50,000}{1 - (0.125)(170/360)}$

(c) $P = \dfrac{20}{0.07(200/360)}$

3.27   Calculate and round to four decimal places:

(a) $r = \dfrac{350}{12,000(270/360)}$

(b) $d = \dfrac{18.75}{758(120/360)}$

(c) $r = \dfrac{0.12}{1 - (0.12)(120/360)}$

3.28   Find:

(a)   8.31% of $300

(b)   102% of 450

(c) $12\frac{1}{4}$% of $18,000

3.29   What percent of 80 is 75?

3.30   What number is 18% more than

(a) 350   (b) 5   (c) 8,000

3.31   What number is 27% less than

(a) 1,200   (b) 78   (c) 27

3.32   The 5% sales tax on a pair of shoes amounted to $1.20. What was the price without the sales tax?

3.33   Find the total price, including 4% sales tax, on an item that is discounted 33% off $189 list price.

3.34   Calculate and round to three decimal places:

(a) 2^{15} (b) 1.03^{15} (c) 0.92^{15}

3.35   Find the value of $(1 + i)^n$ to four decimal places, given:

(a) $i = 0.0725$ and $n = 15$

(b) $i = 0.12/365$ and $n = 730$

(c) $i = 0.08/12$ and $n = 120$

3.36   Find the value of $\dfrac{1}{(1+i)^n}$ to six decimal places, given:

(a) $i = 0.0125$ and $n = 180$

(b) $i = 0.12$ and $n = 3$

(c) $i = \dfrac{0.07}{12}$ and $n = 240$

3.37   Calculate and round to two decimal places:

(a) $200(1.11)^5$ (b) $8,800\left(1+\dfrac{0.08}{12}\right)^{36}$ (c) $3,580\left(1+\dfrac{0.1}{365}\right)^{97}$

3.38   Calculate and round to two decimal places:

(a) $\dfrac{1,800}{(1.05)^{16}}$ (b) $\dfrac{5,720}{(1.01)^{300}}$ (c) $\dfrac{380}{[1+(0.12/365)]^{730}}$

Answers to Supplementary Problems

3.20   (a) $1,415.84, (b) 5,140.73, (c) 20.61507

3.21   (a) 273, (b) $831.71, (c) 4.9079

3.22   (a) 131.90, (b) 40,431.02, (c) 1,393.45

3.23   (a) 19.0, (b) 610.4, (c) 6.5

3.24   (a) 21, (b) 10, (c) 1

3.25   (a) 10.32, (b) 4,406.50, (c) 2,757.69

3.26   (a) 2,758.29, (b) 53,136.53, (c) 514.29

3.27   (a) 0.0389, (b) 0.0742, (c) 0.1250

3.28   (a) $24.93, (b) 459, (c) $2,205

3.29   93.75%

3.30   (a) 413, (b) 5.9, (c) 9,440

3.31   (a) 876, (b) 56.94, (c) 19.71

3.32 $24

3.33 $131.70

3.34   (a) 32,768, (b) 1.558, (c) 0.286

3.35   (a) 2.8573, (b) 1.2712, (c) 2.2196

3.36   (a) 0.106879, (b) 0.711780, (c) 0.247602

3.37   (a) 337.01, (b) 11,178.09, (c) 3,676.40

3.38   (a) 824.60, (b) 289.06, (c) 298.93

Chapter 4

Metric System

The metric system of measurement is used throughout most of the world. The United States is gradually moving from the U.S. customary system to the metric system. The main advantage of the metric system is that it is based on powers of 10. Since each unit is 10 times greater than the next smaller unit, it is easy to convert from one unit to another.

The basic units in the metric system are the meter (m) for length, the gram (g) for mass (weight), the liter (L) for volume, and the degree Celsius (°) for temperature.

4.1 METRIC PREFIXES

Common prefixes used with all basic units are milli, centi, deci, deka, hecto, and kilo. The following is a list of the *measures of length*; the basic unit is the *meter* (m).

> 1 *milli*meter (mm) = 0.001 of a meter
> 1 *centi*meter (cm) = 0.01 of a meter
> 1 *deci*meter (dm) = 0.1 of a meter
> meter (m) = 1
> 1 *deka*meter (dkm) = 10 meters
> 1 *hecto*meter (hm) = 100 meters
> 1 *kilo*meter (km) = 1,000 meters

EXAMPLE 1

Conversion from one unit to another is done by multiplying by a conversion factor equal to 1. To create the conversion factor, express the relationship between the units as a ratio.

(*a*) How many meters are there in 71.8 dekameters?

1. Create a conversion factor.

   Relationship between units: 1 dkm = 10 m

   Relationship expressed as a ratio: $1 = \dfrac{10 \text{ m}}{1 \text{ dkm}}$

   Note that the term in the numerator is the unit to which we are converting.

2. Multiply the quantity by the conversion factor.

$$71.8 \text{ dkm} \times \frac{10 \text{ m}}{1 \text{ dkm}} = 718 \text{ m}$$

(*b*) How many millimeters equal 0.735 meters?

1. Create a conversion factor.

   Relationship between units: 1 mm = 0.001 m

   Relationship expressed as a ratio: $\dfrac{1 \text{ mm}}{0.001 \text{ m}} = 1$

2. Multiply the quantity by the conversion factor.

$$0.735 \text{ m} \times \frac{1 \text{ mm}}{0.001 \text{ m}} = 0.735 \times 1,000 \text{ mm} = 735 \text{ mm}$$

(c)   How many centimeters are there in 2.52 kilometers?

    1.   Create the conversion factors.

       Relationship between units: $1 \text{ km} = 1{,}000 \text{ m}$ $1 \text{ cm} = 0.01 \text{ m}$

       Relationship expressed as ratio: $1 = \dfrac{1{,}000 \text{ m}}{1 \text{ km}}$ $\dfrac{1 \text{ cm}}{0.01 \text{ m}} = 1$

    2.   Multiply the quantity by the conversion factors.

$$2.52 \text{ km} \times \frac{1{,}000 \text{ m}}{1 \text{ km}} \times \frac{1 \text{ cm}}{0.01 \text{ m}} = 2.52 \times 100{,}000 \text{ cm} = 252{,}000 \text{ cm}$$

(d)   Express 3,800 millimeters in dekameters.

    1.   Create the conversion factors.

       Relationship between units: $1 \text{ mm} = 0.001 \text{ m}$ $1 \text{ dkm} = 10 \text{ m}$

       Relationship expressed as a ratio: $1 = \dfrac{0.001 \text{ m}}{1 \text{ mm}}$ $\dfrac{1 \text{ dkm}}{10 \text{ m}} = 1$

    2.   Multiply the quantity by the conversion factors.

$$3{,}800 \text{ mm} \times \frac{0.001 \text{ m}}{1 \text{ mm}} \times \frac{1 \text{ dkm}}{10 \text{ m}} = 3{,}800 \times 0.0001 \text{ dkm} = 0.38 \text{ dkm}$$

The following is a list of the *measures of mass weight*; the basic unit is the *gram* (g).

> 1 *milli*gram (mg) = 0.001 of a gram
> 1 *centi*gram (cg) = 0.01 of a gram
> 1 *deci*gram (dg) = 0.1 of a gram
> gram (g) = 1
> 1 *deka*gram (dkg) = 10 grams
> 1 *hecto*gram (hg) = 100 grams
> 1 *kilo*gram (kg) = 1,000 grams
> 1 metric ton (t) = 1,000 kilograms

Note that since the gram is too small a unit for practical measurements (1 gram is about 1/30 of an ounce), the kilogram is used as the basic unit of weight measurement.

EXAMPLE 2

(a)   How many grams equal 589 milligrams?

    1.   Write a conversion factor.

$$1 \text{ mg} = 0.001 \text{ g}$$
$$1 = 0.001 \text{ g/mg}$$

    2.   Multiply by the conversion factor.

$$589 \text{ mg} \times 0.001 \text{ g/mg} = 0.589 \text{ g}$$

(b)   Change 8.465 kilograms to dekagrams.

    1.   Write the conversion factors.

$$1 \text{ kg} = 1{,}000 \text{ g} \qquad 1 \text{ dkg} = 10 \text{ g}$$
$$1 = 1{,}000 \text{ g/kg} \qquad 1 \text{ dkg/10 g} = 1$$

2. Multiply by the conversion factors.

$$8.465 \text{ kg} \times 1{,}000 \text{ g/kg} \times 1 \text{ dkg}/10 \text{ g} = 8.465 \times 100 \text{ dkg} = 846.5 \text{ dkg}$$

Alternative method:

1. Using the basic unit (in this case, grams), state the relationship between the units as a proportion, with the numerator being the unit desired in the answer.

$$\frac{1 \text{ dkg}}{1 \text{ kg}} = \frac{10 \text{ g}}{1{,}000 \text{ g}} = \frac{1}{100}$$

Note that the units are *inversely* proportional in the ratio of 1/100, since there can only be more of the smaller unit (dkg) in the larger unit (kg)

2. Multiply by the *reciprocal* of the ratio.

$$8.465 \text{ kg} \times 100 \text{ dkg/kg} = 846.5 \text{ dkg}$$

This is a shortcut to the steps in the actual calculations, which are as follows:
   1. Cross multiply.

$$\frac{1 \text{ dkg}}{1 \text{ kg}} \diagdown\!\!\!\!\diagup \frac{10 \text{ g}}{1{,}000 \text{ g}}$$

$$1{,}000 \text{ dkg} = 10 \text{ kg}$$

   2. Solve for either unit of measurement.

$$\text{dkg} = 0.01 \text{ kg} \qquad \text{or} \qquad 100 \text{ dkg} = \text{kg}$$

   3. Write the conversion factor.

$$\frac{1 \text{ dkg}}{0.01 \text{ kg}} \qquad \text{or} \qquad \frac{100 \text{ dkg}}{1 \text{ kg}}$$

   4. Multiply the quantity by the conversion factor.

$$8.465 \text{ kg} \times \frac{100 \text{ dkg}}{\text{kg}} = 8.465 \times 100 \text{ dkg} = 846.5 \text{ dkg}$$

or

$$8.465 \text{ kg} \times \frac{\text{dkg}}{0.01 \text{ kg}} = 8.465 \times 100 \text{ dkg} = 846.5 \text{ dkg}$$

The following is a list of the *measures* of volume; the basic unit is the liter (L).

> 1 *milli*liter (mL) = 0.001 of a liter
> 1 *centi*liter (cL) = 0.01 of a liter
> 1 *deci*liter (dL) = 0.1 of a liter
> liter (L) = 1
> 1 *deka*liter (dkL) = 10 liters
> 1 *hecto*liter (hL) = 100 liters
> 1 *kilo*liter (kL) = 1,000 liters

EXAMPLE 3

(*a*) Express 85 centiliters in dekaliters.

$$1 \text{ cL} = 0.01 \text{ L} \qquad 1 \text{ dkL} = 10 \text{ L}$$

$$1 = \frac{0.01 \text{ L}}{1 \text{ cL}} \qquad \frac{1 \text{ dkL}}{10 \text{ L}} = 1$$

$$85 \text{ cL} \times \frac{0.01 \text{ L}}{1 \text{ cL}} \times \frac{1 \text{ dkL}}{10 \text{ L}} = \frac{0.85}{10} \text{ dkL} = 0.085 \text{ dkL}$$

Alternative method:

$$\frac{\text{dkL}}{\text{cL}} = \frac{10 \, \cancel{\text{L}}}{0.01 \, \cancel{\text{L}}}$$

$$= \frac{1000}{1}$$ This is an inverse proportion as there can only be more of the smaller unit (cL) in the larger unit (dkL)

$$85 \, \cancel{\text{cL}} \times \frac{1 \, \text{dkL}}{1000 \, \cancel{\text{cL}}} = 0.085 \, \text{dkL}$$

(b) **Three** containers with 2,880 milliliters, 692 centiliters, and 120 deciliters of liquid are emptied into a tub. How many liters of liquid are in the tub?

$$2,880 \, \cancel{\text{mL}} \times \frac{\text{L}}{0.001 \, \cancel{\text{mL}}} = 2.88 \, \text{L}$$

$$692 \, \cancel{\text{cL}} \times \frac{\text{L}}{0.01 \, \cancel{\text{cL}}} = 6.92 \, \text{L}$$

$$120 \, \cancel{\text{dL}} \times \frac{\text{L}}{0.1 \, \cancel{\text{dL}}} = \frac{12.00 \, \text{L}}{21.80 \, \text{L}} \quad \text{Total}$$

SOLVED PROBLEMS

4.1   How many meters are 5,825 centimeters?

SOLUTION

Relationship between units: 1 cm = 0.01 m

Conversion factor: $1 = \dfrac{0.01 \, \text{m}}{1 \, \text{cm}}$

$$5,825 \, \cancel{\text{cm}} \times 0.01 \, \text{m}/1 \, \cancel{\text{cm}} = 58.25 \, \text{m}$$

4.2   Change 0.0985 kilometers to decimeters.

SOLUTION

Relationship between units: 1 km = 1,000 m   1 dm = 0.1 m

Conversion factors: $1 = \dfrac{1,000 \, \text{m}}{1 \, \text{km}}$ $\dfrac{1 \, \text{dm}}{0.1 \, \text{m}} = 1$

$$0.0985 \, \cancel{\text{km}} \times 1,000 \, \cancel{\text{m}}/1 \, \cancel{\text{km}} \times 1 \, \text{dm}/0.1 \, \cancel{\text{m}} = 0.0985 \times 10,000 \, \text{dm} = 985 \, \text{dm}$$

Alternative solution:
     Using the base unit, write a proportion with the numerator being the unit desired in the answer:

$$\text{dm/km} = 0.1 \, \cancel{\text{m}}/1,000 \, \cancel{\text{m}}$$

Multiply the quantity by the *inverse* of the base unit ratio (there are 1,000 dm/0.1 km):

$$0.0985 \, \cancel{\text{km}} \times 1,000 \, \text{dm}/0.1 \, \cancel{\text{km}} = 0.0985 \times 10,000 \, \text{dm} = 985 \, \text{dm}$$

4.3   Find the total distance in meters for 580 mm + 350 cm + 0.13 dkm + 0.032 hm.

SOLUTION

1 mm = 0.001 m	1 cm = 0.01 m	1 dkm = 10 m	1 hm = 100 m
1 = 0.001 m/1 mm	1 = 0.01 m/1 cm	1 = 10 m/1 dkm	1 = 100 m/1 hm

$$580 \, \cancel{\text{mm}} \times 0.001 \, \text{m}/1 \, \cancel{\text{mm}} = 0.58 \, \text{m}$$

$$350 \, \cancel{\text{cm}} \times 0.01 \, \text{m}/1 \, \cancel{\text{cm}} = 3.50 \, \text{m}$$

$$0.13 \, \cancel{\text{dkm}} \times 10 \, \text{m}/1 \, \cancel{\text{dkm}} = 1.30 \, \text{m}$$

$$0.032 \, \cancel{\text{hm}} \times 100 \, \text{m}/1 \, \cancel{\text{hm}} = \underline{3.20 \, \text{m}}$$

$$8.58 \, \text{m} \quad \text{Total}$$

4.4   Change 0.227 dekagrams to milligrams.

SOLUTION

$$1 \text{ dkg} = 10 \text{ g} \qquad\qquad 1 \text{ mg} = 0.001 \text{ g}$$
$$1 = 10 \text{ g}/1 \text{ dkg} \qquad 1 \text{ mg}/0.001 \text{ g} = 1$$

$$0.227 \text{ dkg} \times 10 \text{ g}/1 \text{ dkg} \times 1 \text{ mg}/0.001 \text{ g} = 0.227 \times 10{,}000 \text{ mg} = 2{,}270 \text{ mg}$$

Alternative solution:

$$\text{mg/dkg} = 0.001 \text{ g}/10 \text{ g} \quad \text{Inverse proportion: there are } 10 \text{ mg}/0.001 \text{ dkg}$$
$$0.227 \text{ dkg} \times 10 \text{ mg}/0.001 \text{ dkg} = 0.227 \times 10{,}000 \text{ mg} = 2{,}270 \text{ mg}$$

4.5   Express 1,340 centigrams in kilograms.

SOLUTION

$$1 \text{ cg} = 0.01 \text{ g} \qquad\qquad 1 \text{ kg} = 1{,}000 \text{ g}$$
$$1 = 0.01 \text{ g}/1 \text{ cg} \qquad 1 \text{ kg}/1{,}000 \text{ g} = 1$$

$$1{,}340 \text{ cg} \times 0.01 \text{ g}/1 \text{ cg} \times 1 \text{ kg}/1{,}000 \text{ g} = 1{,}340 \times 0.00001 \text{ kg} = 0.0134 \text{ kg}$$

Alternative solution:

$$1 \text{ kg}/1 \text{ cg} = 1{,}000 \text{ g}/0.01 \text{ g}$$
$$= 100{,}000/1 \quad \text{Inverse proportion: there are } 100{,}000 \text{ cg/kg}$$

$$1{,}340 \text{ cg} \times 1 \text{ kg}/100{,}000 \text{ cg} = 0.0134 \text{ kg}$$

4.6   Give the total weight in kilograms for 6,000 dg + 500 dkg + 15 hg.

SOLUTION

$$\text{kg/dg} = 1{,}000 \text{ g}/0.1 \text{ g} \qquad \text{kg/dkg} = 1{,}000 \text{ g}/10 \text{ g} \qquad \text{kg/hg} = 1{,}000 \text{ g}/100 \text{ g}$$
$$= 10{,}000/1 \qquad\qquad = 100/1 \qquad\qquad = 10/1$$

Note that all the above are inverse proportions.

$$6{,}000 \text{ dg} \times 1 \text{ kg}/10{,}000 \text{ dg} = 0.6 \text{ kg}$$
$$500 \text{ dkg} \times 1 \text{ kg}/100 \text{ dkg} = 5.0 \text{ kg}$$
$$15 \text{ hg} \times 1 \text{ kg}/10 \text{ hg} = \underline{1.5 \text{ kg}}$$
$$7.1 \text{ kg} \quad \text{Total}$$

4.7   A truck delivered thirty 45-kilogram bags, ninety 20-kilogram bags, and forty 10-kilogram bags of fertilizer. What is the total weight of fertilizer in metric tons?

SOLUTION

$$30 \times 45 \text{ kg} = 1{,}350 \text{ kg}$$
$$90 \times 20 \text{ kg} = 1{,}800 \text{ kg}$$
$$40 \times 10 \text{ kg} = \underline{\;\;400 \text{ kg}}$$
$$3{,}550 \text{ kg}$$

$$1 \text{ t} = 1{,}000 \text{ kg}$$
$$1 \text{ t}/1{,}000 \text{ kg} = 1$$

$$3{,}550 \text{ kg} \times 1 \text{ t}/1{,}000 \text{ kg} = 3.55 \text{t}$$

4.8   Change 21.36 hectoliters to liters.

     SOLUTION

$$1 \text{ hL} = 10 \text{ L}$$
$$1 = 100 \text{ L}/1 \text{ hL}$$
$$21.36 \text{ hL} \times 100 \text{ L}/1 \text{ hL} = 2{,}136 \text{ L}$$

4.9   Express 855 deciliters in dekaliters.

     SOLUTION

$$\text{dkL}/\text{dcL} = 10 \text{ L}/0.1 \text{ L} = 100/1$$

There are 100 dcL/dkL. Therefore

$$855 \text{ dcL} \times 1 \text{ dkL}/100 \text{ dcL} = 8.55 \text{ dkL}$$

4.10   Find the total volume in liters for 12,800 mL + 420 cL + 0.32 hL.

     SOLUTION

$$1 \text{ mL} = 0.001 \text{ L} \qquad 1 \text{ cL} = 0.01 \text{ L} \qquad \text{hL} = 100 \text{ L}$$
$$1 = 0.001 \text{ L}/1 \text{ mL} \qquad 1 = 0.01 \text{ L}/1 \text{ cL} \qquad 1 = 100 \text{ L}/1 \text{ hL}$$

$$12{,}800 \text{ mL} \times 0.001 \text{ L}/1 \text{ mL} = 12.8 \text{ L}$$
$$420 \text{ cL} \times 0.01 \text{ L}/1 \text{ cL} = 4.2 \text{ L}$$
$$0.32 \text{ hL} \times 100 \text{ L}/1 \text{ hL} = \underline{32.0 \text{ L}}$$
$$49.0 \text{ L} \quad \text{Total}$$

4.2   CONVERSION BETWEEN U.S. CUSTOMARY SYSTEM AND METRIC SYSTEM

    To convert from U.S. customary units to metric units, simply multiply by the metric equivalent. To convert from metric units to U.S. customary units, multiply by the *reciprocal* of the metric equivalent.

    Equivalent measures are given in Table 4-1.

Table 4-1

	U.S. Customary Units	Metric Equivalent
Length	inch (in)	2.540 centimeters (cm)
	foot (ft)	30.480 centimeters (cm)
	yard (yd)	0.914 meters (m)
	mile (mi)	1.609 kilometers (km)
Weight	ounce (oz)	28.349 grams (g)
	pound (lb)	0.453 kilograms (kg)
	short ton (2,000 lb)	907.18 kilograms (kg)
		0.907 metric tons (t)
Volume	teaspoon (tsp)	5 milliliters (mL)
	tablespoon (tbs)	15 milliliters (mL)
	fluid ounce (fl oz)	29.573 milliliters (mL)
	cup (C)	0.236 liters (L)
	pint (pt)	0.473 liters (L)
	quart (qt)	0.946 liters (L)
	gallon (gal)	3.785 liters (L)

EXAMPLE 4

(a) The Andersons returned from their winter trip to Florida. The odometer read 38,905 miles when they departed and 42,321 miles when they returned. How many kilometers did they travel?

$$\text{Miles traveled: } 42,321 - 38,905 = 3,416 \text{ mi}$$

Conversion to kilometers:

Relationship between units: 1 mi = 1.609 km

Conversion factor: $1 = \dfrac{1.609 \text{ km}}{1 \text{ mi}}$

Metric equivalent ⎯⎯⎯

$$3,416 \text{ mi} \times 1.609 \text{ km/mi} = 5,496.344 \text{ km}$$

(b) On a recent European trip Harry traveled 1,200 kilometers in 5 days. How many miles did he average per day?

$$\text{Average km/day: } 1,200 \text{ km/5 days} = 240 \text{ km/day}$$

Conversion to miles:

Relationship between units: 1 mi = 1.609 km

Conversion factor: $\dfrac{1 \text{ mi}}{1.609 \text{ km}} = 1$

Reciprocal of metric equivalent
↓

$$240 \text{ km/day} \times 1 \text{ mi/1.609 km} = 149.16 \text{ mi/day}$$

(c) What is the total weight in kilograms of the following fruit order: 5 pounds of apples, $3\frac{1}{2}$ pounds of bananas, $2\frac{1}{2}$ pounds of grapes?

Total pounds: 5 lb + 3.5 lb + 2.5 lb = 11 lb

Conversion to kilograms:

Relationship to units: 1 lb = 0.453 kg

1 = 0.453 kg/lb

Metric equivalent
↓

$$11 \text{ lb} \times 0.453 \text{ kg/lb} = 4.983 \text{ kg}$$

(d) How many yards are there in 100 meters?

$$1 \text{ yd} = 0.914 \text{ m}$$

$$1 \text{ yd/0.914 m} = 1$$

Reciprocal of metric equivalent
↘

$$100 \text{ m} \times 1 \text{ yd/0.914 m} \cong 109.409 \text{ yd}$$

EXAMPLE 5

(a) If gasoline costs $1.824 per gallon, what is the cost per liter?

$$1 \text{ gal} = 3.785 \text{ L}$$

Substitute the metric equivalent for the gallon, as follows:

$$\$1.824\text{/gal} = \$1.824/3.785 \text{ L} = \$0.4819\text{/L} \cong \$0.482\text{/L}$$

Alternative method:

Conversion factor: 1 = 3.785 L/gal

Multiply by the conversion factor so that like units cancel:

$$\frac{\$1.824}{\cancel{gal}} \times \frac{\cancel{gal}}{3.785\,L} = \frac{\$1.824}{3.785\,L} \cong \frac{\$0.482}{L}$$

This is a shortcut to the actual steps in the calculation, which are as follows:

$$\frac{\$1.824}{gal} \times \frac{1}{\dfrac{3.785\,L}{gal}} = \frac{\$1.824}{\cancel{gal}} \times \frac{\cancel{gal}}{3.785\,L} = \frac{\$1.824}{3.785\,L} \cong \frac{\$0.482}{L}$$

Note that the conversion
takes place in the
denominator only

(b) If a $2\frac{1}{2}$-gallon jug of juice sells for \$4.98, what is the cost per liter?

$$1\,gal = 3.785\,L$$

Conversion factor: $1 = 3.785\,L/gal$
Multiply by the conversion factor so that like units cancel:

$$\frac{\$4.98}{2.5\,\cancel{gal}} \times \frac{\cancel{gal}}{3.785\,L} = \frac{\$4.98}{2.5(3.785)\,L} = \frac{\$4.98}{9.4625\,L} = \frac{\$0.526}{L} \cong \frac{\$0.53}{L}$$

To convert temperature from degrees Fahrenheit (°F) to degrees Celsius (°C), subtract 32 and then multiply by $\frac{5}{9}$. To convert from degrees Celsius to degrees Fahrenheit, multiply by $\frac{9}{5}$, then add 32.

EXAMPLE 6

(a) How many degrees Celsius is 65° Fahrenheit?

$$°C = (°F - 32) \times \frac{5}{9} = (65 - 32) \times \frac{5}{9} = 33 \times \frac{5}{9} = \frac{165}{9} = 18.\dot{3}$$

(b) Convert 25°C to degrees Fahrenheit.

$$°F = \left(°C \times \frac{9}{5}\right) + 32 = \left(25 \times \frac{9}{5}\right) + 32 = (5 \times 9) + 32 = 45 + 32 = 77$$

SOLVED PROBLEMS

4.11 How many linear meters of fencing will be required to enclose a rectangular area 120 feet long and 60 feet wide?

SOLUTION

$$120\,ft + 120\,ft + 60\,ft + 60\,ft = 360\ \text{linear ft total}$$

$$1\,ft = 30.480\,cm \qquad\qquad 1\,cm = 0.01\,m$$
$$1 = 30.480\,cm/ft \qquad\qquad 1 = 0.01\,m/cm$$

$$360\,\cancel{ft} \times 30.480\,\cancel{cm}/\cancel{ft} \times 0.01\,m/\cancel{cm} = 360 \times 0.3048\,m = 109.728\,m$$

4.12 The Dawsons are planning to serve 48 quarter-pound hamburgers at their barbecue party. How many kilograms of ground beef must they order?

SOLUTION

$$48 \times 1/4\,lb = 12\,lb\ \text{total}$$
$$1\,lb = 0.453\,kg$$
$$1 = 0.453\,kg/lb$$

$$12\,\cancel{lb} \times 0.453\,kg/\cancel{lb} = 5.436\,kg \cong 5.4\,kg$$

4.13   A supermarket received the following shipment of vegetables: $11\frac{1}{2}$ short tons of potatoes, 4 short tons of carrots, and $3\frac{1}{4}$ short tons of tomatoes. What is the total weight of the three shipments in metric tons?

SOLUTION

$$11.5 \text{ short tons} + 4 \text{ short tons} + 3.25 \text{ short tons} = 18.75 \text{ short tons} \quad \text{total}$$

$$1 \text{ short ton} = 0.907 \text{ metric tons (t)}$$

$$1 = 0.907 \text{ t/short ton}$$

$$18.75 \text{ short tons} \times 0.907 \text{ t/short ton} = 17.006 \text{ t} \cong 17 \text{ t}$$

4.14   A recipe for a cake requires 6 ounces of unsalted butter. How many dekagrams of butter are needed for two cakes?

SOLUTION

$$2 \times 6 \text{ oz} = 12 \text{ oz}$$

$$1 \text{ oz} = 28.349 \text{ g} \qquad\qquad 1 \text{ dkg} = 10 \text{ g}$$

$$1 = 28.349 \text{ g/oz} \qquad\qquad \frac{1 \text{ dkg}}{10 \text{ g}} = 1$$

$$12 \text{ oz} \times 28.349 \text{ g/oz} \times 1 \text{ dkg}/10 \text{ g} = 12 \times 2.8349 \text{ dkg} = 34.0188 \text{ dkg} \cong 34.02 \text{ dkg}$$

4.15   Bob Schaub's cows produce 12,000 quarts of milk per week. (*a*) How many hectoliters do they produce weekly? (*b*) If Bob sells the milk at $0.56 per liter, what is his weekly income?

SOLUTION

(*a*) $1 \text{ qt} = 0.946 \text{ L} \qquad\qquad 1 \text{ hL} = 100 \text{ L}$

$$1 = 0.946 \text{ L/qt} \qquad\qquad \frac{1 \text{ hL}}{100 \text{ L}} = 1$$

$$12,000 \text{ qt} \times 0.946 \text{ L/qt} \times 1 \text{ hL}/100 \text{ L} = 12,000 \times 0.00946 \text{ hL} = 113.52 \text{ hL}$$

(*b*) $113.52 \text{ hL} \times 100 \text{ L/hL} \times \$0.56/\text{L} = \$6,357.12$

4.16   If $1\frac{1}{2}$ fluid ounces of a perfume sell for $129, what is the price per milliliter?

SOLUTION

$$1 \text{ fl oz} = 29.573 \text{ mL}$$

$$1 = 29.573 \text{ mL/fl oz}$$

$$1.5 \text{ fl oz} \times 29.573 \text{ mL/fl oz} = 44.3595 \text{ mL}$$

$$\$129.00/44.3595 \text{ mL} = \$2.908/\text{mL} \cong \$2.91/\text{mL}$$

Alternative solution:

$$\frac{\$129.00}{1.5 \text{ fl oz}} \times \frac{1}{\dfrac{29.573 \text{ mL}}{\text{fl oz}}} = \frac{\$86.00}{\text{fl oz}} \times \frac{\text{fl oz}}{29.573 \text{ mL}} = \$2.908/\text{mL} \cong \$2.91/\text{mL}$$

4.17   A recipe calls for $\frac{3}{4}$ teaspoon salt, $\frac{1}{4}$ teaspoon freshly ground black pepper, 1 tablespoon soy sauce, 2 tablespoons oil, and $\frac{1}{2}$ cup water. What is the combined volume of the ingredients in centiliters?

SOLUTION

$$1\text{ tsp} = 5\text{ mL} \qquad 1\text{ tbs} = 15\text{ mL} \qquad 1\text{ c} = 0.236\text{ L} \qquad 1\text{ cL} = 0.01\text{ L}$$
$$1 = 5\text{ mL/tsp} \qquad 1 = 15\text{ mL/tbs} \qquad 1 = 0.236\text{ L/c} \qquad 1\text{ cL/0.01 L} = 1$$

$$\frac{1\text{ cL}}{1\text{ mL}} = \frac{0.01\text{ L}}{0.001\text{ L}} = \frac{10}{1} \quad \leftarrow \text{Note that this is an inverse}$$

proportion: $10\text{ mL} = 1\text{ cL}$
$$1 = 1\text{ cL/10 mL}$$

$$0.75\text{ tsp} \times 5\text{ mL/tsp} \times \text{cL/10 mL} = \quad 0.375\text{ cL}$$
$$0.25\text{ tsp} \times 5\text{ mL/tsp} \times \text{cL/10 mL} = \quad 0.125\text{ cL}$$
$$1\text{ tbs} \times 15\text{ mL/tbs} \times \text{cL/10 mL} = \quad 1.500\text{ cL}$$
$$2\text{ tbs} \times 15\text{ mL/tbs} \times \text{cL/10 mL} = \quad 3.000\text{ cL}$$
$$0.5\text{ c} \times 0.236\text{ L/c} \times \text{cL/0.01 L} = \underline{11.800\text{ cL}}$$
$$16.800\text{ cL} \quad \text{Total}$$

4.18 Convert 86°F to Celsius scale.

SOLUTION

$$°C = (°F - 32) \times \frac{5}{9}$$
$$= (86 - 32) \times \frac{5}{9} = 54 \times \frac{5}{9} = 6 \times 5 = 30$$

4.19 An outdoor thermometer registers a reading of −13°F. What is the temperature in degrees Celsius?

SOLUTION

$$°C = (°F - 32) \times \frac{5}{9}$$
$$= (-13 - 32) \times \frac{5}{9} = -45 \times \frac{5}{9} = -5 \times 5 = -25$$

4.20 An imported car weighs 1.82 metric tons. What is the weight in pounds?

SOLUTION

$$1\text{ t} = 1,000\text{ kg} \qquad 1\text{ lb} = 0.453\text{ kg}$$
$$1 = 1,000\text{ kg/t} \qquad \frac{1\text{ lb}}{0.453\text{ kg}} = 1$$

$$1.82\text{ t} \times 1,000\text{ kg/t} \times 1\text{ lb/0.453 kg} = 1,820\text{ lb/0.453} = 4,017.66\text{ lb}$$

4.21 If 1 kg of beef costs \$3.41, what is the equivalent price per pound?

SOLUTION

$$1\text{ lb} = 0.453\text{ kg}$$
$$\frac{1\text{ lb}}{0.453\text{ kg}} = 1$$

$$\frac{\$3.41}{\text{kg}} \times \frac{1}{\dfrac{1\text{ lb}}{0.453\text{ kg}}} = \$3.41 \times \frac{0.453}{\text{lb}} = \$1.54473/\text{lb} \cong \$1.54/\text{lb}$$

4.22   A 400-gram can of mixed nuts costs \$4.20. What is the unit price per ounce?

SOLUTION

$$1 \text{ oz} = 28.349 \text{ g}$$

$$1 \text{ oz}/28.349 \text{ g} = 1$$

$$\frac{\$4.20}{400 \text{ g}} \times \frac{1}{\dfrac{1 \text{ oz}}{28.349 \text{ g}}} = \frac{\$4.20}{400} \times \frac{28.349}{\text{oz}} = 0.0105 \times 28.349/\text{oz} = \$0.297 \text{ oz} \cong \$0.30/\text{oz}$$

4.23   How many fluid ounces are in a 2-liter bottle of wine?

SOLUTION

$$1 \text{ fl oz} = 29.573 \text{ mL} \qquad\qquad 1 \text{ mL} = 0.001 \text{ L}$$

$$\frac{1 \text{ fl oz}}{29.573 \text{ mL}} = 1 \qquad\qquad \frac{1 \text{ mL}}{0.001 \text{ L}} = 1$$

$$2 \text{ L} \times \text{mL}/0.001 \text{ L} \times \text{fl oz}/29.573 \text{ mL} = \frac{2,000}{29.573} = 67.629 \text{ fl oz} \cong 67.63 \text{ fl oz}$$

4.24   Which is colder, 10°C or 45°F?

SOLUTION

$$
\begin{array}{lll}
\text{°C} = (\text{°F} - 32) \times 5/9 & \quad\text{or}\quad & \text{°F} = (\text{°C} \times 9/5) + 32 \\
\quad = (45 - 32) \times 5/9 & & \quad = (10 \times 9/5) + 32 \\
\quad = 13 \times 5/9 & & \quad = (2 \times 9) + 32 \\
\quad = 65/9 & & \quad = 18 + 32 \\
\quad = 7.2 & & \quad = 50
\end{array}
$$

From 45°F = 7.2°C or 10°C = 50°F, we know that 45°F is colder than 10°C.

4.25   What is the width in inches of 35-millimeter film?

SOLUTION

$$\frac{1 \text{ cm}}{1 \text{ mm}} = \frac{0.01 \text{ m}}{0.001 \text{ m}} = \frac{10}{1} \qquad \text{inverse proportion: } 10 \text{ mm} = 1 \text{ cm}$$
$$1 = 1 \text{ cm}/10 \text{ mm}$$

$$1 \text{ in} = 2.540 \text{ cm}$$

$$\frac{1 \text{ in}}{2.540 \text{ cm}} = 1$$

$$35 \text{ mm} \times \text{cm}/10 \text{ mm} \times \text{in}/2.540 \text{ cm} = \frac{3.5 \text{ in}}{2.540} = 1.3779 \text{ in} \cong 1.38 \text{ in}$$

4.26   If the width of a door is 3 feet, will a box 95 centimeters wide fit through the door?

SOLUTION

$$1 \text{ ft} = 30.480 \text{ cm}$$

$$1 = \frac{30.480 \text{ cm}}{\text{ft}}$$

Width of door: $3 \text{ ft} \times \dfrac{30.480 \text{ cm}}{\text{ft}} = 91.44 \text{ cm}$

or width of box: $95 \text{ cm} \times \text{ft}/30.480 \text{ cm} = 3.11679 \text{ ft} \cong 3.12 \text{ ft}$

No. The door is narrower than the box.

4.27 A bag contains 40 kilograms of crystal salt. How many pounds does it weigh?

SOLUTION

$$1\ lb = 0.453\ kg$$
$$1\ lb/0.453\ kg = 1$$
$$40\ kg \times 1\ lb/0.453\ kg \cong 88.30\ lb$$

4.28 A recipe for a pastry requires 200 grams of sweet butter. How many ounces of butter are required?

SOLUTION

$$1\ oz = 28.349\ g$$
$$1\ oz/28.349\ g = 1$$
$$200\ g \times 1\ oz/28.349\ g \cong 7.05\ oz$$

4.29 Jerry's car consumes 15 liters of gasoline per 100 kilometers. Paula's car travels 15 miles on 1 gallon of gasoline. Which car gets better mileage? Give your answer in miles per gallon.

SOLUTION

$$\text{Jerry's car: }15\ L/100\ km \qquad \text{Paula's car: }15\ mi/gal$$

Write both cars' consumption in the same order:

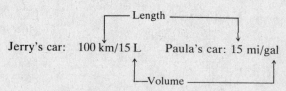

Convert Jerry's gasoline consumption to miles/gallon.

$$1\ mi = 1.609\ km \qquad\qquad 1\ gal = 3.785\ L$$
$$1\ mi/1.609\ km = 1 \qquad\qquad 1\ gal/3.785\ L = 1$$

$$\frac{100\ km \times 1\ mi/1.609\ km}{15\ L \times 1\ gal/3.785\ L} = \frac{100/1.609\ mi}{15/3.785\ gal} = \frac{62.15\ mi}{3.963\ gal} = 15.682\ mi/gal \cong 15.68\ mi/gal$$

Jerry's car gets slightly better mileage than Paula's.

4.30 A warehouse received a shipment of 10 metric tons of sugar. Will it be enough to fill orders for 20,000 pounds of sugar?

SOLUTION

$$1\ t = 1{,}000\ kg \qquad\qquad 1\ lb = 0.453\ kg$$
$$1 = 1{,}000\ kg/t \qquad 1\ lb/0.453\ kg = 1$$

$$10\ t \times 1{,}000\ kg/t \times 1\ lb/0.453\ kg = \frac{10{,}000}{0.453}\ lb = 22{,}075.055\ lb$$

Yes. The shipment will be sufficient to fill orders for 20,000 pounds of sugar.

4.31 How many gallons are required to fill a 2-hectoliter tank?

SOLUTION

$$hL = 100\ L \qquad\qquad 1\ gal = 3.785\ L$$
$$1 = 100\ L/hL \qquad 1\ gal/3.785\ L = 1$$

$$2\ hL \times 100\ L/hL \times 1\ gal/3.785\ L \cong 52.84\ gal$$

4.32 A dairy farm produces 1,500 liters of milk daily. If the milk is sold for $0.50 per quart, what is the farmer's daily income?

SOLUTION

$$1 \text{ qt} = 0.946 \text{ L}$$
$$1 \text{ qt}/0.946 \text{ L} = 1$$
$$1{,}500 \cancel{L} \times 1 \text{ qt}/0.946 \cancel{L} \cong 1{,}582.62 \text{ qt}$$
$$1{,}585.62 \cancel{qt} \times \$0.50/\cancel{qt} = \$792.81$$

4.33 Sonia Higginson paid $1.06 per liter for gasoline while traveling in Denmark. How much would that be per gallon?

SOLUTION

$$1 \text{ gal} = 3.785 \text{ L}$$
$$1 \text{ gal}/3.785 \text{ L} = 1$$

$$\frac{\$1.06}{\cancel{L}} \times \frac{1}{\dfrac{1 \text{ gal}}{3.785 \cancel{L}}} = \$1.06 \times \frac{3.785}{\text{gal}} = \$4.0121/\text{gal} \cong \$4.01/\text{gal}$$

4.34 The average daily temperature in Mexico City is about 15°C. What is the equivalent temperature in degrees Fahrenheit?

SOLUTION

$$°F = \left(°C \times \frac{9}{5} \right) + 32$$

$$= \left(15 \times \frac{9}{5} \right) + 32 = (3 \times 9) + 32 = 27 + 32 = 59$$

4.3 MEASURES OF AREA

Area is measured in square units. In the metric system, the basic unit of area is the square meter (m^2). Each square unit is 100 times greater than the next smaller square unit. Thus, $1 \text{ m}^2 = 100 \text{ dm}^2$, $1 \text{ dm}^2 = 100 \text{ cm}^2$, $1 \text{ cm}^2 = 100 \text{ mm}^2$, etc.

Approximate equivalent measures for metric and U.S. customary units appear in Table 4-2. As before, to convert from U.S. customary to metric units, multiply by the metric equivalent. To convert from metric to U.S. customary units, multiply by the *reciprocal* of the metric equivalent.

EXAMPLE 7

(*a*) Mr. Whyte needs 120 square yards of imported fabric for drapes. How many square meters of the fabric should he order?

$$1 \text{ yd}^2 = 0.83 \text{ m}^2$$
$$1 = 0.83 \text{ m}^2/\text{yd}^2$$
$$120 \cancel{\text{yd}^2} \times 0.83 \text{ m}^2/\cancel{\text{yd}^2} = 99.6 \text{ m}^2$$

Mr. Whyte should order 100 square meters of the fabric.

(*b*) The Andersons' house is situated on a 6-acre plot of land. The county intends to buy 2,000 square meters of the land for widening a county road. How many acres will the Andersons have left?

$$1 \text{ ha} = 10{,}000 \text{ m}^2 \qquad\qquad 1 \text{ acre} = 0.4 \text{ ha}$$
$$\text{ha}/10{,}000 \text{ m}^2 = 1 \qquad\qquad \text{acre}/0.4 \text{ ha} = 1$$

The county intends to buy:

$$2{,}000 \cancel{\text{m}^2} \times \cancel{\text{ha}}/10{,}000 \cancel{\text{m}^2} \times \text{acre}/0.4 \cancel{\text{ha}} = \frac{2{,}000}{4{,}000} \text{ acre} = 0.5 \text{ acre}$$

Number of acres to remain in Andersons' possession:

$$6 \text{ acres} - 0.5 \text{ acres} = 5.5 \text{ acres}$$

Table 4-2

U.S. Customary Units	Metric Equivalent
square inch (in^2)	6.45 square centimeters (cm^2)
square foot (ft^2)	9.29 square decimeters (dm^2)
square yard (yd^2)	0.83 square meters (m^2)
square mile (mi^2)	2.59 square kilometers (km^2)
acre	0.4 hectares (10,000 m^2) (ha)

(*c*) The Waltons wish to put new carpeting in their family room, which measures 4.98 meters by 6 meters. If the carpeting they want sells for $16 per square yard, how much will it cost to recarpet the room?

Amount of carpeting needed:

$$\text{Area} = \text{length} \times \text{width}$$
$$= 6 \text{ m} \times 4.98 \text{ m} = 29.88 \text{ m}^2$$

$$1 \text{ yd}^2 = 0.83 \text{ m}^2$$
$$1 \text{ yd}^2/0.83 \text{ m}^2 = 1$$

$$29.88 \text{ m}^2 \times \text{yd}^2/0.83 \text{ m}^2 = 36 \text{ yd}^2$$

Total cost:

$$36 \text{ yd}^2 \times \$16/\text{yd}^2 = \$576$$

(*d*) A fire destroyed 155,400 hectares of a forest. How many square miles of forest were destroyed?

Since the metric equivalent of square miles is given in square kilometers, we first need to convert hectares into square kilometers. We know that each square unit in the metric system is 100 times greater than the next smaller unit, so that we can make the needed conversion by going up the scale of units and dividing each by 100:

$$1 \text{ ha} = 10,000 \text{ m}^2 = 100 \text{ dkm}^2 = 1 \text{ hm}^2 = 0.01 \text{ km}^2$$

$$1 \text{ ha} = 0.01 \text{ km}^2$$
$$1 = 0.01 \text{ km}^2/\text{ha}$$

Alternatively, we can calculate the number of square meters in a square kilometer and then determine the conversion factor from a proportion.

Since $1 \text{ km} = 1,000 \text{ m}$

Then $1 \text{ km}^2 = 1,000 \text{ m} \times 1,000 \text{ m} = 1,000,000 \text{ m}^2$

$$\frac{\text{ha}}{\text{km}^2} = \frac{10,000 \text{ m}^2}{1,000,000 \text{ m}^2} = \frac{1}{100}$$

This is an inverse proportion. If we cross multiply, we get

$$100 \text{ ha} = \text{km}^2$$
$$1 = \text{km}^2/100 \text{ ha} = 0.01 \text{ km}^2/\text{ha}$$

Conversion of hectares into square miles:

$$155,400 \text{ ha} \times 0.01 \text{ km}^2/\text{ha} \times \text{mi}^2/2.59 \text{ km}^2 = 600 \text{ mi}^2$$
$$\uparrow$$

Since we are converting from metric
to U.S. customary units, we multiply
by the *reciprocal* of the metric equivalent

(e) A bag of fertilizer covers an area of 400 square meters. Will one bag be enough to fertilize an area 60 feet by 80 feet?

$$\text{Area} = \text{length} \times \text{width} = 80 \text{ ft} \times 60 \text{ ft} = 4{,}800 \text{ ft}^2$$

Because the metric equivalent for square feet is given in square decimeters, we must calculate the conversion factor from square decimeters to square meters. Since metric units of area progress by a factor of 100, then

$$1 \text{ dm}^2 = 0.01 \text{ m}^2$$
$$1 = 0.01 \text{ m}^2/\text{dm}^2$$

Alternatively:

$$1 \text{ dm} = 0.1 \text{ m}$$
$$1 \text{ dm}^2 = 0.1 \text{ m} \times 0.1 \text{ m} = 0.01 \text{ m}^2$$
$$1 = 0.01 \text{ m}^2/\text{dm}^2$$

Conversion of area to square meters:

$$1 \text{ ft}^2 = 9.29 \text{ dm}^2$$
$$4{,}800 \text{ ft}^2 \times 9.29 \text{ dm}^2/\text{ft}^2 \times 0.01 \text{ m}^2/\text{dm}^2 = 455.92 \text{ m}^2$$

Thus, one bag of fertilizer will not be sufficient.

SOLVED PROBLEMS

4.35 It costs \$432 to pave a driveway that is 12.45 meters by 5 meters. What is the cost per square yard?

SOLUTION

$$\text{Area} = \text{length} \times \text{width}$$
$$= 12.45 \text{ m} \times 5 \text{ m} = 62.25 \text{ m}^2$$

Conversion:

$$1 \text{ yd}^2 = 0.83 \text{ m}^2$$
$$62.25 \text{ m}^2 \times \text{yd}^2/0.83 \text{ m}^2 = 75 \text{ yd}^2$$

Cost:

$$\$432 \div 75 \text{ yd}^2 = \$5.76/\text{yd}^2$$

4.36 How many square meters of floor space are contained in an area 16 feet long by $12\frac{1}{2}$ feet wide?

SOLUTION

$$\text{Area} = \text{length} \times \text{width}$$
$$= 16 \text{ ft} \times 12.5 \text{ ft} = 200 \text{ ft}^2$$

Conversion:

$$\text{ft}^2 = 9.29 \text{ dm}^2$$

Since

$$1 \text{ dm} = 0.1 \text{ m}$$

then

$$1 \text{ dm}^2 = 0.1 \text{ m} \times 0.1 \text{ m} = 0.01 \text{ m}^2$$
$$1 = 0.01 \text{ m}^2/\text{dm}^2$$
$$200 \text{ ft}^2 \times 9.29 \text{ dm}^2/\text{ft}^2 \times 0.01 \text{ m}^2/\text{dm}^2 = 18.58 \text{ m}^2$$

4.37 A farmer purchased a piece of land that measured 1.24 miles by 2.25 miles. How many square kilometers of land did she purchase?

SOLUTION

$$\text{Area} = \text{length} \times \text{width}$$
$$= 2.25 \text{ mi} \times 1.24 \text{ mi} = 2.79 \text{ mi}^2$$

Conversion:

$$1 \text{ mi}^2 = 2.59 \text{ km}^2$$
$$2.79 \text{ mi}^2 \times 2.59 \text{ km}^2/\text{mi}^2 = 7.2261 \text{ km}^2$$

4.38   How many hectares of land did the farmer in Prob. 4.37 buy?

   SOLUTION

$$1 \text{ km} = 1{,}000 \text{ m} \text{ then } 1 \text{ km}^2 = 1{,}000 \text{ m} \times 1{,}000 \text{ m} = 1{,}000{,}000 \text{ m}^2$$

$$\frac{\text{ha}}{\text{km}^2} = \frac{10{,}000 \text{ m}^2}{1{,}000{,}000 \text{ m}^2} = \frac{1}{100}$$

$$100 \text{ ha} = \text{km}^2$$

$$7.2261 \text{ km}^2 \times 100 \text{ ha/km}^2 = 722.61 \text{ ha}$$

4.39   A page measures 20.3 centimeters by 25.4 centimeters. How many square inches does it contain?

   SOLUTION

$$\text{Area} = \text{length} \times \text{width}$$
$$= 25.4 \text{ cm} \times 20.3 \text{ cm} = 515.62 \text{ cm}^2$$

   Conversion:
$$1 \text{ in}^2 = 6.45 \text{ cm}^2$$

$$515.62 \text{ cm}^2 \times \text{in}^2/6.45 \text{ cm}^2 \cong 79.94 \text{ in}^2$$

4.40   A house with 2,400 square feet of living space is offered for sale. What should be the listing of living area in square meters?

   SOLUTION

$$1 \text{ ft}^2 = 9.29 \text{ dm}^2$$

   Since
$$1 \text{ dm} = 0.1 \text{ m}$$

   then
$$1 \text{ dm}^2 = 0.1 \text{ m} \times 0.1 \text{ m}$$
$$= 0.01 \text{ m}^2$$

$$2{,}400 \text{ ft}^2 \times 9.29 \text{ dm}^2/\text{ft}^2 \times 0.01 \text{ m}^2/\text{dm}^2 = 222.96 \text{ m}^2$$

4.4 MEASURES OF VOLUME

The basic unit of volume in the metric system is the liter (see Sec. 4.1). Volume, or capacity, is also measured in cubic meters (m^3), or portions thereof. Each cubic unit is 1,000 times greater than the next smaller unit. Thus

$$1 \text{ m}^3 = 1{,}000 \text{ dm}^3, \quad 1 \text{ dm}^3 = 1{,}000 \text{ cm}^3, \quad 1 \text{ cm}^3 = 1{,}000 \text{ mm}^3$$

The relationship between liters and cubic metric units is

$$1 \text{ liter (L)} = 1 \text{ cubic decimeter (dm}^3)$$

Approximate conversion factors between metric cubic units and U.S. customary units appear in Table 4-3.

Table 4-3

U.S. Customary Units	Metric Equivalent
cubic inch (in^3)	16.387 cubic centimeters (cm^3)
cubic foot (ft^3)	0.028 cubic meters (m^3)
cubic yard (yd^3)	0.764 cubic meters (m^3)

To convert from U.S. customary units to metric units, multiply by the metric equivalent. To convert from metric units to U.S. customary units, multiply by the *reciprocal* of the metric equivalent.

EXAMPLE 8

(a)   How many cubic meters are there in a 20-cubic foot refrigerator?

Conversion: $1 \text{ ft}^3 = 0.028 \text{ m}^3$

$$20 \text{ ft}^3 \times 0.028 \text{ m}^3/\text{ft}^3 = 0.56 \text{ m}^3$$

(b)   What is the capacity in cubic meters of a tub that is 4.5 feet long, 2.5 feet wide, and 2 feet deep?

$$\text{Volume} = \text{length} \times \text{width} \times \text{height}$$
$$= 4.5 \text{ ft} \times 2.5 \text{ ft} \times 2 \text{ ft} = 22.5 \text{ ft}^3$$

Conversion: $1 \text{ ft}^3 = 0.028 \text{ m}^3$

$$22.5 \text{ ft}^3 \times 0.028 \text{ m}^3/\text{ft}^3 = 0.63 \text{ m}^3$$

(c)   How many gallons of water can the tub in part (b) hold?
     Since the metric equivalent for gallons is given in liters (1 gal = 3.785 L), we must first convert cubic meters to liters and then liters to gallons.

$$1 \text{ L} = 1 \text{ dm}^3$$

Since $1 \text{ m} = 10 \text{ dm}$

then $1 \text{ m}^3 = 10 \text{ dm} \times 10 \text{ dm} \times 10 \text{ dm} = 1{,}000 \text{ dm}^3$

$$0.63 \text{ m}^3 \times 1{,}000 \text{ dm}^3/\text{m}^3 \times \text{L}/\text{dm}^3 \times \text{gal}/3.785 \text{ L} = 166.4465 \text{ gal} \cong 166 \text{ gal}$$

SOLVED PROBLEMS

4.41   Elise Hutcheson wants to cover a 20 foot by 30 foot garden with 6 inches of topsoil. What will it cost her if topsoil sells for $15 per cubic meter?

SOLUTION

Amount needed:

$$\text{Volume} = \text{length} \times \text{width} \times \text{height}$$
$$= 30 \text{ ft} \times 20 \text{ ft} \times 0.5 \text{ ft} = 300 \text{ ft}^3$$

Conversion: $1 \text{ ft}^3 = 0.028 \text{ m}^3$

$$300 \text{ ft}^3 \times 0.028 \text{ m}^3/\text{ft}^3 = 8.4 \text{ m}^3$$

Cost: $8.4 \text{ m}^3 \times \$15/\text{m}^3 = \$126$

4.42   What is the capacity in liters of a plastic container that is 30 inches long, 18 inches wide, and 6 inches deep?

SOLUTION

$$\text{Volume} = \text{length} \times \text{width} \times \text{height}$$
$$= 30 \text{ in} \times 18 \text{ in} \times 6 \text{ in} = 3{,}240 \text{ in}^3$$

Conversion: $1 \text{ in}^3 = 16.387 \text{ cm}^3$ and $1 \text{ L} = 1 \text{ dm}^3$

Since $1 \text{ dm} = 10 \text{ cm}$

then $1 \text{ dm}^3 = 10 \text{ cm} \times 10 \text{ cm} \times 10 \text{ cm} = 1{,}000 \text{ cm}^3$

$$3{,}240 \text{ in}^3 \times 16.387 \text{ cm}^3/\text{in}^3 \times \text{dm}^3/1{,}000 \text{ cm}^3 \times \text{L}/\text{dm}^3 = 53.09388 \text{ L} \cong 53.09 \text{ L}$$

4.43 How many cubic feet of sand are needed to fill a sandbox that is 12 decimeters long, 8 decimeters wide, and 16 centimeters deep?

SOLUTION

$$1 \text{ dm} = 10 \text{ cm}$$
$$16 \text{ cm} \times \text{dm}/10 \text{ cm} = 1.6 \text{ dm}$$
$$\text{Volume} = \text{length} \times \text{width} \times \text{height} = 12 \text{ dm} \times 8 \text{ dm} \times 1.6 \text{ dm} = 153.6 \text{ dm}^3$$

$$1 \text{ ft}^3 = 0.028 \text{ m}^3$$

Since
$$1 \text{ m} = 10 \text{ dm}$$

then
$$1 \text{ m}^3 = 1{,}000 \text{ dm}^3$$

$$153.6 \text{ dm}^3 \times \text{m}^3/1{,}000 \text{ dm}^3 \times \text{ft}^3/0.028 \text{ m}^3 = 5.4857 \text{ ft}^3 \cong 5.49 \text{ ft}^3$$

4.44 How many cubic meters of water are there in a swimming pool 60 feet long, 30 feet wide, and 6 feet deep?

SOLUTION

$$\text{Volume} = \text{length} \times \text{width} \times \text{height} = 60 \text{ ft} \times 30 \text{ ft} \times 6 \text{ ft} = 10{,}800 \text{ ft}^3$$

Conversion:
$$1 \text{ ft}^3 = 0.028 \text{ m}^3$$

$$10{,}800 \text{ ft}^3 \times 0.028 \text{ m}^3/\text{ft}^3 = 302.4 \text{ m}^3$$

4.45 (*a*) How many hectoliters of water are there in the pool in Prob. 4.44? (*b*) How many gallons are there?

SOLUTION

(*a*)
$$1 \text{ m}^3 = 1{,}000 \text{ dm}^3 \qquad 1 \text{ L} = 1 \text{ dm}^3 \qquad 1 \text{ hL} = 100 \text{ L}$$
$$302.4 \text{ m}^3 \times 1{,}000 \text{ dm}^3/\text{m}^3 \times \text{L}/\text{dm}^3 \times \text{hL}/100 \text{ L} = 3{,}024 \text{ hL}$$

(*b*)
$$1 \text{ gal} = 3.785 \text{ L}$$
$$3{,}024 \text{ hL} \times 100 \text{ L}/\text{hL} \times \text{gal}/3.785 \text{ L} = 79{,}894.32 \text{ gal}$$

4.46 Find the capacity in cubic yards of a storage area that is 3 meters long, 2 meters wide, and 4 meters high.

SOLUTION

$$\text{Volume} = \text{length} \times \text{width} \times \text{height} = 3 \text{ m} \times 2 \text{ m} \times 4 \text{ m} = 24 \text{ m}^3$$

Conversion:
$$1 \text{ yd}^3 = 0.764 \text{ m}^3$$

$$24 \text{ m}^3 \times \text{yd}^3/0.764 \text{ m}^3 = 31.4136 \text{ yd}^3 \cong 31.41 \text{ yd}^3$$

4.47 What is the capacity in milliliters of a container that is 2 inches long, $\frac{1}{2}$ inch wide, and $\frac{1}{4}$ inch deep?

SOLUTION

$$\text{Volume} = \text{length} \times \text{width} \times \text{height} = 2 \text{ in} \times 0.5 \text{ in} \times 0.25 \text{ in} = 0.25 \text{ in}^3$$

Conversion:
$$1 \text{ in}^3 = 16.387 \text{ cm}^3$$

Since
$$1 \text{ dm} = 10 \text{ cm}$$

then
$$1 \text{ dm}^3 = 1{,}000 \text{ cm}^3$$

$$1 \text{ L} = 1 \text{ dm}^3 \qquad \text{and} \qquad 1 \text{ L} = 1{,}000 \text{ mL}$$

$$0.25 \text{ in}^3 \times 16.387 \text{ cm}^3/\text{in}^3 \times \text{dm}^3/1{,}000 \text{ cm}^3 \times \text{L}/\text{dm}^3 \times 1{,}000 \text{ mL}/\text{L} = 4.09675 \text{ mL} \cong 4.1 \text{ mL}$$

4.48   How many centiliters are in 1 cubic foot?

SOLUTION

$$1 \text{ ft}^3 = 0.028 \text{ m}^3$$

Since $$1 \text{ m} = 10 \text{ dm}$$

then $$1 \text{ m}^3 = 1{,}000 \text{ dm}^3$$

$$1 \text{ L} = 1 \text{ dm}^3 \quad \text{and} \quad 1 \text{ L} = 100 \text{ cL}$$

$$\cancel{\text{ft}^3} \times 0.028 \text{ } \cancel{\text{m}^3}/\cancel{\text{ft}^3} \times 1{,}000 \text{ } \cancel{\text{dm}^3}/\cancel{\text{m}^3} \times \cancel{\text{L}}/\cancel{\text{dm}^3} \times 100 \text{ cL}/\cancel{\text{L}} = 2{,}800 \text{ cL}$$

Supplementary Problems

4.49   Change each of the following to decimeters:

(*a*)   7,200 mm   (*b*)   1.3 m   (*c*)   0.01 km

4.50   Change each of the following to kilograms:

(*a*)   250 dkg   (*b*)   50,000 mg   (*c*)   0.03 t

4.51   Change each of the following to dekaliters:

(*a*)   1.25 hL   (*b*)   60,000 cL   (*c*)   380 L

4.52   Add the following distances and give the answer in meters: 3,900 cm, 1.7 hm, 0.012 km, and 12,000 mm.

4.53   Add the following weights and give the answer in grams: 5,800 mg, 820 cg, 150 dg, 1.3 dkg, and 0.08 kg.

4.54   In a laboratory experiment, Jody prepared a solution that required 350 milliliters of one liquid, 15 centiliters of another, 0.2 dekaliters of a third, and 2.5 deciliters of a fourth. How many liters did Jody prepare?

4.55   How many linear meters of fencing are required to enclose an area of 60 feet by 80 feet?

4.56   The Johnsons traveled 6,520 miles during their 20-day trip to California. To the nearest tenth, how many kilometers did they average daily?

4.57   There are 12 wieners in a 1-pound package. To the nearest hundredth, how many kilograms of wieners are needed to serve 150 hot dogs?

4.58   A pound of shelled peanuts sells for $1.62. To the nearest cent, how much would 10 dekagrams of peanuts cost?

4.59   To the nearest tenth, how many liters will it take to fill an automobile's 25-gallon gas tank?

4.60   To the nearest kilometer, what is the metric equivalent of the national highway speed limit of 55 miles per hour?

4.61   Convert $-10°C$ to the Fahrenheit scale.

4.62   Would a truck weighing 25,000 pounds and carrying a load of 15,000 pounds be allowed to cross a bridge with a weight limit of 18.5 metric tons?

4.63   At what degree Celsius would you set your thermostat if you wanted a room temperature of 77°F?

4.64   Would 20 liters of gasoline fit in a 5-gallon can?

4.65   To the nearest tenth, what metric measure in milliliters would be placed on cans containing 12 fluid ounces?

4.66   A man is 6 feet 3 inches tall and weight 198 pounds. To the nearest tenth, what is (*a*) his height in centimeters and (*b*) his weight in kilograms?

4.67   Jack owns 4 hectares of land and Paula owns 10 acres of land. Who owns more land and by how much?

4.68   Bob Gilbert wants to panel a room that is 10 feet 6 inches wide and 11 feet 3 inches long. The walls are 8 feet high. To the nearest hundredth, how many square meters of paneling are required?

4.69   Sandra Higgins wants to seed a lawn that measures 10 meters by 12 meters. If 1 pound of seed covers 100 square feet and costs $3, what will it cost (to the nearest cent) to seed the lawn?

4.70   A concrete mix sells for $52 per cubic meter. To the nearest cent, state the equivalent price per cubic yard.

4.71   Your car gets 32 miles per gallon of gasoline. If gasoline costs $0.45 per liter (*a*) what is the cost per gallon (to the nearest cent) and (*b*) how much did you spend on gasoline last year if you traveled 11,200 miles?

4.72   A recipe calls for an oven temperature of 200°C. What would be the equivalent Fahrenheit temperature?

4.73   How many hectoliters of water are needed to fill a container 120 centimeters long, 50 centimeters wide, and 20 centimeters deep?

4.74   What is the capacity in liters of a container 2 feet long, 18 inches wide, and 6 inches deep?

4.75   To the nearest tenth, how many square feet of living space are contained in a house with a living area of 120 square meters?

4.76   A cake weighing $\frac{1}{2}$ kilogram contains 560 calories. To the nearest hundredth, how many calories are there in a 2-ounce serving? (There are 16 ounces in 1 pound.)

4.77   The Dawsons wish to install a new vinyl floor in their kitchen, which is 10 feet wide and 12 feet long. If flooring costs $25 per square meter, how much will the Dawsons pay for their new floor?

Answers to Supplementary Problems

4.49   (*a*) 72 dm, (*b*) 13 dm, (*c*) 100 dm

4.50   (*a*) 2.5 kg, (*b*) 0.05 kg, (*c*) 30 kg

4.51   (*a*) 12.5 dkL, (*b*) 60 dkL, (*c*) 38 dkL

4.52   233 m

4.53   122 g

4.54   2.75 L

4.55   85.344 m

4.56   524.5 km

4.57   5.66 kg

4.58 $0.36

4.59   94.6 L

4.60   88 km/h

4.61   14°F

4.62   Yes, the truck would be allowed to cross the bridge since the truck with its load weighs 18.14 metric tons, which is 0.36 metric tons below the limit.

4.63   25°C

4.64   No. Only about 19 liters of gasoline would fit in a 5-gallon can.

4.65   354.9 mL

4.66   (a) 190.5 cm, (b) 89.7 kg

4.67   They own the same amount of land.

4.68   32.33 m^2

4.69 $38.75

4.70 $39.73/yd^3

4.71   (a) $1.70/gal, (b) $595

4.72   392°F

4.73   1.2 hL

4.74   42 L

4.75   1,291.7 ft^2

4.76   63.42 calories

4.77 $278.70

Chapter 5

Payroll

5.1 GROSS PAY

Gross pay is the total amount of money—before any deductions—that an employer will pay and is generally determined through negotiations between the employer and the employee. The employer, however, must conform with all applicable federal and state laws (minimum wage, and so on).

Gross pay for wage earners is generally computed by using an individual time card.

Time Card

Name _____	Pay Rate/Hour _____	
Week Ended _____		
	Time In	Time Out	Hours
Monday _____	_____	_____
Tuesday _____	_____	_____
Wednesday _____	_____	_____
Thursday _____	_____	_____
Friday _____	_____	_____
Approved _____	Total Hours for Week _____

EXAMPLE 1

Ms. Horesnick's weekly time card is shown below.

Time Card

Name Dotty Horesnick	Pay Rate/Hour $5.00	
Week Ended 3/3/82		
	Time In	Time Out	Hours
Monday	8:00 a.m.	4:00 p.m.	8
Tuesday	8:00 a.m.	4:00 p.m.	8
Wednesday	8:00 a.m.	3:00 p.m.	7
Thursday	8:00 a.m.	2:00 p.m.	6
Friday	8:00 a.m.	4:00 p.m.	8
Approved *Joel Lerner*	Total Hours for Week	37

From the time card, we can compute the gross pay as follows:

$$\text{Hours worked} \times \text{hourly rate} = \text{gross pay}$$
$$37\,\text{h} \times \$5/\text{h} = \$185.00$$

84

SOLVED PROBLEMS

5.1 Leo Forman worked $36\frac{1}{2}$ hours last week at an hourly rate of $3.60. Find his gross pay.

SOLUTION

$$\text{Hours worked} \times \text{hourly rate} = \text{gross pay}$$
$$36.5 \times \$3.60 = \$131.40$$

5.2 For the week ending June 5, Roberta Butler worked 40 hours at an hourly rate of $3.35. Determine her gross pay for the week.

SOLUTION

$$\text{Hours worked} \times \text{hourly rate} = \text{gross pay}$$
$$40 \times \$3.35 = \$134.00$$

5.3 Find, to the nearest cent, the gross pay of an employee who worked $26\frac{1}{4}$ hours at an hourly rate of $4.25.

SOLUTION

$$\text{Hours worked} \times \text{hourly rate} = \text{gross pay}$$
$$26.25 \times \$4.25 = \$111.56$$

5.4 For the following employees of Honeywell Advertising Company, determine the total hours worked and the gross pay, to the nearest cent.

Name	Mon.	Tues.	Wed.	Thurs.	Fri.	Hourly Rate
M. Bury	$7\frac{1}{2}$	$7\frac{1}{2}$	$7\frac{1}{2}$	$7\frac{1}{2}$	$7\frac{1}{2}$	$4.25
J. Cahn	7	5	$2\frac{1}{2}$	8	6	$3.60
P. Gallagher	8	8	8	8	8	$5.00
S. Klein	8	$3\frac{1}{4}$	8	4	0	$4.10
H. Walter	$6\frac{3}{4}$	5	4	3	$7\frac{1}{4}$	$3.35

SOLUTION

Name	Total Hours	$\times$	Hourly Rate	$=$	Gross Pay
M. Bury	37.5	$\times$	$4.25	$=$	$159.38
J. Cahn	28.5	$\times$	$3.60	$=$	$102.60
P. Gallagher	40	$\times$	$5.00	$=$	$200.00
S. Klein	23.25	$\times$	$4.10	$=$	$ 95.33
H. Walter	26	$\times$	$3.35	$=$	$ 87.10

5.2 HOURLY RATE AND HOURS WORKED

We can rewrite the formula for gross pay to solve for hours worked or hourly rate:

$$\text{Hours worked} \times \text{hourly rate} = \text{gross pay}$$

$$\text{Hourly rate} = \frac{\text{gross pay}}{\text{hours worked}} \qquad \text{Hours worked} = \frac{\text{gross pay}}{\text{hourly rate}}$$

EXAMPLE 2

Marlene's gross pay is $15 for 3 hours of work. What is her hourly rate?

$$\text{Hourly rate} = \frac{\text{gross pay}}{\text{hours worked}}$$

$$= \frac{\$15}{3} = \$5$$

EXAMPLE 3

Ivan's gross pay is $24 and his hourly rate is $4. How many hours has he worked?

$$\text{Hours worked} = \frac{\text{gross pay}}{\text{hourly rate}}$$

$$= \frac{\$24}{\$4} = 6$$

SOLVED PROBLEMS

5.5 Robert Hamilton received $154 gross pay for 28 hours worked. What is his hourly rate?

SOLUTION

$$\text{Hourly rate} = \frac{\text{gross pay}}{\text{hours worked}}$$

$$= \frac{\$154}{28} = \$5.50$$

5.6 If Margaret Van Norden worked $37\frac{1}{2}$ hours and received $150 gross pay, what is her hourly rate?

SOLUTION

$$\text{Hourly rate} = \frac{\text{gross pay}}{\text{hours worked}}$$

$$= \frac{\$150}{37.5} = \$4$$

5.7 An employee received $226 gross pay and worked 40 hours. What is this employee's hourly rate?

SOLUTION

$$\text{Hourly rate} = \frac{\text{gross pay}}{\text{hours worked}}$$

$$= \frac{\$226}{40} = \$5.65$$

5.8 If Harry Black received $175 as his gross pay and worked 35 hours, what is his hourly rate?

SOLUTION

$$\text{Hourly rate} = \frac{\text{gross pay}}{\text{hours worked}}$$

$$= \frac{\$175}{35} = \$5$$

5.9   Given the gross pay and the hours worked, find the hourly rate for the following:

	Gross Pay	Hours Worked
(a)	$198.00	36
(b)	$105.80	23
(c)	$117.25	35
(d)	$220.10	$35\frac{1}{2}$
(e)	$106.25	25
(f)	$152.25	$26\frac{1}{4}$
(g)	$253.20	40
(h)	$117.25	$33\frac{1}{2}$

SOLUTION

	Gross Pay	÷	Hours Worked	=	Hourly Rate
(a)	$198.00	÷	36	=	$5.50
(b)	$105.80	÷	23	=	$4.60
(c)	$117.25	÷	35	=	$3.35
(d)	$220.10	÷	35.5	=	$6.20
(e)	$106.25	÷	25	=	$4.25
(f)	$152.25	÷	26.25	=	$5.80
(g)	$253.20	÷	40	=	$6.33
(h)	$117.25	÷	33.5	=	$3.50

5.10   Determine the total hours worked by Wilma Wade if her hourly rate is $4.40 and her gross pay is $88.

SOLUTION

$$\text{Hours worked} = \frac{\text{gross pay}}{\text{hourly rate}}$$

$$= \frac{\$88.00}{\$4.40/h} = 20$$

5.11   If an employee received $150 gross pay at an hourly rate of $3.75, how many hours did he work?

SOLUTION

$$\text{Hours worked} = \frac{\text{gross pay}}{\text{hourly rate}}$$

$$= \frac{\$150.00}{\$3.75/h} = 40$$

5.12   Renée Aronow works as a painter for Maplewood Painting Company. Her gross pay for last week was $102.60 and her hourly rate is $3.60. Calculate her total hours worked.

SOLUTION

$$\text{Hours worked} = \frac{\text{gross pay}}{\text{hourly rate}}$$

$$= \frac{\$102.60}{\$3.60/h} = 28.5$$

5.13 Determine the total hours worked by an employee if the employee's gross pay is $206.98 and hourly rate is $5.24.

SOLUTION

$$\text{Hours worked} = \frac{\text{gross pay}}{\text{hourly rate}}$$

$$= \frac{\$206.98}{\$5.24/\text{h}} = 39.5$$

5.14 Determine the hours worked for each of the following:

	Gross Pay	Hourly Rate
(a)	$ 77.00	$3.50
(b)	$199.51	$5.62
(c)	$175.20	$4.38
(d)	$172.38	$6.76
(e)	$180.88	$5.44
(f)	$132.05	$3.80
(g)	$169.56	$6.28
(h)	$197.60	$4.94

SOLUTION

	Gross Pay	÷	Hourly Rate	=	Hours Worked
(a)	$ 77.00	÷	$3.50	=	22
(b)	$199.51	÷	$5.62	=	35.5
(c)	$175.20	÷	$4.38	=	40
(d)	$172.38	÷	$6.76	=	25.5
(e)	$180.88	÷	$5.44	=	33.25
(f)	$132.05	÷	$3.80	=	34.75
(g)	$169.56	÷	$6.28	=	27
(h)	$197.60	÷	$4.94	=	40

5.3 OVERTIME

Overtime generally refers to the hours worked in excess of 8 in 1 day or 40 in 1 week. For example, if John worked 10 h yesterday he will be paid overtime for 2 hours (10 − 8 = 2). If Mary worked 43 hours last week, she will be paid overtime for 3 hours (43 − 40 = 3).

Overtime pay is usually $1\frac{1}{2}$ times the regular hourly rate. This overtime rate is called time-and-a-half. For example, if your hourly rate is $6, then your overtime rate is $1.5 \times \$6 = \$9$ per hour. Work on Sundays or legal holidays is usually paid for at 2 times the regular hourly rate. This rate is called double time. Therefore, for an hourly rate of $6, the overtime rate for work on Sundays or holidays is $2 \times \$6 = \$12/\text{h}$.

SOLVED PROBLEMS

5.15 Steven Edward's time card shows the following hours worked:

Mon.	Tues.	Wed.	Thurs.	Fri.
$8\frac{3}{4}$	9	7	$7\frac{1}{4}$	10

His hourly rate is $6.50 plus time-and-a-half for any hours worked over 40 per week. Determine (*a*) his total hours worked and (*b*) his gross pay.

SOLUTION

(*a*)
$$\text{Hours worked} = \text{total hours worked}$$
$$8.75 + 9 + 7 + 7.25 + 10 = 42$$

(*b*) The gross pay in this instance is the sum of Steven's regular pay and his overtime pay. We determine the regular pay as follows:

$$\text{Regular hours} \times \text{hourly rate} = \text{regular pay}$$
$$40 \times \$6.50 = \$260.00$$

To calculate overtime pay, we must first determine the overtime hours worked and the hourly rate for working overtime.

$$\text{Overtime hours} = 42\,\text{h worked} - 40\,\text{h} = 2\,\text{h}$$
$$\text{Overtime rate} = \$6.50 \times 1.5 = \$9.75$$

The overtime pay then is

$$\text{Overtime hours} \times \text{overtime rate} = \text{overtime pay}$$
$$2 \times \$9.75 = \$19.50$$

Steven Edward's gross pay for the week is

$$\text{Regular pay} + \text{overtime pay} = \text{gross pay}$$
$$\$260.00 + \$19.50 = \$279.50$$

5.16 An employee worked the following hours during the week:

Mon.	Tues.	Wed.	Thurs.	Fri.
8	9	$8\frac{1}{2}$	10	$7\frac{1}{2}$

Calculate her gross pay at an hourly rate of $5.40 plus time-and-a-half for any work hours over 40 per week.

SOLUTION

$$\text{Regular hours} \times \text{hourly rate} = \text{regular pay}$$
$$40 \times \$5.40 = \$216.00$$

$$\text{Overtime hours*} \times \text{overtime rate**} = \text{overtime pay}$$
$$2.5 \times \$8.10 = \$20.25$$

$$\text{Regular pay} + \text{overtime pay} = \text{gross pay}$$
$$\$216.00 + \$20.25 = \$236.25$$

---

*Overtime hours: $42.5 - 40 = 2.5$
**Overtime rate: $1.5 \times \$5.40 = \$8.10$

5.17 On Monday, Wednesday, and Friday, Joseph Reed worked 10 hours each day. On Tuesday and Thursday he worked 5 hours each day. His hourly rate is $5.70 plus time-and-a-half for any hours worked in excess of 8 per day. What is his gross pay?

SOLUTION

$$\text{Regular hours*} \times \text{hourly rate} = \text{regular pay}$$
$$34 \times \$5.70 = \$193.80$$

$$\text{Overtime hours**} \times \text{overtime rate†} = \text{overtime pay}$$
$$6 \times \$8.55 = \$51.30$$

$$\text{Regular pay} + \text{overtime pay} = \text{gross pay}$$
$$\$193.80 + \$51.30 = \$245.10$$

---

*Regular hours = total hours − overtime hours
$$= (10 \text{ h/day} \times 3 \text{ days} + 5 \text{ h/day} \times 2 \text{ days}) - (10 \text{ h/day} - 8 \text{ h/day}) \times 3 \text{ days}$$
$$= (30 \text{ h} + 10 \text{ h}) - 2 \text{ h/day} \times 3 \text{ days} = 40 \text{ h} - 6 \text{ h} = 34 \text{ h}$$
**Overtime hours: $(10 \text{ h/day} - 8 \text{ h/day}) \times 3 \text{ days}$ (Mon., Wed., and Fri.)
†Overtime rate: $\$5.70 \times 1.5 = \$8.55$

5.18 Find the gross pay for Nancy Solomon if she earns \$5.80 per hour, time-and-a-half for working any hours over 8 per day, and double time for working on Sundays. Her time card for the week ending May 16 is as follows:

Mon.	Tues.	Wed.	Thurs.	Fri.	Sat.	Sun.
$5\frac{1}{2}$	$9\frac{1}{4}$	0	$6\frac{1}{2}$	$8\frac{1}{4}$	5	$4\frac{1}{2}$

SOLUTION

$$\text{Regular hours*} \times \text{hourly rate} = \text{regular pay}$$
$$33 \times \$5.80 = \$191.40$$

$$\text{Overtime hours**} \times \text{overtime rate†} = \text{overtime pay}$$
$$1.5 \times \$8.70 = \$13.05$$
$$4.5 \text{ (Sun.)} \times \$11.60 = \underline{\$52.20}$$
$$\text{Total overtime pay} = \$65.25$$

$$\text{Regular pay} + \text{overtime pay} = \text{gross pay}$$
$$\$191.40 + \$65.25 = \$256.65$$

---

*Regular hours = total hours − overtime hours
$$= 39 - (1.25 + 0.25 + 4.5) = 39 - 6 = 33$$
**Overtime hours: 1.25 h (Tues.) $+ 0.25 \text{ h}$ (Fri.) $= 1.5 \text{ h}$ at time-and-a-half; 4.5 h (Sun.) at double time
†Overtime rates: $\$5.80 \times 1.5 = \$8.70$ for Tues. and Fri.
$$\$5.80 \times 2 = \$11.60 \text{ for Sun.}$$

5.19 At ABC Lighting Manufacturers the employees are paid an hourly rate of \$6.50 plus time-and-a-half for any hours worked over 8 per day. Find the gross pay for Greg Johnston when his time card shows the following:

Mon.	Tues.	Wed.	Thurs.	Fri.
9	$6\frac{1}{2}$	8	10	$7\frac{1}{2}$

SOLUTION

$$\text{Regular hours* } \times \text{ hourly rate} = \text{regular pay}$$
$$38 \times \$6.50 = \$247.00$$

$$\text{Overtime hours** } \times \text{ overtime rate†} = \text{overtime pay}$$
$$3 \times \$9.75 = \$29.25$$

$$\text{Regular pay} + \text{overtime pay} = \text{gross pay}$$
$$\$247.00 + \$29.25 = \$276.25$$

*Regular hours = total hours − overtime hours
$$= 41 - 3 = 38$$
**Overtime hours: 1 (Mon.) + 2 (Thurs.) = 3
†Overtime rate: $6.50 × 1.5 = $9.75

5.20 The following employees of Colonial Contractors each receive an hourly rate of $4.40 plus time-and-a-half for working in excess of 8 hours per day and double time for working Sundays and holidays. (December 25 is Christmas, which is a legal holiday.) Calculate each employee's gross pay.

Name	Dec. 22 Mon.	Dec. 23 Tues.	Dec. 24 Wed.	Dec. 25 Thurs.	Dec. 26 Fri.	Dec. 27 Sat.	Dec. 28 Sun.
P. Glick	$7\frac{3}{4}$	0	$9\frac{1}{4}$	8	0	$7\frac{1}{2}$	8
D. Golden	0	$6\frac{1}{4}$	$9\frac{3}{4}$	0	8	4	$6\frac{1}{2}$
V. Kaplan	10	$5\frac{1}{2}$	0	$8\frac{3}{4}$	$7\frac{1}{2}$	0	$9\frac{3}{4}$
M. Liff	$8\frac{1}{2}$	6	$7\frac{1}{4}$	0	$9\frac{3}{4}$	$7\frac{1}{4}$	0
K. Waite	0	$6\frac{3}{4}$	$9\frac{3}{4}$	10	$6\frac{1}{4}$	0	$7\frac{1}{4}$

SOLUTION

Name	Regular* Hours	×	Hourly Rate	=	Regular Pay	Over-time Hours	×	Over-time Rate**	=	Over-time Pay	Sun. and Holiday Hours	×	Sun. and Holiday Rate†	=	Sun. and Holiday Pay	Gross Pay‡
P. Glick	23.25	×	$4.40	=	$102.30	1.25	×	$6.60	=	$ 8.25	16	×	$8.80	=	$140.80	$251.35
D. Golden	25.5	×	$4.40	=	$112.20	1.75	×	$6.60	=	$11.55	6.5	×	$8.80	=	$ 57.20	$180.95
V. Kaplan	21	×	$4.40	=	$ 92.40	2	×	$6.60	=	$13.20	18.5	×	$8.80	=	$162.80	$268.40
M. Liff	36.5	×	$4.40	=	$160.60	2.25	×	$6.60	=	$14.85	0	×	$8.80	=	$ 0.00	$175.45
K. Waite	21	×	$4.40	=	$ 92.40	1.75	×	$6.60	=	$11.55	17.25	×	$8.80	=	$151.80	$255.75

*Regular hours = total hours − overtime hours
**Overtime rate: $4.40 × 1.5 = $6.60
†Sunday and holiday rate: $4.40 × 2 = $8.80
‡Gross pay = regular pay + overtime pay + Sun. and holiday pay

5.21 Victoria Sullivan worked 46 hours last week at an hourly rate of $4.20 plus time-and-a-half for working over 40 hours per week. What is her gross pay?

SOLUTION

$$\text{Regular hours} \times \text{hourly rate} = \text{regular pay}$$
$$40 \times \$4.20 = \$168$$

$$\text{Overtime hours} \times \text{overtime rate*} = \text{overtime pay}$$
$$6 \times \$6.30 = \$37.80$$

$$\text{Regular pay} + \text{overtime pay} = \text{gross pay}$$
$$\$168 + \$37.80 = \$205.80$$

*Overtime rate: $4.20 × 1.5 = $6.30

5.22 Calculate, to the nearest cent, the gross pay of Harry Rogers. His time card for the week ending February 11 shows $48\frac{1}{2}$ hours worked. His rate of pay is $5.50 per hour plus time-and-a-half for any hours over 40.

SOLUTION

$$\text{Regular hours} \times \text{hourly rate} = \text{regular pay}$$
$$40 \times \$5.50 = \$220$$

$$\text{Overtime hours} \times \text{overtime rate}^* = \text{overtime pay}$$
$$8.5 \times \$8.25 = \$70.13$$

$$\text{Regular pay} + \text{overtime pay} = \text{gross pay}$$
$$\$220 + \$70.13 = \$290.13$$

_____

*Overtime rate: $5.50 \times 1.5 = \$8.25$

5.23 An employee worked the following hours:

Mon.	Tues.	Wed.	Thurs.	Fri.	Sat.	Sun.
$9\frac{3}{4}$	$10\frac{1}{4}$	$6\frac{1}{2}$	8	$7\frac{1}{2}$	0	5

Find her gross pay, to the nearest cent, if she is paid $6.75 per hour plus time-and-a-half for hours in excess of 40 and double time for any hours worked on Sunday.

SOLUTION:

$$\text{Regular hours} \times \text{regular rate} = \text{regular pay}$$
$$40 \times \$6.75 = \$270$$

$$\text{Overtime hours} \times \text{overtime rate}^* = \text{overtime pay}$$
$$2 \times \$10.125 = \$20.25$$
$$5 \text{ (Sun.)} \times \$13.50 = \underline{\$67.50}$$
$$\text{Total overtime pay} = \$87.75$$

$$\text{Regular pay} + \text{overtime pay} = \text{gross pay}$$
$$\$270 + \$87.75 = \$357.75$$

_____

*Overtime rates: $6.75 \times 1.5 = \$10.125$ for weekdays
$6.75 \times 2 = \$13.50$ for Sundays

5.24 For each of the following cases, find the overtime rate (time-and-a-half) and gross pay, to the nearest cent.

	Hours Worked	Hourly Rate
(a)	$46\frac{1}{2}$	$5.75
(b)	52	$4.35
(c)	$40\frac{1}{2}$	$6.25
(d)	$42\frac{3}{4}$	$3.35
(e)	$49\frac{1}{4}$	$6.75
(f)	45	$5.55
(g)	$43\frac{1}{2}$	$4.97
(h)	$47\frac{1}{4}$	$3.66
(i)	$41\frac{3}{4}$	$7.45
(j)	$44\frac{3}{4}$	$6.87

SOLUTION

	Hours Worked	Regular Hours	×	Hourly Rate	=	Regular Pay	Overtime Hours	×	Overtime Rate*	=	Overtime Pay	Gross Pay**
(a)	$46\frac{1}{2}$	40	×	$5.75	=	$230.00	6.5	×	$ 8.625	=	$56.06	$286.06
(b)	52	40	×	$4.35	=	$174.00	12	×	$ 6.525	=	$78.30	$252.30
(c)	$40\frac{1}{2}$	40	×	$6.25	=	$250.00	.5	×	$ 9.375	=	$ 4.69	$254.69
(d)	$42\frac{3}{4}$	40	×	$3.35	=	$134.00	2.75	×	$ 5.025	=	$13.82	$147.82
(e)	$49\frac{1}{4}$	40	×	$6.75	=	$270.00	9.25	×	$10.125	=	$93.66	$363.66
(f)	45	40	×	$5.55	=	$222.00	5	×	$ 8.325	=	$41.63	$263.63
(g)	$43\frac{1}{2}$	40	×	$4.97	=	$198.80	3.5	×	$ 7.455	=	$26.09	$224.89
(h)	$47\frac{1}{4}$	40	×	$3.66	=	$146.40	7.25	×	$ 5.49	=	$39.80	$186.20
(i)	$41\frac{3}{4}$	40	×	$7.45	=	$298.00	1.75	×	$11.175	=	$19.56	$317.56
(j)	$44\frac{3}{4}$	40	×	$6.87	=	$274.60	4.75	×	$10.305	=	$48.95	$323.75

*Overtime rate = hourly rate × 1.5
**Gross pay = regular pay + overtime pay

5.25 For the following employees of Wilson Boat Company, calculate (a) regular hours, (b) regular pay, (c) overtime hours (hours in excess of 40 per week), (d) overtime rate (time-and-a-half), (e) overtime pay, and (f) gross pay.

Name	Mon.	Tues.	Wed.	Thurs.	Fri.	Sat.	Hourly Rate
T. Arsen	8	$7\frac{3}{4}$	8	8	$4\frac{3}{4}$	$5\frac{1}{2}$	$4.30
J. Charm	8	0	8	$7\frac{1}{4}$	6	$7\frac{1}{2}$	$6.10
A. Churchill	$7\frac{1}{2}$	10	$9\frac{1}{4}$	$8\frac{3}{4}$	8	8	$4.50
R. Darcy	7	7	8	8	$6\frac{3}{4}$	$3\frac{1}{4}$	$5.40
C. Lenox	$7\frac{3}{4}$	5	$7\frac{1}{4}$	8	$6\frac{1}{2}$	$4\frac{3}{4}$	$6.20
M. Steltz	$4\frac{1}{2}$	8	$6\frac{1}{4}$	$8\frac{1}{4}$	$7\frac{1}{2}$	$9\frac{1}{2}$	$5.60

SOLUTION

Name	(a) Regular Hours	×	Hourly Rate	=	(b) Regular Pay	(c) Overtime Hours	×	(d) Overtime Rate*	=	(e) Overtime Pay	(f) Gross Pay**
T. Arsen	40	×	$4.30	=	$172.00	2	×	$6.45	=	$12.90	$184.90
J. Charm	36.75	×	$6.10	=	$224.18	0	×	$9.15	=	$ 0.00	$224.18
A. Churchill	40	×	$4.50	=	$180.00	11.5	×	$6.75	=	$77.63	$257.63
R. Darcy	40	×	$5.40	=	$216.00	0	×	$8.10	=	$ 0.00	$216.00
C. Lenox	39.25	×	$6.20	=	$243.35	0	×	$9.30	=	$ 0.00	$243.35
M. Steltz	40	×	$5.60	=	$224.00	4	×	$8.40	=	$33.60	$257.60

*Overtime rate = hourly rate × 1.5
**Gross pay = regular pay + overtime pay

5.4 SALARY

If instead of being paid on an hourly basis, an employee is paid by the week, the month, or the year, he or she is said to be "on salary."

EXAMPLE 4

Joe's salary is $400 a week. What is his annual salary? Since there are 52 weeks in a year, we multiply $400 by 52.

$$\$400/wk \times 52 \text{ wk/yr} = \$20,800/yr$$

Now assume the reverse situation. You know your annual salary is $18,200, but you want to determine your weekly salary. In this case you divide by 52.

$$\$18,200/yr \div 52 \text{ wk/yr} = \$350/wk$$

EXAMPLE 5

Suppose that your salary is $600 per month. What is your annual salary?
A year has 12 months; therefore, to find your annual salary, multiply the monthly salary by 12.

$$\$600/mo \times 12 \text{ mo/yr} = \$7,200/yr$$

Similarly, if we know the annual salary, we can divide by 12 to find the monthly salary. Assume that Jane Tobber has an annual salary of $17,400. What is her monthly salary?

$$\$17,400/yr \div 12 \text{ mo/yr} = \$1,450/mo$$

SOLVED PROBLEMS

5.26   P. Bloomfeld is paid $40,000 annually. His pay period is biweekly. What is his salary per pay period to the nearest cent?

SOLUTION

To find the salary per pay period, we need to divide the annual pay by the number of pay periods in a year. Note that Bloomfeld gets paid only once every two weeks (biweekly) rather than once every week. We must therefore divide the number of weeks in a year by 2 to get the number of pay periods in a year.

$$52 \text{ wk/yr} \div 2 = 26 \text{ pay periods/yr}$$

We can now calculate Bloomfeld's salary per pay period.

$$\text{Annual salary} \div \text{pay periods/yr} = \text{salary/pay period}$$
$$\$40,000 \div 26 = \$1,538.46$$

5.27   Determine the salary per pay period, to the nearest cent, if an employee receives $25,000 per year and is paid monthly.

SOLUTION

$$\text{Annual salary} \div \text{pay periods/yr} = \text{salary/pay period}$$
$$\$25,000 \div 12 \text{ mo} = \$2,083.33$$

5.28   Theresa Toomey's annual salary is $13,000. What is her weekly salary?

SOLUTION

$$\text{Annual salary} \div \text{pay periods/yr} = \text{salary/pay period}$$
$$\$13,000 \div 52 \text{ wk} = \$250$$

5.29 Determine the annual salary of an employee who is paid $897.33 biweekly.

   SOLUTION

$$\text{Salary/pay period} \times \text{pay periods/yr} = \text{annual salary}$$
$$\$897.33 \times 26 \text{ wk} = \$23,330.58$$

5.30 Solve the following to the nearest cent:

	Annual Salary	Pay Period	Salary/Pay Period
(a)	$33,333	Biweekly	?
(b)	$10,400	?	$200
(c)	?	Weekly	$325.67
(d)	?	Monthly	$2,593.86
(e)	$47,980	Weekly	?
(f)	$42,312	?	$3,526
(g)	?	Biweekly	$765.43
(h)	$25,198	Monthly	?
(i)	$25,678.90	?	$987.65
(j)	$55,555	Biweekly	?
(k)	?	Weekly	$254.90
(l)	$18,000	?	$1,500

   SOLUTION

$$(a) \quad \$33,333 \quad \div \quad 26 \text{ wk} \quad = \$1,282.04$$

If we divide annual salary by the salary per pay period, we get the number of pay periods in a year.

$$(b) \quad \$10,400 \quad \div \quad \$200.00/\text{pay period} \quad = 52 \text{ pay periods/yr}$$

The pay period is *weekly*, since there are 52 wk in a year.

(c)	52 wk	× $325.67	= $16,934.84
(d)	12 mo	× $2,593.86	= $31,126.32
(e)	$47,980	÷ 52 wk	= $922.69
(f)	$42,312	÷ $3,526	= 12 pay periods/yr or monthly
(g)	26 wk	× $765.43	= $19,901.18
(h)	$25,198	÷ 12 mo	= $2,099.83
(i)	$25,678.90	÷ $987.65	= 26 pay periods/yr or biweekly
(j)	$55,555	÷ 26 wk	= $2,136.73
(k)	524 wk	× $254.90	= $13,254.80
(l)	$18,000	÷ $1,500	= 12 pay periods/yr or monthly

5.5 COMMISSION

At times it becomes impractical for business owners to assume all the functions of buying and selling. In order to relieve their work load, business owners hire salespeople. The means of paying such employees varies. Some receive a salary (see previous section), others receive a commission on the sales they make, and some are paid through a combination of both salary and commission. A *commission* is a fee paid for a service rendered (such as selling) and is usually expressed as a percentage of the money received by the business.

EXAMPLE 6

Suppose that you are working on a 25% commission basis. This means that your employer gives you 25¢ out of every dollar that you bring into the company through sales. The commission rate multiplied by the sales in dollars equals the amount of commission earned. Your commission on $80 of sales would therefore be

$$\text{Commission rate} \times \text{sales} = \text{commission earned}$$
$$25\% \times \$80 = \$20$$

If the commission is based on a single percent (as in the preceding example), it is called *straight* commission. In *variable* or *sliding scale* commission, two or more percents are used.

EXAMPLE 7

An employer pays 25% commission on sales up to $800 and 10% on the amount of sales above $800. How much does a salesperson earn on a sale of $1,200?

$$\text{Commission rate} \times \text{sales} = \text{commission earned}$$
$$0.25 \times \$800 = \$200$$
$$0.10 \times \$400^* = \underline{40}$$
$$\text{Total earned} = \$240$$

---

*The amount above $800 is $1,200 − $800 = $400

A *draw* is an advance, or sort of loan, against future commissions. An employer may allow a salesperson to draw a regular amount of money each week to help the employee get through "slow" sales periods.

EXAMPLE 8

Suppose an employee draws $200 at the beginning of a week and earns a commission of $240 by the end of the week. How much of the commission does the employee collect at the end of the week?

$$\text{Commission} - \text{draw} = \text{difference to be paid employee}$$
$$\$240 - \$200 = \$40$$

SOLVED PROBLEMS

5.31 Robert Wright receives a 7% commission from Sullivan Motor Sales. What is his commission on $12,000 in sales?

SOLUTION

$$\text{Commission rate} \times \text{sales} = \text{commission earned}$$
$$0.07 \times \$12,000 = \$840$$

5.32 Harriet Tapper receives a 6% commission on all her real estate sales. Half her commission goes to her broker. What is Harriet's portion of the commission on $150,000 in sales?

SOLUTION

$$\text{Commission rate} \times \text{sales} = \text{commission earned}$$
$$0.06 \times \$150,000 = \$9,000$$

Harriet gets to keep only half the commission she earns. Therefore, her portion in this instance is

$$\$9,000 \times \frac{1}{2} = \$4,500$$

5.33 During a month's time a furniture salesman receives 4% commission on the first $12,000 in sales, 5% commission on the next $12,000 in sales, and 6% commission on anything over $24,000. What is his commission on $42,000 in sales?

SOLUTION

$$\text{Commission rate} \times \text{sales} = \text{commission earned}$$
$$0.04 \times \$12,000 = \$\ \ 480$$
$$0.05 \times \$12,000 = \ \ \ \ 600$$
$$0.06 \times \$18,000^* = \underline{\ \ 1,080}$$
$$\text{Total commission} = \$2,160$$

$$^*\$42,000 - \$24,000 = \$18,000$$

5.34 Cohen Music Company pays its salespeople the following commissions on all sales:

2% on the first $1,000 in sales
5% on the next $1,000 in sales
8% on any sales over $2,000

Commissions are paid monthly. Determine to the nearest cent the commissions earned by the following employees:

Employee	Sales
P. Lacey	$1,569.80
E. Marks	$3,486.00
S. Norris	$2,371.99
F. Pinto	$4,507.27
P. Robinson	$2,597.00
K. Stewart	$1,625.30
C. Valley	$4,375.01
T. Yates	$3,625.54

SOLUTION

Employee	Sales	×	Commission Rate	=	Commission Earned
P. Lacey	$1,000.00	×	0.02	=	$ 20.00
	569.80	×	0.05	=	28.49
Total sales	$1,569.80		Total commission	=	$ 48.49
E. Marks	$1,000.00	×	0.02	=	$ 20.00
	1,000.00	×	0.05	=	50.00
	1,486.00	×	0.08	=	118.88
Total sales	$3,486.00		Total commission	=	$188.88
S. Norris	$1,000.00	×	0.02	=	$ 20.00
	1,000.00	×	0.05	=	50.00
	371.99	×	0.08	=	29.76
Total sales	$2,371.99		Total commission	=	$ 99.76
F. Pinto	$1,000.00	×	0.02	=	$ 20.00
	1,000.00	×	0.05	=	50.00
	2,507.27	×	0.08	=	200.58
Total sales	$4,507.27		Total commision	=	$270.58

Employee	Sales	×	Commission Rate	=	Commission Earned
P. Robinson	$1,000.000	×	0.02	=	$ 20.00
	1,000.00	×	0.05	=	50.00
	597.00	×	0.08	=	47.76
Total sales	$2,597.00		Total commission	=	$117.76
K. Stewart	$1,000.00	×	0.02	=	$ 20.00
	625.30	×	0.05	=	31.27
Total sales	$1,625.30		Total commission	=	$ 51.27
C. Valley	$1,000.00	×	0.02	=	$ 20.00
	1,000.00	×	0.05	=	50.00
	2,375.01	×	0.08	=	190.00
Total sales	$4,375.01		Total commission	=	$260.00
T. Yates	$1,000.00	×	0.02	=	$ 20.00
	1,000.00	×	0.05	=	50.00
	1,625.54	×	0.08	=	130.04
Total sales	$3,625.54		Total commission	=	$200.04

5.35 Ruth Gates receives a weekly salary of $200 *plus* a 4% commission on her total sales for the month. What are her gross monthly earnings, if her total sales for the month are $8,400?

SOLUTION

Salary: $200/wk × 4 wk = $ 800
Commission: $8,400 × 0.04 =   336
                        Gross monthly earnings = $1,136

5.36 The employees of Wagner Real Estate receive a weekly salary of $250 *plus* a 5% commission on their first $10,000 in monthly sales and 7% on any monthly sales over $10,000. What are the gross monthly earnings, to the nearest cent, of the following employees:

Name	Sales
B. Eddy	$15,943.87
K. Katz	$ 9,500.69
C. Polster	$35,196.50

SOLUTION

B. Eddy
Salary: $250.00/wk × 4 wk = $1,000.00
Commission: $10,000.00 × 0.05 =   500.00
                                  $5,943.87 × 0.07 =   416.07
                        Gross monthly earnings = $1,916.07

K. Katz
Salary: $250.00/wk × 4 wk = $1,000.00
Commission: $9,500.69 × 0.05 =   475.03
                        Gross monthly earnings = $1,475.03

C. Polster
Salary: $250.00/wk × 4 wk = $1,000.00
Commission: $10,000.00 × 0.05 =   500.00
                                  $25,196.50 × 0.07 = 1,763.76
                        Gross monthly earnings = $3,263.76

5.37 Brown's Sportswear Company pays its salespeople a straight commission of $8\frac{1}{2}\%$ on net sales for the month. Each salesperson also receives a draw of $150 per week. James Conway's sales for the month were $9,860. At the end of the month he is paid the difference between the draw and commission. What is owed James Conway?

SOLUTION

Commission:	$9,860 × 0.085 = $838.10
Draw:	$150/wk × 4 wk = <u> 600.00</u>
	Owed James Conway at end of mo = $238.10

5.38 Jean Gluck is paid a 7% commission on the first $1,500 in carpet sales, 8% on the next $1,500 and 9% on anything over $3,000 in sales. She also receives a $175 per week draw. To the nearest cent, find the difference between the draw and the commission that Jean receives at the end of the month. Her net sales for the month totaled $9,694.66.

SOLUTION

Commission:	$1,500.00 × 0.07	= $105.00
	1,500.00 × 0.08	= 120.00
	<u>6,694.66</u> × 0.09	= <u> 602.52</u>
Total sales $9,694.66	Total commission = $827.52
Draw:	$175/wk × 4 wk = <u> 700.00</u>
	Owed Jean Gluck at end of mo = $127.52

5.6 NET PAY

A deduction is anything that decreases gross pay. For instance, gross pay may be reduced by deductions for union dues or for taxes (either federal, state, or city). *Net pay* is the amount of money that an employee takes home and is equal to gross pay less any deductions.

EXAMPLE 9

If Bob's gross pay is $300 and if his employer deducts $10 for union dues and $30 for taxes, how much does Bob take home?

$$\text{Total deductions: } \$10 + \$30 = \$40$$

$$\text{Gross pay} - \text{total deductions} = \text{take-home or net pay}$$

$$\$300 - \$40 = \$260$$

Deductions required by law are called *mandatory deductions* and include:

Federal Withholding Taxes. Under the federal withholding tax system (commony known as "pay as you go"), federal income tax is collected in the year in which the income is received, rather than in the following year. Thus, employers must withhold funds for the payment of their employees' federal income taxes that will come due the following year. The amount to be withheld depends upon the number of exemptions the employee is allowed (on Form W-4), the amount of the employee's earnings, and the employee's marital status. An employee is entitled to one personal exemption and one for his or her spouse, each dependent, and extra exemption if either the employee or spouse is blind or over 65 years of age.

Social Security Taxes (Federal Insurance Contribution Act—FICA). The FICA tax helps pay for such federal programs as old age and disability benefits, Medicare, and insurance benefits to survivors. During the working years of an employee, funds are set aside from his or her earnings (Social Security taxes). When the employee's earnings cease because of disability, retirement, or death, the funds are made available to the employee or to his or her dependents or survivors. Under the act both employee and employer are required to contribute equally, with the amount being based on the employee's earnings.

An exception to equal contributions occurred in 1984, when the amount paid by the employer was 7% and the employee 6.7%. This difference was the result of a 0.3% government credit against the employee's 7% withholding. This exception notwithstanding, all computations in this text are based on a 7% FICA tax for employees on the first $37,800 earned.

EXAMPLE 10

If, in a given payroll period, a total of $85 was withheld from employees' wages for Social Security taxes, the employer must remit $170 to the government. The $170 represents the $85 contribution by the employees plus the employer's matching share. [In 1984, the employer would have had to remit $173.81 since the employer's rate was 0.3% greater than the employees' rate: $x/\$85 = (7\%/6.7\%)$.]

Wages in excess of $37,800 paid to a worker in one calendar year by one employer are not subject to FICA taxes.

EXAMPLE 11

Barbara's earnings prior to this week were $37,000. This week her salary is $200. Her FICA deduction is $14 ($200 × 7%). If Barbara had earned $37,750 prior to this pay period, only $50 of this week's $200 salary would be subject to FICA tax, and the deduction would be only $3.50 ($50 × 7%).

If an individual works for more than one employer during a year, each employer must withhold and pay taxes on the first $37,800. However, the employee is granted a refund from the government if his or her salary exceeds the $37,800 base.

Notice that the withholding of any wages represents, from the employer's viewpoint, a liability, because the employer must pay to the government the amount withheld from the employee.

In addition to taxes, or involuntary deductions, there may be a number of voluntary deductions made for the convenience of the employee, such as group insurance premiums, hospitalization programs, savings plans, retirement payments, union dues, and charitable contributions.

EXAMPLE 12

Harold Eccleston earned $300 for the week. Deductions from his pay were: Federal withholding taxes of $50, FICA tax of $21, insurance of $6, and union dues of $10. What is his net pay?

$$\text{Net pay} = \text{gross pay} - \text{deductions}$$
$$= \$300 - (\$50 + \$21 + \$6 + \$10) = \$300 - \$87 = \$213$$

SOLVED PROBLEMS

5.39 The federal income tax withheld from B. Sheppard's gross pay is $17.56 and the FICA tax is 7%. What is her net pay, to the nearest cent, if her gross earnings for the week ending January 7 are $236.87?

SOLUTION

Gross pay		$236.87
Deductions		
Federal income tax	$17.56	
FICA tax*	16.58	
Total deductions		34.14
Net pay		$202.73

*FICA tax: $236.87 × 0.07 = $16.58

5.40 If H. Bart has $25 withheld from his gross pay for U.S. savings bonds and also contributes $15 per week directly through his employer to his favorite charitable organization, what is his net pay, to the nearest cent, if his gross pay is $489.55 per week, federal income tax deduction is $33.98, and the FICA tax is 7%? (His year-to-date gross earnings are $24,562.)

SOLUTION

Gross pay		$489.55
Deductions		
Federal income tax	$33.98	
FICA tax*	34.27	
U.S. savings bonds	25.00	
Charitable organization	15.00	
Total deductions		108.25
Net pay		$381.30

*FICA tax: $489.55 × 0.07 = $34.27

5.41 The following deductions were made from S. Sarles's gross pay:

Federal income tax	$35.89
FICA tax	23.32
Life insurance	10.44

If her gross pay is $333.33, what is her net pay?

SOLUTION

Gross pay		$333.33
Deductions		
Federal income tax	$35.89	
FICA tax	23.31	
Life insurance	10.44	
Total deductions		69.64
Net pay		$263.69

5.42 At Schmidt Electric the employees' contribution to the pension plan is 3% of their gross pay. If A. Levinson's gross pay is $543.21, federal income tax withheld is $40.65 and FICA tax is 7%, what is his net pay?

SOLUTION

Gross pay		$543.21
Deductions		
Federal income tax	$40.65	
FICA tax*	38.02	
Pension plan**	16.30	
Total deductions		94.96
Net pay		$448.24

*FICA tax: $543.21 × 0.07 = $38.02
**Pension plan: $543.21 × 0.03 = $16.30

5.43 Find the net pay for P. Doyle if her gross pay is $257.34 per week and her deductions are $20.57 in federal income tax per week, $17.99 in FICA tax per week, and $20 in hospitalization insurance per month.

SOLUTION

Gross pay		$257.34
Deductions		
Federal income tax	$20.57	
FICA tax	17.99	
Hospitalization ins.*	5.00	
Total deductions		43.56
Net pay		$213.78

*Hospitalization insurance: $20/mo ÷ 4 wk/mo = $5/wk

5.44 D. Feldman pays $5.75 per week union dues. If his gross pay is $445.98 for the pay period and $23,190.96 for the year to date, his federal income tax withholding is $32.67, and his FICA tax is 7%, what is his net pay?

SOLUTION

Gross pay		$445.98
Deductions		
Federal income tax	$32.67	
FICA tax*	31.22	
Union dues	5.75	
Total deductions		69.64
Net pay		$376.34

*FICA tax: $445.98 × 0.07 = $31.22

5.45 An employee's year-to-date gross pay is $36,799. Her current week's earnings amount to $735.98, her federal income tax withheld is $52.67, and her FICA tax is 7%. What is her net pay?

SOLUTION

Gross pay		$735.98
Deductions		
Federal income tax	$52.67	
FICA tax	51.52	
Total deductions		104.19
Net pay		$631.79

5.46 At Lord Enterprise the employees contribute 1% of their gross pay to their favorite charitable organization, 2% toward union dues, 3% toward life insurance, and 4% toward hospitalization insurance. If B. Hill's gross pay is $675, federal income tax withholding is $49.87, and FICA tax is $47.25, what is his net pay?

SOLUTION

Gross pay		$675.00
Deductions		
Federal income tax	$49.87	
FICA tax	47.25	
Charitable organization*	6.75	
Union dues**	13.50	
Life insurance***	20.25	
Hospitalization ins.†	27.00	
Total deductions		164.62
Net pay		$510.38

*Charitable organization: $675.00 × 0.01 = $6.75
**Union dues: $675.00 × 0.02 = $13.50
***Life insurance: $675.00 × 0.03 = $20.25
†Hospitalization insurance: $675.00 × 0.04 = $27.00

5.47 L. Bolt's gross pay so far this year totals $38,678.40. Her gross pay for the week ending December 27 is $640.75, federal income tax withheld is $50.87, FICA tax is 7%, and union dues deduction is $7.50. She also has deducted $50 for U.S. savings bonds and $50 for her automatic savings account. Find her net pay.

SOLUTION

Gross pay		$640.75
Deductions		
Federal income tax	$50.87	
FICA tax*	0.00	
Union dues	7.50	
U.S. savings bonds	50.00	
Savings	50.00	
Total deductions		158.37
Net pay		$482.38

*FICA tax is taken only on the first $37,800 in gross yearly earnings.

5.48 Ascertain the net pay for an employee whose gross pay is $256.93 per week, federal income tax withheld is $20.41, FICA tax is 7%, hospitalization insurance is $6.70, union dues deduction is $4.60, and life insurance is $5. In addition, the employee has made a loan through his employer whereby the employee agreed to a deduction of $25 per week from his paycheck until said load is paid.

SOLUTION

Gross pay		$256.93
Deductions		
Federal income tax	$20.41	
FICA tax*	17.99	
Hospitalization ins.	6.70	
Union dues	4.60	
Life insurance	5.00	
Loan	25.00	
Total deductions		79.70
Net pay		$177.23

*FICA tax: $256.93 × 0.07 = $17.99

5.49 Kaufmann Insulation pays its employees biweekly. In addition to the federal income tax withheld, each employee's deductions are as follows:

FICA tax	7%
Union dues	$5.50
Hospitalization ins.	$3.20
Life insurance	$4.20

Each employee also receives a $20 uniform allowance. Given the following gross pay, federal income tax withheld, and year-to-date gross pay for each employee, find the respective net pay to the nearest cent.

Name	Gross Pay	Federal Income Tax Withheld	Year-to-Date Gross Pay
P. Basso	$1,570.90	$111.52	$37,418.00
F. Ericson	1,734.66	121.98	38,693.20
C. Johanson	1,269.70	97.10	25,434.00
G. Markie	1,041.12	77.54	20,822.40
N. Schmitz	867.24	60.96	17,344.80

SOLUTION

P. Basso

Gross pay		$1,570.90
Deductions		
Federal income tax	$111.52	
FICA tax*	26.74	
Union dues	5.50	
Hospitalization ins.	3.20	
Life insurance	4.20	
Total deductions		151.16
		1,419.74
Uniform allowance		20.00
Net pay		$1,439.74

*FICA tax: ($37,800 − $37,418) × 7% = $382 × 0.07 = $26.74

F. Ericson

Gross pay		$1,734.66
Deductions		
Federal income tax	$121.98	
FICA tax*	0.00	
Union dues	5.50	
Hospitalization ins.	3.20	
Life insurance	4.20	
Total deductions		134.88
		$1,599.78
Uniform allowance		20.00
Net pay		$1,619.78

*FICA tax is taken only on the first $37,800 in gross yearly earnings.

C. Johanson

Gross pay		$1,269.70
Deductions		
Federal income tax	$97.10	
FICA tax*	88.88	
Union dues	5.50	
Hospitalization ins.	3.20	
Life insurance	4.20	
Total deductions		198.88
		$1,070.82
Uniform allowance		20.00
Net pay		$1,090.82

*FICA tax: $1,269.70 × 0.07 = $88.88

G. Markie

Gross pay		$1,041.12
Deductions		
Federal income tax	$77.54	
FICA tax*	72.88	
Union dues	5.50	
Hospitalization ins.	3.20	
Life insurance	4.20	
Total deductions		163.32
		$ 877.80
Uniform allowance		20.00
Net pay		$ 897.80

*FICA tax: $1,041.12 × 0.07 = $72.88

N. Schmitz

Gross pay		$867.24
Deductions		
Federal income tax	$60.96	
FICA tax*	60.71	
Union dues	5.50	
Hospitalization ins.	3.20	
Life insurance	4.20	
Total deductions		134.57
		$732.67
Uniform allowance		20.00
Net pay		$752.67

-----

*FICA tax: $867.24 \times 0.07 = \$60.71$

5.50 At Pond Computer Systems, the following deductions are made from the employees' pay, in addition to the federal income tax withheld:

Mandatory
- (a) FICA tax   7% of gross
- (b) State tax   5.50% of gross
- (c) Union dues   2.00% of gross
- (d) Hospitalization ins. 1.50% of gross
- (e) Pension   3.00% of gross

Optional
- (f) Life insurance   2.25% of gross
- (g) Charitable organ.   5.00% of gross
- (h) Savings   7.00% of gross
- (i) U.S. savings bonds $25.00 per paycheck
- (j) Loan payment   8.00% of gross (if loan outstanding)

Given the gross pay, federal income tax withheld, year-to-date gross pay, and optional deductions, find the net pay to the nearest cent for the following employees:

Name	Gross Pay	Federal Income Tax Withheld	Year-to-Date Gross Pay	Optional Deductions
G. Abplanalp	$687.57	$52.99	$38,378.50	f, i, j
M. Cassidy	577.66	40.55	28,883.00	f, g, h
S. Catania	666.66	47.88	38,333.00	g, h, i
J. Doyle	489.76	35.92	24,488.00	f, g, i, j
D. Mabey	599.35	43.76	29,967.50	h, i

SOLUTION

G. Abplanalp

Gross pay		$687.57
Deductions		
Federal income tax	$52.99	
FICA tax	0.00	
State tax	37.82	
Union dues	13.75	
Hospitalization ins.	10.31	
Pension	20.63	
Life insurance	15.47	
U.S. savings bonds	25.00	
Loan	55.01	
Total deductions		230.98
Net pay		$456.59

M. Cassidy

Gross pay		$577.66
Deductions		
Federal income tax	$40.55	
FICA tax	40.44	
State tax	31.77	
Union dues	11.55	
Hospitalization ins.	8.66	
Pension	17.33	
Life insurance	13.00	
Charitable organization	28.88	
Savings	40.44	
Total deductions		232.62
Net pay		$345.04

S. Catania

Gross pay		$666.66
Deductions		
Federal income tax	$47.88	
FICA tax	0.00	
State tax	36.67	
Union dues	13.33	
Hospitalization ins.	10.00	
Pension	20.00	
Charitable organization	33.33	
Savings	46.67	
U.S. savings bonds	25.00	
Total deductions		232.88
Net pay		$433.78

J. Doyle

Gross pay		$489.76
Deductions		
Federal income tax	$35.92	
FICA tax	34.28	
State tax	26.94	
Union dues	9.80	
Hospitalization ins.	7.35	
Pension	14.69	
Life insurance	11.02	
Charitable organization	24.49	
U.S. savings bonds	25.00	
Loans	39.18	
Total deductions		228.57
Net pay		$261.09

D. Mabey

Gross pay		$599.35
Deductions		
Federal income tax	$43.76	
FICA tax	41.95	
State tax	32.96	
Union dues	11.99	
Hospitalization ins.	8.99	
Pension	17.98	
Savings	41.95	
U.S. savings bonds	25.00	
Total deductions		224.58
Net pay		$374.77

Note that for all deductions except (i), the calculation is:

$$\text{Gross pay} \times \text{deduction \%}$$

Where the year-to-date gross pay exceeds $37,800, no further FICA tax is withheld.

Supplementary Problems

5.51 Sarah Litt worked $32\frac{1}{4}$ hours last week at an hourly rate of $5.20. Find her gross pay.

5.52 Find, to the nearest cent, the gross pay of an employee who worked $22\frac{3}{4}$ hours at an hourly rate of $3.35.

5.53 Richard Hammer's time card shows the following hours worked:

Mon.	Tues.	Wed.	Thurs.	Fri.
$7\frac{1}{2}$	$8\frac{3}{4}$	$9\frac{3}{4}$	6	8

His hourly rate is $5.75 plus time-and-a-half for any hours worked over 40 per week. Determine (a) his total hours worked and (b) gross pay.

5.54 Determine the total hours worked and the gross pay (to the nearest cent) for the following employees of Tyson Automotive:

	Name	Mon.	Tues.	Wed.	Thurs.	Fri.	Hourly Rate
(a)	D. Earle	$6\frac{1}{2}$	8	$7\frac{1}{4}$	5	8	$4.95
(b)	N. McHugh	8	$6\frac{1}{4}$	8	$7\frac{3}{4}$	6	$3.50

5.55 Patricia Gray received $140.25 gross pay for 33 hours worked. What is her hourly rate?

5.56 An employee received $221 gross pay and worked 34 hours. What is the employee's hourly rate?

5.57 Given the gross pay and the hours worked, find the hourly rate for the following:

	Gross Pay	Hours Worked
(a)	$115.00	$28\frac{3}{4}$
(b)	$210.00	$37\frac{1}{2}$
(c)	$270.80	40
(d)	$130.90	34

5.58 Determine the total hours worked by George Townsend if his hourly rate is $5.25 and his gross pay is $168.

5.59 Janis Klein works as a carpenter for Johnston Construction Company. Her gross pay for last week was $162.40 and her hourly rate is $5.60. Calculate her total hours worked.

5.60 Given the following information, determine the hours worked.

	Gross Pay	Hourly Rate
(a)	$131.00	$5.24
(b)	$140.40	$3.90
(c)	$190.00	$4.75
(d)	$144.10	$6.55

5.61 An employee worked the following hours during the week:

Mon.	Tues.	Wed.	Thurs.	Fri.
10	6	7	11	8

Calculate his gross pay at an hourly rate of $4.60 plus time-and-a-half for any hours over 8 per day.

5.62 On Tuesday and Thursday Margaret Darder worked $9\frac{1}{2}$ hours each day. On Monday, Wednesday, and Friday, she worked 7 hours each day. Her hourly rate is $4.50 plus time-and-a-half for any hours in excess of 8 per day. What is her gross pay?

5.63 Find the gross pay for John Devore if he earns $3.40 per hour, time-and-a-half for any hours over 8 per day, and double time for working on Sundays. His time card for the week ending September 24 is as follows:

Mon.	Tues.	Wed.	Thurs.	Fri.	Sat.	Sun.
0	10	4	$7\frac{1}{2}$	$6\frac{3}{4}$	$9\frac{1}{2}$	5

5.64 The following employees of B&B Concrete, Inc. each receive an hourly rate of $6.20, plus time-and-a-half for hours in excess of 8 per day, and double time for Sundays and holidays. (New Year's Day is designated as a holiday.) Calculate each employee's gross pay.

	Name	1/1 Mon.	1/2 Tues.	1/3 Wed.	1/4 Thurs.	1/5 Fri.	1/6 Sat.	1/7 Sun.
(a)	L. Smith	6	9	0	$7\frac{1}{4}$	0	$7\frac{3}{4}$	5
(b)	K. Young	7	$7\frac{1}{2}$	$8\frac{1}{2}$	0	$9\frac{1}{2}$	0	6

5.65 Calculate, to the nearest cent, the gross pay for Rita Hansen. Her time card for the week ending June 27 shows $51\frac{1}{4}$ hours worked. Her rate of pay is $4.30 per hour plus time-and-a-half for any hours over 40 per week.

5.66 An employee worked the following hours:

Mon.	Tues.	Wed.	Thurs.	Fri.	Sat.	Sun.
$5\frac{1}{2}$	$9\frac{3}{4}$	7	0	$8\frac{1}{4}$	10	3

Find his gross pay, to the nearest cent, if he is paid $5.65 per hour plus time-and-a-half for hours in excess of 40 per week and any hours worked on Sunday.

5.67 Given the hours worked and hourly rate of pay, find the overtime rate (at time-and-a-half) and gross pay to the nearest cent for the following. Overtime is paid for hours worked in excess of 40 per week.

	Hours Worked	Hourly Rate
(a)	$48\frac{1}{2}$	$4.63
(b)	$45\frac{3}{4}$	$6.35
(c)	$54\frac{1}{4}$	$5.28

5.68 For the following employees of Brog Sewing Machine Company, calculate

(a) Regular hours

(b) Regular pay

(c) Overtime hours (hours in excess of 40 per week)

(d) Overtime rate (time-and-a-half)

(e) Overtime pay

(f) Gross pay

Name	Mon.	Tues.	Wed.	Thurs.	Fri.	Sat.	Sun.	Hourly Rate
B. Halper	$7\frac{1}{2}$	8	$9\frac{3}{4}$	$6\frac{1}{4}$	8	0	$2\frac{1}{2}$	$6.50
T. Shaver	$3\frac{1}{2}$	$5\frac{1}{4}$	0	8	$4\frac{3}{4}$	8	$6\frac{3}{4}$	$5.80

5.69   V. Friedman is paid $35,600 annually. Her pay period is biweekly. What are her gross earnings per pay period to the nearest cent?

5.70   An employee receives $17,900 per year and is paid monthly. Determine the gross earnings per pay period to the nearest cent.

5.71   Given the following, find the annual salary for (a), the pay period for (b), and the gross earnings per pay period for (c).

	Annual Salary	Pay Period	Gross Earnings/Pay Period
(a)	?	Weekly	$279.88
(b)	$17,573.14	?	$675.89
(c)	$21,000.00	Monthly	?

5.72   Harry Lober receives a $7\frac{1}{2}$% commission on all his real estate sales. Half the commission goes to his broker. Of his commission on $133,300 in sales how much does Harry get to keep?

5.73   During a month's time an automobile salesperson receives 6% commission on the first $5,000 in sales, 7% commission on the next $5,000 in sales, and 8% commission on anything over $10,000. What is her commission on $36,000 in sales?

5.74   Victor Link receives a biweekly salary of $500 plus a $5\frac{1}{2}$% commission on his total sales for the month. What are his gross monthly earnings, if his total sales for the month were $3,485?

5.75   Elise Thompson is paid a 5% commission on the first $800 in paint sales, 6% on the next $800, and 7% on anything over $1,600 in sales. She also receives a $150 per week draw. To the nearest cent, find the difference she receives at the end of the week between the draw and the commission. Her net sales for the week totaled $3,600.

5.76   Assuming the federal income tax withheld from C. Thomas's gross pay is $26.94 and the FICA tax is 7%, what is his net pay to the nearest cent, if his gross earnings for the week ending January 5 are $345.70?

5.77   At Vallone Computer Company the employees' contribution to the pension plan is $2\frac{1}{2}$% of their gross pay. If B. Kinney's gross pay is $467.36, federal income tax withheld is $38.62, and FICA tax is 7%, what is her net pay?

5.78   Find the net pay for T. Fagan if his gross pay is $298.76 per week and his deductions are $23.69 federal income tax per week, $20.86 FICA tax per week, and $10 life insurance per month.

5.79   An employee's year-to-date gross pay is $38,670. Her current week's earnings amount to $660.20, her federal income tax withheld is $47.81, and her FICA tax is 7%. What is her net pay?

5.80   Bush Inc. pays its employees biweekly. In addition to the federal income tax withheld, each employee's deductions are as follows:

FICA tax	7%
Union dues	$8.30
Hospitalization ins.	$6.50
Life insurance	$4.50

Each employee also receives a $30 uniform allowance. Given gross pay, federal income tax withheld, and year-to-date gross pay, find the net pay to the nearest cent for the following employees:

	Name	Gross Pay	Federal Income Tax Withheld	Year-to-Date Gross Pay
(a)	J. Dalby	$1,222.24	$ 90.72	$30,556.00
(b)	B. Hahn	1,895.33	137.60	47,383.25

Answers to Supplementary Problems

5.51 $167.70

5.52 $76.21

5.53   (a) 40, (b) $230

5.54   (a) 34.75 h, $172.01; (b) 36 h, $126

5.55 $4.25/h

5.56 $6.50/h

5.57   (a) $4.00/h, (b) $5.60/h, (c) $6.77/h, (d) $3.85/h

5.58   32

5.59   29

5.60   (a) 25, (b) 36, (c) 40, (d) 22

5.61 $204.70

5.62 $186.75

5.63 $168.30

5.64   (a) $288.30, (b) $325.50

5.65 $244.56

5.66 $255.67

5.67   (a) $6.945/h, $244.23; (b) $9.525/h, $308.77; (c) $7.92/h, $324.06

5.68   B. Halper: (*a*) 40, (*b*) $260, (*c*) 2, (*d*) $9.75/h, (*e*) $19.50, (*f*) $279.50
           T. Shaver: (*a*) 36.25, (*b*) $210.25, (*c*) 0, (*d*) $8,70/h, (*e*) $0, (*f*) $210.25

5.69 $1,369.23

5.70 $1,491.67

5.71   (*a*) $14,553.76, (*b*) 26 pay periods/per year or biweekly, (*c*) $1,750

5.72 $4,998.75

5.73 $2,730

5.74 $1,191.68

5.75 $78

5.76 $294.56

5.77 $384.34

5.78 $251.71

5.79 $612.39

5.80   (*a*) $1,056.66, (*b*) $1,768.43

Chapter 6

Depreciation

6.1 DEPRECIATION AND SALVAGE VALUE

Although the useful life of equipment (a fixed asset) may be long, it is nonetheless limited. Eventually the equipment will lose all productive worth and will possess only salvage value (scrap value). Accounting demands a period-by-period matching of costs against income. Hence, the cost of a fixed asset (over and above its salvage value) is distributed over the asset's estimated lifetime. This spreading of the cost over the periods which receive benefits is known as *depreciation*.

The depreciable amount of a fixed asset—that is, cost minus salvage value—may be written off in different ways. For example, the amount may be spread evenly over the years affected, as in the straight-line method. The units of production method bases depreciation for each period on the amount of output. Two accelerated methods, the double declining balance method and the sum-of-the-years'-digits method, provide for greater amounts of depreciation in the earlier years.

6.2 STRAIGHT-LINE METHOD

This is the simplest and most widely used depreciation method. Under this method an equal portion of the cost (above salvage value) of the asset is allocated to each period of use. The periodic depreciation charge is expressed as

$$\frac{\text{Cost} - \text{salvage value}}{\text{Estimated life}} = \text{depreciation}$$

EXAMPLE 1

If the cost of a machine is $17,000, its salvage value $2,000, and its estimated useful life 5 yr, the straight-line depreciation is

$$\frac{\$17,000 - \$2,000}{5 \text{ yr}} = \$3,000/\text{yr}$$

The date on which a piece of equipment is bought has an effect on the amount of depreciation taken for the first year. Similarly, if the equipment is later sold, the sale date determines the amount of depreciation taken in the year of sale.

EXAMPLE 2

Suppose the machine in Example 1 was bought on March 26. Since this date is closer to April 1 than March 1, the depreciation for the first year (ending December 31) is based on April 1 acquisition.

From the yearly depreciation of $3,000 (Example 1), we determine the monthly depreciation as follows:

$$\$3,000/\text{yr} \div 12 \text{ mo/yr} = \$250/\text{mo depreciation}$$

Since April 1 through December 31 encompasses 9 months, we multiply the monthly depreciation by 9 to find the depreciation applicable to the first year.

$$\$250/\text{mo} \times 9 \text{ mo} = \$2,250 \text{ depreciation for 1st year}$$

For the second through the fifth years, the full $3,000 per year depreciation is taken, unless the machine is sold. If the machine is sold *before* the end of a given year, the amount of depreciation applied in that year is calculated on the fraction of the year during which the machine was used, as above.

At any point in time, the *book value* is the cost of the equipment less any depreciation to date.

EXAMPLE 3

If bought on March 26 (Example 2), the end of the first year (December 31) book value of the machine in Example 1 is

$$\text{Book value} = \text{cost} - \text{depreciation}$$
$$= \$17,000 - \$2,250 = \$14,750$$

At the end of the fifth year, the book value of this machine is its salvage value, $2,000.

SOLVED PROBLEMS

6.1 On January 1 Greenwood Industries purchased machinery for $5,000. It is estimated that the machinery will have a useful life of 5 years and a salvage value of $500. Using the straight-line method, determine the depreciation per year.

SOLUTION

$$\frac{\text{Cost} - \text{salvage}}{\text{Estimated life}} = \text{depreciation}$$
$$\frac{\$5,000 - \$500}{5 \text{ yr}} =$$
$$\frac{\$4,500}{5 \text{ yr}} =$$
$$\$900/\text{yr} =$$

6.2 Find the amount of depreciation per year if a fixed asset bought on January 1 for $15,000 has an estimated life of 10 years and a salvage value of $3,000.

SOLUTION

$$\frac{\text{Cost} - \text{salvage}}{\text{Estimated life}} = \text{depreciation}$$
$$\frac{\$15,000 - \$3,000}{10 \text{ yr}} =$$
$$\frac{\$12,000}{10 \text{ yr}} =$$
$$\$1,200/\text{yr} =$$

6.3 If Miller Farms purchased equipment on January 5 for $35,000, calculate the depreciation per year using the straight-line method. The salvage value is $7,000, and the estimated useful life is 10 years.

SOLUTION

$$\frac{\text{Cost} - \text{salvage}}{\text{Estimated life}} = \text{depreciation}$$
$$\frac{\$35,000 - \$7,000}{10 \text{ yr}} =$$
$$\frac{\$28,000}{10 \text{ yr}} =$$
$$\$2,800/\text{yr} =$$

6.4 Harold Enterprises bought office furniture on May 12. The purchase price was $4,000 and the estimated useful life is 5 years. The salvage value is $550. Find the depreciation as of December 31 (same year).

SOLUTION

$$\frac{\text{Cost} - \text{salvage}}{\text{Estimated life}} = \text{depreciation}$$

$$\frac{\$4,000 - \$550}{5 \text{ yr}} =$$

$$\frac{\$3,450}{5 \text{ yr}} =$$

$$\$690/\text{yr} =$$

First-year depreciation:

$$\$690/\text{yr} \div 12 \text{ mo/yr} = \$57.50/\text{mo depreciation}$$
$$\$57.50 \times 8 \text{ mo}^* = \$460 \text{ depreciation as of Dec. 31}$$

_____

*May through December = 8 mo

6.5   A delivery truck was purchased by Wade Florists on September 12. The initial cost of the truck was $9,000, but some new parts were needed, totaling $800. Under the straight-line method, what is the depreciation to the nearest cent at the end of the year if the estimated useful life of the truck is 5 years and the salvage value is $1,200?

SOLUTION

$$\frac{\text{Cost} - \text{salvage}}{\text{Estimated life}} = \text{depreciation}$$

$$\frac{\$9,800 - \$1,200}{5 \text{ yr}} =$$

$$\frac{\$8,600}{5 \text{ yr}} =$$

$$\$1,720/\text{yr} =$$

First-year depreciation:

$$\$1,720 \div 12 \text{ mo} = \$143.33/\text{mo}$$
$$\$143.33 \times 4 \text{ mo} = \$573.32 \text{ depreciation at end of yr}$$

6.6   What is the amount of depreciation at the end of the second year, if a piece of equipment was purchased on July 24 for $1,300, its estimated useful life is 8 years and trade-in value is $100?

SOLUTION

$$\frac{\text{Cost} - \text{salvage}}{\text{Estimated life}} = \text{depreciation}$$

$$\frac{\$1,300 - \$100}{8 \text{ yr}} =$$

$$\frac{\$1,200}{8 \text{ yr}} =$$

$$\$150/\text{yr} =$$

End of second-year depreciation:

$$\$150 \div 12 \text{ mo} = \$12.50/\text{mo}$$
$$\$12.50 \times 5 \text{ mo}^* = \$62.50 \text{ depreciation for 1st yr}$$
$$\$62.50 + \$150 = \$212.50 \text{ depreciation at end of 2d yr}$$

_____

*The month of July is not included since July 24 is closer to August 1 than to July 1.

6.7   A dishwasher was purchased by the Check-Inn Restaurant on October 1. The purchase price was $1,200 and the installation cost was $300. The estimated useful life of the dishwasher is 6 years and its salvage value is $300. What is the amount of depreciation to the nearest cent at the end of the fourth year?

SOLUTION

$$\frac{\text{Cost} - \text{salvage}}{\text{Estimated life}} = \text{depreciation}$$

$$\frac{\$1,500 - \$300}{6 \text{ yr}} =$$

$$\frac{\$1,200}{6 \text{ yr}} =$$

$$\$200/\text{yr} =$$

End of fourth-year depreciation:

$$\$200 \div 12 \text{ mo} = \$16.67/\text{mo}$$

$$\$16.67 \times 3 \text{ mo} = \$50.01 \text{ depreciation for 1st yr}$$

$$\$200 \times 3 \text{ yr}^* = \$600 \text{ depreciation for years 2, 3, and 4}$$

$$\$600 + \$50.01 = \$650.01 \text{ depreciation at end of 4th yr}$$

————————

*For the second, third, and fourth years the full depreciation of $200 per year is applied.

6.8   If office furniture purchased on January 2 for $8,100 has an estimated useful life of 6 years and a trade-in value of $750, what is the book value at the end of the fifth year?

SOLUTION

$$\frac{\text{Cost} - \text{salvage}}{\text{Estimated life}} = \text{depreciation}$$

$$\frac{\$8,100 - \$750}{6 \text{ yr}} =$$

$$\$7,350/6 \text{ yr} =$$

$$\$1,225/\text{yr} =$$

End of fifth-year depreciation:

$$\$1,225 \times 5 \text{ yr} = \$6,125 \text{ depreciation for 5 yr}$$

Book value at end of fifth year:

$$\text{Cost} - \text{depreciation} = \text{book value}$$

$$\$8,100 - \$6,125 =$$

$$\$1,975 =$$

6.9   Lorino Plumbing and Heating purchased tools on February 18 for $800. The salvage value of the tools is $200, and the estimated life is 10 years. What is the book value at the end of the fourth year?

SOLUTION

$$\frac{\text{Cost} - \text{salvage}}{\text{Estimated life}} = \text{depreciation}$$

$$\$800 - \$200 =$$

$$\frac{\$600}{10 \text{ yr}} =$$

$$\$60/\text{yr} =$$

End of fourth-year depreciation:

$$\$60 \div 12 \text{ mo} = \$5/\text{mo}$$

$$\$5 \times 10 \text{ mo} = \$50 \text{ depreciation for 1st year}$$

$$\$60 \times 3 \text{ yr} = \$180 \text{ depreciation for years 2, 3, and 4}$$

$$\$180 + \$50 = \$230 \text{ depreciation at end of 4th yr}$$

Book value at end of fourth year:

$$Cost - depreciation = book\ value$$
$$\$800 - \$230 =$$
$$\$570 =$$

6.10 Determine the depreciation rate per year for an estimated useful life of (a) 10 yr, (b) 50 yr, (c) 8 yr, (d) 5 yr, (e) 16 yr, and (f) 20 yr.

SOLUTION

$$\frac{100\%}{Estimated\ life} = depreciation\ rate/yr$$

(a) $100\% \div 10\ yr = 10\%$ (d) $100\% \div 5\ yr = 20\%$

(b) $100\% \div 50\ yr = 2\%$ (e) $100\% \div 16\ yr = 6\frac{1}{4}\%$

(c) $100\% \div 8\ yr = 12\frac{1}{2}\%$ (f) $100\% \div 20\ yr = 5\%$

6.11 Determine the (a) depreciation rate, (b) yearly depreciation, and (c) book value after 10 years of a building that cost \$100,000 on January 7. After its estimated useful life of 25 yr, the salvage value is \$20,000.

SOLUTION

$$\frac{100\%}{Estimated\ life} = depreciation\ rate/yr$$
$$100\% \div 25\ yr =$$
$$4\% =$$

(b) We can rewrite formula 5.1 in terms of depreciation rate, as follows:

$$(Cost - salvage) \times depreciation\ rate/yr = depreciation$$
$$(\$100,000 - \$20,000) \times 0.04 =$$
$$\$80,000 \times 0.04 =$$
$$\$3,200/yr =$$

(c) Book value after 10 yr:

$$\$3,200 \times 10\ yr = \$32,000\ depreciation\ for\ 10\ yr$$
$$Cost - depreciation = book\ value$$
$$\$100,000 - \$32,000 = \$68,000$$

6.12 Find the annual depreciation for the following:

Purchase Cost	Additional Cost Involved	Estimated Life (Years)	Salvage Value
\$120,000	\$ 0	30	\$30,000
50,000	0	20	10,000
7,000	200	6	1,200
3,000	0	10	0
150,000	0	50	25,000
10,000	500	8	3,500
33,000	900	20	1,300
100,000	0	50	20,000
650	75	3	125
5,400	600	5	1,500

SOLUTION

Cost* − Salvage Value	÷	Estimated Life (Years)	=	Annual Depreciation
($120,000 − $30,000)	÷	30	=	$3,000
($50,000 − $10,000)	÷	20	=	$2,000
($7,200 − $1,200)	÷	6	=	$1,000
($3,000 − $0)	÷	10	=	$300
($150,000 − $25,000)	÷	50	=	$2,500
($10,500 − $3,500)	÷	8	=	$875
($33,900 − $1,300)	÷	20	=	$1,630
($100,000 − $20,000)	÷	50	=	$1,600
($725 − $125)	÷	3	=	$200
($6,000 − $1,500)	÷	5	=	$900

*Purchase cost + additional cost involved

6.13 Prepare a depreciation schedule for a piece of machinery purchased January 10 for $7,700. Transportation costs amounted to $300. The estimated useful life is 10 years, and the machine has a salvage value of $800. The depreciation schedule spans the estimated life of the machine and includes the depreciation rate for each year, the dollar amount of that year's depreciation, the book value, and each year's accumulated depreciation.

SOLUTION

$$\text{Cost} = \text{purchase cost} + \text{any additional cost involved}$$
$$= \$7,700 + \$300 = \$800$$

$$\frac{100\%}{\text{Estimated life}} = \text{depreciation rate/yr}$$

$$\frac{100\%}{10 \text{ yr}} =$$

$$10\% =$$

$$(\text{Cost} - \text{salvage}) \times \text{depreciation rate/yr} = \text{annual depreciation}$$
$$(\$8,000 - \$800) \times 0.10 =$$
$$\$7,200 \times 0.10 =$$
$$\$720 =$$

Year	Depreciation Rate (%)	Yearly Depreciation	Book Value	Accumulated Depreciation
0			$8,000	
1	10	$720	7,280	$ 720
2	10	720	6,560	1,440
3	10	720	5,840	2,160
4	10	720	5,120	2,880
5	10	720	4,400	3,600
6	10	720	3,680	4,320
7	10	720	2,960	5,040
8	10	720	2,240	5,760
9	10	720	1,520	6,480
10	10	720	800	7,200

6.14 Marshall Painters bought 15 paint sprayers at a cost of $80 each. The delivery charge for all 15 sprayers was $80, and delivery was on August 16. Each sprayer has an estimated useful life of 8 years and no salvage value. What is the depreciation on December 31 of the sixth year?

SOLUTION

Cost:

$$15 \text{ sprayers} \times \$80 \text{ each} = \$1,200$$
$$\$1,200 + \$80 \text{ (delivery charge)} = \$1,280$$

$$\frac{\text{Cost} - \text{salvage}}{\text{Estimated life}} = \text{depreciation}$$

$$\frac{\$1,280}{8 \text{ yr}} =$$

$$\$160/\text{yr} =$$

Depreciation at end of sixth year:

$$\$160/\text{yr} \div 12 \text{ mo/yr} = \$13.33/\text{mo}$$

$$\$13.33 \times 4 \text{ mo} = \$53.32 \text{ depreciation for 1st yr}$$

$$\$160 \times 5 \text{ yr} = \$800 \text{ depreciation for years 2–6}$$

$$\$800 + \$53.32 = \$853.32 \text{ depreciation Dec. 31 of 6th yr}$$

6.15 What is the book value at the end of the third year for each of the following:

(*a*) Cost $10,000   (*d*) Cost $900
       Salvage value $2,000   Salvage value $0
       Estimated life   5 yr   Estimated life   3 yr

(*b*) Cost $8,500   (*e*) Cost $5,000
       Salvage value $1,000   Salvage value $500
       Estimated life   6 yr   Estimated life   9 yr

(*c*) Cost $26,000   (*f*) Cost $750
       Salvage value $3,000   Salvage value $50
       Estimated life   10 yr   Estimated life   4 yr

SOLUTION

	Cost − Salvage Value	÷	Estimated Life (Years)	×	No. Years	=	Depreciation for 3 Years	Cost −	Depreciation for 3 Years	=	Book Value
(*a*)	($10,000 − $2,000)	÷	5	×	3	=	$4,800	$10,000 −	$4,800	=	$5,200
(*b*)	($8,500 − $1,000)	÷	6	×	3	=	$3,750	$8,500 −	$3,750	=	$4,750
(*c*)	($26,000 − $3,000)	÷	10	×	3	=	$6,900	$26,000 −	$6,900	=	$19,100
(*d*)	($900 − $0)	÷	3	×	3	=	$900	$900 −	$900	=	$0
(*e*)	($5,000 − $500)	÷	9	×	3	=	$1,500	$5,000 −	$1,500	=	$3,500
(*f*)	($750 − $50)	÷	4	×	3	=	$525	$750 −	$525	=	$225

6.3 UNITS OF PRODUCTION

Where the use of equipment varies substantially from year to year, the units of production method is appropriate for determining the depreciation. For example, in some years logging operations may be carried on for 200 days, in other years for 230 days, in still other years for only 160 days, depending on weather conditions. Under this method, depreciation is computed for the appropriate unit of output or production (such as hours, miles, or pounds) by the following formula:

$$\frac{\text{Cost} - \text{salvage}}{\text{Estimated units of production during lifetime}} = \text{unit depreciation}$$

The total number of units used in a year is then multiplied by the unit depreciation to arrive at the depreciation amount for that year. We can express this as

$$\text{Unit depreciation} \times \text{usage} = \text{depreciation}$$

or $$\frac{\text{Cost} - \text{salvage}}{\text{Estimated life (in units)}} \times \text{usage} = \text{depreciation}$$

This method has the advantage of relating depreciation cost directly to income.

EXAMPLE 4

Cost of a machine, $17,000; salvage, $2,000; estimated life, 8,000 hours.

$$\frac{\$17,000 - \$2,000}{8,000\ \text{h}} = \$1.875\ \text{depreciation/h}$$

Over a 5-year lifetime, the machine was in operation for 1,800, 1,200, 2,000, 1,400, and 1,600 hours for years 1 to 5, respectively. The computation of the depreciation for those years is

Year 1	1,800 h × $1.875/h =	$ 3,375
Year 2	1,200 h × $1.875/h =	2,250
Year 3	2,000 h × $1.875/h =	3,750
Year 4	1,400 h × $1.875/h =	2,625
Year 5	1,600 h × $1.875/h =	3,000
	Total depreciation (8,000 h) =	$15,000

SOLVED PROBLEMS

6.16   An item of machinery, bought on January 5 for $15,000, has an estimated useful life of 30,000 hours and a salvage value of $3,000. In its first year of operation the machine was used for 15,000 hours. What is the depreciation when calculated by the units of production method?

SOLUTION

$$\frac{\text{Cost} - \text{salvage}}{\text{Estimated life}} \times \text{usage} = \text{depreciation}$$

$$\frac{\$15,000 - \$3,000}{30,000\ \text{h}} \times 15,000\ \text{h} =$$

$$\frac{\$12,000}{30,000\ \text{h}} \times 15,000\ \text{h} =$$

$$\$0.40/\text{h} \times 15,000\ \text{h} =$$

$$\$6,000 =$$

6.17   Marion Enterprises bought a photocopier for $5,000. If it was used 3,000 hours the first year, 4,500 hours the second year, and 3,900 hours the third year, find the depreciation for the 3 years, using the units of production method. The trade-in value of the copier is $1,000, and its useful life is estimated to be 40,000 hours.

SOLUTION

$$\frac{\text{Cost} - \text{salvage}}{\text{Estimated life}} = \text{unit depreciation}$$

$$\frac{\$5,000 - \$1,000}{40,000} =$$

$$\frac{\$4,000}{40,000 \text{ h}} =$$

$$\$0.10/\text{h} =$$

Unit depreciation × usage = depreciation

Year 1 $0.10/h × 3,000 h = $ 300
Year 2 $0.10/h × 4,500 h = $ 450
Year 3 $0.10/h × 3,900 h = $ 390
          Depreciation for 3 yr = $1,140

6.18   Steph Pest Control bought a truck costing $11,000 that has an estimated useful life of 100,000 miles and a trade-in value of $2,000. Determine the depreciation if the truck was driven 7,000 miles the first year.

SOLUTION

$$\frac{\text{Cost} - \text{salvage}}{\text{Estimated life}} \times \text{usage} = \text{depreciation}$$

$$\frac{\$11,000 - \$2,000}{100,000 \text{ m}} \times 7,000 \text{ m} =$$

$$\frac{\$9,000}{100,000 \text{ m}} \times 7,000 \text{ m} =$$

$$\$0.09 \text{ m} \times 7,000 \text{ m} =$$

$$\$630 =$$

6.19   A used floor polisher was purchased by Liberty Floor Maintenance Company on March 25 for $750. Some repair work amounting to $75 was needed to put the machine into operating condition. Use the units of production method to determine the depreciation after 1,000 hours of use. The salvage value of the machine is $25, and its estimated useful life is 5,000 hours.

SOLUTION

$$\$750 + \$75 = \$825 \text{ cost}$$

$$\frac{\text{Cost} - \text{salvage}}{\text{Estimated life}} \times \text{usage} = \text{depreciation}$$

$$\frac{\$825 - \$25}{5,000 \text{ h}} \times 1,000 \text{ h} =$$

$$\frac{\$800}{5,000 \text{ h}} \times 1,000 \text{ h} =$$

$$\$0.16/\text{h} \times 1,000 \text{ h} =$$

$$\$160 =$$

6.20   Using the units of production method, find the depreciation of a machine that produced 3,600 units in its first year of operation. The cost of the machine was $17,000. It has a salvage value of $3,000 and an estimated lifetime output of 50,000 units.

SOLUTION

$$\frac{\text{Cost} - \text{salvage}}{\text{Estimated life}} \times \text{usage} = \text{depreciation}$$

$$\frac{\$17,000 - \$3,000}{50,000 \text{ units}} \times 3,600 \text{ units} =$$

$$\frac{\$14,000}{50,000 \text{ units}} \times 3,600 \text{ units} =$$

$$\$0.28/\text{unit} \times 3,600 \text{ units} =$$

$$\$1,008 =$$

6.21 If Miller & Co. bought a used truck for their lumber business for $6,000 and it cost them $1,500 in repairs before they were able to use it, what is the depreciation according to the units of production method at the end of the second year in operation if the truck has a trade-in value of $1,500 and an estimated useful life of an additional 85,000 miles? In the first year, they drove the truck 12,000 miles and in the second year, 14,000 miles.

SOLUTION

$$\$6,000 + \$1,500 = \$7,500 \text{ cost}$$

$$\frac{\text{Cost} - \text{salvage}}{\text{Estimated life}} = \text{unit depreciation}$$

$$\frac{\$7,500 - \$1,500}{85,000 \text{ mi}} =$$

$$\frac{\$6,000}{85,000 \text{ mi}} =$$

$$\$0.07/\text{mi} =$$

Unit depreciation $\times$ usage = depreciation

Year 1	$0.07/mi $\times$ 12,000 mi =	$ 840
Year 2	$0.07/mi $\times$ 14,000 mi =	$ 980
	Depreciation for 2 yr =	$1,820

6.22 Use the units of production method to find the depreciation for the following:

Cost	Salvage Value	Estimated Life	Usage
$25,000	$ 2,500	75,000 h	16,450 h
70,000	5,000	100,000 units	75,500 units
99,000	10,000	85,000 h	37,750 h
8,000	1,400	75,000 mi	55,600 mi
13,500	2,300	100,000 mi	66,000 mi

SOLUTION

$\left[\left(\text{Cost} - \dfrac{\text{Salvage}}{\text{Value}}\right) \div \dfrac{\text{Estimated}}{\text{Life}}\right]$		$\times$	Usage	=	Depreciation
[($25,000 - $2,500)	$\div$ 75,000 h]	$\times$	16,450 h	=	$4,935.00
[($70,000 - $5,000)	$\div$ 100,000 units]	$\times$	75,500 units	=	$49,075.00
[($99,000 - $10,000)	$\div$ 85,000 h]	$\times$	37,750 h	=	$39,526.47
[($8,000 - $1,400)	$\div$ 75,000 mi]	$\times$	55,600 mi	=	$4,892.80
[($13,500 - $2,300)	$\div$ 100,000 mi]	$\times$	66,000 mi	=	$7,392.00

6.23 Using the units of production method, find the depreciation of a tractor bought by Misner Farms on April 6 for $23,000. Mr. Misner paid $750 in transportation costs to have the tractor delivered. The tractor has an estimated useful life of 70,000 hours, and its salvage value is $2,750. Misner used the tractor 4,000 hours the first year and 3,950 hours the second year.

SOLUTION

$$\$23,000 + \$750 = \$23,750 \text{ cost}$$

$$\frac{\text{Cost} - \text{salvage}}{\text{Estimated life}} = \text{unit depreciation}$$

$$\frac{\$23,750 - \$2,750}{70,000 \text{ h}} =$$

$$\frac{\$21,000}{70,000 \text{ h}} =$$

$$\$0.30/\text{h} =$$

Unit depreciation × usage = depreciation

Year 1 $0.30/h × 4,000 h = $1,200

Year 2 $0.30/h × 3,950 h = $1,185

Depreciation for 2 yr = $2,385

6.24 Katz Home Builders started business on October 18. One month prior they purchased a truck for $5,000 and spent an additional $500 to get the truck in operating condition. They also bought a band saw for $500. The truck has an estimated useful life of 50,000 miles and a trade-in value of $1,500. The band saw has an estimated useful life of 5,000 hours and a trade-in value of $50. What is each item's depreciation at the end of the year if they (a) put 2,085 miles on the truck as of December 31 and (b) used the saw 300 hours?

SOLUTION

(a) Truck

$$\$5,000 + \$500 = \$5,500 \text{ cost}$$

$$\frac{\text{Cost} - \text{salvage}}{\text{Estimated life}} \times \text{usage} = \text{depreciation}$$

$$\frac{\$5,500 - \$1,500}{50,000 \text{ mi}} \times 2,085 \text{ mi} =$$

$$\frac{\$4,000}{50,000 \text{ mi}} \times 2,085 \text{ mi} =$$

$$\$0.08/\text{mi} \times 2,085 \text{ mi} =$$

$$\$166.80 =$$

(b) Band saw

$$\frac{\text{Cost} - \text{salvage}}{\text{Estimated life}} \times \text{usage} = \text{depreciation}$$

$$\frac{\$500 - \$50}{5,000 \text{ h}} \times 300 \text{ h} =$$

$$\frac{\$450}{5,000 \text{ h}} \times 300 \text{ h} =$$

$$\$0.09/\text{h} \times 300 \text{ h} =$$

$$\$27 =$$

6.25 Payne Electronics bought an assembler that would assemble 30 transformers per hour. If during the first year of operation 43,200 transformers were assembled, find the depreciation by using the units of production method. The assembler cost $150,000 and has a salvage value of $5,000. It is expected to assemble 500,000 transformers during its useful life.

SOLUTION

$$\frac{\text{Cost} - \text{salvage}}{\text{Estimated life}} \times \text{usage} = \text{depreciation}$$

$$\frac{\$150,000 - \$5,000}{500,000 \text{ units}} \times 43,200 \text{ units} =$$

$$\frac{\$145,000}{500,000 \text{ units}} \times 43,200 \text{ units} =$$

$$\$0.29/\text{unit} \times 43,200 \text{ units} =$$

$$\$12,528 =$$

6.26 An item of equipment that has a production capacity of 50 units per hour and an estimated life of 200,000 hours was purchased. The costs involved to get the equipment into operation were $257,500 price, $700 transportation charges, $300 insurance while in transit, and $1,500 installation charge. The trade-in value is $10,000. If it produced 125,000 units in 2,500 hours, what is the depreciation according to the units of production method?

SOLUTION

$$\$257,500 + \$700 + \$300 + \$1,500 = \$260,000 \text{ cost}$$

$$\frac{\text{Cost} - \text{salvage}}{\text{Estimated life}} \times \text{usage} = \text{depreciation}$$

$$\frac{\$260,000 - \$10,000}{200,000 \text{ h}} \times 2,500 \text{ h} =$$

$$\frac{\$250,000}{200,000 \text{ h}} \times 2,500 \text{ h} =$$

$$\$1.25 \times 2,500 \text{ h} =$$

$$\$3,125 =$$

6.27 What is the book value of a piece of machinery with an estimated useful life of 750,000 hours and a trade-in value of $6,000, if the machine cost $81,000 and was used for 300,500 hours?

SOLUTION

$$\frac{\text{Cost} - \text{salvage}}{\text{Estimated life}} \times \text{usage} = \text{depreciation}$$

$$\frac{\$81,000 - \$6,000}{750,000 \text{ h}} \times 300,500 \text{ h} =$$

$$\frac{\$75,000}{750,000 \text{ h}} \times 300,500 \text{ h} =$$

$$\$0.10/\text{h} \times 300,500 \text{ h} =$$

$$\$30,050 =$$

$$\text{Cost} - \text{depreciation} = \text{book value}$$

$$\$81,000 - \$30,050 =$$

$$\$50,950 =$$

6.28 Find (a) the depreciation and (b) the book value at the end of the third year for an item of equipment that cost $60,000. Delivery of the equipment cost an additional $500, and its estimated useful life is 125,000 miles. The salvage value is $5,500. The equipment was used 22,000 miles the first year, 25,600 miles the second year, and 19,680 miles the third year.

SOLUTION

(*a*)
$$\$60,000 + \$500 = \$60,500 \text{ cost}$$

$$\frac{\text{Cost} - \text{salvage}}{\text{Estimated life}} = \text{unit depreciation}$$

$$\frac{\$60,500 - \$5,500}{125,000 \text{ mi}} =$$

$$\frac{\$55,000}{125,000 \text{ mi}} =$$

$$\$0.44/\text{mi} =$$

Unit depreciation × usage = depreciation

Year 1	$0.44/mi × 22,000 mi = \$ 9,680.00
Year 2	$0.44/mi × 25,600 mi = 11,264.00
Year 3	$0.44/mi × 19,680 mi = 8,659.20

Depreciation at end of 3 yr = $29,603.20

(*b*)
$$\text{Cost} - \text{depreciation} = \text{book value}$$
$$\$60,500.00 - \$29,603.20 =$$
$$\$30,896.80 =$$

6.29 Using the units of production method, find the depreciation of a used truck which cost $4,400. Additional costs incurred were $125.89 parts, $258.43 repairs, and $215.68 repainting. The original estimated useful life was 100,000 miles, but the truck had 57,500 miles on it when purchased. Its trade-in value is $750, and the truck was driven 15,899 miles the first year.

SOLUTION

$$\$4,400 + \$125.89 + \$258.43 + \$215.68 = \$5,000 \text{ cost}$$

$$\frac{\text{Cost} - \text{salvage}}{\text{Estimated life}} \times \text{usage} = \text{depreciation}$$

$$\frac{\$5,000 - \$750}{100,000 \text{ mi} - 57,500 \text{ mi}} \times 15,899 \text{ mi} =$$

$$\frac{\$4,250}{42,500 \text{ mi}} \times 15,899 \text{ mi} =$$

$$\$0.10 \times 15,899 \text{ mi} =$$

$$\$1,589.90 =$$

6.30 Cook Computer Systems, Inc. purchased a machine that welds components onto printed circuit boards at a rate of 20 per hour. The machine cost $125,000 plus $2,000 in transportation costs and $3,000 in installation costs. Its estimated useful life is the welding of 100,000 components, and its salvage value is $10,000. Using the units of production method, determine the depreciation after 76,550 components have been welded.

SOLUTION

$$\$125,000 + \$2,000 + \$3,000 = \$130,000 \text{ cost}$$

$$\frac{\text{Cost} - \text{salvage}}{\text{Estimated life}} \times \text{usage} = \text{depreciation}$$

$$\frac{\$130,000 - \$10,000}{100,000 \text{ units}} \times 76,550 \text{ units} =$$

$$\frac{\$120,000}{100,000 \text{ units}} \times 76,550 \text{ units} =$$

$$\$1.20/\text{unit} \times 76,550 \text{ units} =$$

$$\$91,860 =$$

6.4 DOUBLE DECLINING BALANCE METHOD

The double declining balance method produces the highest amount of depreciation in the earlier years. *It does not recognize salvage or scrap value.* Instead, the book value of the asset remaining at the end of the depreciation period becomes the salvage or scrap value. Under this method, the straight-line rate is doubled and applied to the declining book balance each year. Many companies prefer the double declining balance method because of the greater "write-off" in the earlier years, a time when the asset contributes most to the business and when the expenditure was actually made. The procedure is to apply a *fixed rate* to the declining book value of the asset each year. As the book value declines, the depreciation becomes smaller.

EXAMPLE 5

A $17,000 asset is to be depreciated over 5 years. The double declining balance rate is thus 40%/yr from

$$\frac{100\%}{\text{Estimated life in years}} \times 2 = \text{depreciation rate}$$

$$\frac{100\%}{5 \text{ yr}} \times 2 = 40\%/\text{yr}$$

The yearly depreciation and book value are shown in the following table.

Year	Book Value at Beginning of Year	Rate (%)	Depreciation for Year	Book Value at End of Year
1	$17,000	40	$6,800	$10,200
2	10,200	40	4,080	6,120
3	6,120	40	2,448	3,672
4	3,672	40	1,468	2,204
5	2,204	40	881	1,323

The $1,322 book value at the end of the fifth year becomes the scrap value. If, however, a scrap value of $2,000 had been determined, the depreciation for the fifth year would be adjusted from $881 to $204 ($2,204 − $2,000).

The date of purchase should also be considered. In the previous example, we assumed that the equipment was purchased at the beginning of the year, which is usually not a common occurrence. Therefore, a change in the computation for the first partial year of service is needed if we determine that the equipment was purchased later in the year.

EXAMPLE 6

If the equipment in Example 5 had been purchased and put to use at the end of the ninth month of the fiscal year, the pro rata portion of the first full year's depreciation would be

$$\frac{3}{12}(40\% \times \$17,000) = \$1,700$$

The method of computation for the remaining years would not be affected (although the *amounts* would change). Thus, the depreciation for the second year would be

$$40\%(\$17,000 - \$1,700) = \$6,120$$

and the book value at the end of the second year would be

$$\$9,180 = [\$17,000 - (\$1,700 + \$6,120)]$$

SOLVED PROBLEMS

6.31 On January 1, Morgan Company purchased office furniture for $1,000. The furniture has an estimated useful life of 10 years, and its salvage value is $100. Using the double declining balance method of depreciation, what is the depreciation at the end of the first year?

SOLUTION

$$\frac{100\%}{\text{Estimated life (yr)}} \times 2 = \text{depreciation rate}$$
$$100\%/10 \text{ yr} \times 2 =$$
$$20\%/\text{yr} =$$

$$\text{Cost} \times \text{depreciation rate} = \text{depreciation}$$
$$\$1,000 \times 0.20/\text{yr} =$$
$$\$200/\text{yr} =$$

Note that the salvage value is not considered when determining depreciation with this method.

6.32 Equipment was bought on January 5 for $25,000. It has an estimated useful life of 40 years and a trade-in value of $5,000. Using the double declining balance method, determine the book value at the end of the third year.

SOLUTION

$$100\%/\text{estimated life (yr)} \times 2 = \text{depreciation rate}$$
$$100\%/40 \text{ yr} \times 2 =$$
$$5\%/\text{yr} =$$

	Cost × depreciation rate = depreciation	Cost − depreciation = book value
Year 1	$25,000.00 × 0.05/yr = $1,250.00	$25,000.00 − $1,250.00 = $23,750.00
Year 2	$23,750.00 × 0.05/yr = $1,187.50	$23,750.00 − $1,187.50 = $22,562.50
Year 3	$22,562.50 × 0.05/yr = $1,128.13	$22,562.50 − $1,128.13 = $21,434.37

Note that in calculating the depreciation for years 2 and 3, we use the preceding year's book value as the cost in each case. We can state this in mathematical terms as follows:

[Cost (from previous yr) − depreciation (from previous yr)] × depreciation rate = depreciation

or more simply,

$$\text{Book value} \times \text{depreciation rate} = \text{depreciation}$$

6.33 Using the double declining balance method of depreciation, determine the book value at the end of the first year on an item that was bought on April 8 for $60,000 and that has a salvage value of $8,000 and an estimated useful life of 50 years.

SOLUTION

$$100\%/\text{estimated life (yr)} \times 2 = \text{depreciation rate}$$
$$100\%/50 \text{ yr} \times 2 =$$
$$4\%/\text{yr} =$$

$$\text{Cost} - \text{depreciation rate} = \text{depreciation}$$
$$\$60,000 \times 0.04/\text{yr} =$$
$$\$2,400/\text{yr} =$$

End of first-year depreciation:

$$\$2,400/\text{yr} \div 12 \text{ mo/yr} = \$200/\text{mo}$$
$$\$200/\text{mo} \times 9 \text{ mo} = \$1,800$$

Book value at end of first year:

$$\text{Cost} - \text{depreciation} = \text{book value}$$
$$\$60,000 - \$1,800 =$$
$$\$58,200 =$$

6.34 Using the double declining balance method, determine the accumulated depreciation at the end of the second year for a bulldozer that cost $6,000. The bulldozer's estimated useful life is 20 years, and its trade-in value is $500. It was bought on November 27.

SOLUTION

$$100\%/\text{estimated life} \times 2 = \text{depreciation rate}$$
$$100\%/20 \text{ yr} \times 2 =$$
$$10\%/\text{yr} =$$

End of first-year depreciation:

$$\text{Cost} \times \text{depreciation rate} = \text{depreciation}$$
$$\$6,000 \times 0.10/\text{yr} =$$
$$\$600/\text{yr} =$$

$$\$600/\text{yr} \div 12 \text{ mo/yr} = \$50/\text{mo}$$
$$\$50/\text{mo} \times 1 \text{ mo} = \$50$$

Depreciation for second year:

$$(\text{Cost} - \text{depreciation})^* \times \text{depreciation rate} = \text{depreciation}$$
$$(\$6,000 - \$50) \times 0.10/\text{yr} =$$
$$\$5,950 \times 0.10/\text{yr} =$$
$$\$595/\text{yr} =$$

Accumulated depreciation at end of second year:

$$\$50 + \$595 = \$645$$

---

*See Prob. 5.32.

6.35 Using the double declining balance method of depreciation, prepare a depreciation schedule for the first 5 years on a piece of machinery that cost $80,000, has a trade-in value of $5,000 and an estimated life of 25 years.

SOLUTION

$$100\%/\text{estimated life} \times 2 = \text{depreciation rate}$$
$$100\%/25 \text{ yr} \times 2 =$$
$$8\%/\text{yr} =$$

Year	Book Value*	Depreciation Rate	Amount of Depreciation	Accumulated Depreciation
1	$80,000.00	.08	$6,400.00	$ 6,400.00
2	73,600.00	.08	5,888.00	12,288.00
3	67,712.00	.08	5,416.96	17,704.96
4	62,295.04	.08	4,983.60	22,688.56
5	57,311.44	.08	4,584.92	27,273.48

*Note that the book values shown are for the *beginning* of each year.

6.36 Using the double declining balance method of depreciation, prepare a depreciation schedule to the end of the third year for the March 29 purchase of 20 typewriters at a cost of $600 each by Starr Office Management, Inc. The typewriters have an estimated useful life of 5 years and a trade-in value of $100 each.

SOLUTION

$$20 \text{ typewriters} \times \$600 \text{ each} = \$12,000 \text{ total cost}$$

$$100\%/\text{estimated life} \times 2 = \text{depreciation rate}$$
$$100\%/5 \text{ yr} \times 2 =$$
$$40\%/\text{yr} =$$

End of first-year depreciation:

$$\text{Cost} \times \text{depreciation rate} = \text{depreciation}$$
$$\$12,000 \times 0.40/\text{yr} =$$
$$\$4,800/\text{yr} =$$

$$\$4,800/\text{yr} \div 12 \text{ mo/yr} = \$400/\text{mo}$$
$$\$400/\text{mo} \times 9 \text{ mo} = \$3,600$$

Year	Book Value	Depreciation Rate	Amount of Depreciation	Accumulated Depreciation
1	$12,000	.40	$3,600	$3,600
2	8,400	.40	3,360	6,960
3	5,040	.40	2,016	8,976

6.37 If machinery that cost $60,000 and has a trade-in value of $5,000 was put into use on January 1, what is the book value at the end of the fifth year, if said machinery has an estimated useful life of 25 years?

SOLUTION

Year	Book Value	Depreciation Rate*	Amount of Depreciation	Accumulated Depreciation
1	$60,000.00	.08	$4,800.00	$ 4,800.00
2	55,200.00	.08	4,416.00	9,216.00
3	50,784.00	.08	4,062.72	13,278.72
4	46,721.28	.08	3,737.70	17,016.42
5	42,983.58	.08	3,438.69	20,455.11

$*100\%/25 \text{ yr} \times 2 = 8\%/\text{yr}$

Book value at *end* of fifth year:

$$\text{Cost (at beginning of year 5)} - \text{depreciation} = \text{book value}$$
$$\$42,983.58 - \$3,438.69 = \$39,544.89$$

or

$$\text{Original cost} - \text{accumulated depreciation to date} = \text{book value}$$
$$\$60,000.00 - \$20,455.11 = \$39,544.89$$

6.38 Wilson Vending Company bought machines costing a total of $27,000. The machines have an estimated trade-in value of $7,000 and a life expectancy of 8 years. Using the double declining balance method, what is the accumulated depreciation at the end of the fourth year?

SOLUTION

Year	Book Value	Depreciation Rate*	Amount of Depreciation	Accumulated Depreciation
1	$27,000.00	.25	$6,750.00	$ 6,750.00
2	20,250.00	.25	5,062.50	11,812.50
3	15,187.50	.25	3,796.88	15,609.38
4	11,390.62	.25	2,847.66	18,457.04

*100%/8 yr × 2 = 25%/yr

6.39　A conveyor with an estimated useful life of 20 years and a salvage value of $700 was purchased for $7,000. Using the double declining balance method of depreciation, determine the book value at the end of the third year.

SOLUTION

Year	Book Value	Depreciation Rate*	Amount of Depreciation	Accumulated Depreciation
1	$7,000	.10	$700	$ 700
2	6,300	.10	630	1,330
3	5,670	.10	567	1,897

*100%/20 yr × 2 = 10%/yr

Book value at end of third year:

Original cost − accumulated depreciation to date = book value
$$\$7,000 - \$1,897 = \$5,103$$

6.40　Using the double declining balance method of depreciation, find the book value to the nearest dollar at the end of the second year for the following:

(a)
Cost	$120,000
Trade-in value	$5,700
Estimated life	25 yr
Purchased	May 3

(b)
Cost	$3,000
Trade-in value	$0
Estimated life	8 yr
Purchased	August 16

(c)
Cost	$18,000
Trade-in value	$3,200
Estimated life	10 yr
Purchased	October 6

SOLUTION

(a)
$$100\%/\text{estimated life} \times 2 = \text{depreciation rate}$$
$$100\%/25 \text{ yr} \times 2 = 8\%/\text{yr}$$

Depreciation at end of year 1:

$$\text{Cost} \times \text{depreciation rate} = \text{depreciation}$$
$$\$120,000 \times 0.08/\text{yr} = \$9,600$$

$$\$9,600/\text{yr} \div 12 \text{ mo/yr} = \$800/\text{mo}$$
$$\$800/\text{mo} \times 8 \text{ mo} = \$6,400$$

Depreciation at end of year 2:

$$(\text{Cost} - \text{depreciation}) \times \text{depreciation rate} = \text{depreciation}$$
$$(\$120,000 - \$6,400) \times 0.08/\text{yr} =$$
$$\$113,600^* \times 0.08/\text{yr} =$$
$$\$9,088 =$$

Book value at end of year 2:

$$\text{Cost (at beginning of year 2)} - \text{depreciation} = \text{book value}$$
$$\$113,600^* - \$9,088 = \$104,512$$

---

*Note that, as before, the original cost less the depreciation for the first year (i.e., the book value) becomes the cost of the item at the beginning of the second year.

(b)
$$100\%/\text{estimated life} \times 2 = \text{depreciation rate}$$
$$100\%/8 \text{ yr} \times 2 = 25\%/\text{yr}$$

Depreciation at end of year 1:

$$\text{Cost} \times \text{depreciation rate} = \text{depreciation}$$
$$\$3,000 \times 0.25/\text{yr} = \$750/\text{yr}$$

$$\$750/\text{yr} \div 12 \text{ mo/yr} = \$62.50/\text{mo}$$
$$\$62.50/\text{mo} \times 4 \text{ mo} = \$250$$

Depreciation at end of year 2:

$$(\text{Cost} - \text{depreciation}) \times \text{depreciation rate} = \text{depreciation}$$
$$(\$3,000 - \$250) \times 0.25/\text{yr} =$$
$$\$2,750 \times 0.25/\text{yr} =$$
$$\$687.50/\text{yr} =$$

Book value at end of year 2:

$$\text{Cost (at beginning of year 2)} - \text{depreciation} = \text{book value}$$
$$\$2,750 - \$687.50 = \$2,062.50$$

(c)
$$100\%/\text{estimated life} \times 2 = \text{depreciation rate}$$
$$100\%/10 \text{ yr} \times 2 = 20\%/\text{yr}$$

Depreciation at end of year 1:

$$\text{Cost} \times \text{depreciation rate} = \text{depreciation}$$
$$\$18,000 \times 0.20/\text{yr} = \$3,600/\text{yr}$$

$$\$3,600/\text{yr} \div 12 \text{ mo/yr} = \$300/\text{mo}$$
$$\$300/\text{mo} \times 3 \text{ mo} = \$900$$

Depreciation at end of year 2:

$$(\text{Cost} - \text{depreciation}) \times \text{depreciation rate} = \text{depreciation}$$
$$(\$18{,}000 - \$900) \times 0.20/\text{yr} =$$
$$\$17{,}100 \times 0.20/\text{yr} =$$
$$\$3{,}420/\text{yr} =$$

Book value at end of year 2:

$$\text{Cost (at beginning of year 2)} - \text{depreciation} = \text{book value}$$
$$\$17{,}100 - \$3{,}420 = \$13{,}680$$

6.41 By preparing a depreciation schedule based on the double declining balance method of depreciation, determine the accumulated depreciation at the end of 5 years on 25 tables purchased at $150 each by Mohawk Restaurant. Their estimated useful life is 16 years, and they have no salvage value. The date of purchase was January 1. (Round the depreciation to the nearest dollar.)

SOLUTION

Year	Book Value	Depreciation Rate*	Amount of Depreciation	Accumulated Depreciation
1	$3,750**	.125	$469	$ 469
2	3,281	.125	410	879
3	2,871	.125	359	1,238
4	2,512	.125	314	1,552
5	2,198	.125	275	1,827

*$100\%/16 \text{ yr} \times 2 = 12\frac{1}{2}/\text{yr}$
**25 tables $\times$ \$150/table = \$3,750 total cost

6.42 Using the double declining balance method, prepare a depreciation schedule for a truck costing $8,800 purchased on January 1. The truck has an estimated useful life of 5 years and a salvage value of $1,000. (Round the depreciation to the nearest dollar.)

SOLUTION

Year	Book Value	Depreciation Rate*	Amount of Depreciation	Accumulated Depreciation
1	$8,800	.40	$3,520	$3,520
2	5,280	.40	2,112	5,632
3	3,168	.40	1,267	6,899
4	1,901	.40	760	7,659
5	1,141		141	7,800

*$100\%/5 \text{ yr} \times 2 = 40\%/\text{yr}$

When an item has a salvage value, the depreciation for the final year of useful life is calculated as follows (see also Example 5):

$$\text{Cost (at beginning of final year)} - \text{salvage value} = \text{depreciation}$$
$$\$1{,}141 - \$1{,}000 = \$141$$

6.43 McGuire Enterprises purchased a copy machine on December 21 for $5,200. The copier has an estimated useful life of 8 years and a salvage value of $500. Using the double declining balance method of depreciation, find the book value at the end of the second year.

SOLUTION

$$100\%/\text{estimated life} \times 2 = \text{depreciation rate}$$
$$100\%/8 \text{ yr} \times 2 = 25\%/\text{yr}$$

Cost × depreciation rate = depreciation   Cost − depreciation = book value

Year 1 $5,200 × 0.25/yr = $1,300* $5,200 − $1,300 = $3,900

Year 2 $3,900 × 0.25/yr = $975 $3,900 − $975 = $2,925

*December 21 to December 31 of the year in which copier was bought is not counted.

6.44 Using the double declining balance method, prepare a depreciation schedule for an item bought on September 1 for $12,000. It has a trade-in value of $1,000 and an estimated useful life of 4 years.

SOLUTION

Year	Book Value	Depreciation Rate*	Amount of Depreciation	Accumulated Depreciation
1	$12,000		$2,000	$ 2,000
2	10,000	.50	5,000	7,000
3	5,000	.50	2,500	9,500
4	2,500		1,500	11,000

*100%/4 yr × 2 = 50%/yr
**Depreciation for year 1:

$$\text{Cost} \times \text{depreciation rate} = \text{depreciation}$$
$$\$12,000 \times 0.50/\text{yr} = \$6,000$$
$$\$6,000/\text{yr} \div 12 \text{ mo/yr} = \$500/\text{mo}$$
$$\$500/\text{mo} \times 4 \text{ mo} = \$2,000$$

Since the item has a salvage value and year 4 is the last year of this item's useful life, the depreciation for year 4 is calculated as follows (see Example 5):

$$\text{Cost (at beginning of final year)} - \text{salvage value} = \text{depreciation}$$
$$\$2,500 - \$1,000 = \$1,500$$

6.45 Using the double declining balance method, what is the accumulated depreciation at the end of 4 years for a piece of equipment bought on January 1 for $6,100, if the equipment has an estimated useful life of 10 years and a salvage value of $570? (Round the depreciation to the nearest dollar.)

SOLUTION

Year	Book Value	Depreciation Rate*	Amount of Depreciation	Accumulated Depreciation
1	$6,100	.20	$1,220	$1,220
2	4,880	.20	976	2,196
3	3,904	.20	781	2,977
4	3,123	.20	625	3,602

*100%/10 yr × 2 = 20%/yr

6.5 SUM-OF-THE-YEARS'-DIGITS METHOD

With this method, the years of the asset's lifetime are labeled 1, 2, 3, etc., and the depreciation amounts are based on a series of fractions that have the sum of the years' digits as their common denominator. The greatest digit assigned to a year is used as the numerator for the first year, the next greatest digit for the second year, and so forth.

EXAMPLE 7

Cost of machine $17,000; salvage value, $2,000; estimated life, 5 years.
The depreciable amount is the cost less any salvage value:

$$\$17,000 - \$2,000 = \$15,000$$

To find the fraction of this amount that is to be written off each year, proceed as follows:

1. Label the years 1, 2, 3, 4, and 5.

2. Calculate the sum (S) of the years' digits by adding the digits assigned in step 1:

$$S = 1 + 2 + 3 + 4 + 5 = 15$$

3. Convert the sum to a series of fractions by placing each digit assigned in step 1 in the numerator of each respective fraction and placing the sum of the digits found in step 2 in the denominator:

$$\frac{1}{15} + \frac{2}{15} + \frac{3}{15} + \frac{4}{15} + \frac{5}{15} = 1$$

4. Take the above series of fractions *in reverse order* as the depreciation rates. Thus,

Year	Fraction	×	Amount	=	Depreciation
1	5/15	×	$15,000	=	$ 5,000
2	4/15	×	$15,000	=	$ 4,000
3	3/15	×	$15,000	=	$ 3,000
4	2/15	×	$15,000	=	$ 2,000
5	1/15	×	$15,000	=	$ 1,000
			Total depreciation	=	$15,000

For a machine that has a short life expectancy, such as the one in the previous example, the method outlined in step 2 for finding the sum of the years' digits suffices. However, for a machine that has a long life expectancy, it is much simpler to use the following formula:

$$S = \frac{N(N+1)}{2}$$

where S is the sum of the years' digits and N is the life expectancy.

For the machine in Example 7, the calculation for the sum of the years' digits would be

$$S = \frac{5(5+1)}{2} = \frac{30}{2} = 15$$

EXAMPLE 8

The life expectancy of a piece of equipment is estimated to be 30 yr. The sum of the years' digits by the formula used in the preceding example would be:

$$S = \frac{N(N+1)}{2}$$

In this case, $N = 30$ yr. Therefore,

$$S = \frac{30(30+1)}{2} = \frac{930}{2} = 465$$

SOLVED PROBLEMS

6.46 Find the sum of the years' digits for the following life expectancies: (*a*) 5 years, (*b*) 10 years, (*c*) 8 years, (*d*) 20 years, and (*e*) 15 years.

SOLUTION

$$S = \text{sum of the years' digits}$$
$$N = \text{estimated life}$$

$$S = \frac{N(N+1)}{2}$$

(*a*) $S = 5(5+1)/2 = 5(3) = 15$

(*b*) $S = 10(10+1)/2 = 5(11) = 55$

(*c*) $S = 8(8+1)/2 = 4(9) = 36$

(*d*) $S = 20(20+1) = 10(21) = 210$

(*e*) $S = 15(15+1) = 15(8) = 120$

6.47 Determine the first year's depreciation fraction that would be used in the sum-of-the-years'-digits method of depreciation for the following estimated useful lives: (*a*) 4 years, (*b*) 12 years, (*c*) 6 years, (*d*) 18 years, and (*e*) 3 years.

SOLUTION

Since N is the estimated life, it would also be the numerator of the first year's fraction. S is the sum of the years' digits, and as such would be the denominator. Therefore, the first year's depreciation fraction may be expressed as N/S.

For each of the given cases, we need to find S first.

$$S = \frac{N(N+1)}{2}$$

		First Year's Fraction
(*a*)	$S = 4(4+1)/2 = 2(5) = 10$	and $N/S = 4/10$
(*b*)	$S = 12(12+1)/2 = 6(13) = 78$	and $N/S = 12/78$
(*c*)	$S = 6(6+1)/2 = 3(7) = 21$	and $N/S = 6/21$
(*d*)	$S = 18(18+1)/2 = 9(19) = 171$	and $N/S = 18/171$
(*e*)	$S = 3(3+1)/2 = 3(2) = 6$	and $N/S = 3/6$

6.48 Using the sum-of-the-years'-digits method, find the first year's depreciation for a snowplow that cost the town of Holiday $8,000 and has an estimated useful life of 15 years and a salvage value of $1,500.

SOLUTION

$$S = \frac{N(N+1)}{2} = \frac{15(15+1)}{2} = 15(8) = 120$$

First year's depreciation fraction = $N/S = 15/120.$*

$$\text{Cost} - \text{salvage} = \text{depreciable amount}$$
$$\$8,000 - \$1,500 = \$6,500$$

$$\text{Depreciable amount} \times \text{depreciation fraction} = \text{depreciation}$$
$$\$6,500 \times 15/120^* = \$812.50$$

---

*Note that for ease of calculation, 15/120 can be reduced to 1/8 and/or written as the decimal 0.125.

6.49 If on January 1 Cliver Transport purchased two vans costing $50,000 each for their moving and storage business, what is the depreciation on both after the first year? The vans have a trade-in value of $5,000 each and an estimated life of 10 years each. (Round the depreciation to the nearest dollar.)

SOLUTION

$$S = \frac{N(N+1)}{2}$$

$$= \frac{10(10+1)}{2} = 55$$

Depreciation fraction for year $1 = N/S = 10/55$.

$$2 \text{ vans} \times \$50{,}000/\text{van} = \$100{,}000 \text{ total cost}$$
$$2 \text{ vans} \times \$5{,}000/\text{van} = \$10{,}000 \text{ total trade-in value}$$

$$\text{Cost} - \text{salvage} = \text{depreciable amount}$$
$$\$100{,}000 - \$10{,}000 = \$90{,}000$$

$$\text{Depreciable amount} \times \text{depreciation fraction} = \text{depreciation}$$
$$\$90{,}000 \times 10/55 = \$16{,}364$$

6.50 ABC Lighting purchased display cases totaling $5,670. Their estimated useful life is 8 years, and their salvage value is $1,200. Using the sum-of-the-years'-digits method, determine the depreciation to the nearest cent for the first 2 years.

SOLUTION

$$S = \frac{N(N+1)}{2}$$

$$= \frac{8(8+1)}{2} = 36$$

Depreciation fraction for year $1 = N/S = 8/36$.

Recall from Example 7 that we take the sequence of fractions in reverse order for our calculations. Hence, the numerator of year 1 fraction is the last year of useful life (i.e., the estimated life) of the item. Since we are moving backward, the numerator of the next year's fraction is the estimated life minus 1 year. This may be stated as follows:

$$\text{Depreciation fraction for year } 2 = \frac{N-1}{S}$$

$$= \frac{8-1}{36} = \frac{7}{36}$$

$$\text{Cost} - \text{salvage} = \text{depreciable amount}$$
$$\$5{,}670 - \$1{,}200 = \$4{,}470$$

$$\text{Depreciable amount} \times \text{depreciation fraction} = \text{depreciation}$$

Year 1	$\$4{,}470 \times 8/36 = \$993.33$
Year 2	$\$4{,}470 \times 7/36 = \$869.17$

6.51 A piano was purchased by Melody Disco for $6,750. Using the sum-of-the-years'-digits method, what is the depreciation to the nearest cent for the first 3 years if the piano has a salvage value of $960 and an estimated useful life of 25 years?

SOLUTION

$$S = \frac{N(N+1)}{2} = \frac{25(25+1)}{2} = 325$$

	Year 1	**Year 2***	**Year 3****
Depreciation fraction	$\frac{N}{S} = \frac{25}{325}$	$\frac{N-1}{S} = \frac{24}{325}$	$\frac{N-2}{S} = \frac{23}{325}$

---

*See previous problem.

**Because we are moving in reverse sequential order from the total years of estimated life, we subtract yet one more year from N to find the numerator of the depreciation fraction for year 3.

$$\text{Cost} - \text{salvage} = \text{depreciable amount}$$
$$\$6,750 - \$960 = \$5,790$$

$$\text{Depreciable amount} \times \text{depreciation fraction} = \text{depreciation}$$

Year 1	$\$5,790 \times 25/325 = \$445.38$
Year 2	$\$5,790 \times 24/325 = \$427.57$
Year 3	$\$5,790 \times 23/325 = \$409.75$

6.52 Using the sum-of-the-years'-digits method of depreciation, what is the book value (to the nearest cent) at the end of the first year on a piece of equipment that cost \$20,650? The equipment has a salvage value of \$3,650 and an estimated useful life of 50 years.

SOLUTION

$$S = \frac{N(N+1)}{2} = \frac{50(50+1)}{2} = 1,275$$

Depreciation fraction for year $1 = N/S = 50/1,275$.

$$\text{Cost} - \text{salvage} = \text{depreciable amount}$$
$$\$20,650 - \$3,650 = \$17,000$$

$$\text{Depreciable amount} \times \text{depreciation fraction} = \text{depreciation}$$

$$\$17,000.00 \times \frac{50}{1,275} = \$666.67$$

$$\text{Cost} - \text{depreciation} = \text{book value}$$
$$\$20,650.00 - \$666.67 = \$19,983.33$$

6.53 Using the sum-of-the-years'-digits method, determine the accumulated depreciation after 3 years on an item that cost \$125,000 and has an estimated useful life of 75 years and a salvage value of \$10,000. (Round the depreciation to the nearest dollar.)

SOLUTION

$$S = \frac{N(N+1)}{2} = \frac{75(75+1)}{2} = 2,850$$

	Year 1	**Year 2***	**Year 3****
Depreciation fraction:	$\frac{N}{S} = \frac{75}{2,850}$	$\frac{N-1}{S} = \frac{74}{2,850}$	$\frac{N-2}{S} = \frac{73}{2,850}$

---

*See Prob. 5.50.

**See Prob. 5.51.

$$\text{Cost} - \text{salvage} = \text{depreciable amount}$$
$$\$125,000 - \$10,000 = \$115,000$$

Depreciable amount × depreciable fraction = depreciation

Year 1 $\$115,000 \times 75/2{,}850 = \$3{,}026$

Year 2 $\$115,000 \times 74/2{,}850 = \$2{,}986$

Year 3 $\$115,000 \times 73/2{,}850 = \$2{,}946$

Accumulated depreciation = $\$8{,}958$

6.54 Using the sum-of-the-years'-digits method, prepare a depreciation schedule for a pizza oven that was purchased for $3,000 and has an estimated useful life of 5 years and a salvage value of $900.

SOLUTION

Year	Depreciable Amount*	Depreciation Fraction	Amount of Depreciation	Accumulated Depreciation	Book Value at End of Year
1	$2,100	5/15**	$700	$ 700	$2,300
2	2,100	4/15	560	1,260	1,740
3	2,100	3/15	420	1,680	1,320
4	2,100	2/15	280	1,960	1,040
5	2,100	1/15	140	2,100	900

*Cost − salvage = depreciable amount

$\$3,000 - \$900 = \$2,100$

$S = \dfrac{N(N+1)}{2} = \dfrac{5(5+1)}{2} = 15$; see also **Example 7.

6.55 Using the sum-of-the-years'-digits method, prepare a depreciation schedule for the first 5 years for machinery that cost $75,000. The machinery has a salvage value of $6,000 and an estimated useful life of 40 years. (Round depreciation to the nearest cent.)

SOLUTION

Year	Depreciable Amount*	Depreciation Fraction	Amount of Depreciation	Accumulated Depreciation	Book Value at End of Year
1	$69,000.00	40/820**	$3,365.85	$ 3,365.85	$71,634.15
2	69,000.00	39/820	3,281.71	6,647.56	68,352.44
3	69,000.00	38/820	3,197.56	9,845.12	65,154.88
4	69,000.00	37/820	3,113.41	12,958.53	62,041.47
5	69,000.00	36/820	3,029.27	15,987.80	59,012.20

*   Cost − salvage = depreciable amount

$\$75,000 - \$6,000 = \$69,000$

**$S = \dfrac{N(N+1)}{2} = \dfrac{40(40+1)}{2} = 820$; see also Probs. 5.50 and 5.51.

6.56 Use the sum-of-the-years'-digits method to find the depreciation (to the nearest cent) for the first year for each of the following:

(*a*) Cost $4,825
Salvage value $600
Estimated life   6 yr

(*b*) Cost $17,164
Salvage value $2,600
Estimated life   12 yr

(*c*) Cost $65,300
Salvage value $9,000
Estimated life   25 yr

(*d*) Cost $9,999
Salvage value $1,000
Estimated life   8 yr

SOLUTION

(*a*) $S = N(N + 1)/2 = 6(6 + 1)/2 = 21$; depreciation fraction $= N/S = 6/21$

$$(\text{Cost} - \text{salvage value})^* \times \text{depreciation fraction} = \text{depreciation}$$
$$(\$4,825 - \$600) \times 6/21 =$$
$$\$4,225 \times 6/21 =$$
$$\$1,207.14 =$$

(*b*) $S = N(N + 1)/2 = 12(12 + 1)/2 = 78$; depreciation fraction $= N/S = 12/78$

$$(\text{Cost} - \text{salvage value})^* \times \text{depreciation fraction} = \text{depreciation}$$
$$(\$17,164 - \$2,600) \times 12/78 =$$
$$\$14,564 \times 12/78 =$$
$$\$2,240.62 =$$

(*c*) $S = N(N + 1)/2 = 25(25 + 1)/2 = 325$; depreciation fraction $= N/S = 25/325$

$$(\text{Cost} - \text{salvage value})^* \times \text{depreciation fraction} = \text{depreciation}$$
$$(\$65,300 - \$9,000) \times 25/325 =$$
$$\$56,300 \times 25/325 =$$
$$\$4,330.77 =$$

(*d*) $S = N(N + 1)/2 = 8(8 + 1)/2 = 36$; depreciation fraction $= N/S = 8/36$

$$(\text{Cost} - \text{salvage value})^* \times \text{depreciation fraction} = \text{depreciation}$$
$$(\$9,999 - \$1,000) \times 8/36 =$$
$$\$8,999 \times 8/36 =$$
$$\$1,999.78 =$$

---

*Depreciable amount = cost − salvage value

6.57 Using the sum-of-the-years'-digits method, prepare a depreciation schedule for the first 5 years for 40 beds purchased by Hansen Motel. The beds cost $200 each. The charge to have all of them delivered was $200. Their life expectancy is 15 years with no salvage value. (Round depreciation to the nearest dollar.)

SOLUTION

Year	Depreciable Amount*	Depreciation Fraction	Amount of Depreciation	Accumulated Depreciation	Book Value at End of Year
1	$8,200	15/120**	$1,025	$1,025	$7,175
2	8,200	14/120	957	1,982	6,218
3	8,200	13/120	888	2,870	5,330
4	8,200	12/120	820	3,690	4,510
5	8,200	11/120	752	4,442	3,758

*40 beds × $200/bed = $8,000 purchase cost
$8,000 + $200 delivery charge = $8,200 total cost
Cost − salvage = depreciable amount
    $8,200 − $0 = $8,200

**$S = N(N+1)/2 = 15(15+1)/2 = 120$

6.58 Using the sum-of-the-years'-digits method, prepare a depreciation schedule for the first 4 years for an item that cost $56,400 and has a salvage value of $4,500 and an estimated useful life of 30 years. (Round the depreciation to the nearest cent.)

SOLUTION

Year	Depreciable Amount*	Depreciable Fraction	Amount of Depreciation	Accumulated Depreciation	Book Value at End of Year
1	$51,900	30/465**	$3,348.39	$3,348.39	$53,051.61
2	51,900	29/465	3,236.77	6,585.16	49,814.84
3	51,900	28/465	3,125.16	9,710.32	46,689.68
4	51,900	27/465	3,013.55	12,723.87	43,676.13

* Cost − salvage = depreciable amount
  $56,400 − $4,500 = $51,900

**$S = N(N+1)/2 = 30(30+1)/2 = 465$

6.59 Use the sum-of-the-years'-digits method to determine the accumulated depreciation at the end of the second year on a backhoe purchased by Van Dyke Excavating, Inc. on April 1 for $8,500. The backhoe has an estimated useful life of 5 years and a trade-in value of $1,000. (Round the depreciation to the nearest dollar.)

SOLUTION

$$S = \frac{N(N+1)}{2}$$

$$= \frac{5(5+1)}{2} = 15$$

Depreciation fraction:

Year 1 $N/S = 5/15$

Year 2 $(N-1)/S = (5-1)/15 = 4/15$

Cost − salvage value = depreciable amount
    $8,500 − $1,000 = $7,500

Year 1.   Depreciable amount × depreciation fraction = depreciation

$$\$7,500 \times 5/15 = \$2,500 \text{ for 1st full year of useful life}$$

Portion applicable to first calendar year:

$$\$2,500 \times 9 \text{ mo}/12 \text{ mo in a year} = \$1,875*$$

Year 2.   Since the first 3 months of the *second calendar* year are still part of the equipment's *first* year of *useful life*, the depreciation for these months is calculated on the basis of the first year's fraction as follows:

Depreciation for first full year × applicable portion of year = depreciation

$$\$2,500 \times 3 \text{ mo}/12 \text{ mo in year} = \$625 \text{ for Jan. 1–Apr. 1 of 2nd year}$$

Depreciation for remaining 9 months of second year:

Depreciable amount × depreciation fraction = depreciation

$$\$7,500 \times 4/15 = \$2,000 \text{ for 2nd full year of useful life}$$

Portion applicable to second calendar year:

$$\$2,000 \times 9 \text{ mo}/12 \text{ mo in a year} = \$1,500*$$

The full depreciation for the second calendar year is therefore

$$\$625 + \$1,500 = \$2,125$$

Accumulated depreciation at end of second year:

$$\$1,875 + \$2,125 = \$4,000$$

---

*Note that this calculation is the same as

$$\text{Depreciation/yr} \div 12 \text{ mo/yr} = \text{depreciation/mo}$$
$$\text{Depreciation/mo} \times \text{applicable mo} = \text{depreciation for applicable portion of yr}$$

6.60   Using the sum-of-the-years'-digits method, determine the depreciation for the second year on an item that cost $22,000, has a salvage value of $2,000, and has an estimated useful life of 10 years. It was purchased on September 24. (Round the depreciation to the nearest dollar.)

SOLUTION

$$S = \frac{N(N+1)}{2}$$

$$= \frac{10(10+1)}{2} = 55$$

Depreciation fraction:

$$\text{Year 1} \qquad N/S = 10/55$$

$$\text{Year 2} \qquad (N-1)/S = (10-1)/55 = 9/55$$

Cost − salvage = depreciable amount

$$\$22,000 - \$2,000 = \$20,000$$

Since the first 9 months of the second calendar year are still part of the item's first year of useful life, the depreciation for these months is calculated on the basis of the first year's fraction as follows:

Depreciable amount × depreciation fraction = depreciation

$$\$20,000 \times 10/55 = \$3,636 \text{ for 1st full year of useful life}$$

Portion applicable to second calendar year:

$$\$3,636 \times 9 \text{ mo}/12 \text{ mo in yr} = \$2,727 \text{ for Jan. 1–Oct. 1 of 2nd calendar year}$$

The last 3 months of the second calendar year are calculated on the basis of the second year's depreciation fraction:

$$\text{Depreciable amount} \times \text{depreciation fraction} = \text{depreciation}$$
$$\$20,000 \times 9/55 = \$3,273 \text{ for 2nd full year of useful life}$$

Portion applicable to second calendar year:

$$\$3,273 \times 3 \text{ mo}/12 \text{ mo in year} = \$818 \text{ for Oct. 1–Dec. 31 of 2nd calendar year}$$

Depreciation for second year:

$$\$2,727 + \$818 = \$3,545$$

6.6 SUMMARY

The four principal methods of depreciation are compared in Table 6-1. Over a 5-year lifetime, the asset was in operation for 1,800, 1,200, 2,000, 1,400, and 1,600 hours per year, respectively. The cost of the asset was $17,000, and the scrap value is $2,000.

Table 6-1   Annual Depreciation Charge

Year	Straight-Line	Sum-of-the-Years' Digits	Double Declining Balance	Units of Production
1	$ 3,000	$ 5,000	$ 6,800	$ 3,375
2	3,000	4,000	4,080	2,250
3	3,000	3,000	2,448	3,750
4	3,000	2,000	1,468	2,625
5	3,000	1,000	204	3,000
Total	$15,000	$15,000	$15,000	$15,000

SOLVED PROBLEM

6.61 A fixed asset costing $60,000 and having an estimated salvage value of $5,000 has a life expectancy of 10 years. Compare the results of the various depreciation methods by filling in the tables below. Take twice the straight-line rate as the rate in the double declining balance method.

Straight-Line Method

Year	Depreciation Expense	Accumulated Depreciation	Book Value at End of Year
1			
2			
3			
4			

Sum-of-theYears'-Digits Method

Year	Fraction	Depreciation Expense	Accumulated Depreciation	Book Value at End of Year
1				
2				
3				
4				

Double Declining Balance Method

Year	Rate	Depreciation Expense	Accumulated Depreciation	Book Value at End of Year
1				
2				
3				
4				

SOLUTION

Straight-Line Method

Year	Depreciation Expense	Accumulated Depreciation	Book Value at End of Year
1	$5,500*	$ 5,500	$54,500**
2	5,500	11,000	49,000
3	5,500	16,500	43,500
4	5,500	22,000	38,000

*($60,000 − $5,000) ÷ 10/yr = $5,500/yr
**$60,000 − $5,500 = $54,500

Sum-of-the-Years'-Digits Method

Year	Fraction*	Depreciation Expense	Accumulated Depreciation	Book Value at End of Year
1	10/55	$10,000	$10,000	$50,000
2	9/55	9,000	19,000	41,000
3	8/55	8,000	27,000	33,000
4	7/55	7,000	34,000	26,000

$$*S = \frac{10(10+1)}{2} = 55$$

Double Declining Balance Method

Year	Rate*	Depreciation Expense	Accumulated Depreciation	Book Value at End of Year
1	0.20	$12,000	$12,000	$48,000
2	0.20	9,600	21,600	38,400
3	0.20	7,680	29,280	30,720
4	0.20	6,144	35,424	24,576

$* \frac{100\%}{10 \text{ yr}} \times 2 = 20\%$; note that this is twice the straight-line rate.
**20% × ($60,000 − $12,000) = $9,600.

Supplementary Problems

6.62   Using the straight-line method of depreciation, find the amount of depreciation per year if a fixed asset bought on January 6 for $17,000 has an estimated life of 15 years and a salvage value of $2,000.

6.63   Muller Printers bought printing equipment on July 6. The purchase price was $3,700, and the estimated useful life is 4 years. The salvage value is $700. Find the depreciation as of December 31 (same year) by using the straight-line method.

6.64   Using the straight-line method, calculate the amount of depreciation at the end of the second year on a piece of machinery purchased on October 28 for $4,650. The estimated useful life is 5 years and the trade-in value is $1,650.

6.65   A computer was purchased by Hill Enterprises on February 1. The purchase price was $2,000, and installation cost was $720. The estimated useful life is 10 years, and the salvage value is $500. What is the amount of straight-line depreciation (to the nearest cent) at the end of the third year?

6.66   If a photocopier purchased on January 3 for $13,400 has an estimated useful life of 15 years and a trade-in value of $950, what is the book value at the end of the sixth year according to the straight-line method of depreciation?

6.67   Determine the depreciation rate per year for the following estimated useful lives: 4 years, 25 years, and 32 years.

6.68   Prepare a depreciation schedule for a piece of equipment purchased on January 8 for $5,000. Transportation costs amounted to $500. The estimated useful life is 4 years, and the salvage value is $500. Use the straight-line method of depreciation.

6.69   Using the straight line method of depreciation, determine the book value at the end of the fourth year for the following:

(*a*)

Cost	$12,000
Salvage value	$1,000
Estimated life	10 yr

(*b*)

Cost	$7,400
Salvage value	$600
Estimated life	8 yr

(*c*)

Cost	$35,000
Salvage value	$4,000
Estimated life	20 yr

6.70   An item of equipment was bought on January 1 for $30,000. It has an estimated useful life of 100,000 hours and a salvage value of $4,000. If it was used for 35,650 hours in its first year of operation, what is the depreciation according to the units of production method?

6.71   A used dishwasher was purchased by Faine Restaurant on April 3 for $1,500. Repair work totaling $300 was needed before putting the machine into operation. Using the units of production method, determine the depreciation after 5,760 hours of use, if the salvage value is $50 and the estimated useful life is 57,750 hours.

6.72   Using the units of production method, find the depreciation on a piece of assembly line equipment that produced 9,750 units during its first year in operation. The cost of the equipment was $40,000. It has a salvage value of $2,500 and an estimated lifetime output of 75,000 units.

6.73 K&M Painting Contractors started business on June 1. One month prior they purchased a van for $8,000 and incurred additional costs amounting to $1,000 to get the van in operating condition. They also bought a paint sprayer for $300. The van has an estimated useful life of 100,000 miles and a trade-in value of $2,000. The paint sprayer has an estimated useful life of 2,750 hours and a trade-in value of $25. What is the depreciation, based on the units of production method, at the end of the year if they put 5,670 miles on the van as of December 31 and used the paint sprayer 250 hours?

6.74 Roe Computers bought an assembler that assembles 50 circuit parts per hour. If during the first year of operation the machine assembled 68,430 circuits, find the depreciation by using the units of production method. The assembler cost $230,000, has a salvage value of $10,000, and is expected to assemble 1 million circuits during its useful life.

6.75 What is the book value of a piece of equipment that cost $70,000, was used 237,000 hours, and has an estimated useful life of 500,000 hours and a trade-in value of $5,000?

6.76 Using the units of production method, find the depreciation of a used truck that cost $3,700. Additional costs incurred were $335.69 parts, $312.97 repairs, and $151.34 repainting. The original estimated useful life was 150,000 miles, but the truck had 87,965 miles on it when purchased. The trade-in value is $500, and the truck was driven 9,623 miles during the year.

6.77 Office furniture was purchased by Chester Company on January 1 for $2,000. Its estimated useful life is 20 years, and it has a salvage value of $250. Using the double declining balance method of depreciation, what is the depreciation at the end of the first year?

6.78 Equipment was bought on January 10 for $30,000. It has an estimated useful life of 25 years and a trade-in value of $3,000. Determine the book value at the end of the first year by using the double declining balance method of depreciation.

6.79 Determine the accumulated depreciation at the end of the second year by using the double declining balance method of depreciation on a tractor that cost $9,000. Its estimated useful life is 10 years, and the trade-in value is $500. It was bought on October 20.

6.80 If equipment that cost $100,000 and has a trade-in value of $10,000 was put into use on January 3, what is the book value at the end of the second year, if said equipment has an estimated useful life of 50 years and the double declining balance method of depreciation is used?

6.81 For the following, find the book value to the nearest dollar at the end of the first year by using the double declining balance method of depreciation:

Cost	$3,000
Trade-in value	$50
Estimated life	10 yr
Purchased	January 1
Cost	$27,000
Trade-in value	$5,000
Estimated life	25 yr
Purchased	May 1

6.82 A conveyor with an estimated useful life of 8 years and a salvage value of $400 was purchased for $5,000. Determine the book value at the end of the second year by using the double declining balance method of depreciation.

6.83 Mullen Corporation purchased a computer on December 31 for $7,000. Its estimated useful life is 20 years, and the salvage value is $1,000. Find the book value at the end of the first year by using the double declining balance method of depreciation.

6.84   According to the double declining balance method, what is the accumulated depreciation at the end of 2 years on a piece of machinery bought on January 13 for $4,000? The estimated useful life is 5 years, and the salvage value is $200. (Round the depreciation to the nearest dollar.)

6.85   Find the sum of the years for the following life expectancies: 4 years, 3 years, and 20 years.

6.86   Determine the first year's depreciation fraction in the sum-of-the-years'-digits method of depreciation for the following estimated useful lives: 15 years, 5 years, and 8 years.

6.87   Using the sum-of-the-years'-digits method, find the first year's depreciation on a tractor that cost the town of Hill $10,000 and has an estimated useful life of 20 years and a salvage value of $1,000.

6.88   Billy purchased three trucks costing $10,000 each for his painting business. The trucks have a trade-in value of $1,000 each and an estimated life of 15 years each. What is the depreciation on all three at the end of the first year if purchase was made on January 10? (Round the depreciation to the nearest dollar.)

6.89   Use the sum-of-the-years'-digits method to find the book value (to the nearest cent) at the end of the first year on a piece of machinery that cost $15,425. It has a salvage value of $2,425 and an estimated useful life of 10 years.

6.90   Using the sum-of-the-years'-digits method, determine the accumulated depreciation at the end of 2 years on an item that cost $90,000 and has an estimated useful life of 50 years and a salvage value of $5,000. (Round the depreciation to the nearest dollar.)

6.91   Use the sum-of-the-years'-digits method to find the depreciation at the end of the first year for the following:

   (*a*)

Cost	$9,687
Salvage value	$500
Estimated life	8 yr

   (*b*)

Cost	$2,450
Salvage value	$250
Estimated life	6 yr

Answers to Supplementary Problems

6.62 $1,000

6.63 $375

6.64 $700

6.65 $647.50

6.66 $8,420

6.67   25%, 4%, $3\frac{1}{8}$%

6.68

Year	Depreciation Rate (%)	Yearly Depreciation	Book Value (End of Year)	Accumulated Depreciation
1	25	$1,250	$4,250	$1,250
2	25	1,250	3,000	2,500
3	25	1,250	1,750	3,750
4	25	1,250	500	5,000

6.69 (a) $7,600, (b) $4,000, (c) $28,800

6.70 $9,269

6.71 $172.80

6.72 $4,875

6.73 $396.90 van, $25 paint sprayer

6.74 $15,054.60

6.75 $39,190

6.76 $577.38

6.77 $200

6.78 $27,600

6.79 $2,040

6.80 $92,160

6.81 $2,400, $25,560

6.82 $2,812.50

6.83 $6,300

6.84 $2,560

6.85 10, 6, 210

6.86 15/120, 5/15, 8/36

6.87 $857.14

6.88 $3,375

6.89 $13,061.36

6.90 $6,600

6.91 (a) $2,041.56, (b) $628.57

Chapter 7

Interest and Discount

7.1 SIMPLE INTEREST

When an investor lends money to a borrower, the borrower must pay back the money originally borrowed, called the *principal*, and also the fee charged for the use of the money, called *interest*. From the investor's point of view, interest is income from invested capital. The sum of the principal and the interest due is called the *amount* or *accumulated value* or *maturity value*.

The amount of interest is based on three factors: the principal, the rate of interest, and the time span of the loan. At *simple interest*, the formula for computing the interest I on principal P for t years at annual rate r is given by

$$\text{Interest} = \text{principal} \times \text{rate} \times \text{time}$$
$$I = Prt$$

The maturity value S is given by

$$\text{Maturity value} = \text{principal} + \text{interest}$$
$$S = P + I$$

EXAMPLE 1

Anne Geisler requests a 2-year loan of $6,500 from Traders Bank. The bank approves the loan at an annual interest rate of 14%. (*a*) What is the simple interest on the loan? (*b*) What is the maturity value of the loan?

(*a*)
$$\text{Principal} = \$6,500$$
$$\text{Rate} = 14\% = 0.14$$
$$\text{Time} = 2 \text{ yr}$$

Substituting these values into $I = Prt$, we get

$$I = Prt$$
$$= \$6,500 \times 0.14 \times 2 = \$1,820$$

(*b*) The maturity value is defined as the sum of the principal and the interest. Hence, the maturity value of this loan is equal to

$$S = P + I = \$6,500 + \$1,820 = \$8,320$$

Although the time span of a loan may be given in days, months, or years, the rate of interest is an annual rate. Thus, when the duration of a loan is given in months or days, the time must be converted to years. When the time is given in months, then

$$t = \frac{\text{number of months}}{12}$$

EXAMPLE 2

Find the simple interest on Anne Geisler's loan of $6,500 if the loan is offered at a rate of 21% and is due in 3 months. What is the maturity value of the loan at these terms?

$$P = \$6,500 \qquad r = 21\% = 0.21 \qquad t = 3/12$$

$$I = Prt$$

$$= \$6,500 \times 0.21 \times \frac{3}{12} = \$341.25$$

149

The maturity value of the loan now equals

$$S = P + I$$
$$= \$6{,}500 + \$341.25 = \$6{,}841.25$$

SOLVED PROBLEMS

7.1 Find the simple interest on $800 loaned at an annual interest rate of 12% for 2 years.

SOLUTION

$$\text{Interest} = \text{principal} \times \text{rate} \times \text{time}$$

The principal $(P) = \$800$, the rate $(r) = 12\% = 0.12$, and time $(t) = 2$.

$$I = Prt$$
$$= \$800 \times 0.12 \times 2 = \$192$$

7.2 What is the maturity value of the loan in Prob. 7.1?

SOLUTION

The maturity value is equal to the principal plus the interest.

$$S = I + P$$
$$= \$800 + \$192 = \$992$$

7.3 (a) Find the simple interest on a $30,000 loan due in 5 years when the annual interest rate on the loan is 16%. (b) What is the maturity value of this loan?

SOLUTION

(a) $P = \$30{,}000 \qquad r = 16\% = 0.16 \qquad t = 5$

$$I = Prt$$
$$= \$30{,}000 \times 0.16 \times 5 = \$24{,}000$$

(b) $$S = P + I$$
$$= \$30{,}000 + \$24{,}000 = \$54{,}000$$

7.4 Find the simple interest on a $3,000 loan at 17% annual interest for 4 months.

SOLUTION

$$P = \$3{,}000 \qquad r = 17\% = 0.17 \qquad t = \frac{4}{12} = \frac{1}{3}$$

$$I = Prt$$
$$= \$3{,}000 \times 0.17 \times \frac{1}{3} = \$170$$

7.5 Find the simple interest on a $5,000 loan at $14\frac{1}{2}\%$ for 7 months.

SOLUTION

$$P = \$5{,}000 \qquad r = 14\frac{1}{2}\% = 0.145 \qquad t = \frac{7}{12}$$

$$I = Prt$$
$$= \$5{,}000 \times 0.145 \times \frac{7}{12} = \$422.92$$

7.2   CALCULATING DUE DATES

If the term of a loan is given in months, the due date of the loan is a corresponding day in the *maturity month*. There are two qualifying conditions:

1. If the maturity month does not have the required number of days, then the last day of the month serves as the maturity date. Thus, a 2-month loan dated December 31 is due on February 28 (or February 29 in a leap year).

2. If the due date of a loan falls on a nonbusiness day, the maturity date is the next business day, with the additional day(s) added to the period, for which interest is charged.

EXAMPLE 3

(*a*) A 15-month loan dated February 2 is due May 2 of the following year. (*b*) A loan dated May 31 and due in 4 months has a maturity date of September 30. (*c*) A 7-month loan dated December 4 is due July 5, since July 4 is a holiday.

Interest is charged for the extra day the loan is outstanding. For simplicity, we have assumed that the maturity dates in (*a*) and (*b*) fall on a business day. Should this not be the case, then the due date is postponed until the next business day and interest is charged [just as in (*c*)].

When the time is given in days, we may calculate either (1) *exact simple interest* on the basis of a 365-day year (leap year or not) or (2) *ordinary simple interest* on the basis of a 360-day year, called a *banker's year*. Of the two, ordinary interest brings greater revenue to the lender.

The formulas for calculating time (t) for exact and ordinary simple interest are:

Exact simple interest:
$$t = \frac{\text{number of days}}{365}$$

Ordinary simple interest:
$$t = \frac{\text{number of days}}{360}$$

EXAMPLE 4

Find the exact and the ordinary simple interest on a 60-day loan of $1,950 at $13\frac{1}{2}\%$.

We know that $P = \$1,950$ and $r = 13\frac{1}{2}\% = 0.135$, but we must calculate t for each type of interest.

$$t_{\text{exact}} = \frac{60}{365} \qquad t_{\text{ordinary}} = \frac{60}{360}$$

The respective simple interests are:

Exact simple interest:
$$I = Prt$$
$$= \$1,950 \times 0.135 \times \frac{60}{365} = \$43.27$$

Ordinary simple interest:
$$I = Prt$$
$$= \$1,950 \times 0.135 \times \frac{60}{360} = \$43.88$$

There are two ways to calculate the number of days between calendar dates.

1. *Exact time* is the count of the actual number of days, including all except the first day. Exact time can be easily found from Table 7-1 by subtracting the serial numbers of the given dates. (April 15, for example, has a serial number of 105 since it is the 105th day of the year.) In leap years, serial numbers of all days after February 28 are increased by 1 (so that the serial number for April 15 would be 106).

2. *Approximate time* is found by assuming that each month has 30 days.

Table 7-1　The Number of Each Day of the Year

Day of Month	Jan.	Feb.	Mar.	Apr.	May	June	July	Aug.	Sept.	Oct.	Nov.	Dec.	Day of Month
1	1	32	60	91	121	152	182	213	244	274	305	335	1
2	2	33	61	92	122	153	183	214	245	275	306	336	2
3	3	34	62	93	123	154	184	215	246	276	307	337	3
4	4	35	63	94	124	155	185	216	247	277	308	338	4
5	5	36	64	95	125	156	186	217	248	278	309	339	5
6	6	37	65	96	126	157	187	218	249	279	310	340	6
7	7	38	66	97	127	158	188	219	250	280	311	341	7
8	8	39	67	98	128	159	189	220	251	281	312	342	8
9	9	40	68	99	129	160	190	221	252	282	313	343	9
10	10	41	69	100	130	161	191	222	253	283	314	344	10
11	11	42	70	101	131	162	192	223	254	284	315	345	11
12	12	43	71	102	132	163	193	224	255	285	316	346	12
13	13	44	72	103	133	164	194	225	256	286	317	347	13
14	14	45	73	104	134	165	195	226	257	287	318	348	14
15	15	46	74	105	135	166	196	227	258	288	319	349	15
16	16	47	75	106	136	167	197	228	259	289	320	350	16
17	17	48	76	107	137	168	198	229	260	290	321	351	17
18	18	49	77	108	138	169	199	230	261	291	322	352	18
19	19	50	78	109	139	170	200	231	262	292	323	353	19
20	20	51	79	110	140	171	201	232	263	293	324	354	20
21	21	52	80	111	141	172	202	233	264	294	325	355	21
22	22	53	81	112	142	173	203	234	265	295	326	356	22
23	23	54	82	113	143	174	204	235	266	296	327	357	23
24	24	55	83	114	144	175	205	236	267	297	328	358	24
25	25	56	84	115	145	176	206	237	268	298	329	359	25
26	26	57	85	116	146	177	207	238	269	299	330	360	26
27	27	58	86	117	147	178	208	239	270	300	331	361	27
28	28	59	87	118	148	179	209	240	271	301	332	362	28
29	29		88	119	149	180	210	241	272	302	333	363	29
30	30		89	120	150	181	211	242	273	303	334	364	30
31	31		90		151		212	243		304		365	31

Note: For leap year add 1 to the tabulated number after February 28.

EXAMPLE 5

(a) Find the exact time from January 18 to July 9 of the same year, when the year is a leap year. From Table 7-1:

Date	Day Number
July 9	$190 + 1^* = 191$
Jan. 18	-18
Exact time	173 days

---

* Since the year is a leap year, 1 is added to all days after February 28.

(b) Find the approximate time between January 18 and July 9. To do this, we set up a table and subtract, as shown:

Date	Month	Day	Month	Day
July 9	7	9 ⟶	6	39*
Jan. 18	1	18	1	18
Difference			5	21

*Although July has 31 days, we assumed that all months have only *30* days to carry out the subtraction. This is because approximate time is based on a year having 12 equal months of 30 days each. Consequently, leap years are also not considered when dealing with approximate time.

To restate in days the approximate time of 5 months and 21 days, we proceed as follows:

$$(5 \text{ mo} \times 30 \text{ days/mo}) + 21 \text{ days} = 150 \text{ days} + 21 \text{ days} = 171 \text{ days}$$

SOLVED PROBLEMS

7.6 Find the exact simple interest on a 90-day loan of $900 at $15\frac{1}{4}\%$.

SOLUTION

$$P = \$900 \qquad r = 15\tfrac{1}{4}\% = 0.1525 \qquad t = \frac{90}{365}$$

$$\begin{aligned} I &= Prt \\ &= \$900 \times 0.1525 \times \frac{90}{365} = \$33.84 \end{aligned}$$

7.7 Find the ordinary simple interest for the loan in Prob. 7.6.

SOLUTION

$$P = \$900 \qquad r = 15\tfrac{1}{4}\% = 0.1525 \qquad t = \frac{90}{360}$$

$$\begin{aligned} I &= Prt \\ &= \$900 \times 0.1525 \times \frac{90}{360} = \$34.31 \end{aligned}$$

7.8 Find the (a) exact and (b) ordinary simple interest on a 120-day loan of $145,000 that has an annual interest rate of $19\frac{3}{4}\%$. (c) Which gives the lender a greater return on the $145,000 investment and by how much?

SOLUTION

(a) Exact simple interest

$$P = \$145,000 \qquad r = 19\tfrac{3}{4}\% = 0.1975 \qquad t = \frac{120}{365}$$

$$\begin{aligned} I &= Prt \\ &= \$145,000 \times 0.1975 \times \frac{120}{365} = \$9,415.07 \end{aligned}$$

(b) Ordinary simple interest

$$P = \$145,000 \qquad r = 19\tfrac{3}{4}\% = 0.1975 \qquad t = \frac{120}{360}$$

$$I = Prt$$

$$= \$145,000 \times 0.1975 \times \frac{120}{360} = \$9,545.83$$

(c) Of the two, ordinary simple interest gives the lender $130.76 more interest on this investment.

7.9 Find the exact time from April 9 to December 3 of the same year.

SOLUTION

From Table 7-1:

Date	Day Number
Dec. 3	337
Apr. 9	−99
Exact time	238 days

7.10 Find the exact time from February 4 to April 21 of the same leap year.

SOLUTION

Date	Day Number
April 21, 1984	111
Add 1 for leap year	+1
	112
Feb. 4, 1984	−35
Exact time	77 days

7.11 Find the exact time from May 18 to July 5 of the following year.

SOLUTION

Date	Day Number
July 5	186
Add 365 for extending into next year	+365
	551
May 18	−138
Exact time	413 days

7.12 Find the approximate time in Prob. 7.9.

SOLUTION

Date	Month	Day	Month	Day
Dec.3	12	3 ⟶	11	33
Apr.9	4	9	4	9
Difference			7	24

The approximate time is 7 months and 24 days, or $(7 \times 30) + 24 = 234$ days.

7.13 Find the approximate time in Prob. 7.11.

SOLUTION

Date	Month	Day	Month	Day
July 5	12 + 7	5 ⟶ 18	18	35
May 18	5	18	5	18
Difference			13	17

The approximate time is 13 months and 17 days, or $(13 \times 30) + 17 = 407$ days.

7.14 Find the maturity date of a 60-day loan dated June 15.

SOLUTION

Date	Day Number
June 15	166
Add term of loan	+ 60
Maturity date	226, which is Aug. 14

7.15 Find the maturity date on a 120-day loan dated October 1, 19X5.

SOLUTION

Date	Day Number
Oct. 1, 1985	274
Add term of loan	+ 120
	394
Subtract 365	− 365
Maturity date	29, which is Jan. 29, 19X6

7.16 Find the due date on a 3-month loan dated April 4.

SOLUTION

Three months after April 4 is July 4, which is a legal holiday. Therefore the due date is July 5 (if a business day), and interest is charged for 91 days if approximate time is used or for 92 days if exact time is used.

7.3 METHODS FOR COMPUTING SIMPLE INTEREST

There are four distinct methods for computing simple interest between two dates:

1. Exact time and ordinary interest
2. Exact time and exact interest
3. Approximate time and ordinary interest
4. Approximate time and exact interest

Method 1 is also known as the "*banker's rule*" and is the common method used in business in the United States and in international business transactions. Method 2 is used by the U.S. government and also is a general practice in Canada. Method 3 is used for periodic repayment plans, such as monthly payments on real estate mortgages, installment purchases, and certain types of personal borrowing, and in computing accrued bond interest on corporate bonds. Method 4 is theoretically possible but never used.

EXAMPLE 6

A sum of $75,000 is invested from March 13 until December 20 of the same year at $15\frac{1}{2}$% simple interest. For each of the four methods, the interest earned is illustrated below.

$$P = \$75,000 \quad \text{and} \quad r = 15\frac{1}{2}\% = 0.1550$$

(a) Exact time and ordinary interest:

The calculation to find the exact time is as follows:

Date	Day Number
Dec. 20	354
Mar. 13	−72
Exact time	282 days

To find t for ordinary interest, we have to use a year based on 360 days:

$$t = \frac{282}{360}$$

We can now calculate the interest:

$$I = Prt$$
$$= \$75,000 \times 0.1550 \times \frac{282}{360} = \$9,106.25$$

(b) Exact time and exact interest:

From (a) we know the exact number of days is 282. To find t for exact interest, we have to use a 365-day year:

$$t = \frac{282}{365}$$

$$I = Prt$$
$$= \$75,000 \times 0.1550 \times \frac{282}{365} = \$8,981.51$$

(c) Approximate time and ordinary interest:

To find approximate time, we construct a table and subtract:

Date	Month	Day
Dec. 20	12	20
Mar. 13	3	13
Difference	9	7

We then convert to approximate time in days:

$$(9 \text{ mo} \times 30 \text{ days/mo}) + 7 \text{ days} = 277 \text{ days}$$

For ordinary interest we use a 360-day year to calculate t:

$$t = \frac{277}{360}$$

$$I = Prt$$
$$= \$75,000 \times 0.1550 \times \frac{277}{360} = \$8,944.79$$

(d) Approximate time and exact interest:

From (c) we know that the number of approximate days is 277. Using a 365-day year to calculate t, we get

$$t = \frac{277}{365}$$

$$I = Prt$$
$$= \$75,000 \times 0.1550 \times \frac{277}{365} = \$8,822.26$$

SOLVED PROBLEMS

7.17　A sum of $2,000 is invested from April 9 to December 3 of the same year at 15% simple interest. Find the interest earned using the four methods.

SOLUTION

From Prob. 7.9 the exact time is 238 days, and from Prob. 7.12 the approximate time is 234 days.

$$P = \$2,000 \qquad r = 15\% = 0.15 \qquad t \text{ depends on the method used}$$

$$I = Prt$$

1.　Exact time and ordinary interest:　　　　$I = \$2,000(0.15)\left(\dfrac{238}{360}\right) = \$198.33$

2.　Exact time and exact interest:　　　　　$I = \$2,000(0.15)\left(\dfrac{238}{365}\right) = \$195.62$

3.　Approximate time and ordinary interest:　$I = \$2,000(0.15)\left(\dfrac{234}{360}\right) = \$195.00$

4.　Approximate time and exact interest:　　$I = \$2,000(0.15)\left(\dfrac{234}{365}\right) = \$192.33$

7.18　Using the banker's rule, find the simple interest on $1,800 at $17\frac{1}{4}\%$ from February 4 to April 21 of the same leap year.

SOLUTION

From Prob. 7.10 the exact time is 77 days.

$$P = \$1,800 \qquad r = 17\tfrac{1}{4}\% = 0.1725 \qquad t = \frac{77}{360}$$

$$I = Prt$$
$$= \$1,800(0.1725)(77/360) = \$66.41$$

7.19　Find the maturity value (See Sec. 7.1) of a note for $1,500 at 12% ordinary simple interest for 182 days.

SOLUTION

$$P = \$1,500 \qquad r = 0.12 \qquad t = 182/360$$

$$I = Prt$$
$$= \$1,500(0.12)(182/360) = \$91$$

$$S = P + I$$
$$= \$1,500 + \$91 = \$1,591$$

7.20　Joe borrowed $1,200 on September 10 to start college. He repaid the loan on July 20 of the following year. What amount did he pay back if the bank calculated the exact interest at 11% and used the exact time?

SOLUTION

Exact time from September 10 to July 20 of the following year:

Date	Day Number
July 20	201
Add 365 for extending into next year	+ 365
	566
Sept. 10	− 253
Exact time	313 days

Interest paid:

$$P = \$1,200 \qquad r = 0.11 \qquad t = \frac{313}{365}$$

$$I = Prt$$

$$= \$1,200 \times 0.11 \times \frac{313}{365} = \$113.19$$

To determine how much Joe paid back, we calculate the maturity value of the loan.

$$S = P + I$$
$$= \$1,200 + \$113.19 = \$1,313.19$$

Joe paid the bank $1,313.19.

7.4 THE FORMULAS FOR P, r, AND t AND PRESENT VALUE

From $I = Prt$ and $S = P + I$, we can obtain several useful formulas. For finding the interest rate, we can rewrite $I = Prt$ in terms of r:

$$r = \frac{I}{Pt}$$

For finding the time period in years, we can rewrite $I = Prt$ in terms of t:

$$t = \frac{I}{Pr}$$

For finding the principal when the maturity value is unknown, we can rewrite $I = Prt$ in terms of P:

$$P = \frac{I}{rt}$$

The formulas for interest and maturity value can be combined as follows to obtain

$$S = P + I$$
$$= P + Prt = P(1 + rt)$$

We can restate the above formula in terms of P to find the principal when the maturity value (S) is known:

$$P = \frac{S}{1 + rt}$$

The principal P computed by this formula is referred to as the *present value* of S.

SOLVED PROBLEMS

7.21 At what rate of simple interest will $500 accumulate interest of $10 in 3 months?

SOLUTION

$$P = \$500 \qquad I = \$10 \qquad t = \frac{3}{12}$$

$$r = \frac{I}{Pt}$$

$$= \frac{\$10}{\$500(3/12)} = 0.08 = 8\%$$

7.22 Judy borrowed $800 and paid off the principal together with interest of $52.58 at the end of 182 days. If the bank used the banker's rule (see Sec. 7.3), what rate of interest did the bank charge?

SOLUTION

$$P = \$800 \qquad I = \$52.58 \qquad t = \frac{182}{360}$$

$$r = \frac{I}{Pt}$$

$$= \frac{\$52.58}{\$800(182/360)} \cong 0.13 = 13\%$$

7.23 If the bank pays exact interest at 11% for exact time, by what date will a deposit of $1,000, made on January 2, earn interest of $100?

SOLUTION

$$P = \$1,000 \qquad I = \$100 \qquad r = 0.11$$

$$t = \frac{I}{Pr}$$

$$= \frac{\$100}{\$1,000(0.11)} = 0.9090909 \text{ yr} \cong 332 \text{ days}$$

Using Table 7-1 we find that 332 days after January 2 is November 30 of the same year.

7.24 What principal will earn interest of $550.75 at 11.015% in 6 months?

SOLUTION

$$I = \$550.75 \qquad r = 0.11015 \qquad t = \frac{6}{12}$$

$$P = \frac{I}{rt}$$

$$= \frac{\$550.75}{(0.11015)(6/12)} = \$10,000$$

7.25 Ninety days after borrowing money a person pays back exactly $870.19. How much was borrowed if the payment includes principal and ordinary simple interest at $9\frac{1}{2}\%$?

SOLUTION

$$S = \$870.19 \qquad r = 0.095 \qquad t = \frac{90}{360}$$

$$P = \frac{S}{1 + rt}$$

$$= \frac{\$870.19}{1 + (0.095)(90/360)} = \$850$$

7.26 Find the present value of $2,100 due in 15 months, if money is worth 11%.

SOLUTION

$$S = \$2,100 \qquad r = 0.11 \qquad t = \frac{15}{12}$$

$$P = \frac{S}{1 + rt}$$

$$= \frac{\$2,100}{1 + (0.11)(15/12)} = \$1,846.15$$

7.27   Recall from Prob. 7.20 that Joe had borrowed $1,200 at 11% exact interest for 313 days. Use $S = P(1 + rt)$ to calculate the maturity value of this loan.

SOLUTION

$$P = \$1,200 \qquad r = 11\% = 0.11 \qquad t = 313/365$$

$$S = P(1 + rt)$$
$$= \$1,200[1 + (0.11)(313/365)] = \$1,313.19$$

7.5 PROMISSORY NOTES AND BANK DISCOUNT

A *promissory note* is a written promise by a debtor, called the *maker* of the note, to pay the creditor, called the *payee* of the note, a sum of money on a specified date. Promissory notes are used when money is borrowed or goods or services are sold on credit. There are two types of promissory notes, *interest-bearing* notes and *non-interest-bearing* notes. Figure 7-1 is an example of an interest-bearing note.

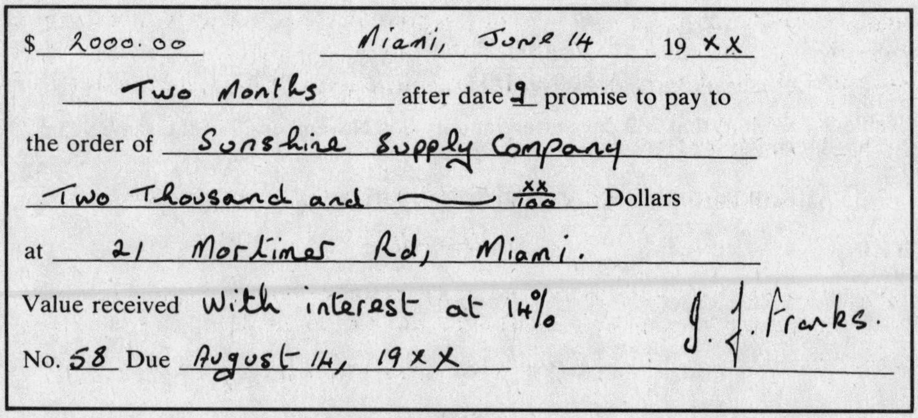

Fig. 7-1

Looking at the promissory note in Fig. 7-1 we learn the following terms:

1. The *face value* of the note, which is the amount of money stated in the note ($2,000)
2. The *date* of the note (June 14, 19XX), which is the date on which the note was made and from which the interest is computed
3. The *term* of the note (2 months)
4. The *payee* of the note (Sunshine Supply Company)
5. The *maker* of the note (I. J. Franks)
6. The *interest rate* on the note (14% ordinary simple interest)
7. The *maturity date* of the note (August 14, 19XX, 2 months after June 14, 19XX)

On the maturity date, August 14, 19XX, the principal of $2,000 and the simple interest at 14% for 2 months must be paid. The total of principal and interest is called the *maturity value* of the note. (If the term of the note is in days, ordinary simple interest is used to calculate the maturity value.)

Figure 7-2 is an example of a non-interest-bearing note.

The interest rate is not stated on the note in Fig. 7-2. The maturity value of the note is equal to its face value and $500 must be paid on May 9, 19XX (assuming a nonleap year). Note that interest is paid on a non-interest-bearing loan. The interest is deducted in advance, at the time the money is borrowed.

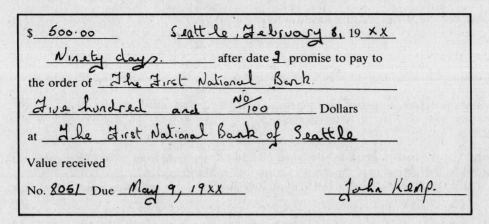

Fig. 7-2

An important feature of a promissory note is that it is *negotiable*. That is, it can be transferred to another payee (a person, company, bank) by the endorsement of the present payee. Cashing a note at a bank is called *discounting a note*. The bank collects interest in advance, called *bank discount* (*D*), which is computed on the *maturity value* (*S*) of the note at a specified annual *discount rate* (*d*) for the *term* (*t*) of the discount in years. The term of the discount is the time (in years) from the date of discount until the maturity date of the note. If the time is given in days, the banker's year of 360 days is used.

Thus the bank discount (*D*) is computed by

$$\text{Discount} = \text{maturity value} \times \text{discount rate} \times \text{term of discount}$$

$$D = Sdt$$

The money received for the discounted note is called the *proceeds*. The proceeds (*P*) are obtained by deducting the bank discount (*D*) from the maturity value (*S*) of the note:

$$\text{Proceeds} = \text{maturity value} - \text{bank discount}$$

$$P = S - D$$

By combining the preceding two formulas, we can calculate proceeds directly from the discount rate and the term:

$$P = S - D = S - Sdt = S(1 - dt)$$

EXAMPLE 7

Refer to Fig. 7-2. If the First National Bank of Seattle charged 18.5% interest in advance on the 90-day, $500 loan, how much did John Kemp actually receive?

$$S = \$500 \qquad d = 18.5\% = 0.185 \qquad t = \frac{90}{360}$$

The interest collected in advance is called the bank discount (*D*):

$$D = Sdt$$

$$= \$500 \times 0.185 \times \frac{90}{360} = \$23.125 \cong \$23.13$$

The money received for the discounted note is called the proceeds (*P*):

$$P = S - D$$

$$= \$500 - \$23.13 = \$476.87$$

John Kemp received $476.87.

We can rewrite the preceding formula to solve for S:

$$P = S(1 - dt)$$

$$\frac{P}{1 - dt} = S$$

This formula is used to calculate the maturity value of a loan for specified proceeds.

EXAMPLE 8

Celeste Curtis wants to get a 180-day, non-interest-bearing note from a bank that charges $14\frac{1}{4}\%$ interest. What should be the face value of the note if Celeste needs $1,000 in cash?

We want to find the maturity value (S) of the 180-day note for specified proceeds (P) of $1,000.

$$S = \frac{P}{1 - dt}$$

$$= \frac{\$1,000}{1 - (0.1425)(180/360)} = \$1,076.72$$

The face value of the note should be $1,076.72.

SOLVED PROBLEMS

7.28   Find the maturity value of the note in Fig. 7-1.

SOLUTION

$$P = \$2,000 \qquad r = 14\% = 0.14 \qquad t = \frac{2}{12}$$

From Sec. 7.4,

$$S = P(1 + rt)$$

$$= \$2,000\left(1 + 0.14 \times \frac{2}{12}\right) = \$2,046.67$$

7.29   Sunshine Supply Company cashed the note in Fig. 7-1 on July 17, 19XX, at their bank at a 12% bank discount rate. Find the bank discount and the proceeds.

SOLUTION

The term of discount is the time from July 17 to August 14, 19XX, that is, 28 days.

$$S = \$2,046.67 \qquad d = 0.12 \qquad t = \frac{28}{360}$$

$$D = Sdt$$

$$= \$2,046.67 \times 0.12 \times \frac{28}{360} = \$19.10$$

$$P = S - D$$

$$= \$2,046.67 - \$19.10 = \$2,027.57$$

The bank discount charged by the bank is $19.10 and Sunshine Supply Company receives proceeds of $2,027.57.

7.30   What rate of interest did the bank in Prob. 7.29 realize on its investment, if it held the note until the maturity date?

SOLUTION

The bank paid $2,027.57 for the note on July 17, 19XX, and received $2,046.67 from I. J. Franks on August 14, 19XX. The bank realized a profit of $2,046.67 - $2,027.57 = $19.10 on their investment of $2,027.57 over a period of 28 days. The rate of interest realized by the bank is

$$r = \frac{I}{Pt}$$

$$= \frac{\$19.10}{\$2,027.57(28/360)} \cong 0.1211 = 12.11\%$$

Note that the interest rate is 0.11% higher than the corresponding discount rate (d). This is because the discount rate (d) is applied to the maturity value (S), whereas the interest rate (r) is applied to the principal (proceeds) (P). Both rates result in the same amount of interest $19.10 and are said to be *equivalent rates*.

7.31 Referring to the note in Fig. 7-2, find the proceeds to John Kemp if the First National Bank of Seattle charged 15% interest in advance on the loan.

SOLUTION

$$S = \$500 \qquad d = 0.15 \qquad t = \frac{90}{360}$$

$$D = Sdt$$

$$= \$500 \times 0.15 \times \frac{90}{360} = \$18.75$$

$$P = S - D$$
$$= \$500 - \$18.75 = \$481.25$$

Alternative solution:
   We may also calculate the proceeds (P) directly:

$$P = S(1 - dt)$$
$$= \$500[1 - (0.15)(90/360)] = \$481.25$$

7.32 What is the true interest rate (at ordinary simple interest) that John Kemp paid on his loan in Prob. 7.31?

SOLUTION

The principal of the loan is $481.25, and the interest is $18.75 for 90 days.

$$P = \$481.25 \qquad I = \$18.75 \qquad t = \frac{90}{360}$$

$$r = \frac{I}{Pt}$$

$$= \frac{\$18.75}{\$481.25(90/360)} \cong 0.1558 = 15.58\%$$

7.33 Find the maturity date and the term of discount for each of the following:

	Date of Note	Term of Note	Date of Discount
(a)	June 12	120 days	July 15
(b)	Nov. 8	3 months	Jan. 10

SOLUTION

(a) Maturity date: June 12 + 120 days = Oct. 10
    Term of discount: Number of days from July 15 to Oct. 10 = 87 days

(b) Maturity date: Nov. 8 + 3 months = Feb. 8
    Term of discount: Number of days from Jan. 10 to Feb. 8 = 29 days

7.34 Gary Becker's own 60-day, non-interest-bearing note is discounted at 16%. If the face of the note is $1,232.88, find the proceeds.

SOLUTION

$$S = \$1,232.88 \qquad d = 0.16 \qquad t = \frac{60}{360}$$

$$P = S(1 - dt)$$
$$= \$1,232.88[1 - (0.16)(60/360)] = \$1,200$$

7.35 The Cooper Corporation receives a 90-day, 14%, $5,000 note from the West Company on February 9, 19XX, and discounts the note at $15\frac{1}{2}$% on March 1, 19XX. Find the proceeds of the note if 19XX is a leap year.

SOLUTION

We must first determine the maturity value of the note.

$$\text{Maturity value} = S$$
$$\text{Principal} = P = \$5,000$$
$$\text{Interest rate} = r = 14\% = 0.14$$
$$\text{Term of the loan} = t = \frac{90}{360}$$

From Sec. 7.4

$$S = P(1 + rt)$$
$$= \$5,000\left(1 + 0.14 \times \frac{90}{360}\right) = \$5,175$$

Next we must calculate the term of the discounted note.

$$\text{Maturity date: Feb. 9, 19XX} + 90 \text{ days} = \text{May 9, 19XX}$$
$$\text{Term of discount: Number of days from March 1 to May 9, 19XX} = 69$$

The proceeds (P) can now be determined.

$$S = \$5,175 \qquad r = 15.5\% = 0.155 \qquad t = \frac{60}{360}$$

$$P = S(1 - rt)$$
$$= \$5,175\left(1 - 0.155 \times \frac{69}{360}\right) = \$5,021.26$$

7.36 Monica borrowed $800 from her bank and signed a 180-day, non-interest-bearing note. If the bank charged 12% interest in advance, what were the proceeds of the loan?

SOLUTION

$$S = \$800 \qquad d = 12\% = 0.12 \qquad t = \frac{180}{360}$$

$$D = Sdt$$
$$= \$800 \times 0.12 \times \frac{180}{360} = \$48$$

$$P = S - D$$
$$= \$800 - \$48 = \$752$$

Although Monica borrowed $800, she received only $752 in cash. At the maturity date, 180 days later, Monica must pay the bank full $800.

7.37 What should be the face value of a non-interest-bearing note in Prob. 7.36 if Monica wants to receive $800 in cash?

SOLUTION

We want to find the maturity value (S) of the 180-day loan for specified proceeds of $P = \$800$.

$$S = \frac{P}{1 - dt}$$

$$= \frac{\$800}{1 - (0.12)(180/360)} = \$851.06$$

Monica should sign a 180-day, non-interest-bearing note for $851.06 to receive $800 in cash.

7.38 On April 21, a retailer buys goods worth $5,000. If he pays cash, he will get a 4% cash discount. To take advantage of this cash discount, he signs a 90-day, non-interest-bearing note at his bank, which discounts notes at a discount rate of 9%. What should the face value of this note be to give the retailer the exact amount needed to pay cash for the goods?

SOLUTION

Cash discount: $4\% \times \$5,000 = \$200$

The retailer needs: $\$5,000 - \$200 = \$4,800$

We now need to determine the maturity value (S) for proceeds of $P = \$4,800$, $d = 9\% = 0.09$, and $t = 90/360$.

$$S = \frac{P}{1 - dt}$$

$$= \frac{\$4,800}{1 - (0.09)(90/360)} = \$4,910.49$$

The face value of the non-interest-bearing note should be $4,910.49.

7.39 A company borrowed $40,000 on June 5 and signed a promissory note bearing interest at 13% for 3 months. On the maturity date, the company paid the interest in full and gave a second note for 6 months without interest and for such an amount that when it was discounted at a 14% discount rate on the day it was signed, the proceeds were just sufficient to pay the $40,000 debt. Find (*a*) the amount of interest paid on the first note and (*b*) the face value of the second note.

SOLUTION

(*a*) Interest on the first note, due September 5, is

$$I = Prt$$

$$= \$40,000 \times 0.13 \times \frac{3}{12} = \$1,300$$

(*b*) We must now calculate the maturity value S of the loan for specified proceeds of $P = \$40,000$, $d = 0.14$, and $t = \frac{6}{12}$.

$$S = \frac{P}{1 - dt}$$

$$= \frac{\$40,000}{1 - (0.14)(6/12)} = \$43,010.75$$

The face value of the second note is $43,010.75.

7.6 COMPOUND INTEREST

If the interest due is added to the principal at the end of each interest period and thereafter earns interest, the interest is said to be *compounded*.

Interest may be compounded (and converted into principal) annually, semiannually, quarterly, monthly, weekly, daily, or continuously. When compounding daily, a 365-day year is generally used. The rate of interest is usually stated as an annual interest rate and is referred to as a *nominal rate of interest*.

For calculating compound interest, the following notations are used:

P = the original principal, or the present value of S, or the discounted value of S
S = the compound amount of P, or the maturity value of P, or the accumulated value of P
m = the number of conversion periods per year, or the frequency of compounding
j_m = the nominal (yearly) interest rate which is compounded (payable, convertible) m times per year
i = the interest rate per interest period
n = the total number of interest (or conversion) periods involved

The interest rate per period (i) equals the nominal interest rate divided by the number of conversion periods per year:

$$i = \frac{j_m}{m}$$

EXAMPLE 9

The nominal interest rate is 10%, and the interest is compounded semiannually. What is the interest per period?

$$m = 2 \text{ (interest is compounded twice per year)}$$

$$j_m = j_2 = 10\%$$

$$i = \frac{j_m}{m}$$

$$= 10\%/2 = 5\%$$

The total number of interest periods n equals the number of years for which interest was collected multiplied by the number of conversion periods per year:

$$n = \text{years} \times m$$

EXAMPLE 10

If nominal interest of 7.5% was compounded quarterly for $2\frac{1}{2}$ years, what was the total number of interest periods?

$$n = \text{years} \times m$$
$$= 2.5 \times 4 = 10$$

The calculations of interest due and the accumulated value at the end of the first three successive interest periods are shown below. (P = original principal and i = interest rate per conversion period.)

End of Period	Interest Due	Accumulated Value (S)
1	Pi	$P + Pi = P(1 + i)$
2	$[P(1 + i)]i$	$P(1 + i) + [P(1 + i)]i = P(1 + i)(1 + i) = P(1 + i)^2$
3	$[P(1 + i)^2]i$	$P(1 + i)^2 + [P(1 + i)^2]i = P(1 + i)^2(1 + i) = P(1 + i)^3$

If we continue in this manner, the accumulated value at the end of n periods is:

$$\text{Accumulated value} = \text{principal} \times \text{accumulation factor}$$
$$S = P(1 + i)^n$$

This is the *fundamental compound interest* formula and its use to calculate S is called *accumulation*. The factor $(1 + i)^n$ is called the *accumulation factor* or the *accumulated value of $1*.*

The formula for compound interest (I) is

$$I = S - P$$

EXAMPLE 11

(a) What is the accumulated value of $2,500 at the end of 2 years if $\frac{1}{2}$% interest was compounded monthly. (b) What is the compound interest?

(a) We need to first determine the total number of conversion periods. Since there are 12 months in a year, $m = 12$. The total number of conversion periods is defined as

$$n = \text{years} \times m$$
$$= 2 \times 12 = 24$$

The accumulated value then is

$$S = P(1 + i)^n$$
$$= \$2,500(1 + 0.005)^{24} = \$2,500 \times 1.1271598 = \$2,817.90$$

On the calculator:

Enter	Press	Display
2500	x	2500.
	(	2500.
1	+	1.
0.005	)	1.005
	y^x	1.005
24	=	2817.8994

(b) The compound interest is

$$I = S - P$$
$$= \$2,817.90 - \$2,500 = \$317.90$$

At the same nominal rate, the accumulated value (S) is directly proportional to the frequency of conversion. When the need arises to compare investment plans or loans that differ in nominal rate and conversion frequency, the *effective annual yield* of interest is calculated. The effective annual yield is defined as a rate (j), which when compounded annually, yields the same amount of yearly interest as the nominal rate. The formula for effective annual yield is derived as follows:

Effective rate: $1 at rate j for 1 year will accumulate to $1 + j$

Nominal rate: $1 at rate j_m for 1 year will accumulate to $\left(1 + \dfrac{j_m}{m}\right)^m$

Since by definition $1 + j = \left(1 + \dfrac{j_m}{m}\right)^m$

then $j = \left(1 + \dfrac{j_m}{m}\right)^m - 1$

---

*It is assumed that students have a pocket calculator equipped with the power function y^x. For the procedure used to calculate the accumulation factor $(1 + i)^n$ on the calculator, see Chap. 3, Example 8(a). In this book, all digits provided by the calculator are used in the calculations, with rounding to the nearest cent being done only in the final answer.

EXAMPLE 12

A credit union offers three types of investment certificates that have nominal interest rates of $j_2 = 11\frac{3}{5}\%$, $j_4 = 11\frac{1}{2}\%$, and $j_{12} = 11\frac{2}{5}\%$, respectively. Which certificate will yield the greatest return on an investment?

To compare the three certificates, we must calculate their effective annual interest rates.

$$j = \left(1 + \frac{j_m}{m}\right)^m - 1$$

For $j_2 = 11\frac{3}{5}\%$: $j = (1 + 0.116/2)^2 - 1 = 0.1193640$

For $j_4 = 11\frac{1}{2}\%$: $j = (1 + 0.115/4)^4 - 1 = 0.1200551$

For $j_{12} = 11\frac{2}{5}\%$: $j = (1 + 0.114/12)^{12} - 1 = 0.1201492$

Since j_{12}, which offers the lowest nominal interest rate, has the greatest effective annual interest rate, it will yield the greatest return on an investment.

Businesspeople often need to determine how much principal to invest now at a given nominal interest rate, so that it will accumulate to a stipulated amount by a specified future date. From Sec. 7.4, we know that principal (P) can be calculated from

$$P = \frac{S}{(1+i)^n}$$

This can be restated as

$$P = S\left[\frac{1}{(1+i)^n}\right]$$

Present value = amount × discount factor

The process of calculating P by this formula is called *discounting* and P is called the *present value* or the *discounted value* of S. The factor $1/(1+i)^n$ is called the *discount factor* or the *discounted value of $1*. Note that the discount factor is the reciprocal of the accumulation factor. To calculate the discount factor on a pocket calculator, first determine the accumulation factor [see Chap. 3, Example 8(a)] and then press the $\boxed{\frac{1}{x}}$ key to find the reciprocal.

When discounting promissory notes at compound interest, we use the same formula, but now P is called the *proceeds* and S the *maturity value* of the note. The *compound discount* is then equal to $S - P$.

EXAMPLE 13

Find the principal which will amount to $5,000 in 2 years at $j_4 = 9\frac{1}{4}\%$.

$$S = \$5,000$$

$$i = \frac{j_m}{m}$$

Since $j_m = 9\frac{1}{4}\%$ and $m = 4$,

$$i = 0.0925/4$$
$$= 0.023125$$

$$n = \text{yr} \times m$$
$$= 2 \times 4 = 8$$

$$P = S\left[\frac{1}{(1+i)^n}\right]$$

$$= \$5,000\left[\frac{1}{(1+0.023125)^8}\right] = \$4,164.2848 \cong \$4,164.28$$

On the calculator:

Enter	Press	Display	OR	Enter	Press	Display	
5000	$\times$	5000.		1	$+$	1.	
1	$\div$	5000.		0.023125	$=$	1.023125	
	(	5000.			y^x	1.023125	
1	$+$	1.		8	$=$	1.2006864	
0.023125	)	1.023125			$\frac{1}{x}$	.83285797	Discount factor
	y^x	1.023125			$\times$	.83285797	
8	$=$	4164.2848		5000	$=$	4164.2848	

SOLVED PROBLEMS

7.40 (a) Find the simple interest on $1,000 for 2 years at an interest rate of 10%. (b) Find the compound interest on $1,000 for 2 years at a nominal rate of 10% compounded semiannually ($j_2 = 10\%$).

SOLUTION

(a) Simple interest:

$$I = Prt$$
$$= \$1,000(0.10)(2) = \$200$$

(b) Compound interest:
Since the interest period is 6 months, interest is earned at the rate $i = 10\%/2 = 5\%$ per period, and there are four interest periods in 2 years.

End of Period	Interest	Accumulated Value
1	$1,000.00(0.05) = $ 50.00	$1,050.00
2	$1,050.00(0.05) = 52.50	1,102.50
3	$1,102.50(0.05) = 55.12	1,157.62
4	$1,157.62(0.05) = 57.88	1,215.50
	Total = $215.50	

The compound interest on $1,000 for 2 years at a nominal rate of 10% is $215.50.

Alternative solution:

$$P = \$1,000 \qquad i = 0.05 \qquad n = 4$$

Accumulated value:

$$S = P(1+i)^n$$
$$= \$1,000(1.05)^4 = \$1,000(1.2155063) = \$1,215.51$$

Compound interest:

$$I = S - P$$
$$= \$1,215.51 - \$1,000 = \$215.51$$

The 1¢ difference in the answer is due to accumulation of roundoff errors in the previous solution.

7.41 Determine the interest rate i per conversion period and the total number of conversion periods n for (a) $j_{12} = 18\%$ for 3 years, (b) 12% compounded daily for 2 years, and (c) $j_4 = 10.108\%$ for 18 months.

SOLUTION

(a)
$$i = \frac{j_m}{m} = \frac{0.18}{12} = 0.015 \text{ (per month)}$$
$$n = \text{yr} \times m = 3 \times 12 = 36 \text{ (months)}$$

(b)
$$i = \frac{j_m}{m} = \frac{0.12}{365} = 0.0003288 \text{ (per day)}$$
$$n = \text{yr} \times m = 2 \times 365 = 730 \text{ (days)}$$

(c)
$$i = \frac{j_m}{m} = \frac{0.10108}{4} = 0.02527 \text{ (per quarter)}$$
$$n = \text{yr} \times m = \frac{18}{12} \times 4 = 6 \text{ (quarters)}$$

7.42 Compute the accumulation factor for each part of Prob. 7.41.

SOLUTION

The accumulation factor is $(1 + i)^n$. On the calculator:

	(a) $i = 0.015$ (per mo) $n = 36$	(b) $i = 0.0003288$ (per day) $n = 730$	(c) $i = 0.02527$ (per qtr) $n = 6$
Enter $(1 + i)$	1.015	1.0003288	1.02527
Press $\boxed{y^x}$	$\boxed{y^x}$	$\boxed{y^x}$	$\boxed{y^x}$
Enter n	36	730	6
Press $\boxed{=}$	$\boxed{=}$	$\boxed{=}$	$\boxed{=}$
Read $(1 + i)^n$	1.7091395	1.2712294	1.1615275

7.43 Compute the accumulation factor $(1 + i)^n$ for (a) 3 years, 12% compounded monthly; (b) 2 years, 10% compounded daily, and (c) 30 months, 15% compounded semiannually.

SOLUTION

$$i = \frac{j_m}{m} \qquad n = \text{years} \times m$$

On the calculator:

		(a) $i = 0.12$ (per mo) $n = 36$	(b) $i = 0.10$ (per day) $n = 730$	(c) $i = 0.15$ (per half-yr) $n = 5$
	Enter 1	1	1	1
	Press $\boxed{+}$	$\boxed{+}$	$\boxed{+}$	$\boxed{+}$
Enter $(1 + i)$ {	Enter j_m	0.12	0.10	0.15
	Press $\boxed{\div}$	$\boxed{\div}$	$\boxed{\div}$	$\boxed{\div}$
	Enter m	12	365	2
	Enter $\boxed{=}$	$\boxed{=}$	$\boxed{=}$	$\boxed{=}$
Press $\boxed{y^x}$		$\boxed{y^x}$	$\boxed{y^x}$	$\boxed{y^x}$
Enter n		36	730	5
Press $\boxed{=}$		$\boxed{=}$	$\boxed{=}$	$\boxed{=}$
Read $(1 + i)^n$		1.4307688	1.2213693	1.4356293

7.44 Find the accumulated value of $1,000 using the times and rates in Prob. 7.43.

SOLUTION

$$S = P(1+i)^n$$

Accumulated value = principal × accumulation factor

(a) $$S = \$1,000(1.01)^{36} = \$1,000(1.4307688) = \$1,430.77$$

(b) $$S = \$1,000(1 + 0.10/365)^{730} = \$1,000(1.2213693) = \$1,221.37$$

(c) $$S = \$1,000(1.075)^5 = \$1,000(1.4356293) = \$1,435.63$$

7.45 Find the compound interest on an investment of $2,000 at $j_{12} = 18\%$ for (a) 5 years and (b) 20 years.

SOLUTION

(a) $$P = \$2,000 \qquad i = \frac{j_m}{m} = \frac{0.18}{12} = 0.015 \qquad n = \text{yr} \times m = 5 \times 12 = 60$$

$$S = P(1+i)^n$$
$$= \$2,000(1.015)^{60} = \$2,000(2.4432198) = \$4,886.44$$

$$I = S - P$$
$$= \$4,886.44 - \$2,000 = \$2,886.44$$

(b) $$P = \$2,000 \qquad i = \frac{j_m}{m} = 0.015 \qquad n = \text{yr} \times m = 20 \times 12 = 240$$

$$S = P(1+i)^n$$
$$= \$2,000(1.015)^{240} = \$2,000(35.632809) = \$71,265.62$$

$$I = S - P$$
$$= \$71,265.62 - \$2,000 = \$69,265.62$$

Note that the compound interest on $2,000 at $j_{12} = 18\%$ for 20 years is $69,265.62, which is almost 35 times the original investment of $2,000. If the investment had been at 18% simple interest, the interest earned would have been only $2,000(0.18)(20) = \$7,200$. This illustrates the power of compound interest at a high rate of interest for a long period of time.

7.46 John Doe deposited $10,000 into a retirement savings plan on May 1, 1984. How much will be in the plan on May 1, 1994, if the plan accumulates interest at 10.21% compounded daily, assuming (a) exact time (1 year = 365 days), (b) approximate time (1 year = 360 days)?

SOLUTION

(a) $$P = \$10,000 \qquad i = \frac{j_m}{m} = \frac{0.1021}{365} \qquad n = \text{yr} \times m = 10 \times 365 = 3,650$$

$$S = P(1+i)^n$$
$$= \$10,000\left(1 + \frac{0.1021}{365}\right)^{3,650} = \$10,000(2.7755729) = \$27,755.73$$

(b) $$P = \$10,000 \qquad i = \frac{j_m}{m} = \frac{0.1021}{360} \qquad n = \text{yr} \times m = 10 \times 360 = 3,600$$

$$S = P(1+i)^n$$
$$= \$10,000\left(1 + \frac{0.1021}{360}\right)^{3,600} = \$10,000(2.7755694) = \$27,755.69$$

The difference between the answers for (a) and (b) is only 4¢. Most U.S. banks use a 365-day year when compounding daily.

7.47 Find the accumulated value of an investment of $1,000 for 10 years at a nominal rate of 10% compounded with frequencies $m = 1, 2, 4, 12$, and 365.

SOLUTION

m	i	n	$(1 + i)^n$	Accumulated Value
1	.10	10	2.5937425	$2593.74
2	.05	20	2.6532977	2653.30
4	.025	40	2.6850638	2685.06
12	$\frac{.10}{12}$	120	2.7070415	2707.04
365	$\frac{.10}{365}$	3,650	2.7179089	2717.91

7.48 Find the effective rate j of (a) 12% compounded quarterly, (b) $10\frac{1}{4}$% compounded daily, and (c) a credit-card charge of 2% per month on the unpaid balance.

SOLUTION

$$j = \left(1 + \frac{j_m}{m}\right)^m - 1$$

(a)
$$j = \left(1 + \frac{0.12}{4}\right)^4 - 1 = 0.1255088 \cong 12.55\%$$

(b)
$$j = \left(1 + \frac{0.1025}{365}\right)^{365} - 1 = 0.1079213 \cong 10.79\%$$

(c)
$$j = (1.02)^{12} - 1 = 0.2682418 \cong 26.82\%$$

7.49 A savings and loan association offers guaranteed investment certificates paying interest at $j_{12} = 12\frac{1}{4}$%, $j_2 = 12\frac{1}{2}$%, and $j_1 = 12\frac{3}{4}$%. Which option is the best?

SOLUTION

We calculate the effective annual rate j for each rate and select the certificate with the highest effective rate.

$$j = \left(1 + \frac{j_m}{m}\right)^m - 1$$

For $j_{12} = 12\frac{1}{4}$%:
$$j = \left(1 + \frac{0.1225}{12}\right)^{12} - 1 = 0.1296174$$

For $j_2 = 12\frac{1}{2}$%:
$$j = \left(1 + \frac{0.125}{2}\right)^2 - 1 = 0.1289063$$

For $j_1 = 12\frac{3}{4}$%:
$$j = j_1 = 0.1275$$

Guaranteed investment certificates at $j_{12} = 12\frac{1}{4}$% offer the best option since they give the best rate of return.

7.50 Compute the discount factor for each part of Prob. 7.41.

SOLUTION

The numerical values of discount factors $1/(1 + i)^n$ are obtained as follows, on the calculator:

	(a) $i = 0.015$ (per mo) $n = 36$	(b) $i = 0.0003288$ (per day) $n = 730$	(c) $i = 0.02527$ (per qtr) $n = 6$
Enter $(1+i)$	1.015	1.0003288*	1.02527
Press $\boxed{y^x}$	$\boxed{y^x}$	$\boxed{y^x}$	$\boxed{y^x}$
Enter n	36	730	6
Press $\boxed{=}$	$\boxed{=}$	$\boxed{=}$	$\boxed{=}$
Press $\boxed{\dfrac{1}{x}}$	$\boxed{\dfrac{1}{x}}$	$\boxed{\dfrac{1}{x}}$	$\boxed{\dfrac{1}{x}}$
Read $\dfrac{1}{(1+i)^n}$	0.5850897	0.78664007	0.86093527

*Note: If $1 + (0.12/365)$ is entered for $(1+i)$, the discount factor read off the calculator will be 0.78665913.

7.51 Find the principal which will amount to $2,000

(a) In 5 years at $j_{12} = 12\%$

(b) In 3 years at 10% compounded daily

SOLUTION

(a) $S = \$2,000 \qquad i = \dfrac{j_m}{m} = \dfrac{0.12}{12} \qquad n = \text{yr} \times m = 5(12) = 60$

$$P = S\left[\frac{1}{(1+i)^n}\right]$$

$$= \$2,000\left[\frac{1}{\left(1+\dfrac{0.12}{12}\right)^{60}}\right] = \$2,000(0.5504496) = \$1,100.90$$

(b) $S = \$2,000 \qquad i = \dfrac{j_m}{m} = \dfrac{0.10}{365} \qquad n = \text{yr} \times m = 3(365) = 1,095$

$$P = S\left[\frac{1}{(1+i)^n}\right]$$

$$= \$2,000\left[\frac{1}{\left(1+\dfrac{0.10}{365}\right)^{1,095}}\right] = \$2,000(0.7408487) = \$1,481.70$$

7.52 Find the present value of $1,000 due in

(a) 5 years, if interest is 16% compounded quarterly

(b) 10 years, if interest is 8% compounded semiannually

SOLUTION

(a) $S = \$1,000 \qquad i = \dfrac{j_m}{m} = \dfrac{0.16}{4} \qquad n = \text{yr} \times m = 5(4) = 20$

$$P = S\left[\frac{1}{(1+i)^n}\right]$$

$$= \$1,000\left[\frac{1}{\left(1+\dfrac{0.16}{4}\right)^{20}}\right] = \$1,000(0.4563869) = \$456.39$$

(b)
$$S = \$1,000 \qquad i = \frac{j_m}{m} = \frac{0.08}{2} \qquad n = \text{yr} \times m = 10(2) = 20$$

$$P = S\left[\frac{1}{(1+i)^n}\right]$$

$$= \$1,000\left[\frac{1}{\left(1+\frac{0.08}{2}\right)^{20}}\right] = \$1,000(0.4563869) = \$456.39$$

7.53 An obligation of \$5,000 is due December 31, 1988. What is the value of this obligation on December 31, 1985, if money is worth $j_{12} = 15\%$?

SOLUTION

$$S = 5,000 \qquad i = \frac{j_m}{m} = \frac{0.15}{12} \qquad n = \text{yr} \times m = 3(12) = 36$$

$$P = S\left[\frac{1}{(1+i)^n}\right]$$

$$= \$5,000\left[\frac{1}{(1.0125)^{36}}\right] = \$5,000(0.6394092) = \$3,197.05$$

The value of the obligation on December 31, 1985, is \$3,197.05.

7.54 You can buy a lot for \$20,000 cash or for payments of \$10,000 now, \$6,000 in 1 year, and \$6,000 in 2 years. Which option is better for you, if money is worth 16% compounded quarterly?

SOLUTION

We must compare the present value of the cash option (\$20,000) to the present value of the payments option at $j_4 = 16\%$.

Present value (P) of payments option:

Due Now +	Present Value of Money Due in 1 Year +	Present Value of Money Due in 2 Years
\$10,000	$S = \$6,000$ $i = \dfrac{j_m}{m} = \dfrac{0.16}{4}$ $n = 4$ $P = S\left[\dfrac{1}{(1+i)^n}\right]$ $= \$6,000\left[\dfrac{1}{\left(1+\frac{0.16}{4}\right)^4}\right]$ $= \$6,000(0.85480419)$ $= \$5,128.83$	$S = \$6,000$ $i = \dfrac{j_m}{m} = \dfrac{0.16}{4}$ $n = \text{yr} \times m = 2 \times 4 = 8$ $P = S\left[\dfrac{1}{(1+i)^n}\right]$ $= \$6,000\left[\dfrac{1}{\left(1+\frac{0.16}{4}\right)^8}\right]$ $= \$6,000(0.73069021)$ $= \$4,384.14$

$$\$10,000 + \$5,128.83 + \$4,384.14 = \underline{\underline{\$19,512.97}}$$

The payments option is better since its present value is less than \$20,000.

7.55 Which of the two options in Prob. 7.54 is better if money is worth $j_{12} = 12\%$?

SOLUTION

Present value (P) of the payments option at $j_{12} = 12\%$:

Due Now	+	Present Value of Money Due in 1 Year	+	Present Value of Money Due in 2 Years
$10,000		$S = \$6,000$ $i = \dfrac{0.12}{12}$ $n = 12$ $P = S\left[\dfrac{1}{(1+i)^n}\right]$ $= \$6,000\left[\dfrac{1}{(1.01)^{12}}\right]$ $= \$6,000(0.88744923)$ $= \$5,324.70$		$S = \$6,000$ $i = \dfrac{0.12}{12}$ $n = 2 \times 12 = 24$ $P = S\left[\dfrac{1}{(1+i)^n}\right]$ $= \$6,000\left[\dfrac{1}{(1.01)^{24}}\right]$ $= \$6,000(0.78756613)$ $= \$4,725.40$

$$\$10,000 + \$5,324.70 + \$4,725.40 = \underline{\underline{\$20,050.10}}$$

The cash option is now the better one, since its present value ($20,000) is less than the payments option.

7.56 Find (a) the proceeds (P) and (b) the compound discount if a promissory note for $1,000 due in 2 years without interest is discounted at $j_{12} = 13\frac{1}{4}\%$.

SOLUTION

(a)
$$S = 1,000 \qquad i = \frac{0.1325}{12} \qquad n = 2(12) = 24$$

$$P = S\left[\frac{1}{(1+i)^n}\right]$$

$$= \$1,000\left[\frac{1}{\left(1+\dfrac{0.1325}{12}\right)^{24}}\right] = \$1,000(0.768321) = \$768.32$$

(b)
$$\text{Compound discount} = S - P$$
$$= \$1,000 - \$768.32 = \$231.68$$

Supplementary Problems

7.57 Find the simple interest on a loan of (a) $500 at $8\frac{1}{4}\%$ for 1 year, (b) $2,000 at $16\frac{1}{2}\%$ for 30 months, and (c) $1,200 at 10.82% for 6 months.

7.58 Find the ordinary simple interest on a loan of (a) $900 at $14\frac{1}{2}\%$ for 120 days, (b) $1,400 at 13% for 90 days, and (c) $750 at 9.21% for 60 days.

7.59 Find the exact simple interest on each loan in Prob. 7.58.

7.60 Find the exact time from (a) April 21 to June 29 of the same year, (b) November 7 to February 28 of the following year, (c) March 17, 19X6, to November 8, 19X6, and (d) July 8, 19X4, to January 18, 19X5.

7.61 Find the approximate time for each term in Prob. 7.60.

7.62 Find the maturity date of (a) a 90-day loan dated August 17, (b) a 60-day loan dated December 8, (c) a 6-month loan dated May 3, and (d) a 182-day loan dated March 7, 19X4.

7.63 Using the four methods (exact time and ordinary interest, exact time and exact interest, approximate time and ordinary interest, and approximate time and exact interest), find the simple interest on (a) an $800 loan at 17% from April 21 to June 29 and (b) a $5,000 loan at $12\frac{3}{4}$% from July 8, 19X4, to January 18, 19X5.

7.64 Using the banker's rule, find the simple interest on investments of (a) $1,500 at 9% from March 17, 19X6 to November 8, 19X6, (b) $650 at $15\frac{1}{2}$% from October 1, 19X4, to January 29, 19X5, (c) $2,000 at $10\frac{5}{8}$% from March 15, 19X5, to September 3, 19X5.

7.65 Using exact time and exact interest, find the simple interest on the investments in Prob. 7.64.

7.66 Find the maturity value of (a) a $2,500 loan for 85 days, (b) a $1,200 loan for 120 days, and (c) a $10,000 loan for 60 days, all at 14% ordinary simple interest.

7.67 Find the maturity value of the loans in Prob. 7.66 at 12% exact simple interest.

7.68 At what rate of simple interest will (a) $500 accumulate $10 interest in 2 months, (b) money double itself in 7 years, and (c) $2,000 grow to $2,100 in 1 year.

7.69 Find the rate of ordinary simple interest charged on the following loans:

	Principal	Maturity Value	Time (Days)
(a)	$800	$830.50	90
(b)	$1,500	$1,640.62	270

7.70 Freda invested $1,200 for 180 days and earned $65.10 interest. What rate of exact simple interest did she earn?

7.71 How many days will it take $1,000 (a) to earn $50 at 12% ordinary simple interest and (b) to accumulate to at least $1,500 at $18\frac{3}{4}$% exact simple interest?

7.72 What principal will earn (a) ordinary simple interest of $25 at 12.5% in 120 days, (b) exact simple interest of $19.50 at 9.75% in 73 days, and (c) simple interest of $21.25 at 10% in 3 months?

7.73 Using ordinary simple interest, find the present value of (a) $600 due in 163 days at 11% and (b) $1,500 due in 71 days at $18\frac{1}{4}$%.

7.74 Using exact simple interest, find the present value of the obligations in Prob. 7.73.

7.75 Find the principal and the interest on the following loans at ordinary simple interest:

	Maturity Value	Time (Days)	Rate (%)
(a)	$856.40	217	16.25
(b)	$11,748.96	730	$8\frac{5}{8}$
(c)	$1,831.25	25	25

7.76 A couple borrows $20,000. The annual interest rate is $12\frac{1}{2}$%, payable monthly, and the monthly payment is $300. How much of the first payment goes to interest and how much to principal?

7.77 Questions (a) through (e) refer to Fig. 7-3.

(a) Who is the maker of the note?

(b) What is the face value?

(c) What is the maturity date of the note?

(d) Who is the payee?

(e) What is the maturity value of the note?

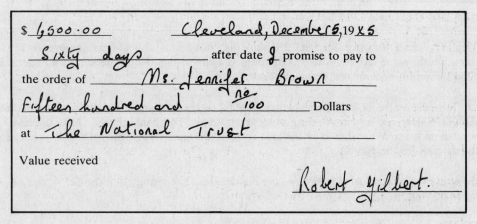

Fig. 7-3

7.78 Find the maturity date and the maturity value of each of the following promissory notes:

	Face	Date	Term	Interest Rate
(a)	$750	Nov. 3	3 mo	$8\frac{1}{4}\%$
(b)	$2,000	June 18	120 days	$17\frac{1}{2}\%$
(c)	$5,000	Sept. 5	341 days	11.073%

7.79 Referring to Fig. 7.3, in Prob. 7.77, find the proceeds to Robert Gilbert if Jennifer Brown charged him 18% interest in advance.

7.80 What is the true interest rate (at ordinary simple interest) that Robert Gilbert paid on the loan in Prob. 7.77?

7.81 Jennifer Brown cashed the note in Prob. 7.77 on December 20, 19X5, at a 14% bank discount rate. Find the bank discount and the proceeds.

7.82 Find the maturity date and the term of discount for each of the following notes:

	Date of Note	Term of Note	Date of Discount
(a)	Sept. 1	60 days	Oct. 7
(b)	Feb. 4	2 mo	Mar. 1
(c)	Dec. 14, 19X4	192 days	Mar. 1, 19X5

7.83 Find the proceeds when each of the following notes is discounted:

	Face Value	Date	Term	Interest Rate	Date of Discount	Discount Rate
(a)	$3,000	Nov. 3	3 mo		Dec. 1	$10\frac{1}{4}\%$
(b)	$1,200	Sept. 1	60 days	$15\frac{1}{2}\%$	Oct. 7	$14\frac{3}{4}\%$
(c)	$500	Dec. 14	192 days	17%	Dec. 24	17%
(d)	$4,000	Feb. 4	2 mo		Mar. 1	$8\frac{1}{2}\%$

7.84   A bank charges 11% interest in advance on short-term loans. Find the proceeds of the loan if the borrower signs a non-interest-bearing note for (a) $1,800 due in 6 months and (b) $600 due in 90 days.

7.85   A bank charges $15\frac{1}{4}$% interest in advance on short-term loans. Find the face value of the non-interest-bearing note given the bank if the borrower receives (a) $800 for 4 months, (b) $1,200 for 90 days, and (c) $2,000 from June 12 to December 12.

7.86   The Travelers Trust discounted at 15% bank discount a non-interest-bearing note for $20,000 due in 180 days. On the same day the note was discounted again at 14% bank discount at a Federal Reserve bank. Find the profit made by the Travelers Trust.

7.87   On June 29, a retailer buys goods worth $3,000. To take advantage of a 5% cash discount, the retailer signs a 60-day non-interest-bearing note at his bank. The bank charges 11% interest in advance on short-term loans. What should be the face value of this note to give the retailer the exact amount needed to pay cash for the goods?

7.88   Compute the face value of a 90-day note dated June 15, bearing interest at 15% and having a maturity value of $788.50.

7.89   Find the compound interest on $2,000 for 1 year at $j_4 = 16\%$ (a) by calculating the interest due and the accumulated value at the end of each of four successive interest periods and (b) by the fundamental compound interest formula.

7.90   Determine i and n for (a) $j_4 = 11\%$ for 18 months, (b) $j_{12} = 24\%$ for 5 years, (c) 13.138% compounded annually for 3 years, (d) 5% compounded daily for 2 years, and (e) $10\frac{5}{8}$% compounded semiannually for 30 months.

7.91   Compute the accumulation factor for each part of Prob. 7.90.

7.92   Find the compound interest on $2,000 invested at the interest rates and for the times given in Prob. 7.90.

7.93   Find the compound interest on (a) $600 for 6 years at 9% compounded quarterly, (b) $1,500 for 1 year at 6.08% compounded daily, (c) $350 for 3 years, 5 months, at $12\frac{1}{4}$% compounded monthly, (d) $10,000 for 10 years at $j_2 = 18\%$.

7.94   In 1492, Queen Isabella sponsored Christopher Columbus's journey by giving him an amount of money equivalent to $10,000. If she had placed this money in a bank account at $j_1 = 2\frac{1}{2}\%$ (interest rates weren't as high as today), how much money (to the nearest million) would be in the account in 1992?

7.95   Carl deposited $500 into a savings account that earns interest at $8\frac{1}{2}$% compounded daily. How much interest will he earn during (a) the first year and (b) the second year?

7.96   Melinda deposited $800 in a savings account. Her deposit earned interest at $j_4 = 6\%$ for 2 years and then at $j_4 = 8\frac{1}{2}\%$ for the next 2 years. How much was in her savings account at the end of 4 years?

7.97   Find the accumulated value of $2,000 for 3 years at 13% compounded

   (a)   Annually   (d)   Monthly

   (b)   Semiannually   (e)   Daily

   (c)   Quarterly

7.98   Find the annual effective rate equivalent to (a) 15% compounded quarterly, (b) $9\frac{1}{2}$% compounded monthly, (c) $11\frac{3}{8}$% compounded semiannually, and (d) 5% compounded daily.

7.99   Steve must borrow $1,500 for 3 years. He is offered the money at (a) $j_{12} = 12\%$, (b) $j_2 = 12\frac{1}{2}\%$, and (c) $13\frac{1}{2}$% simple interest. Which offer should he accept?

7.100   If $j_{12} = 14\frac{1}{8}\%$, $j_4 = 14\frac{1}{4}\%$, and $j_{365} = 14\%$, which rate gives you the best and which gives you the worst rate of return on your investment?

7.101   Compute the discount factor for each part in Prob. 7.90.

7.102   Find the present value of (a) $2,000 due in 3 years if money is worth $j_{12} = 12\%$, (b) $900 due in 2 years if money is worth $j_4 = 9\frac{3}{4}\%$, and (c) $1,500 with interest at $j_2 = 13\%$ due in 2 years if money is worth $j_1 = 15\%$.

7.103   On his 18th birthday, Bruce received $2,000 as a result of a deposit his parents made on the day he was born. How much was originally deposited if the deposit earned interest at (a) 7% compounded semiannually and (b) 12% compounded annually?

7.104   Find the compound discount if $1,200 due in 3 years with interest at $16\frac{1}{4}\%$ compounded monthly is discounted at a nominal rate of 14% compounded

    (a)   Annually   (d)   Monthly

    (b)   Semiannually   (e)   Daily

    (c)   Quarterly

7.105   A note for $2,500 dated June 1, 19X4, compound interest at $j_2 = 15\%$, is due in 5 years. On November 1, 19X5, the holder of the note cashed the note at a bank that discounts notes at 13% compounded monthly. Find the (a) proceeds and (b) compound discount.

Answers to Supplementary Problems

7.57   (a) $41.25, (b) $825, (c) $64.92

7.58   (a) $43.50, (b) $45.50, (c) $11.51

7.59   (a) $42.90, (b) $44.88, (c) $11.35

7.60   (a) 69 days, (b) 113 days, (c) 236 days, (d) 194 days

7.61   (a) 68 days, (b) 111 days, (c) 231 days, (d) 190 days

7.62   (a) November 15, (b) February 6, (c) November 3, (d) September 5, 19X4

7.63   (a) $26.07, $25.71, $25.69, $25.34

    (b) $343.54, $338.84, $336.46, $331.85

7.64   (a) $88.50, (b) $33.58, (c) $101.53

7.65   (a) $87.29, (b) $33.12, (c) $100.14

7.66   (a) $2,582.64, (b) $1,256, (c) $10,233.33

7.67   (a) $2,569.86, (b) $1,247.34, (c) $10,197.26

7.68   (a) 12%, (b) 14.29%, (c) 5%

7.69   (a) $15\frac{1}{4}\%$, (b) $12\frac{1}{2}\%$

7.70   11%

7.71   (*a*) 150 days, (*b*) 974 days

7.72   (*a*) $600, (*b*) $1,000, (*c*) $850

7.73   (*a*) $571.53, (*b*) $1,447.89

7.74   (*a*) $571.91, (*b*) $1,448.58

7.75   (*a*) $P = \$780$, $I = \$76.40$; (*b*) $P = \$10,000$, $I = \$1,748.96$; (*c*) $P = \$1,800$, $I = \$31.25$

7.76 $I = \$208.33$, $P = \$91.67$

7.77   (*a*) Robert Gilbert, (*b*) $1,500, (*c*) February 3, 19X6, (*d*) Jennifer Brown, (*e*) $1,500

7.78   (*a*) Feb. 3, $765.47; (*b*) Oct. 16, $2,116.67; (*c*) Aug. 12, $5,524.43

7.79 $1,455

7.80   18.56%

7.81 $D = \$26.25$, $P = \$1,473.75$

7.82   (*a*) Oct. 31, $t = 24$ days; (*b*) Apr. 4, $t = 34$ days; (*c*) June 24, 19X5, $t = 115$ days

7.83   (*a*) $2,945.33, (*b*) $1,218.90, (*c*) $498.46, (*d*) $3,967.89

7.84   (*a*) $1,701, (*b*) $583.50

7.85   (*a*) $842.84, (*b*) $1,247.56, (*c*) $2,168.07

7.86 $100

7.87 $2,903.23

7.88 $760

7.89   (*a*)

End of Period	Interest Due	Accumulated Value (S)
1	$2,000.00 × 0.04 = $ 80.00	$2,080.00
2	$2,080.00 × 0.04 = $ 83.20	$2,163.20
3	$2,163.20 × 0.04 = $ 86.53	$2,249.73
4	$2,249.73 × 0.04 = $ 89.99	$2,339.72
	Total = $339.72	

(*b*) $339.72

7.90   (*a*) $i = 0.0275$, $n = 6$; (*b*) $i = 0.02$, $n = 60$; (*c*) $i = 0.13138$, $n = 3$; (*d*) $i = 0.05/365 = 0.00013699$, $n = 730$; (*e*) $i = 0.053125$, $n = 5$

7.91   (*a*) 1.1767684, (*b*) 3.2810308, (*c*) 1.4481898, (*d*) 1.1051632 $\left[\text{from } \left(1 + \dfrac{0.05}{365}\right)^{730}\right]$, (*e*) 1.2953872

7.92   (*a*) $353.54, (*b*) $4,562.06, (*c*) $896.38, (*d*) $210.33, (*e*) $590.77

7.93   (a) \$423.46, (b) \$94.02, (c) \$180.78, (d) \$46,044.11

7.94   \$2,301,000,000

7.95   (a) \$44.35, (b) \$48.29

7.96   \$1,066.29

7.97   (a) \$2,885.79, (b) \$2,918.28, (c) \$2,935.69, (d) \$2,947.77, (e) \$2,953.76

7.98   (a) 15.87%, (b) 9.92%, (c) 11.70%, (d) 5.13%

7.99   (c)

7.100 Best is $j_{12} = 14\frac{1}{8}\%$; worst is $j_{365} = 14\%$

7.101 (a) 0.8497849, (b) 0.3047823, (c) 0.6905172, (d) 0.9048436, (e) 0.7719699

7.102 (a) \$1,397.85, (b) \$742.29, (c) \$1,459.13

7.103 (a) \$579.67, (b) \$260.08

7.104 (a) \$633, (b) \$649.80, (c) \$658.68, (d) \$664.79, (e) \$667.80

7.105 (a) \$3,241.93, (b) \$1,910.65

Chapter 8

Annuities and Their Applications

8.1 ANNUITIES

An *annuity* is a sequence of payments, usually equal, made at equal intervals of time. Premiums on insurance, mortgage payments, payments of rent, payments on installment purchases, bond interest payments, pension and retirement plan payments are just a few examples of annuities.

The time between successive payments of an annuity is called the *payment interval*. The time from the beginning of the first payment interval to the end of the last payment interval is called the *term* of an annuity. When the term of an annuity is fixed, the annuity is called an *annuity certain*. When the term of an annuity depends on some uncertain event, the annuity is called *a contingent annuity*. In this text the word annuity will refer to an annuity certain.

When the payment interval and interest conversion period coincide, the annuity is called a *simple annuity*; otherwise it is a *general annuity*. Only simple annuities are discussed in this text.

For calculating annuity, the following notations are used:

R = the periodic payment of the annuity
n = the number of payments
i = the interest rate per conversion period
S = the *accumulated value*, or the *amount of an annuity*, which is the value of all the payments at the end of the term of the annuity
A = the *discounted value*, or the *present value of an annuity*, which is the value of all the payments at the beginning of the term of an annuity.

When the payments are made at the end of each payment interval, the annuity is called an *ordinary annuity* (Fig. 8-1).

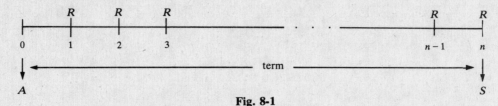

Fig. 8-1

The formula for the accumulated value (S) of an ordinary simple annuity is

$$S = Rs_{\overline{n}|i} = R\left[\frac{(1+i)^n - 1}{i}\right]$$

Accumulated value = payment × accumulation factor

The factor $s_{\overline{n}|i}$ (read "*s* angle *n* at *i*") is the accumulated value of an ordinary simple annuity having n payments of \$1 each; it is called the *accumulated value of \$1 per period*, or the *accumulation factor for n payments*.

EXAMPLE 1

(*a*) Compute the accumulation factor $s_{\overline{n}|i}$ when $i = 4.25\%$ and $n = 18$.

$$s_{\overline{n}|i} = \frac{(1+i)^n - 1}{i}$$

$$= \frac{(1+0.0425)^{18} - 1}{0.0425} = 26.24203$$

On the calculator:

Enter $(1+i)$	1.0425
Press $\boxed{y^x}$	$\boxed{y^x}$
Enter n	18
Press $\boxed{=}$	$\boxed{=}$
Press $\boxed{-}$	$\boxed{-}$
Enter 1	1
Press $\boxed{=}$	$\boxed{=}$
Press $\boxed{\div}$	$\boxed{\div}$
Enter i	0.0425
Press $\boxed{=}$	$\boxed{=}$
Read $s_{\overline{n}|i}$	26.24203

(b) Find the accumulated value of $1,000 invested at the end of each quarter for 3 years at $6\frac{1}{2}\%$ compounded quarterly.

$$R = \$1,000 \qquad i = \frac{0.065}{4} = 0.01625 \qquad n = 3 \times 4 = 12$$

(See Chap. 7, Examples 9 and 10 for explanations of i and n calculations.)

$$S = Rs_{\overline{n}|i} = R\left[\frac{(1+i)^n - 1}{i}\right] = \$1,000\left[\frac{(1+0.01625)^{12} - 1}{0.01625}\right] = \$13,132.77$$

The formula for the discounted (or present) value (A) of an ordinary simple annuity is

$$A = Ra_{\overline{n}|i} = R\left[1 - \frac{1}{(1+i)^n}\bigg/ i\right]$$

Discounted value = payment $\times$ discount factor

The factor $a_{\overline{n}|i}$ (read "a angle n at i") is called the *discount factor for n payments*.

EXAMPLE 2

(a) Compute the discount factor $a_{\overline{n}|i}$ when $i = 4\frac{1}{2}\%$ and $n = 8$.

$$a_{\overline{n}|i} = \frac{1 - \dfrac{1}{(1+i)^n}}{i} = \frac{1 - \dfrac{1}{(1+0.045)^8}}{0.045} = 6.5958862$$

On the calculator:

Enter $(1+i)$	1.045
Press $\boxed{y^x}$	$\boxed{y^x}$
Enter n	8
Press $\boxed{=}$	$\boxed{=}$
Press $\boxed{\dfrac{1}{x}}$	$\boxed{\dfrac{1}{x}}$
Press $\boxed{+/-}$	$\boxed{+/-}$
Press $\boxed{+}$	$\boxed{+}$
Enter 1	1
Press $\boxed{=}$	$\boxed{=}$
Press $\boxed{\div}$	$\boxed{\div}$
Enter i	0.045
Press $\boxed{=}$	$\boxed{=}$
Read $a_{\overline{n}|i}$	6.5958862

*The $\boxed{+/-}$ key changes the sign of the number already displayed on the calculator.

(b) How much money deposited now will provide payments of \$2,000 at the end of each half-year for 10 years if interest is 11% compounded semiannually?

$$R = \$2,000 \qquad i = \frac{0.11}{2} = 0.055 \qquad n = 10 \times 2 = 20$$

$$A = Ra_{\overline{n}|i} = R \left[\frac{1 - \dfrac{1}{(1+i)^n}}{i} \right]$$

$$= \$2,000 \left[\frac{1 - \dfrac{1}{(1+0.055)^{20}}}{0.055} \right] = \$2,000(11.950383) = \$23,900.77$$

If we solve the preceding formulas for R, we obtain

$$R = \frac{S}{s_{\overline{n}|i}}$$

and

$$R = \frac{A}{a_{\overline{n}|i}}$$

We can now calculate the periodic payment of an ordinary simple annuity if we know either its accumulated value (S) or its discounted value (A).

EXAMPLE 3

(a) If you want to accumulate \$500,000 in 30 years, how much money should you deposit at the end of each quarter in a retirement plan that earns interest at 10% compounded quarterly?

$$S = \$500,000 \qquad i = \frac{0.10}{4} = 0.025 \qquad n = 30 \times 4 = 120$$

$$R = \frac{S}{s_{\overline{n}|i}} \qquad \qquad \left\{ \begin{aligned} s_{\overline{n}|i} &= \frac{(1+i)^n - 1}{i} \\ \end{aligned} \right.$$

$$= \frac{\$500,000}{s_{\overline{120}|0.025}} \qquad \qquad = \frac{(1+0.025)^{120} - 1}{0.025}$$

$$= \frac{\$500,000}{734.32605}$$

$$= \$680.90$$

(b) A home computer with a price tag of \$1,500 may be purchased for \$300 down and the balance may be paid in equal monthly installments for 1 year. What is the monthly installment if interest is charged at 18% compounded monthly?

$$A = \$1,500 - \$300 = \$1,200 \qquad i = 0.18/12 = 0.015 \qquad n = 12$$

$$R = \frac{A}{a_{\overline{n}|i}} \qquad \qquad \left\{ \begin{aligned} a_{\overline{n}|i} &= \frac{1 - \dfrac{1}{(1+i)^n}}{i} \\ \end{aligned} \right.$$

$$= \frac{\$1,200}{a_{\overline{12}|0.015}} \qquad \qquad = \frac{1 - \dfrac{1}{(1+0.015)^{12}}}{0.015}$$

$$= \frac{\$1,200}{10.907505}$$

$$= \$110.02$$

An *annuity due* is an annuity whose payments are due at the *beginning* of each payment interval (Fig. 8-2). If we compare Figs. 8-1 and 8-2, we see that an annuity due is simply a "slipped" ordinary annuity. To find the accumulated value (S) and the discounted value (A) of an annuity due, we must therefore modify the formulas as follows:

$$S = Rs_{\overline{n}|i}(1+i)$$
$$A = Ra_{\overline{n}|i}(1+i)$$

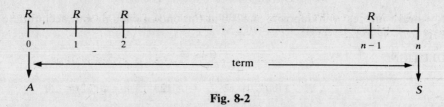

Fig. 8-2

SOLVED PROBLEMS

8.1   Compute the accumulation factor

$$s_{\overline{n}|i} = \frac{(1+i)^n - 1}{i}$$

for (a) $i = 0.02$, $n = 20$; (b) $i = 0.055$, $n = 12$; (c) $i = 0.0125$, $n = 120$.

SOLUTION

The numerical values of the accumulation factors are obtained on a calculator as follows.

	(a)	(b)	(c)
Enter $(1+i)$	1.02	1.055	1.0125
Press y^x	y^x	y^x	y^x
Enter n	20	12	120
Press $=$	$=$	$=$	$=$
Press $-$	$-$	$-$	$-$
Enter 1	1	1	1
Press $=$	$=$	$=$	$=$
Press $\div$	$\div$	$\div$	$\div$
Enter i	0.02	0.055	0.0125
Press $=$	$=$	$=$	$=$
Read $s_{\overline{n}|i}$	24.29737	16.385591	275.21706

8.2   Find the accumulated value of $500 invested at the end of each quarter-year for 5 years at 8% compounded quarterly.

SOLUTION

$$R = \$500 \qquad i = \frac{0.08}{4} = 0.02 \qquad n = 5(4) = 20$$

Note that the accumulation factor is the same as the one in Prob. 8.1(a).

$$S = R s_{\overline{n}|i}$$
$$= \$500 s_{\overline{20}|0.02} = \$500 \times 24.29737 = \$12,148.69$$

8.3   Find the amount of $1,200 invested at the end of each half-year for 6 years at $j_2 = 11\%$.

SOLUTION

$$R = \$1,200 \qquad i = \frac{0.11}{2} = 0.055 \qquad n = 6(2) = 12$$

Note that the accumulation factor is the same as the one in Prob. 8.1(b).

$$S = R s_{\overline{n}|i}$$
$$= \$1,200 s_{\overline{12}|0.055} = \$1,200 \times 16.385591 = \$19,662.71$$

8.4   How much interest will deposits of \$100 at the end of each month accumulate by the end of 10 years at $j_{12} = 15\%$?

SOLUTION

$$R = \$100 \qquad i = \frac{0.15}{12} = 0.0125 \qquad n = 10(12) = 120$$

Note that the accumulation factor is the same as the one in Prob. 8.1(*c*).

$$S = Rs_{\overline{n}|i}$$
$$= \$100 s_{\overline{120}|0.0125} = \$100 \times 275.21706 = \$27,521.71$$

The face value of the deposits is:

$$120 \times \$100 = \$12,000$$

The interest is:

$$\$27,521.71 - \$12,000 = \$15,521.71$$

8.5   Jeff deposits \$150 every 3 months into a savings account that pays interest at $j_4 = 12\%$. If he made his first deposit on February 1, 19X2, find his total savings just after he makes a deposit on May 1, 19X6.

SOLUTION

We arrange the data as in Fig. 8-3, noting that the ordinary annuity starts one interest period before the first deposit, that is, on November 1, 19X1.

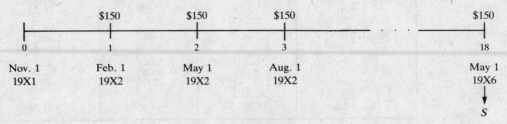

Fig. 8-3

We want to calculate the accumulated value (*S*) of 18 deposits of \$150 each at $j_4 = 12\%$.

$$S = Rs_{\overline{n}|i}$$
$$= \$150 s_{\overline{18}|0.03} = \$150 \left[\frac{(1.03)^{18} - 1}{0.03} \right] = \$150 \times 23.414435 = \$3,512.17$$

8.6   Andrea is repaying a debt with payments of \$300 a month. If she misses her payments for April, May, and June, what payment will be required in July to put her back on schedule, if interest is at $j_{12} = 18\%$?

SOLUTION

Andrea will have to pay three overdue payments with interest together with the July payment. We need to determine the accumulated value of these payments.

$$R = \$300 \qquad i = \frac{0.18}{12} = 0.015 \qquad n = 4 \text{ (for 3 missed payments plus July)}$$

$$S = Rs_{\overline{n}|i}$$

$$= \$300 s_{\overline{4}|0.015} = \$300 \left[\frac{(1.015)^4 - 1}{0.015} \right] = \$1,227.27$$

8.7   Compute the discount factor

$$a_{\overline{n}|i} = \frac{1 - \dfrac{1}{(1+i)^n}}{i}$$

when (a) $i = 0.0075$ and $n = 60$; (b) $i = 0.128$ and $n = 5$; (c) $i = 0.035$ and $n = 20$.

SOLUTION

The numerical values of the discount factors are obtained on a calculator as follows.

	(a)	(b)	(c)
Enter $(1+i)$	1.0075	1.128	1.035
Press $\boxed{y^x}$	$\boxed{y^x}$	$\boxed{y^x}$	$\boxed{y^x}$
Enter n	60	5	20
Press $\boxed{=}$	$\boxed{=}$	$\boxed{=}$	$\boxed{=}$
Press $\boxed{\frac{1}{x}}$	$\boxed{\frac{1}{x}}$	$\boxed{\frac{1}{x}}$	$\boxed{\frac{1}{x}}$
Press $\boxed{+/-}$	$\boxed{+/-}$	$\boxed{+/-}$	$\boxed{+/-}$
Press $\boxed{+}$	$\boxed{+}$	$\boxed{+}$	$\boxed{+}$
Enter 1	1	1	1
Press $\boxed{=}$	$\boxed{=}$	$\boxed{=}$	$\boxed{=}$
Press $\boxed{\div}$	$\boxed{\div}$	$\boxed{\div}$	$\boxed{\div}$
Enter i	0.0075	0.128	0.035
Press $\boxed{=}$	$\boxed{=}$	$\boxed{=}$	$\boxed{=}$
Read $a_{\overline{n}|i}$	48.173374	3.534463	14.212403

8.8   Find the present value of an annuity of $350 at the end of each month for 5 years at 9% compounded monthly.

SOLUTION

$$R = \$350 \qquad i = \frac{0.09}{12} = 0.0075 \qquad n = 5(12) = 60$$

Note that the discount factor is the same as the one in Prob. 8.7(a).

$$A = Ra_{\overline{n}|i}$$
$$= \$350 a_{\overline{60}|0.0075} = \$350 \times 48.173374 = \$16,860.68$$

8.9   How much money deposited now would provide payments of $10,000 at the end of each year for 5 years if interest is at 12.8% compounded annually?

SOLUTION

$$R = \$10,000 \qquad i = 0.128 \qquad n = 5(1) = 5$$

Note that the discount factor is the same as the one in Prob. 8.7(b).

$$A = Ra_{\overline{n}|i}$$
$$= \$10,000 a_{\overline{5}|0.128} = \$10,000 \times 3.534463 = \$35,344.63$$

8.10   A contract that calls for 20 payments of $800 at the end of each 3 months is sold to a buyer at a price that will yield the buyer 14% compounded quarterly. What does the buyer pay?

SOLUTION

The price to yield $j_4 = 14\%$ is equal to the discounted value (A) of this ordinary annuity.

$$R = \$800 \qquad i = \frac{0.14}{4} = 0.035 \qquad n = 20$$

Note that the discount factor is the same as the one in Prob. 8.7(c).

$$A = Ra_{\overline{n}|i}$$
$$= \$800 a_{\overline{20}|0.035} = \$800 \times 14.212403 = \$11,369.92$$

8.11   A refrigerator can be bought for \$150 down and \$50 a month for 18 months. What is the cash price of the refrigerator if the interest on the installment plan is 15% compounded monthly?

SOLUTION

Letting C denote the cash price, we arrange the data as in Fig. 8-4. The cash price of the refrigerator is the down payment plus the discounted value of the ordinary simple annuity. Thus $C = \$150 + A$.

$$R = \$50 \qquad i = \frac{0.15}{12} = 0.0125 \qquad n = 18$$

$$C = \$150 + A$$
$$= \$150 + \$50 a_{\overline{18}|0.0125}$$
$$= \$150 + \$50 \left[\frac{1 - \dfrac{1}{(1.0125)^{18}}}{0.0125} \right] = \$150 + \$801.48 = \$951.48$$

```
   $150      $50       $50                              $50

    ├─────────┼─────────┼──────  ·  ·  ·  ──────────────┤
    0         1         2                               18
    │
    ↓
    C
```

Fig. 8-4

8.12   How much money should you deposit at the end of each year in a retirement fund that earns interest at $11\frac{1}{4}\%$ compounded annually if you want to accumulate \$150,000 in 20 years?

SOLUTION

$$S = \$150,000 \qquad i = 0.1125 \qquad n = 20$$

$$R = \frac{S}{s_{\overline{n}|i}}$$

$$= \frac{\$150,000}{s_{\overline{20}|0.1125}} = \frac{\$150,000}{66.074269} = \$2270.17$$

8.13   A company estimates that its computer equipment will need replacement 5 years fron now at a cost of \$90,000. How much must be set aside each month to provide that money if the company can earn interest at 12% compounded monthly?

SOLUTION

$$S = \$90,000 \qquad i = \frac{0.12}{12} = 0.01 \qquad n = 5(12) = 60$$

$$R = \frac{S}{s_{\overline{n}|i}}$$

$$= \frac{\$90,000}{s_{\overline{60}|0.01}} = \frac{\$90,000}{81.66967} = \$1,102.00$$

8.14 A car selling for $7,800 may be purchased for $1,800 down and the balance in equal monthly payments for 2 years. Find (a) the monthly payment and (b) the total interest paid if the interest is charged at 15% compounded monthly.

SOLUTION

Present value of loan:

$$A = \$7,800 - \$1,800 = \$6,000$$

$$i = \frac{0.15}{12} = 0.0125 \qquad n = 2(12) = 24$$

(a)

$$R = \frac{A}{a_{\overline{n}|i}}$$

$$= \frac{\$6,000}{a_{\overline{24}|0.0125}} = \frac{\$6,000}{20.624235} = \$290.92$$

(b) Total interest:

$$(24 \times \$290.92) - \$6,000 = \$982.08$$

8.15 Find the monthly payment in Prob. 8.14 if the down payment is $800, the term of loan is 3 years, and interest is charged at 18% compounded monthly.

SOLUTION

$$A = \$7,800 - \$800 = \$7,000$$

$$i = \frac{0.18}{12} = 0.015 \qquad n = 3(12) = 36$$

$$R = \frac{A}{a_{\overline{n}|i}}$$

$$= \frac{\$7,000}{a_{\overline{36}|0.015}} = \frac{\$7,000}{27.660684} = \$253.07$$

8.16 Upon her husband's death, a widow is the beneficiary of her husband's $60,000 life insurance policy. One option available to her is a monthly annuity over a 10-year period. If the insurance company pays interest at 9% compounded monthly, what payments at the end of each month will the widow receive?

SOLUTION

$$A = \$60,000 \qquad i = \frac{0.09}{12} = 0.0075 \qquad n = 10(12) = 120$$

$$R = \frac{A}{a_{\overline{n}|i}}$$

$$= \frac{\$60,000}{a_{\overline{120}|0.0075}} = \frac{\$60,000}{78.941693} = \$760.05$$

8.17 At age 65 Mr. Smith takes his life savings of $100,000 and buys a 15-year annuity with monthly payments. Find the size of these payments at $j_{12} = 12\%$.

SOLUTION

$$A = \$100,000 \qquad i = \frac{0.12}{12} = 0.01 \qquad n = 15(12) = 180$$

$$R = \frac{A}{a_{\overline{n}|i}}$$

$$= \frac{\$100,000}{a_{\overline{180}|0.01}} = \frac{\$100,000}{83.321664} = \$1,200.17$$

8.18 A couple is trying to decide which of two houses to buy. The smaller house would require a $50,000 mortgage, the larger house a $60,000 mortgage. If the rate on the loan is 15% compounded monthly and the term is 29 years, what would be the difference in the monthly payments?

SOLUTION

For the smaller house:

$$A = \$50,000 \qquad i = \frac{0.15}{12} = 0.0125 \qquad n = 29(12) = 348$$

$$R = \frac{A}{a_{\overline{n}|i}}$$

$$= \frac{\$50,000}{a_{\overline{348}|0.0125}} = \frac{\$50,000}{78.939236} = \$633.40$$

For the larger house:

$$A = \$60,000 \qquad i = \frac{0.15}{12} = 0.0125 \qquad n = 29(12) = 348$$

$$R = \frac{A}{a_{\overline{n}|i}}$$

$$= \frac{\$60,000}{a_{\overline{348}|0.0125}} = \frac{\$60,000}{78.939236} = \$760.08$$

The difference in the monthly payment is $760.08 − $633.40 = $126.68.

8.19 Deposits of $1,000 are made at the beginning of each year for 5 years into an account paying interest at 11.058% effective. How much is in the account at the end of 5 years?

SOLUTION

We arrange the data as in Fig. 8-5. Note that this is an annuity due.

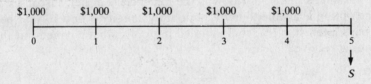

Fig. 8-5

$$R = \$1,000 \qquad i = 0.11058 \qquad n = 5$$

We calculate the accumulated value (S) of an annuity due:

$$S = R s_{\overline{n}|i}(1 + i)$$
$$= \$1,000 s_{\overline{5}|0.11058}(1.11058)$$
$$= \$1,000(6.2349897)(1.11058) = \$6924.45$$

8.20 The monthly rent for a three-bedroom apartment is $450, payable at the beginning of each month. If money is worth $j_{12} = 18\%$, what is the equivalent yearly rental payable in advance?

SOLUTION

We arrange the data as in Fig. 8-6.

$$R = \$450 \qquad i = \frac{0.18}{12} = 0.015 \qquad n = 12$$

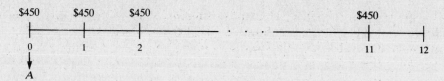

Fig. 8-6

We calculate the discounted value (A) of an annuity due:

$$A = Ra_{\overline{n}|i}(1 + i)$$
$$= \$450a_{\overline{12}|0.015}(1.015) = \$450(10.907505)(1.015) = \$4,982$$

8.21 Using the data given in Prob. 8.20, find the cash equivalent of 5 years of rent if money is worth $j_{12} = 12\%$.

SOLUTION

$$R = \$450 \qquad i = \frac{0.12}{12} = 0.01 \qquad n = 5(12) = 60$$

$$A = Ra_{\overline{n}|i}(1 + i)$$
$$= \$450a_{\overline{60}|0.01}(1.01) = \$450(44.955038)(1.01) = \$20,432.06$$

8.22 The premium on a life insurance policy can be paid either yearly or monthly in advance. If the annual premium is $210, what monthly premium would be equivalent at 9% compounded monthly?

SOLUTION

We arrange the data as in Fig. 8-7.

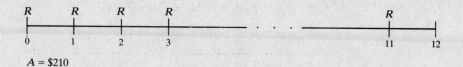

$$A = \$210$$

Fig. 8-7

$$A = \$210 \qquad i = \frac{0.09}{12} = 0.0075 \qquad n = 12$$

$$R = \frac{A}{a_{\overline{n}|i}(1 + i)}$$

$$= \frac{\$210}{a_{\overline{12}|0.0075}(1.0075)} = \frac{\$210}{(11.434913)(1.0075)} = \$18.23$$

8.23 Derive the following formula:

$$S = Rs_{\overline{n}|i} = R\,\frac{(1 + i)^n - 1}{i}$$

SOLUTION

Consider an ordinary simple annuity of n payments of $1 each, as shown in Fig. 8-8.

Let $s_{\overline{n}|i}$ denote the accumulated value of this annuity. To obtain $s_{\overline{n}|i}$, accumulate each $1 payment to the date of the last payment:

$$s_{\overline{n}|i} = 1 + (1 + i)^1 + (1 + i)^2 + \cdots + (1 + i)^{n-1}$$

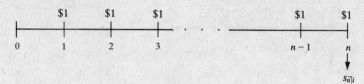

Fig. 8-8

Note that this is the sum of a geometric progression of n terms, with first term 1 and common ratio $(1 + i)$. From algebra, the formula for the sum of a geometric progression is

$$S_n = t_1 \frac{r^n - 1}{r - 1}$$

where S_n = the sum of n terms
   t_1 = the first term
   r = the common ratio

We can substitute the values of $s_{\overline{n}|i}$ into this formula as follows:

Sum of geometric progression: $S_n = s_{\overline{n}|i}$

First term: $t_1 = 1$

Common ratio: $r = (1 + i)$

Thus $$s_{\overline{n}|i} = 1 \left[\frac{(1 + i)^n - 1}{(1 + i) - 1} \right] = \frac{(1 + i)^n - 1}{i}$$

The accumulated value (S) of an ordinary simple annuity of n payments of R dollars each is then

$$S = R s_{\overline{n}|i} = R \frac{(1 + i)^n - 1}{i}$$

8.24   Derive the following formula:

$$A = R \frac{1 - \dfrac{1}{(1 + i)^n}}{i}$$

SOLUTION

The discounted value (or present value) A of an ordinary simple annuity of n payments is the value of all payments at the beginning of the term of the annuity.

From Chap. 7, Sec. 7.6, we know that the formula for discounted or present value is

$$P = S \frac{1}{(1 + i)^n}$$

Since P = present value = A, we may write

$$A = S \frac{1}{(1 + i)^n}$$

Since $$S = R \frac{(1 + i)^n - 1}{i}$$

by substituting the value for S in the above formula, we get

$$A = S \frac{1}{(1 + i)^n}$$

$$= R \left[\frac{(1 + i)^n - 1}{i} \right] \left[\frac{1}{(1 + i)^n} \right] = R \frac{1 - \dfrac{1}{(1 + i)^n}}{i}$$

8.2 AMORTIZATION OF A DEBT

Amortization is a method of payment in which an interest-bearing debt is repaid in equal periodic payments. When a debt is amortized by equal periodic payments, the debt becomes the discounted value (A) or an ordinary annuity. The size of the payment (R) is calculated by using the formula $R = A/a_{\overline{n}|i}$ (see section 8.1). The common practice is to round the payment up to the nearest cent. This avoids the problem of being short on the last payment, which is adjusted downward if necessary.

EXAMPLE 4

Find the monthly payment on a loan of $4,500, to be amortized over 2 years at 21% compounded monthly.

$$A = \$4,500 \qquad i = \frac{0.21}{12} = 0.0175 \qquad n = 2 \times 12 = 24$$

$$
\begin{aligned}
R &= \frac{A}{a_{\overline{n}|i}} \\
&= \frac{\$4,500}{a_{\overline{24}|0.0175}} \\
&= \frac{\$4,500}{19.460686} \\
&= \$231.23543 \cong \$231.24
\end{aligned}
\qquad
\left\{
\begin{aligned}
a_{\overline{n}|i} &= \frac{1 - \dfrac{1}{(1+i)^n}}{i} \\[2mm]
&= \frac{1 - \dfrac{1}{(1+0.0175)^{24}}}{0.0175} \\[2mm]
&= 19.460686
\end{aligned}
\right.
$$

Each payment pays the interest on unpaid balance and also repays a part of the outstanding principal. As time goes on and the outstanding principal is gradually reduced, the amount applied to interest decreases while the amount applied to principal increases. An *amortization schedule* shows the progress of the amortization of a debt.

EXAMPLE 5

For the debt in Example 4, construct an amortization schedule showing the distribution of the payments between interest and principal.

$$A = \$4,500 \qquad i = 0.0175 \qquad n = 24 \qquad R = \$321.24 \text{ (rounded up)}$$

Payment 1:

The interest due at the end of the first month is

$$0.0175 \times \$4,500 = \$78.75$$

Of the first $231.24 payment, $78.75 will be applied toward interest and $152.49 (from $231.24 − $78.75) will go toward repayment of the principal. Thus, the outstanding principal after the first payment will be

$$\$4,500 - \$152.49 = \$4,347.51$$

Payment 2:

The interest due at the end of the second month is calculated on the *outstanding* loan balance:

$$0.0175 \times \$4,347.51 = \$76.08$$

Of the second $231.24 monthly payment, $76.08 will go toward interest and $155.16 (from $231.24 − $76.08) will be applied toward repayment of the principal. The principal outstanding after the second payment will be

$$\$4,347.51 - \$155.16 = \$4,192.35$$

By continuing in this way for 24 payments, we can construct the amortization schedule shown in Table 8-1.

Suppose we want to know the outstanding balance after k number of payments have been made (see Fig. 8-9). Rather than going through the tedious process outlined in Example 5 until we reach payment number k, we can see from Fig. 8-9 that the outstanding principal is the difference between the accumulated values of the debt (A) and the payments (R) already made, or

$$P_k = A(1+i)^k - Rs_{\overline{k}|i}$$

where P_k = outstanding principal after k payment
        k = number of payments made

Table 8-1

Payment		Applied to		
Number	Amount	Interest	Principal	Outstanding Principal
Start				$4,500.00
1	$ 231.24	$ 78.75	$ 152.49	4,347.51
2	231.24	76.08	155.16	4,192.35
3	231.24	73.37	157.87	4,034.48
4	231.24	70.60	160.64	3,873.84
5	231.24	67.79	163.45	3,710.39
6	231.24	64.93	166.31	3,544.08
7	231.24	62.02	169.22	3,374.86
8	231.24	59.06	172.18	3,202.68
9	231.24	56.05	175.19	3,027.49
10	231.24	52.98	178.26	2,849.23
11	231.24	49.86	181.38	2,667.85
12	231.24	46.69	184.55	2,483.30
13	231.24	43.46	187.78	2,295.52
14	231.24	40.17	191.07	2,104.45
15	231.24	36.83	194.41	1,910.04
16	231.24	33.43	197.81	1,712.23
17	231.24	29.96	201.28	1,510.95
18	231.24	26.44	204.80	1,306.15
19	231.24	22.86	208.38	1,097.77
20	231.24	19.21	212.03	885.74
21	231.24	15.50	215.74	670.00
22	231.24	11.73	219.51	450.49
23	231.24	7.88	223.36	227.13
24	231.13*	4.00**	227.13	
Total	$5,549.65	$1,049.65	$4,500.00	

*Adjusted down as follows: $231.23543/mo × 24 mo = $5,549.65 total

$5549.65 − ($231.24 × 23) = $231.13

**Adjusted up as follows: $5,549.65 − $4,500 = $1,049.65 total interest

$1,049.65 − $1,045.65 (the sum of 23 interest payments) = $4

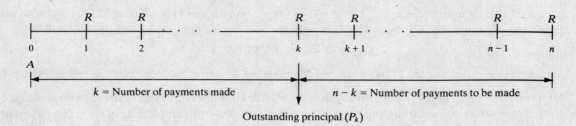

Fig. 8-9

EXAMPLE 6

Calculate the outstanding principal at the end of the first year (i.e., after 12 payments) on the loan in Example 4.

$$A = \$4{,}500 \qquad i = 0.0175 \qquad k = 12 \qquad R = \$231.24$$

$$
\begin{aligned}
P_k &= A(1+i)^k - Rs_{\overline{k}|i} \\
&= \$4{,}500(1.0175)^{12} - \$231.24 s_{\overline{12}|0.0175} \\
&= \$4{,}500(1.2314393) - \$231.24(13.225104) \longleftarrow \\
&= \$5{,}541.4769 - \$3{,}058.173 \\
&= \$2{,}483.3039 \cong \$2{,}483.30
\end{aligned}
$$

$$
\begin{aligned}
s_{\overline{k}|i} &= \frac{(1+i)^k - 1}{i} \\
&= \frac{(1.0175)^{12} - 1}{0.0175} \\
&= 13.225104
\end{aligned}
$$

If all the payments, including the last one, are equal, the outstanding principal is simply the discounted value of $(n - k)$, the payments yet to be made:

$$P_k = Ra_{\overline{n-k}|i}$$

EXAMPLE 7

Linda Klein is repaying a loan in 18 monthly payments of \$106.35. Interest on the loan is 15% compounded monthly. After making the tenth payment, Linda wants to pay the remainder of the loan in full. Find (*a*) the outstanding principal after the tenth payment and (*b*) the unearned interest charge.

(*a*) Outstanding principal after tenth payment:

$$R = \$106.35 \qquad n - k = 18 - 10 = 8 \qquad i = \frac{0.15}{12} = 0.0125$$

$$
\begin{aligned}
P_k &= Ra_{\overline{n-k}|i} \\
&= \$106.35 a_{\overline{8}|0.0125} \\
&= \$106.35(7.5681242) \\
&= \$804.87
\end{aligned}
$$

$$
\begin{aligned}
a_{\overline{n-k}|i} &= \frac{1 - \dfrac{1}{(1+i)^{n-k}}}{i} \\
&= \frac{1 - \dfrac{1}{(1.0125)^8}}{0.0125} \\
&= 7.5681242
\end{aligned}
$$

(*b*) Unearned interest charge:

Total of remaining payments ($8 \times \$106.35$)	\$850.80
Less outstanding principal	804.87
Unearned interest charge	\$ 45.93

Annual percentage rate tables (see Table 8-2), prepared by the Federal Reserve Board and contained in Regulation Z, are used to determine the annual percentage rate (APR) of credit plans. APR is the true or effective annual rate of interest. The tables list the finance charge (FC) per \$100 of the amount financed (usually abbreviated as FC/100). To calculate the FC/100, let

$$
\begin{aligned}
FC &= \text{finance charge (interest)} \\
B &= \text{amount financed (principal)} \\
\frac{B}{100} &= \text{amount financed in hundreds}
\end{aligned}
$$

Then

$$\frac{FC}{100} = FC \div \frac{B}{100}$$

$$= FC \times \frac{100}{B} = \frac{FC(100)}{B}$$

Table 8-2   Annual Percentage Rate Table For Monthly Payment Plans*

Number of Payments	Annual Percentage Rate							
	10.00%	10.25%	10.50%	10.75%	11.00%	11.25%	11.50%	11.75%
	(Finance charge per $100 of amount financed)							
1	0.83	0.85	0.87	0.90	0.92	0.94	0.96	0.98
2	1.25	1.28	1.31	1.35	1.38	1.41	1.44	1.47
3	1.67	1.71	1.76	1.80	1.84	1.88	1.92	1.96
4	2.09	2.14	2.20	2.25	2.30	2.35	2.41	2.46
5	2.51	2.58	2.64	2.70	2.77	2.83	2.89	2.96
6	2.94	3.01	3.08	3.16	3.23	3.31	3.38	3.45
7	3.36	3.45	3.53	3.62	3.70	3.78	3.87	3.95
8	3.79	3.88	3.98	4.07	4.17	4.26	4.36	4.46
9	4.21	4.32	4.43	4.53	4.64	4.75	4.85	4.96
10	4.64	4.76	4.88	4.99	5.11	5.23	5.35	5.46
11	5.07	5.20	5.33	5.45	5.58	5.71	5.84	5.97
12	5.50	5.64	5.78	5.92	6.06	6.20	6.34	6.48
13	5.93	6.08	6.23	6.38	6.53	6.68	6.84	6.99
14	6.36	6.52	6.69	6.85	7.01	7.17	7.34	7.50
15	6.80	6.97	7.14	7.32	7.49	7.66	7.84	8.01
16	7.23	7.41	7.60	7.78	7.97	8.15	8.34	8.53
17	7.67	7.86	8.06	8.25	8.45	8.65	8.84	9.04
18	8.10	8.31	8.52	8.73	8.93	9.14	9.35	9.56
19	8.54	8.76	8.98	9.20	9.42	9.64	9.86	10.08
20	9.89	9.21	9.44	9.67	9.90	10.13	10.37	10.60
21	9.42	9.66	9.90	10.15	10.39	10.63	10.88	11.12
22	9.86	10.12	10.37	10.62	10.88	11.13	11.39	11.64
23	10.30	10.57	10.84	11.10	11.37	11.63	11.90	12.17
24	10.75	11.02	11.30	11.58	11.86	12.14	12.42	12.70
25	11.19	11.48	11.77	12.06	12.35	12.64	12.93	13.22
26	11.64	11.94	12.24	12.54	12.85	13.15	13.45	13.75
27	12.09	12.40	12.71	13.03	13.34	13.66	13.97	14.29
28	12.53	12.86	13.18	13.51	13.84	14.16	14.49	14.82
29	12.98	13.32	13.66	14.00	14.33	14.67	15.01	15.35
30	13.43	13.78	14.13	14.48	14.83	15.19	15.54	15.89
31	13.89	14.25	14.61	14.97	15.33	15.70	16.06	16.43
32	14.34	14.71	15.09	15.46	15.84	16.21	16.59	16.97
33	14.79	15.18	15.57	15.95	16.34	16.73	17.12	17.51
34	15.25	15.65	16.05	16.44	16.85	17.25	17.65	18.05
35	15.70	16.11	16.53	16.94	17.35	17.77	18.18	18.60
36	16.16	16.58	17.01	17.43	17.86	18.29	18.71	19.14
37	16.62	17.06	17.49	17.93	18.37	18.81	19.25	19.69
38	17.08	17.53	17.98	18.43	18.88	19.33	19.78	20.24
39	17.54	18.00	18.46	18.93	19.39	19.86	20.32	20.79
40	18.00	18.48	18.95	19.43	19.90	20.38	20.86	21.34
41	18.47	18.95	19.44	19.63	20.42	20.91	21.40	21.89
42	18.93	19.43	19.93	20.43	20.93	21.44	21.94	22.45
43	19.40	19.91	20.42	20.95	21.45	21.97	22.49	23.01
44	19.86	20.39	20.91	21.44	21.97	22.50	23.03	23.57
45	20.33	20.87	21.41	21.95	22.49	23.03	23.58	24.12
46	20.80	21.35	21.90	22.46	23.01	23.57	24.13	24.69
47	21.27	21.83	22.40	22.97	23.53	24.10	24.68	25.25
48	21.74	22.32	22.90	23.48	24.06	24.64	25.23	25.81
49	22.21	22.80	23.39	23.99	24.58	25.18	25.78	26.38
50	22.69	23.29	23.89	24.50	25.11	25.72	26.33	26.95
51	23.16	23.78	24.40	25.02	25.64	26.26	26.89	27.52
52	23.64	24.27	24.90	25.53	26.17	26.81	27.45	28.09
53	24.11	24.76	25.40	26.05	26.70	27.35	28.00	28.66
54	24.59	25.25	25.91	26.57	27.23	27.90	28.56	29.23
55	25.07	25.74	26.41	27.09	27.77	28.44	29.13	29.81
56	25.55	26.23	26.92	27.61	28.30	28.99	29.69	30.39
57	26.03	26.73	27.43	28.13	28.84	29.54	30.25	30.97
58	26.51	27.23	27.94	28.66	29.37	30.10	30.82	31.55
59	27.00	27.72	28.45	29.18	29.91	30.65	31.39	32.13
60	27.48	28.22	28.96	29.71	30.45	31.20	31.96	32.71

*Truth in Lending, Regulation Z, Annual Percentage Rate Tables, vol. 1, *Board of Governors of the Federal Reserve System, Washington, DC.*

Table 8-2 (*cont.*)   197

Number of Payments	Annual Percentage Rate							
	12.00%	12.25%	12.50%	12.75%	13.00%	13.25%	13.50%	13.75%
	(Finance charge per $100 of amount financed)							
1	1.00	1.02	1.04	1.06	1.08	1.10	1.12	1.15
2	1.50	1.53	1.57	1.60	1.63	1.66	1.69	1.72
3	2.01	2.05	2.09	2.13	2.17	2.22	2.26	2.30
4	2.51	2.57	2.62	2.67	2.72	2.78	2.83	2.88
5	3.02	3.08	3.15	3.21	3.27	3.34	3.40	3.46
6	3.53	3.60	3.68	3.75	3.83	3.90	3.97	4.05
7	4.04	4.12	4.21	4.29	4.38	4.47	4.55	4.64
8	4.55	4.65	4.74	4.84	4.94	5.03	5.13	5.22
9	5.07	5.17	5.28	5.39	5.49	5.60	5.71	5.82
10	5.58	5.70	5.82	5.94	6.05	6.17	6.29	6.41
11	6.10	6.23	6.36	6.49	6.62	6.75	6.88	7.01
12	6.62	6.76	6.90	7.04	7.18	7.32	7.46	7.60
13	7.14	7.29	7.44	7.59	7.75	7.90	8.05	8.20
14	7.66	7.82	7.99	8.15	8.31	8.48	8.64	8.81
15	8.19	8.36	8.53	8.71	8.88	9.06	9.23	9.41
16	8.71	8.90	9.08	9.27	9.46	9.64	9.83	10.02
17	9.24	9.44	9.63	9.83	10.03	10.23	10.43	10.63
18	9.77	9.98	10.19	10.40	10.61	10.82	11.03	11.24
19	10.30	10.52	10.74	10.96	11.18	11.41	11.63	11.85
20	10.83	11.06	11.30	11.53	11.76	12.00	12.23	12.46
21	11.36	11.61	11.85	12.10	12.34	12.59	12.84	13.08
22	11.90	12.16	12.41	12.67	12.93	13.19	13.44	13.70
23	12.44	12.71	12.97	13.24	13.51	13.78	14.05	14.32
24	12.98	13.26	13.54	13.82	14.10	14.38	14.66	14.95
25	13.52	13.81	14.10	14.40	14.69	14.98	15.28	15.57
26	14.06	14.36	14.67	14.97	15.28	15.59	15.89	16.20
27	14.60	14.92	15.24	15.56	15.87	16.19	16.51	16.83
28	15.15	15.48	15.81	16.14	16.47	16.80	17.13	17.46
29	15.70	16.04	16.38	16.72	17.07	17.41	17.75	18.10
30	16.24	16.60	16.95	17.31	17.66	18.02	18.38	18.74
31	16.79	17.16	17.53	17.90	18.27	18.63	19.00	19.38
32	17.35	17.73	18.11	18.49	18.87	19.25	19.63	20.02
33	17.90	18.29	18.69	19.08	19.47	19.87	20.26	20.66
34	18.46	18.86	19.27	19.67	20.08	20.49	20.90	21.31
35	19.01	19.43	19.85	20.27	20.69	21.11	21.53	21.95
36	19.57	20.00	20.43	20.87	21.30	21.73	22.17	22.60
37	20.13	20.58	21.02	21.46	21.91	22.36	22.81	23.25
38	20.69	21.15	21.61	22.07	22.52	22.99	23.45	23.91
39	21.26	21.73	22.20	22.67	23.14	23.61	24.09	24.56
40	21.82	22.30	22.79	23.27	23.76	24.25	24.73	25.22
41	22.39	22.88	23.38	23.88	24.38	24.88	25.38	25.88
42	22.96	23.47	23.98	24.49	25.00	25.51	26.03	26.55
43	23.53	24.05	24.57	25.10	25.62	26.15	26.68	27.21
44	24.10	24.64	25.17	25.71	26.25	26.79	27.33	27.88
45	24.67	25.22	25.77	26.32	26.88	27.43	27.99	28.55
46	25.25	25.81	26.37	26.94	27.51	28.08	28.65	29.22
47	25.82	26.40	26.98	27.56	28.14	28.72	29.31	29.89
48	26.40	26.99	27.58	28.18	28.77	29.37	29.97	30.57
49	26.98	27.59	28.19	28.80	29.41	30.02	30.63	31.24
50	27.56	28.18	28.80	29.42	30.04	30.67	31.29	31.92
51	28.15	28.78	29.41	30.05	30.68	31.32	31.96	32.60
52	28.73	29.38	30.02	30.67	31.32	31.98	32.63	33.29
53	29.32	29.98	30.64	31.30	31.97	32.63	33.30	33.97
54	29.91	30.58	31.25	31.93	32.61	33.29	33.98	34.66
55	30.50	31.18	31.87	32.56	33.26	33.95	34.65	35.35
56	31.09	31.79	32.49	33.20	33.91	34.62	35.33	36.04
57	31.68	32.39	33.11	33.83	34.56	35.28	36.01	36.74
58	32.27	33.00	33.74	34.47	35.21	35.95	36.69	37.43
59	32.87	33.61	34.36	35.11	35.86	36.62	37.37	38.13
60	33.47	34.23	34.99	35.75	36.52	37.29	38.06	38.83

Table 8-2 (*cont.*)

Number of Payments	Annual Percentage Rate							
	10.00%	10.25%	10.50%	10.75%	11.00%	11.25%	11.50%	11.75%
(Finance charge per $100 of amount financed)								
301	173.31	178.64	184.00	189.40	194.83	200.29	205.78	211.30
302	174.02	179.37	184.75	190.17	195.62	201.11	206.62	212.17
303	174.73	180.10	185.50	190.95	196.42	201.93	207.46	213.03
304	175.43	180.83	186.26	191.72	197.22	202.75	208.31	213.90
305	176.14	181.56	187.01	192.49	198.01	203.57	209.15	214.76
306	176.85	182.29	187.76	193.27	198.81	204.39	209.99	215.63
307	177.55	183.02	188.51	194.05	199.61	205.21	210.84	216.50
308	178.26	183.75	189.27	194.82	200.41	206.03	211.68	217.37
309	178.97	184.48	190.02	195.60	201.21	206.85	212.53	218.23
310	179.68	185.21	190.78	196.38	202.01	207.68	213.38	219.10
311	180.39	185.95	191.53	197.16	202.81	208.50	214.22	219.97
312	181.10	186.68	192.29	197.94	203.62	209.33	215.07	220.85
313	181.82	187.41	193.05	198.72	204.42	210.15	215.92	221.72
314	182.53	188.15	193.81	199.50	205.22	210.98	216.77	222.59
315	183.24	188.89	194.56	200.28	206.03	211.81	217.62	223.46
316	183.96	189.62	195.32	201.06	206.83	212.63	218.47	224.34
317	184.67	190.36	196.08	201.84	207.64	213.46	219.32	225.21
318	185.39	191.10	196.84	202.63	208.44	214.29	220.17	226.09
319	186.10	191.83	197.60	203.41	209.25	215.12	221.03	226.96
320	186.82	192.57	198.37	204.19	210.06	215.95	221.88	227.84
321	187.53	193.31	199.13	204.98	210.86	216.78	222.73	228.71
322	188.25	194.05	199.89	205.76	211.67	217.61	223.59	229.59
323	188.97	194.79	200.65	206.55	212.48	218.45	224.44	230.47
324	189.69	195.53	201.42	207.34	213.29	219.28	225.30	231.35
325	190.41	196.28	202.18	208.13	214.10	220.11	226.15	232.23
326	191.13	197.02	202.95	208.91	214.91	220.95	227.01	233.11
327	191.85	197.76	203.71	209.70	215.72	221.78	227.87	233.99
328	192.57	198.51	204.48	210.49	216.54	222.62	228.73	234.87
329	193.29	199.25	205.25	211.28	217.35	223.45	229.59	235.75
330	194.01	199.99	206.01	212.07	218.16	224.29	230.45	236.64
331	194.73	200.74	206.78	212.86	218.98	225.13	231.31	237.52
332	195.46	201.49	207.55	213.65	219.79	225.96	232.17	238.40
333	196.18	202.23	208.32	214.45	220.61	226.80	233.03	239.29
334	196.90	202.98	209.09	215.24	221.42	227.64	233.89	240.17
335	197.63	203.73	209.86	216.03	222.24	228.48	234.75	241.06
336	198.35	204.47	210.63	216.83	223.06	229.32	235.62	241.94
337	199.08	205.22	211.40	217.62	223.87	230.16	236.48	242.83
338	199.81	205.97	212.18	218.42	224.69	231.00	237.34	243.72
339	200.53	206.72	212.95	219.21	225.51	231.84	238.21	244.61
340	201.26	207.47	213.72	220.01	226.33	232.69	239.08	245.50
341	201.99	208.22	214.50	220.81	227.15	233.53	239.94	246.38
342	202.72	208.98	215.27	221.60	227.97	234.37	240.81	247.27
343	203.45	209.73	216.05	222.40	228.79	235.22	241.68	248.16
344	204.18	210.48	216.82	223.20	229.61	236.06	242.54	249.06
345	204.91	211.23	217.60	224.00	230.44	236.91	243.41	249.95
346	205.64	211.99	218.38	224.80	231.26	237.75	244.28	250.84
347	206.37	212.74	219.15	225.60	232.08	238.60	245.15	251.73
348	207.10	213.50	219.93	226.40	232.91	239.45	246.02	252.63
349	207.83	214.25	220.71	227.20	233.73	240.29	246.89	253.52
350	208.57	215.01	221.49	228.00	234.56	241.14	247.76	254.41
351	209.30	215.76	222.27	228.81	235.38	241.99	248.63	255.31
352	210.03	216.52	223.05	229.61	236.21	242.84	249.51	256.20
353	210.77	217.28	223.83	230.41	237.03	243.69	250.38	257.10
354	211.50	218.04	224.61	231.22	237.86	244.54	251.25	258.00
355	212.24	218.80	225.39	232.02	238.69	245.39	252.13	258.89
356	212.98	219.55	226.17	232.83	239.52	246.24	253.00	259.79
357	213.71	220.31	226.95	233.63	240.35	247.09	253.88	260.69
358	214.45	221.07	227.74	234.44	241.18	247.95	254.75	261.59
359	215.19	221.84	228.52	235.25	242.01	248.80	255.63	262.49
360	215.93	222.60	229.31	236.05	242.84	249.65	256.50	263.39

Table 8-2 (*cont.*) 199

Number of Payments	Annual Percentage Rate							
	12.00%	12.25%	12.50%	12.75%	13.00%	13.25%	13.50%	13.75%
	(Finance charge per $100 of amount financed)							
301	216.85	222.43	228.04	233.67	239.33	245.01	250.72	256.45
302	217.74	223.34	228.97	234.63	240.31	246.01	251.74	257.50
303	218.63	224.25	229.91	235.58	241.29	247.02	252.77	258.55
304	219.52	225.16	230.84	236.54	242.27	248.02	253.80	259.60
305	220.41	226.08	231.77	237.50	243.25	249.03	254.82	260.65
306	221.30	226.99	232.71	238.46	244.23	250.03	255.85	261.70
307	222.19	227.90	233.65	239.42	245.21	251.04	256.88	262.75
308	223.08	228.82	234.58	240.38	246.20	252.04	257.91	263.80
309	223.97	229.73	235.52	241.34	247.18	253.05	258.94	264.86
310	224.86	230.65	236.46	242.30	248.17	254.06	259.97	265.91
311	225.75	231.56	237.40	243.26	249.15	255.07	261.01	266.97
312	226.65	232.48	238.34	244.23	250.14	256.08	262.04	268.02
313	227.54	233.40	239.28	245.19	251.13	257.09	263.07	269.08
314	228.44	234.32	240.22	246.16	252.11	258.10	264.11	270.14
315	229.33	235.24	241.17	247.12	253.10	259.11	265.14	271.19
316	230.23	236.16	242.11	248.09	254.09	260.12	266.18	272.25
317	231.13	237.08	243.05	249.05	255.08	261.13	267.21	273.31
318	232.03	238.00	244.00	250.02	256.07	262.15	268.25	274.37
319	232.93	238.92	244.94	250.99	257.06	263.16	269.29	275.43
320	233.83	239.84	245.89	251.96	258.06	264.18	270.32	276.49
321	234.73	240.77	246.83	252.93	259.05	265.19	271.36	277.55
322	235.63	241.69	247.78	253.90	260.04	266.21	272.40	278.62
323	236.53	242.61	248.73	254.87	261.04	267.23	273.44	279.68
324	237.43	243.54	249.68	255.84	262.03	268.24	274.48	280.74
325	238.33	244.46	250.62	256.81	263.02	269.26	275.52	281.81
326	239.23	245.39	251.57	257.78	264.02	270.28	276.57	282.87
327	240.14	246.32	252.52	258.76	265.02	271.30	277.61	283.94
328	241.04	247.25	253.47	259.73	266.01	272.32	278.65	285.01
329	241.95	248.17	254.43	260.71	267.01	273.34	279.70	286.07
330	242.85	249.10	255.38	261.68	268.01	274.36	280.74	287.14
331	243.76	250.03	256.33	262.66	269.01	275.39	281.79	288.21
332	244.67	250.96	257.28	263.63	270.01	276.41	282.83	289.28
333	245.58	251.89	258.24	264.61	271.01	277.43	283.88	290.35
334	246.48	252.82	259.19	265.59	272.01	278.46	284.93	291.42
335	247.39	253.76	260.15	266.57	273.01	279.48	285.97	292.49
336	248.30	254.69	261.10	267.54	274.01	280.50	287.02	293.56
337	249.21	255.62	262.06	268.52	275.02	281.53	288.07	294.63
338	250.12	256.56	263.02	269.50	276.02	282.56	289.12	295.70
339	251.03	257.49	263.97	270.49	277.02	283.58	290.17	296.78
340	251.95	258.42	264.93	271.47	278.03	284.61	291.22	297.85
341	252.86	259.36	265.89	272.45	279.03	285.64	292.27	298.93
342	253.77	260.30	266.85	273.43	280.04	286.67	293.32	300.00
343	254.68	261.23	267.81	274.41	281.04	287.70	294.37	301.08
344	255.60	262.17	268.77	275.40	282.05	288.73	295.43	302.15
345	256.51	263.11	269.73	276.38	283.06	289.76	296.48	303.23
346	257.43	264.05	270.69	277.37	284.06	290.79	297.54	304.30
347	258.34	264.99	271.65	278.35	285.07	291.82	298.59	305.38
348	259.26	265.93	272.62	279.34	286.08	292.85	299.64	306.46
349	260.18	266.87	273.58	280.32	287.09	293.88	300.70	307.54
350	261.10	267.81	274.54	281.31	288.10	294.92	301.76	308.62
351	262.01	268.75	275.51	282.30	289.11	295.95	302.81	309.70
352	262.93	269.69	276.47	283.29	290.12	296.99	303.87	310.78
353	263.85	270.63	277.44	284.27	291.13	298.02	304.93	311.86
354	264.77	271.57	278.41	285.26	292.15	299.06	305.99	312.94
355	265.69	272.52	279.37	286.25	293.16	300.09	307.05	314.02
356	266.61	273.46	280.34	287.24	294.17	301.13	308.11	315.11
357	267.53	274.41	281.31	288.23	295.19	302.16	309.17	316.19
358	268.45	275.35	282.27	289.23	296.20	303.20	310.23	317.27
359	269.38	276.30	283.24	290.22	297.22	304.24	311.29	318.36
360	270.30	277.24	284.21	291.21	298.23	305.28	312.35	319.44

200

Table 8-2 (cont.)

Number of Payments	Annual Percentage Rate							
	14.00%	14.25%	14.50%	14.75%	15.00%	15.25%	15.50%	15.75%
(Finance charge per $100 of amount financed)								
1	1.17	1.19	1.21	1.23	1.25	1.27	1.29	1.31
2	1.75	1.78	1.82	1.85	1.88	1.91	1.94	1.97
3	2.34	2.38	2.43	2.47	2.51	2.55	2.59	2.64
4	2.93	2.99	3.04	3.09	3.14	3.20	3.25	3.30
5	3.53	3.59	3.65	3.72	3.78	3.84	3.91	3.97
6	4.12	4.20	4.27	4.35	4.42	4.49	4.57	4.64
7	4.72	4.81	4.89	4.98	5.06	5.15	5.23	5.32
8	5.32	5.42	5.51	5.61	5.71	5.80	5.90	6.00
9	5.92	6.03	6.14	6.25	6.35	6.46	6.57	6.68
10	6.53	6.65	6.77	6.88	7.00	7.12	7.24	7.36
11	7.14	7.27	7.40	7.53	7.66	7.79	7.92	8.05
12	7.74	7.89	8.03	8.17	8.31	8.45	8.59	8.74
13	8.36	8.51	8.66	8.81	8.97	9.12	9.27	9.43
14	8.97	9.13	9.30	9.46	9.63	9.79	9.96	10.12
15	9.59	9.76	9.94	10.11	10.29	10.47	10.64	10.82
16	10.20	10.39	10.58	10.77	10.95	11.14	11.33	11.52
17	10.82	11.02	11.22	11.42	11.62	11.82	12.02	12.22
18	11.45	11.66	11.87	12.08	12.29	12.50	12.72	12.93
19	12.07	12.30	12.52	12.74	12.97	13.19	13.41	13.64
20	12.70	12.93	13.17	13.41	13.64	13.88	14.11	14.35
21	13.33	13.58	13.82	14.07	14.32	14.57	14.82	15.06
22	13.96	14.22	14.48	14.74	15.00	15.26	15.52	15.78
23	14.59	14.87	15.14	15.68	15.68	15.96	16.23	16.50
24	15.23	15.51	15.80	16.08	16.37	16.65	16.94	17.22
25	15.87	16.17	16.46	16.76	17.06	17.35	17.65	17.95
26	16.51	16.82	17.13	17.44	17.75	18.06	18.37	18.68
27	17.15	17.47	17.80	18.12	18.44	18.76	19.09	19.41
28	17.80	18.13	18.47	18.80	19.14	19.47	19.81	20.15
29	18.45	18.79	19.14	19.49	19.83	20.18	20.53	20.88
30	19.10	19.45	19.81	20.17	20.54	20.90	21.26	21.62
31	19.75	20.12	20.49	20.87	21.24	21.61	21.99	22.37
32	20.40	20.79	21.17	21.56	21.95	22.33	22.72	23.11
33	21.06	21.46	21.85	22.25	22.65	23.06	23.46	23.86
34	21.72	22.13	22.54	22.95	23.37	23.78	24.19	24.61
35	22.38	22.80	23.23	23.65	24.08	24.51	24.94	25.36
36	23.04	23.48	23.92	24.35	24.80	25.24	25.68	26.12
37	23.70	24.16	24.61	25.06	25.51	25.97	26.42	26.88
38	24.37	24.84	25.30	25.77	26.24	26.70	27.17	27.64
39	25.04	25.52	26.00	26.48	26.96	27.44	27.92	28.41
40	25.71	26.20	26.70	27.19	27.69	28.18	28.68	29.18
41	26.39	26.89	27.40	27.91	28.41	28.92	29.44	29.95
42	27.06	27.58	28.10	28.62	29.15	29.67	30.19	30.72
43	27.74	28.27	28.81	29.34	29.88	30.42	30.96	31.50
44	28.42	28.97	29.52	30.07	30.62	31.17	31.72	32.28
45	29.11	29.67	30.23	30.79	31.36	31.92	32.49	33.06
46	29.79	30.36	30.94	31.52	32.10	32.68	33.26	33.84
47	30.48	31.07	31.66	32.25	32.84	33.44	34.03	34.63
48	31.17	31.77	32.37	32.98	33.59	34.20	34.81	35.42
49	31.86	32.48	33.09	33.71	34.34	34.96	35.59	36.21
50	32.55	33.18	33.82	34.45	35.09	35.73	36.37	37.01
51	33.25	33.89	34.54	35.19	35.84	36.49	37.15	37.81
52	33.95	34.61	35.27	35.93	36.60	37.27	37.94	38.61
53	34.65	35.32	36.00	36.68	37.36	38.04	38.72	39.41
54	35.35	36.04	36.73	37.42	38.12	38.82	39.52	40.22
55	36.05	36.76	37.46	38.17	38.88	39.60	40.31	41.03
56	36.76	37.48	38.20	38.92	39.65	40.38	41.11	41.84
57	37.47	38.20	38.94	39.68	40.42	41.16	41.91	42.65
58	38.18	38.93	39.68	40.43	41.19	41.95	42.71	43.47
59	38.89	39.66	40.42	41.19	41.96	42.74	43.51	44.29
60	39.61	40.39	41.17	41.95	42.74	43.53	44.32	45.11

Table 8-2 (*cont.*)   201

Number of Payments	Annual Percentage Rate							
	16.00%	16.25%	16.50%	16.75%	17.00%	17.25%	17.50%	17.75%
	(Finance charge per $100 of amount financed)							
1	1.33	1.35	1.37	1.40	1.42	1.44	1.46	1.48
2	2.00	2.04	2.07	2.10	2.13	2.16	2.19	2.22
3	2.68	2.72	2.76	2.80	2.85	2.89	2.93	2.97
4	3.36	3.41	3.46	3.51	3.57	3.62	3.67	3.73
5	4.04	4.10	4.16	4.23	4.29	4.35	4.42	4.48
6	4.72	4.79	4.87	4.94	5.02	5.09	5.17	5.24
7	5.40	5.49	5.58	5.66	5.75	5.83	5.92	6.00
8	6.09	6.19	6.29	6.38	6.48	6.58	6.67	6.77
9	6.78	6.89	7.00	7.11	7.22	7.32	7.43	7.54
10	7.48	7.60	7.72	7.84	7.96	8.08	8.19	8.31
11	8.18	8.31	8.44	8.57	8.70	8.83	8.96	9.09
12	8.88	9.02	9.16	9.30	9.45	9.59	9.73	9.87
13	9.58	9.73	9.89	10.04	10.20	10.35	10.50	10.66
14	10.29	10.45	10.62	10.78	10.95	11.11	11.28	11.45
15	11.00	11.17	11.35	11.53	11.71	11.88	12.06	12.24
16	11.71	11.90	12.09	12.28	12.46	12.65	12.84	13.03
17	12.42	12.62	12.83	13.03	13.23	13.43	13.63	13.83
18	13.14	13.35	13.57	13.78	13.99	14.21	14.42	14.64
19	13.86	14.09	14.31	14.54	14.76	14.99	15.22	15.44
20	14.59	14.82	15.06	15.30	15.54	15.77	16.01	16.25
21	15.31	15.56	15.81	16.06	16.31	16.56	16.81	17.07
22	16.04	16.30	16.57	16.83	17.09	17.36	17.62	17.88
23	16.78	17.05	17.32	17.60	17.88	18.15	18.43	18.70
24	17.51	17.80	18.09	18.37	18.66	18.95	19.24	19.53
25	18.25	18.55	18.85	19.15	19.45	19.75	20.05	20.36
26	18.99	19.30	19.62	19.93	20.24	20.56	20.87	21.19
27	19.74	20.06	20.39	20.71	21.04	21.37	21.69	22.02
28	20.48	20.82	21.16	21.50	21.84	22.18	22.52	22.86
29	21.23	21.58	21.94	22.29	22.64	22.99	23.35	23.70
30	21.99	22.35	22.72	23.08	23.45	23.81	24.18	24.55
31	22.74	23.12	23.50	23.88	24.26	24.64	25.02	25.40
32	23.50	23.89	24.28	24.68	25.07	25.46	25.86	26.25
33	24.26	24.67	25.07	25.48	25.88	26.29	26.70	27.11
34	25.03	25.44	25.86	26.28	26.70	27.12	27.54	27.97
35	25.79	26.23	26.66	27.09	27.52	27.96	28.39	28.83
36	26.57	27.01	27.46	27.90	28.35	28.80	29.25	29.70
37	27.34	27.80	28.26	28.72	29.18	29.64	30.10	30.57
38	28.11	28.59	29.06	29.53	30.01	30.49	30.96	31.44
39	28.89	29.38	29.87	30.36	30.85	31.34	31.83	32.32
40	29.68	30.18	30.68	31.18	31.68	32.19	32.69	33.20
41	30.46	30.97	31.49	32.01	32.52	33.04	33.56	34.08
42	31.25	31.78	32.31	32.84	33.37	33.90	34.44	34.97
43	32.04	32.58	33.13	33.67	34.22	34.76	35.31	35.86
44	32.83	33.39	33.95	34.51	35.07	35.63	36.19	36.76
45	33.63	34.20	34.77	35.35	35.92	36.50	37.08	37.66
46	34.43	35.01	35.60	36.19	36.78	37.37	37.96	38.56
47	35.23	35.83	36.43	37.04	37.64	38.25	38.86	39.46
48	36.03	36.65	37.27	37.88	38.50	39.13	39.75	40.37
49	36.84	37.47	38.10	38.74	39.37	40.01	40.65	41.29
50	37.65	38.30	38.94	39.59	40.24	40.89	41.55	42.20
51	38.46	39.12	39.79	40.45	41.11	41.78	42.45	43.12
52	39.28	39.96	40.63	41.31	41.99	42.67	43.36	44.04
53	40.10	40.79	41.48	42.17	42.87	43.57	44.27	44.97
54	40.92	41.63	42.33	43.04	43.75	44.47	45.18	45.90
55	41.74	42.47	43.19	43.91	44.64	45.37	46.10	46.83
56	42.57	43.31	44.05	44.79	45.53	46.27	47.02	47.77
57	43.40	44.15	44.91	45.66	46.42	47.18	47.94	48.71
58	44.23	45.00	45.77	46.54	47.32	48.09	48.87	49.65
59	45.07	45.85	46.64	47.42	48.21	49.01	49.80	50.60
60	45.91	46.71	47.51	48.31	49.12	49.92	50.73	51.55

202

Table 8-2 (*cont.*)

Number of Payments	Annual Percentage Rate							
	22.00%	22.25%	22.50%	22.75%	23.00%	23.25%	23.50%	23.75%
	(Finance charge per $100 of amount financed)							
1	1.83	1.85	1.87	1.90	1.92	1.94	1.96	1.98
2	2.76	2.79	2.82	2.85	2.88	2.92	2.95	2.98
3	3.69	3.73	3.77	3.82	3.86	3.90	3.94	3.98
4	4.62	4.68	4.73	4.78	4.84	4.89	4.94	5.00
5	5.57	5.63	5.69	5.76	5.82	5.89	5.95	6.02
6	6.51	6.59	6.66	6.74	6.81	6.89	6.96	7.04
7	7.47	7.55	7.64	7.73	7.81	7.90	7.99	8.07
8	8.42	8.52	8.62	8.72	8.82	8.91	9.01	9.11
9	9.39	9.50	9.61	9.72	9.83	9.94	10.04	10.15
10	10.36	10.48	10.60	10.72	10.84	10.96	11.08	11.21
11	11.33	11.47	11.60	11.73	11.86	12.00	12.13	12.26
12	12.31	12.46	12.60	12.75	12.89	13.04	13.18	13.33
13	13.30	13.46	13.61	13.77	13.93	14.08	14.24	14.40
14	14.29	14.46	14.63	14.80	14.97	15.13	15.30	15.47
15	15.29	15.47	15.65	15.83	16.01	16.19	16.37	16.56
16	16.29	16.48	16.68	16.87	17.06	17.26	17.45	17.65
17	17.30	17.50	17.71	17.92	18.12	18.33	18.53	18.74
18	18.31	18.53	18.75	18.97	19.19	19.41	19.62	19.84
19	19.33	19.56	19.79	20.02	20.26	20.49	20.72	20.95
20	20.35	20.60	20.84	21.09	21.33	21.58	21.82	22.07
21	21.38	21.64	21.90	22.16	22.41	22.67	22.93	23.19
22	22.42	22.69	22.96	23.23	23.50	23.77	24.04	24.32
23	23.46	23.74	24.03	24.31	24.60	24.88	25.17	25.45
24	24.51	24.80	25.10	25.40	25.70	25.99	26.29	26.59
25	25.56	25.87	26.18	26.49	26.80	27.11	27.43	27.74
26	26.62	26.94	27.26	27.59	27.91	28.24	28.56	28.89
27	27.68	28.02	28.35	28.69	29.03	29.37	29.71	30.05
28	28.75	29.10	29.45	29.80	30.15	30.51	30.86	31.22
29	29.82	30.19	30.55	30.92	31.28	31.65	32.02	32.39
30	30.90	31.28	31.66	32.04	32.04	32.80	33.18	33.57
31	31.98	32.38	32.77	33.17	33.56	33.96	34.35	34.75
32	33.07	33.48	33.89	34.30	34.71	35.12	35.53	35.94
33	34.17	34.59	35.01	35.44	35.86	36.29	36.71	37.14
34	35.27	35.71	36.14	36.58	37.02	37.46	37.90	38.34
35	36.37	36.83	37.28	37.73	38.18	38.64	39.09	39.55
36	37.49	37.95	38.42	38.89	39.35	39.82	40.29	40.77
37	38.60	39.08	39.56	40.05	40.53	41.02	41.50	41.99
38	39.72	40.22	40.72	41.21	41.71	42.21	42.71	43.22
39	40.85	41.36	41.87	42.39	42.90	43.42	43.93	44.45
40	41.98	42.51	43.04	43.56	44.09	44.62	45.16	45.69
41	43.12	43.66	44.20	44.75	45.29	45.84	46.39	46.94
42	44.26	44.82	45.38	45.94	46.50	47.06	47.62	48.19
43	45.41	45.98	46.56	47.13	47.71	48.29	48.87	49.45
44	46.56	47.15	47.74	48.33	48.93	49.52	50.11	50.71
45	47.72	48.33	48.93	49.54	50.15	50.76	51.37	51.98
46	48.89	49.51	50.13	50.75	51.37	52.00	52.63	53.26
47	50.06	50.69	51.33	51.97	52.61	53.25	53.89	54.54
48	51.23	51.88	52.54	53.19	53.85	54.51	55.16	55.83
49	52.41	53.08	53.75	54.42	55.09	55.77	56.44	57.12
50	53.59	54.28	54.96	55.65	56.34	57.03	57.73	58.42
51	54.78	55.48	56.19	56.89	57.60	58.30	59.01	59.73
52	55.98	56.69	57.41	58.13	58.86	59.58	60.31	61.04
53	57.18	57.91	58.65	59.38	60.12	60.87	61.61	62.35
54	58.38	59.13	59.88	60.64	61.40	62.16	62.92	63.68
55	59.59	60.36	61.13	61.90	62.67	63.45	64.23	65.01
56	60.80	61.59	62.38	63.17	63.96	64.75	65.54	66.34
57	62.02	62.83	63.63	64.44	65.25	66.06	66.87	67.68
58	63.25	64.07	64.89	65.71	66.54	67.37	68.20	69.03
59	64.48	65.32	66.15	67.00	67.84	68.68	69.53	70.38
60	65.71	66.57	67.42	68.28	69.14	70.01	70.87	71.74

Table 8-2 (*cont.*)

203

Number of Payments	Annual Percentage Rate							
	24.00%	24.25%	24.50%	24.75%	25.00%	25.25%	25.50%	25.75%
	(Finance charge per $100 of amount financed)							
1	2.00	2.02	2.04	2.06	2.08	2.10	2.12	2.15
2	3.01	3.04	3.07	3.10	3.14	3.17	3.20	3.23
3	4.03	4.07	4.11	4.15	4.20	4.24	4.28	4.32
4	5.05	5.10	5.16	5.21	5.26	5.32	5.37	5.42
5	6.08	6.14	6.21	6.27	6.34	6.40	6.46	6.53
6	7.12	7.19	7.27	7.34	7.42	7.49	7.57	7.64
7	8.16	8.24	8.33	8.42	8.51	8.59	8.68	8.77
8	9.21	9.31	9.40	9.50	9.60	9.70	9.80	9.90
9	10.26	10.37	10.48	10.59	10.70	10.81	10.92	11.03
10	11.33	11.45	11.57	11.69	11.81	11.93	12.06	12.18
11	12.40	12.53	12.66	12.80	12.93	13.06	13.20	13.33
12	13.47	13.62	13.76	13.91	14.05	14.20	14.34	14.49
13	14.55	14.71	14.87	15.03	15.18	15.34	15.50	15.66
14	15.64	15.81	15.98	16.15	16.32	16.49	16.66	16.83
15	16.74	16.92	17.10	17.28	17.47	17.65	17.83	18.02
16	17.84	18.03	18.23	18.42	18.62	18.81	19.01	19.21
17	18.95	19.16	19.36	19.57	19.78	19.99	20.20	20.40
18	20.06	20.28	20.50	20.72	20.95	21.17	21.39	21.61
19	21.19	21.42	21.65	21.89	22.12	22.35	22.59	22.82
20	22.31	22.56	22.81	23.05	23.30	23.55	23.79	24.04
21	23.45	23.71	23.97	24.23	24.49	24.75	25.01	25.27
22	24.59	24.86	25.13	25.41	25.68	25.96	26.23	26.50
23	25.74	26.02	26.31	26.60	26.88	27.17	27.46	27.75
24	26.89	27.19	27.49	27.79	28.09	28.39	28.69	29.00
25	28.05	28.36	28.68	28.99	29.31	29.62	29.94	30.25
26	29.22	29.55	29.87	30.20	30.53	30.86	31.19	31.52
27	30.39	30.73	31.07	31.42	31.76	32.10	32.45	32.79
28	31.57	31.93	32.28	32.64	33.00	33.35	33.71	34.07
29	32.76	33.13	33.50	33.87	34.24	34.61	34.98	35.36
30	33.95	34.33	34.72	35.10	35.49	35.88	36.26	36.65
31	35.15	35.55	35.95	36.35	36.75	37.15	37.55	37.95
32	36.35	36.77	37.18	37.60	38.01	38.43	38.84	39.26
33	37.57	37.99	38.42	38.85	39.28	39.71	40.14	40.58
34	38.78	39.23	39.67	40.11	40.56	41.01	41.45	41.90
35	40.01	40.47	40.92	41.38	41.84	42.31	42.77	43.23
36	41.24	41.71	42.19	42.66	43.14	43.61	44.09	44.57
37	42.48	42.96	43.45	43.94	44.43	44.93	45.42	45.91
38	43.72	44.22	44.73	45.23	45.74	46.25	46.75	47.26
39	44.97	45.49	46.01	46.53	47.05	47.57	48.10	48.62
40	46.22	46.76	47.29	47.83	48.37	48.91	49.45	49.99
41	47.48	48.04	48.59	49.14	49.69	50.25	50.80	51.36
42	48.75	49.32	49.89	50.46	51.03	51.60	52.17	52.74
43	50.03	50.61	51.19	51.78	52.36	52.95	53.54	54.13
44	51.31	51.91	52.51	53.11	53.71	54.31	54.92	55.52
45	52.59	53.21	53.82	54.44	55.06	55.68	56.30	56.92
46	53.89	54.52	55.15	55.78	56.42	57.05	57.69	58.33
47	55.18	55.83	56.48	57.13	57.78	58.44	59.09	59.75
48	56.49	57.15	57.82	58.49	59.15	59.82	60.50	61.17
49	57.80	58.48	59.16	59.85	60.53	61.22	61.91	62.60
50	59.12	59.81	60.51	61.21	61.92	62.62	63.33	64.03
51	60.44	61.15	61.87	62.59	63.31	64.03	64.75	65.47
52	61.77	62.50	63.23	63.97	64.70	65.44	66.18	66.92
53	63.10	63.85	64.60	65.35	66.11	66.86	67.62	68.38
54	64.44	65.21	65.98	66.75	67.52	68.29	69.07	69.84
55	65.79	66.57	67.36	68.14	68.93	69.72	70.52	71.31
56	67.14	67.94	68.74	69.55	70.36	71.16	71.97	72.79
57	68.50	69.32	70.14	70.96	71.78	72.61	73.44	74.27
58	69.86	70.70	71.54	72.38	73.22	74.06	74.91	75.76
59	71.23	72.09	72.94	73.80	74.66	75.52	76.39	77.25
60	72.61	73.48	74.35	75.23	76.11	76.99	77.87	78.76

EXAMPLE 8

The Felds bought appliances costing $7,800 on a 36-month deferred payment plan by paying $900 down. Their monthly add-on charge is $56.93. What true annual rate of interest are the Felds paying?

$$B = \$7,800 - \$900 = \$6,900 \qquad FC = \$56.93/\text{mo} \times 36 \text{ mo} = \$2,049.48$$

$$\frac{FC}{100} = \frac{FC(100)}{B}$$

$$= \frac{\$2,049.48(100)}{\$6,900} = 29.70$$

Refer to Table 8-2 and locate the number of payments (36 in this case) in the far left column. Read across this line until you reach the value nearest the $FC/100$ value found in your calculations (29.70). The APR listed at the top of this column is the true or effective annual rate of interest. From the table, we see that the Felds are paying interest at a rate of 17.75% annually.

SOLVED PROBLEMS

8.25   Find the monthly payment on a loan of $2,000 to be amortized over 2 years at 18% compounded monthly.

SOLUTION

$$A = \$2,000 \qquad i = \frac{0.18}{12} = 0.015 \qquad n = 2(12) = 24$$

$$R = \frac{A}{a_{\overline{n}|i}}$$

$$= \frac{\$2,000}{a_{\overline{24}|0.015}} = \frac{\$2,000}{20.030405} = \$99.85 \text{ (rounded up to the cent)}$$

8.26   What is the total interest on the loan in Prob. 8.25?

SOLUTION

Total payments (24 × $99.85)	$2,396.40
Less principal of loan	2,000.00
Interest on loan	$ 396.40

8.27   A debt of $10,000 is to be amortized with six equal semiannual payments. Find the semiannual payment if interest is at 14% compounded semiannually.

SOLUTION

$$A = \$10,000 \qquad i = \frac{0.14}{2} = 0.07 \qquad n = 6$$

$$R = \frac{A}{a_{\overline{n}|i}}$$

$$= \frac{\$10,000}{a_{\overline{6}|0.07}} = \frac{\$10,000}{4.7665397} = \$2,097.96 \text{ (rounded up to the cent)}$$

8.28   For the debt in Prob. 8.27, make out a complete amortization schedule, showing the distribution of the payments between interest and principal.

SOLUTION

Payment 1: The interest due at the end of the first half-year is

$$7\% \times \$10,000 = \$700$$

The first payment of $2,097.96 will pay the interest $700 and will also reduce the outstanding principal by $1,397.96 (from $2,097.96 − $700). Thus the outstanding principal after the first payment is

$$\$10,000 - \$1,397.96 = \$8,602.04$$

Payment 2: The interest due at the end of the second period is calculated on the outstanding principal.

$$7\% \times \$8,602.04 = \$602.14$$

The outstanding principal is reduced by $1,495.82 (from $2,097.96 − $602.14). The new outstanding principal after the second payment is

$$\$8,602.04 - \$1,495.82 = \$7,106.22$$

This procedure is repeated for all six payments, and the results are shown in the following amortization schedule.

Payment		Applied to		Outstanding Principal
Number	Amount	Interest	Principal	
Start				$10,000.00
1	$ 2,097.96	$ 700.00	$ 1,397.96	8,602.04
2	2,097.96	602.14	1,495.82	7,106.22
3	2,097.96	497.44	1,600.52	5,505.70
4	2,097.96	385.40	1,712.56	3,793.14
5	2,097.96	265.52	1,832.44	1,960.70
6	2,097.95*	137.25	1,960.70	
Total	$12,587.75	$2,587.75	$10,000.00	

*To adjust final balance to zero.

The totals at the bottom are for checking the results of the calculations. The total amount applied to principal must equal the original debt. The total amount of payments must equal the total amount applied to interest plus the total amount applied to principal.

8.29 A loan of $1,000 with interest at $j_4 = 12\%$ is to be amortized by payments of $300 at the end of each quarter for as long as necessary. Make out the amortization schedule.

SOLUTION

To make out the amortization schedule, follow the method outlined in Example 5 and Prob. 8.28, with $i = 0.12/4 = 0.03$.

Payment		Applied to		Outstanding Principal
Number	Amount	Interest	Principal	
Start				$1,000.00
1	$ 300.00	$30.00	$ 270.00	730.00
2	300.00	21.90	278.10	451.90
3	300.00	13.56	286.44	165.46
4	170.42	4.96	165.46	
Total	$1,070.42	$70.42	$1,000.00	

Note that the fourth payment is only $170.42, which is the sum of the outstanding principal after the third payment plus the interest due at 3%.

8.30 A couple purchased a home and signed a mortgage contract for $50,000 to be paid in equal monthly payments over 29 years with interest at 12% compounded monthly. (*a*) Find the monthly payment and (*b*) make out a partial amortization schedule showing the distribution of the first six payments between payment of interest and repayment of the principal.

SOLUTION

(*a*)
$$A = \$50,000 \qquad i = \frac{0.12}{12} = 0.01 \qquad n = 29(12) = 348$$

$$R = \frac{A}{a_{\overline{n}|i}}$$
$$= \frac{\$50,000}{a_{\overline{348}|0.01}} = \frac{\$50,000}{96.865546} = \$516.18$$

(*b*) Using the results from part (*a*), we can construct a partial amortization schedule using $i = 0.12/12 = 0.01$ and the procedure shown in Example 5.

Payment		Applied to		Outstanding
Number	Amount	Interest	Principal	Principal
Start				$50,000.00
1	$ 516.18	$ 500.00	$16.18	49,983.82
2	516.18	499.84	16.34	49,967.48
3	516.18	499.67	16.51	49,950.97
4	516.18	499.51	16.67	49,934.30
5	516.18	499.34	16.84	49.917.46
6	516.18	499.17	17.01	49,900.45
Total	$3,097.08	$2,997.53	$99.55	

During the first 6 months, only $99.55 of the original $50,000 mortgage loan is repaid. It should be noted that about 97% of each of the first six payments is applied to interest and about 3% is applied to reduce the outstanding principal.

8.31 Find the outstanding principal on the mortgage loan in Prob. 8.30 after 5 years (i.e., after 60 payments).

SOLUTION

$$A = \$50,000 \qquad i = 0.01 \qquad k = 60 \qquad R = \$516.18$$

$$P_k = A(1+i)^k - Rs_{\overline{k}|i}$$
$$= \$50,000(1.01)^{60} - \$516.18s_{\overline{60}|0.01}$$
$$= \$50,000(1.8166967) - \$516.18(81.66967)$$
$$= \$90,834.84 - \$42,156.25 = \$48,678.59$$

8.32 How much interest did the couple in Prob. 8.30 pay in the first 5 years?

SOLUTION

Total payments (60 × $516.18)	$30,970.80
Less amount applied to principal ($50,000 − $48,678.59)	1,321.41
Amount applied to interest	$29,649.39

8.33 How much of the one hundredth payment of Prob. 8.30 is applied to interest and how much to principal?

SOLUTION

First we have to find the outstanding principal after 99 payments.

$$A = \$50,000 \qquad i = 0.01 \qquad k = 99 \qquad R = \$516.18$$

$$\begin{aligned} P_k &= A(1+i)^k - Rs_{\overline{k}|i} \\ &= \$50,000(1.01)^{99} - \$516.18 s_{\overline{99}|0.01} \\ &= \$50,000(2.6780335) - \$516.18(167.80335) \\ &= \$133,901.67 - \$86,616.73 = \$47,284.94 \end{aligned}$$

The one hundredth payment pays interest at 1% of the outstanding principal:

$$0.01 \times \$47,284.94 = \$472.85$$

The outstanding principal is reduced by:

$$\$516.18 - \$472.85 = \$43.33$$

8.34 Doug is repaying a loan with 24 monthly payments of $68.85 each. After making his fourteenth payment, Doug wants to pay the loan in full. If interest on the loan is 18% per annum payable monthly, find (*a*) the amount of the loan payoff (outstanding principal) and (*b*) the unearned finance charge (interest rebate).

SOLUTION

(*a*)
$$R = \$68.85 \qquad \text{and} \qquad i = \frac{0.18}{12} = 0.015$$

The number of payments remaining is

$$n - k = 24 - 14$$

$$\begin{aligned} P_k &= Ra_{\overline{n-k}|i} \\ &= \$68.85 a_{\overline{10}|0.015} = \$68.85(9.2221846) = \$634.95 \end{aligned}$$

(*b*)

Total amount of remaining payments (10 × $68.85)	$688.50
Less amount of the loan payoff	634.95
Unearned finance charge	$ 53.55

8.35 A used car with a cash price of $3,200 is purchased on a deferred payment plan, with $200 down and a 7% add-on charge. Repayment is to be made over 12 months. Find (*a*) the monthly payment and (*b*) the true annual rate of interest, using Table 8-1.

SOLUTION

(*a*) The principal to be financed equals the cash price minus the down payment:

$$\$3,200 - \$200 = \$3,000$$

The interest (finance charge) is

$$7\% \times \$3,000 = \$210$$

The monthly payment is obtained by dividing the sum of principal plus interest by the number of payments:

$$(\$3,000 + \$210) \div 12 = \$267.50$$

(b) To use Table 8-1 to find the true annual rate of interest, we have to calculate the finance charge per $100 of amount financed, denoted by $FC/100$. Let FC = finance charge (interest) and B = amount financed (principal). Then

$$FC/100 = FC \div B/100 = \$210 \div (\$3{,}000/100) = 7$$

In Table 8-1, locate the number of payments (12) in the far left column. Read across this line until you reach the value closest to 7, which is 7.04. The APR at the top of this column is 12.75%. Thus, the true annual percentage rate charged on this loan is 12.75%.

8.36 A finance company charges 13% "interest in advance" and allows the client to repay the loan in 12 equal monthly payments. The monthly payment is calculated as one twelfth of the total of principal and interest. Using Table 8-1 find the annual rate of interest.

SOLUTION

The finance charge per $100 of the amount financed ($FC/100$) is:

$$13\% \times \$100 = \$13$$

In the payments column of Table 8-1, on the line showing 12 payments, we locate 13.04 as the number closest to 13. The column heading at the top is 23.25%, the true annual percentage rate. Note that although the stated rate is 13%, the true rate is 23.25%. This is because the interest charge is calculated on the full principal of a loan, and the amount (principal + interest) is then divided into equal payments. An amortization schedule would show that the outstanding principal decreases over time, but the payments remain constant. The difference (amount allocated to interest) thereby increases over time.

8.37 Wanda Tober wants to pay a maximum of $700 a month for a $60,000 mortgage. If she is able to get a 29-year term, what is the maximum rate she can afford?

SOLUTION

Total of payments ($700 × 348)	$243,600
Less principal of loan	60,000
Finance charge	$183,600

$$FC = \$183{,}600 \quad \text{and} \quad B = \$60{,}000$$

$$FC/100 = FC \div B/100$$
$$= (\$183{,}600) \div (\$60{,}000/100) = 306$$

In the payments column of Table 8-1, on the line showing 348 payments, we locate 306.46. The column heading at the top is 13.75%, the true annual percentage rate. Thus the maximum rate Wanda Taber can afford to pay is 13.75%.

8.3 SINKING FUNDS

When a specified amount of money is needed at a specified future date it may be accumulated systematically in a fund by means of equal periodic deposits. Such a fund is called a *sinking fund*. Sinking funds are used to pay off debts, to redeem bond issues, to replace worn-out equipment, or to buy new equipment.

When an amount of money is accumulated by equal periodic deposits, the amount becomes the accumulated value (S) of an ordinary annuity and is calculated from $S = Rs_{\overline{n}|i}$. The size of the deposit (R) is determined by

$$R = \frac{S}{s_{\overline{n}|i}}$$

EXAMPLE 9

The owners of Sunrise Farms set up a sinking fund to accumulate $60,000 by the end of 5 years. What monthly deposit is required if the fund earns interest at $10\frac{1}{2}\%$ compounded monthly?

$$S = \$60,000 \qquad i = \frac{0.105}{12} = 0.00875 \qquad n = 5 \times 12 = 60$$

$$R = \frac{S}{s_{\overline{n}|i}} \qquad\qquad\qquad \begin{cases} s_{\overline{n}|i} = \dfrac{(1+i)^n - 1}{i} \\[2mm] = \dfrac{(1.00875)^{60} - 1}{0.00875} \\[2mm] = 78.468914 \end{cases}$$

$$= \frac{\$60,000}{s_{\overline{60}|0.00875}}$$

$$= \frac{\$60,000}{78.468914}$$

$$= \$764.63$$

A *sinking fund schedule* shows how the fund accumulates to the desired amount. The amount in the fund after k deposits equals the accumulated value of the k deposits.

EXAMPLE 10

For the fund in Example 9, construct a sinking fund schedule for the first year's deposits.

First month:
Amount at beginning:	0
Interest:	0
Monthly deposit:	$764.63
Amount at end:	$764.63

Total increase: $764.63

Second month:
Amount at beginning:	$ 764.63
Interest ($764.63 × 0.875%):	6.69
Monthly deposit:	764.63
Amount at end:	$1,535.95

Total increase: $771.32

Third month:
Amount at beginning:	$1,535.95
Interest ($1,535.95 × 0.875%):	13.44
Monthly deposit:	764.63
Amount at end:	$2,314.02

Total increase: $778.07

If we continue in this manner for 12 months, we can then construct the following sinking fund schedule:

Month	Amount at Beginning	Interest at 0.875%	+	Monthly Deposit	=	Total Increase	Amount at End
1	0	0	+	$764.63	=	$764.63	$ 764.63
2	$ 764.63	$ 6.69	+	764.63	=	771.32	1,535.95
3	1,535.95	13.44	+	764.63	=	778.07	2,314.02
4	2,314.02	20.25	+	764.63	=	784.88	3.098.90
5	3,098.90	27.12	+	764.63	=	791.75	3,890.65
6	3,890.65	34.04	+	764.63	=	798.67	4,689.32
7	4,689.32	41.03	+	764.63	=	805.66	5,494.98
8	5,494.98	48.08	+	764.63	=	812.71	6,307.69
9	6,307.69	55.19	+	764.63	=	819.82	7,127.51
10	7,127.51	62.37	+	764.63	=	827.00	7,954.51
11	7,954.51	69.60	+	764.63	=	834.23	8,788.74
12	8,788.74	76.90	+	764.63	=	841.53	9,630.27

We can check the amount in the fund at the end of the first year by finding the accumulated value of 12 monthly deposits as follows:

$$R = \$764.63 \qquad i = 0.00875 \qquad k = 12$$

$$
\begin{aligned}
S_k &= Rs_{\overline{k}|i} \\
&= \$764.63 s_{\overline{12}|0.00875} \\
&= \$764.63(12.59468) \longleftarrow \\
&= \$9,630.27
\end{aligned}
\qquad
\left\{
\begin{aligned}
s_{\overline{k}|i} &= \frac{(1+i)^k - 1}{i} \\
&= \frac{(1.00875)^{12} - 1}{0.00875} \\
&= 12.59468
\end{aligned}
\right.
$$

In the sinking fund method of discharging a debt, the debtor pays the interest on the loan at the end of each interest period and makes equal periodic deposits into a sinking fund that will accumulate the principal borrowed by the end of the term of the loan. The sum of the interest payment and the sinking fund deposit is called the *periodic expense* or the *periodic cost of the debt*. At the end of the term of the loan, the borrower transfers the amount in the sinking fund to the lender. The *book value* of the debt at any time is the original principal minus the amount in the sinking fund.

EXAMPLE 11

J. Krieger borrows \$15,000 at 18% payable monthly and makes monthly deposits into a sinking fund to discharge the debt at the end of 1 year. The sinking fund earns interest at 9% compounded monthly. (*a*) What is the monthly expense of the debt? (*b*) At the end of 6 months, what is the book value of the debt?

(*a*)   Monthly deposit in sinking fund:

$$S = \$15,000 \qquad i = \frac{0.09}{12} = 0.0075 \qquad n = 12$$

$$
\begin{aligned}
R &= \frac{S}{s_{\overline{n}|i}} \\
&= \frac{\$15,000}{s_{\overline{12}|0.0075}} \\
&= \frac{\$15,000}{12.507587} \longleftarrow \\
&= \$1,199.27
\end{aligned}
\qquad
\left\{
\begin{aligned}
s_{\overline{n}|i} &= \frac{(1+i)^n - 1}{i} \\
&= \frac{(1.0075)^{12} - 1}{0.0075} \\
&= 12.507587
\end{aligned}
\right.
$$

Monthly interest on loan at $i = 0.18/12 = 0.015$:

$$\$15,000 \times 0.015 = \$225$$

Monthly expense of debt = deposit into sinking fund + interest on loan
$$= \$1,199.27 + \$225 = \$1,424.27$$

(*b*)   Amount in sinking fund at the end of 6 months:

$$R = \$1,199.27 \qquad i = 0.0075 \qquad k = 6$$

$$
\begin{aligned}
S_k &= Rs_{\overline{k}|i} \\
&= \$1,199.27 s_{\overline{6}|0.0075} \\
&= \$1,199.27(6.1136315) \longleftarrow \\
&= \$7,331.89
\end{aligned}
\qquad
\left\{
\begin{aligned}
s_{\overline{k}|i} &= \frac{(1+i)^k - 1}{i} \\
&= \frac{(1.0075)^6 - 1}{0.0075} \\
&= 6.1136315
\end{aligned}
\right.
$$

Book value = original principal − amount in sinking fund
$$= \$15,000 - \$7,331.89 = \$7,668.11$$

SOLVED PROBLEMS

8.38 A condominium association decided to set up a sinking fund to accumulate $40,000 by the end of 3 years to build a new swimming pool.

(a) What monthly deposits are required if the fund earns interest at 9% compounded monthly?

(b) If there are 120 apartment units in the condominium, what is the monthly sinking fund assessment per unit?

SOLUTION

(a) The sinking fund deposits form an ordinary annuity.

$$S = \$40,000 \qquad i = \frac{0.09}{12} = 0.0075 \qquad n = 3 \times 12 = 36$$

$$R = \frac{S}{s_{\overline{n}|i}}$$

$$= \frac{\$40,000}{s_{\overline{36}|0.0075}} = \frac{\$40,000}{41.152716} = \$971.99$$

(b) The monthly assessment per unit is:

$$\frac{\$971.99}{120 \text{ units}} = \$8.10/\text{unit}$$

8.39 For the fund in Prob. 8.38, show the first six lines of the sinking fund schedule.

SOLUTION

The monthly deposit is:

$$120 \text{ units} \times \$8.10/\text{unit} = \$972$$

First month:

Amount at beginning:	0.00	
Interest:	0.00	Total
Monthly deposit:	$972.00	increase: $972.00
Amount at end:	$972.00	

Second month:

Amount at beginning:	$ 972.00	
Interest ($972 × 0.0075):	7.29	Total
Monthly deposit:	972.00	increase: $979.29
Amount at end:	$1,951.29	

Third month:

Amount at beginning:	$1,951.29	
Interest ($1,951.29 × 0.0075):	14.63	Total
Monthly deposit:	972.00	increase: $986.63
Amount at end:	$2,937.92	

Fourth month:

Amount at beginning:	$2,937.92	
Interest ($2,937.92 × 0.0075):	22.03	Total
Monthly deposit:	972.00	increase: $994.03
Amount at end:	$3,931.95	

Fifth month:

Amount at beginning:	$3,931.95	
Interest ($3,931.95 × 0.0075):	29.49	Total
Monthly deposit:	972.00	increase: $1,001.49
Amount at end:	$4,933.44	

Sixth month:

Amount at beginning:	$4,933.44	
Interest ($4,933.44 × 0.0075):	37.00	Total
Monthly deposit:	972.00	increase: $1,009.00
Amount at end:	$5,942.44	

Month	Amount at Beginning	Interest at $\frac{3}{4}$%	+	Monthly Deposit	=	Total Increase	Amount at End
1	0	0		$972.00		$ 972.00	$ 972.00
2	$ 972.00	$ 7.29		972.00		979.29	1,951.29
3	1,951.29	14.63		972.00		986.63	2,937.92
4	2,937.92	22.03		972.00		994.03	3,931.95
5	3,931.95	29.49		972.00		1,001.49	4,933.44
6	4,933.44	37.00		972.00		1,009.00	5,942.44

We may check the amount in the fund at the end of 6 months by finding the accumulated value of six deposits as follows:

$$R = \$972 \qquad i = 0.0075 \qquad k = 6$$

$$S_k = Rs_{\overline{k}|i}$$
$$= \$972 s_{\overline{6}|0.0075} = \$972 \times 6.1136314 = \$5,942.45$$

8.40   Show the last two lines of the sinking fund schedule in Prob. 8.39.

SOLUTION

First we must calculate the amount in the fund at the end of the 34th month as the accumulated value of 34 payments:

$$R = \$972 \qquad i = 0.0075 \qquad k = 34$$

$$S_k = Rs_{\overline{k}|i}$$
$$= \$972 s_{\overline{34}|0.0075} = \$972 \times 38.564578 = \$37,484.77$$

By using the procedure shown in Prob. 8.39, we can now complete the last two lines of the sinking fund schedule. The results are shown below.

Month	Amount at Beginning	Interest at $\frac{3}{4}$%	+	Monthly Deposit	=	Total Increase	Amount at End
35	$37,484.77	$281.14		$972.00		$1,253.14	$38,737.91
36	38,737.91	290.53		972.00		1,262.53	40,000.44

The final amount is 44¢ over, due to rounding.

8.41 How much interest did the sinking fund in Prob. 8.40 accumulate?

SOLUTION

The final amount in the fund	$40,000.44
Less total deposits (36 deposits × $972)	34,992.00
Total interest earned	$ 5,008.44

8.42 On a debt of $20,000, interest is at 16% payable quarterly, and quarterly deposits are made into a sinking fund to discharge the debt at the end of 5 years. If the sinking fund earns interest at 10% compounded quarterly, what is the quarterly expense of the debt?

SOLUTION

Quarterly interest on the debt at $i = 0.16/4 = 0.04$:

$$\$20,000 \times 0.04 = \$800$$

Quarterly deposit (R) into the sinking fund:

$$S = \$20,000 \qquad i = \frac{0.10}{4} = 0.025 \qquad n = 4 \times 5 = 20$$

$$R = \frac{S}{s_{\overline{n}|i}}$$

$$= \frac{\$20,000}{s_{\overline{20}|0.025}} = \frac{\$20,000}{25.544656} = \$782.94$$

Quarterly expense of the debt = interest on loan + deposit in sinking fund

$$= \$800 + \$782.94 = \$1,582.94$$

8.43 Find the book value of the borrower's debt in Prob. 8.42 at the end of 3 years.

SOLUTION

The amount in the sinking fund at the end of the third year is the accumulated value of 12 deposits.

$$R = \$782.94 \qquad i = 0.025 \qquad k = 12$$

$$S_k = Rs_{\overline{k}|i}$$

$$= \$782.94 s_{\overline{12}|0.025} = \$782.94 \times 13.795553 = \$10,801.09$$

Book value = original principal − amount in sinking fund

$$\doteq \$20,000 - \$10,801.09 = \$9,198.91$$

8.44 A city issues $1,000,000 worth of bonds to raise capital to improve the sewage treatment system. Interest on bonds is at 13% per annum payable semiannually.

(*a*) What semiannual deposits must be made into a sinking fund earning interest at 9% compounded semiannually in order to redeem the bonds at the end of 15 years?

(*b*) What is the semiannual expense of the debt?

SOLUTION

(*a*) The sinking fund deposits form an ordinary annuity.

$$S = \$1,000,000 \qquad i = \frac{0.09}{2} = 0.045 \qquad n = 15 \times 2 = 30$$

$$R = \frac{S}{s_{\overline{n}|i}}$$

$$= \frac{\$1,000,000}{s_{\overline{30}|0.045}} = \frac{\$1,000,000}{61.00707} = \$16,391.54$$

(b)   Semiannual interest on bonds:

$$6\tfrac{1}{2}\% \times \$1,000,000 = \$65,000$$

Semiannual expense of the debt = interest + deposit in sinking fund
$$= \$65,000 + \$16,391.54 = \$81,391.54$$

8.45   Instead of issuing bonds, should the city in Prob. 8.44 borrow $1,000,000 at 14% compounded annually and amortize the debt by equal semiannual payments?

SOLUTION:

$$A = \$1,000,000 \qquad i = \frac{0.14}{2} = 0.07 \qquad n = 15 \times 2 = 30$$

$$R = \frac{A}{a_{\overline{n}|i}}$$

$$= \frac{\$1,000,000}{a_{\overline{30}|0.07}} = \frac{\$1,000,000}{12.409041} = \$80,586.41$$

Since the semiannual expense under amortization is less than the expense in the sinking fund method, the city should borrow $1,000,000 at 14% compounded semiannually and amortize the debt. By doing so, the city could save $805.15 (from $81,391.56 − $80,586.41) semiannually.

8.4   CAPITAL BUDGETING

Capital budgeting involves choosing among investment alternatives such as which assets to acquire or replace or whether to buy or lease. Comparing the present values of cash flows of the different alternatives is therefore essential to capital budgeting.

EXAMPLE 12

An investor must decide between two investment alternatives. Alternative 1 will give the investor a return of $2,700 at the end of 2 years plus $11,500 at the end of 6 years. Alternative 2 will give a return of $2,000 at the end of each year for 6 years. Which alternative is preferable if money is worth 12%?

Alternative 1:

There are two components to this investment, and the present value of each must be determined. The sum of the present value of the components is then the present value of this alternative. Since each component consists of a lump sum payment, we use the formula for present value presented in Prob. 8.24:

$$A = S\,\frac{1}{(1+i)^n}$$

Component 1	Component 2
$S_1 = \$2,700 \qquad i = 0.12 \qquad n_1 = 2$	$S_2 = \$11,500 \qquad i = 0.12 \qquad n_2 = 6$

$$A_1 = S_1\,\frac{1}{(1+i)^{n_1}} \qquad\qquad A_2 = S_2\,\frac{1}{(1+i)^{n_2}}$$

$$= \$2,700\left[\frac{1}{(1.12)^2}\right] \qquad\qquad = \$11,500\left[\frac{1}{(1.12)^6}\right]$$

$$= \$2,700\left(\frac{1}{1.2544}\right) = \$2,152.42 \qquad = \$11,500\left(\frac{1}{1.9738227}\right) = \$5,826.26$$

$$A_{\text{total}} = A_1 + A_2$$
$$= \$2,152.42 + \$5,826.26 = \$7,978.68$$

Alternative 2:

Since the return on the investment is in equal periodic payments, the formula for present value used is

$$A = Ra_{\overline{n}|i}$$

$$R = \$2,000 \qquad i = 0.12 \qquad n = 6$$

$$\begin{aligned}
A &= Ra_{\overline{n}|i} \\
&= \$2,000 a_{\overline{6}|0.12} \\
&= \$2,000(4.1114073) \leftarrow \\
&= \$8,222.81
\end{aligned}$$

$$\left\{\begin{aligned}
a_{\overline{n}|i} &= \dfrac{1 - \dfrac{1}{(1+i)^n}}{i} \\[2ex]
&= \dfrac{1 - \dfrac{1}{(1.12)^6}}{0.12} \\[2ex]
&= 4.1114073
\end{aligned}\right.$$

Alternative 2 is the preferable investment since the present value of its return on investment exceeds that of alternative 1.

Capital investment projects involve cash outflows (costs) and cash inflows (returns). The difference between the present value of cash inflows and outflows is the *net present value*.

$$\text{Net present value} = \text{present value of inflows} - \text{present value of outflows}$$

For a given rate of return, the investor should accept those capital investment projects having a positive or zero net present value and reject those having a negative net present value. Because the application of present value techniques to capital investment projects usually involves estimates, the amounts in this section are rounded to the nearest dollar.

EXAMPLE 13

A publishing company is considering publishing a book. Cost and sales estimates for the book are as follows:

Acquisition cost	$10,000
Prepublication (editorial and production) costs	37,000
Yearly reprinting cost	11,900
Yearly distribution cost	2,000
Net return at the end of each year for 5 years	33,413
Yearly royalty to author	7,425

If the company requires an 18% return on its investment, would the company find it profitable to publish this book? See Fig. 8-10, below.

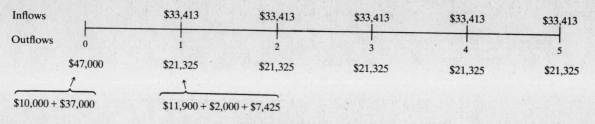

Fig. 8-10

Present value of inflows:

$$R = \$33,413 \qquad i = 0.18 \qquad n = 5$$

$$\begin{aligned}
A &= Ra_{\overline{n}|i} \\
&= \$33,413 a_{\overline{5}|0.18} \\
&= \$33,413(3.127171) \leftarrow \\
&= \$104,488
\end{aligned}$$

$$\left\{\begin{aligned}
a_{\overline{n}|i} &= \dfrac{1 - \dfrac{1}{(1+i)^n}}{i} \\[2ex]
&= \dfrac{1 - \dfrac{1}{(1.18)^5}}{0.18} \\[2ex]
&= 3.127171
\end{aligned}\right.$$

Present value of outflows:

$$R = \$21,325 \qquad i = 0.18 \qquad n = 5$$

$$A = Ra_{\overline{n}|i}$$
$$= \$21,325a_{\overline{5}|0.18} = \$21,325(3.127171) = \$66,687$$

$$A_{\text{total}} = \$47,000 \text{ (from year 0)} + \$66,687 = \$113,687$$

Net present value = present value of inflows − present value of outflows
$$= \$104,488 - \$113,687 = -\$9,199$$

The negative net present value indicates that the project is not profitable since it does not meet the required 18% return on investment required by the publisher.

SOLVED PROBLEMS

8.46 A company must decide whether to buy computer equipment for $380,000 and enter a service contract requiring the payment of $1,200 at the end of each month for 5 years or whether to enter a 5-year lease agreement requiring the payment of $9,000 at the beginning of each month. If leased, the equipment may be purchased at the end of 5 years for $50,000. If the company can earn 15% compounded monthly on its capital, should the company buy or lease?

SOLUTION

The cash outflows (costs) for the two alternatives are shown in Fig. 8-11.

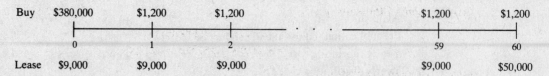

Fig. 8-11

Present value of the costs to buy:

Present value of cash payment for the equipment:

$$\$380,000$$

Present value of the service contract:

$$R = \$1,200 \qquad i = 0.0125 \qquad n = 60$$

$$A = Ra_{\overline{n}|i}$$
$$= \$1,200a_{\overline{60}|0.0125} = \$1,200 \times 42.034592 = \$50,442$$

$$A_{\text{total}} = \$380,000 + \$50,442 = \$430,442$$

Present value of the costs to lease:

Present value of the monthly lease (annuity due):

$$R = \$9,000 \qquad i = 0.0125 \qquad n = 60$$

$$A = Ra_{\overline{n}|i}(1 + i)$$
$$= \$9,000a_{\overline{60}|0.0125}(1.0125) = \$9,000(42.034592)(1.0125) = \$383,040$$

Present value of purchase price after 5 years:

$$A = S \frac{1}{(1+i)^n}$$

$$= \$50,000 \left[\frac{1}{(1.0125)^{60}} \right] = \$23,728$$

$$A_{total} = \$383,040 + \$23,728 = \$406,768$$

Since the present value of the costs to lease is less than the present value of the costs to buy, the company should lease the computer equipment.

8.47 What would be the outcome in Prob. 8.46 if (a) the time value of money is not considered; (b) the rate of return is 9% compounded monthly?

SOLUTION

(a) If we do not take into account the time value of money, the present value of the costs to buy is simply

$$\$380,000 + 60(\$1,200) = \$452,000$$

and the present value of the costs to lease is

$$60(\$9,000) + \$50,000 = \$590,000$$

Since the cost to buy is less than the cost to lease, the company would probably decide to buy the computer equipment.

(b) Using $i = 0.09/12 = 0.0075$, we repeat the calculations of Prob. 8.46.

Present value of the costs to buy:

$$A_{total} = \$380,000 + \$1,200 a_{\overline{60}|0.0075}$$
$$= \$380,000 + \$57,808 = \$437,808$$

Present value of the costs to lease:

$$A_{total} = \$9,000 a_{\overline{60}|0.0075}(1.0075) + \$50,000 \left[\frac{1}{(1.0075)^{60}} \right]$$

$$= \$436,812 + \$31,935 = \$468,747$$

At 9% compounded monthly, the company would find it more profitable to buy the computer equipment than to lease it.

8.48 An investor must decide between two investment alternatives. Alternative 1 will give the investor a return of $15,000 at the end of 3 years plus $40,000 at the end of 5 years. Alternative 2 will give the investor a return of $9,000 at the end of each of the next 5 years. Which alternative is preferable if money is worth (a) 11%, (b) 20%?

SOLUTION

(a) For $i = 11\%$

Present value of alternative 1:

There are two components to this alternative. Since each is a lump sum payment, to find the present value we use:

$$A = S \frac{1}{(1+i)^n}$$

$$\text{Component 1}$$

$$S_1 = \$15,000 \qquad i = 0.11 \qquad n_1 = 3$$

$$A_1 = S_1 \frac{1}{(1+i)^{n_1}}$$

$$= \$15,000 \left[\frac{1}{(1.11)^3}\right]$$

$$= \$10,968$$

$$\text{Component 2}$$

$$S_2 = \$40,000 \qquad i = 0.11 \qquad n_2 = 5$$

$$A_2 = S_2 \frac{1}{(1+i)^{n_2}}$$

$$= \$40,000 \left[\frac{1}{(1.11)^5}\right]$$

$$= \$23,738$$

$$A_{\text{total}} = A_1 + A_2$$
$$= \$10,968 + \$23,738 = \$34,706$$

Present value of alternative 2:

Since the return on investment is in equal periodic payments to find the present value we use:

$$A = Ra_{\overline{n}|i}$$

$$R = \$9,000 \qquad i = 0.11 \qquad n = 5$$

$$A = Ra_{\overline{n}|i}$$
$$= \$9,000 a_{\overline{5}|0.11}$$
$$= \$9,000(3.695897) \leftarrow$$
$$= \$33,263$$

$$a_{\overline{n}|i} = \frac{1 - \dfrac{1}{(1+i)^n}}{i}$$

$$= \frac{1 - \dfrac{1}{(1.11)^5}}{0.11}$$

$$= 3.695897$$

Since at 11% the present value of alternative 1 is greater than that of alternative 2, alternative 1 is the preferable investment.

(b)   For $i = 20\%$

Present value of alternative 1:

$$A_{\text{total}} = S_1 \frac{1}{(1+i)^{n_1}} + S_2 \frac{1}{(1+i)^{n_2}}$$

$$= \$15,000 \left[\frac{1}{(1.20)^3}\right] + \$40,000 \left[\frac{1}{(1.20)^5}\right]$$

$$= \$8,681 + \$16,075 = \$24,756$$

Present value of alternative 2:

$$A = Ra_{\overline{n}|i}$$
$$= \$9,000 a_{\overline{5}|0.20}$$
$$= \$9,000(2.9906121) \leftarrow$$
$$= \$26,916$$

$$a_{\overline{n}|i} = \frac{1 - \dfrac{1}{(1+i)^n}}{i}$$

$$= \frac{1 - \dfrac{1}{(1.20)^5}}{0.20}$$

$$= 2.9906121$$

At 20%, alternative 2 is the preferable investment.

8.49   The Southern Manufacturing Company completed a feasibility study concerning the development of a new product. The study includes the following estimates:

Initial cost outlay	$1,500,000
Further outlay at the end of 3 years	800,000
Residual value after 5 years	500,000
Net returns at the end of each year for 5 years	550,000

SOLUTION

Present value of inflows:

$$A_{total} = Ra_{\overline{n}|i} + S\frac{1}{(1+i)^n}$$

$$= \$550,000a_{\overline{5}|0.15} + \$500,000\left[\frac{1}{(1.15)^5}\right]$$

$$= \$550,000(3.3521551) + \$500,000(0.49717673) = \$1,843,685 + \$248,588 = \$2,092,273$$

Present value of outflows:

$$A_{total} = \text{current outflow (year 0)} + S\frac{1}{(1+i)^n}$$

$$= \$1,500,000 + \$800,000\left[\frac{1}{(1.15)^3}\right] = \$1,500,000 + \$526,013 = \$2,026,013$$

Net present value = present value of inflow − present value of outflow
$$= \$2,092,273 - \$2,026,013 = \$66,260$$

Since the net present value is positive, the rate of return on the investment is greater than 15% and the venture is profitable and should be undertaken.

8.50 A businesswoman is presented with two alternative projects with the following cash flows:

End of Year	Project A		Project B	
	Inflows	Outflows	Inflows	Outflows
0		$90,000		$50,000
1	$20,000		$30,000	
2	20,000		30,000	40,000
3	20,000		30,000	
4	70,000		30,000	

Which proposal is more desirable if the required rate of return is 12%?

SOLUTION

Project A

Present value of inflows:

$$A_{total} = Ra_{\overline{n}|i} + S\frac{1}{(1+i)^n}$$

$$= \$20,000a_{\overline{3}|0.12} + \$70,000\left[\frac{1}{(1.12)^4}\right]$$

$$= \$48,037 + \$44,486 = \$92,523$$

Present value of outflows: $90,000

Net present value = present value of inflow − present value of outflow
$$\$92,523 - \$90,000 = \$2,523$$

Project B

Present value of inflows:

$$A = Ra_{\overline{n}|i}$$

$$= \$30,000a_{\overline{4}|0.12} = \$91,120$$

Present value of outflows:

$$A_{total} = \text{current outflow (year 0)} + S\,\frac{1}{(1+i)^n}$$

$$= \$50,000 + \$40,000\left[\frac{1}{(1.12)^2}\right]$$

$$= \$50,000 + \$31,888$$

$$= \$81,888$$

Net present value = present value of inflow − present value of outflow

$$= \$91,120 - \$81,888 = \$9,232$$

Since the net present value of project B is greater than the net present value of project A, project B is the more desirable one.

Supplementary Problems

8.51 Compute the accumulation factor $s_{\overline{n}|i}$ when (a) $i = 0.0105$ and $n = 15$, (b) $i = 0.088$ and $n = 25$, and (c) $i = 0.10/12$ and $n = 120$.

8.52 Find the accumulated value of an ordinary simple annuity of \$1,500 per year for 10 years if money is worth (a) $j_1 = 6\%$, (b) $j_1 = 12\%$, and (c) 18% effective.

8.53 Find the amount of the following investments:

(a) \$500 at the end of each quarter for 4 years and 3 months at 10% compounded quarterly,

(b) \$80 at the end of each month for 3 years at $13\frac{1}{2}\%$ compounded monthly,

(c) \$2,000 at the end of each half year for 6 years at $11\frac{1}{2}\%$ compounded semiannually.

8.54 Elizabeth deposits \$180 every month into a savings account that pays interest at $j_{12} = 12\%$. How much money is in her account on June 1, 19X7, if the first deposit is made on October 1, 19X4?

8.55 How much interest did Elizabeth accumulate by June 1, 19X7, in Prob. 8.54?

8.56 A couple wants to save enough money to open their own business. If they deposit \$1,200 at the end of every 3 months into a fund that earns interest at 11% compounded quarterly, how much would be in the fund at the end of (a) 3 years, (b) 5 years?

8.57 At the end of each month John makes regular deposits of \$100 for 2 years and then \$150 for the next 2 years. Find the accumulated value of his deposits at the end of 4 years if interest is at $j_{12} = 10\frac{1}{2}\%$.

8.58 Compute the discount factor $a_{\overline{n}|i}$ when (a) $i = 0.005$ and $n = 300$; (b) $i = 0.11$ and $n = 10$; and (c) $i = 0.055$ and $n = 18$.

8.59 Find the present value of an ordinary simple annuity of \$800 per half-year for 15 years at (a) $j_2 = 8\%$, (b) $j_2 = 10\%$, (c) $j_2 = 12\%$.

8.60 Find the discounted value of the following ordinary annuities: (a) \$100 a month for 50 months at $j_{12} = 7\frac{1}{2}\%$, (b) \$5,000 a year for 20 years at 12.148% effective, and (c) \$1,200 per quarter for 5 years, 6 months at $j_4 = 9\frac{3}{4}\%$.

8.61   The Hutchesons want to save enough money to send their two children to college. The children are 4 years apart in age, so the parents want to have a sum of money that will provide $4,000 a year for 8 years. Find the sum required 1 year before the first withdrawal if interest is 11% per annum.

8.62   Monica receives an inheritance of $500 at the end of each quarter for 10 years. If money is worth $j_4 = 14\%$, what is the cash value of this inheritance?

8.63   Mr. McDonald signed a contract that calls for a down payment of $3,000 and for payments of $350 a month for 4 years. Money is worth $j_{12} = 13\frac{1}{2}\%$. What is the cash value of the contract?

8.64   The contract of Prob. 8.63 is sold to Ms. Goddard after the twelfth payment has been made. What price did Ms. Goddard pay to yield her $j_{12} = 15\%$?

8.65   To settle a debt with interest at $10\frac{1}{2}\%$ compounded semiannually, Mrs. Bauer agrees to make eight payments of $500 at the end of each half-year and a balloon payment of $2,854.07 six months later. What is the debt?

8.66   Mr. Wilson wants to sell his car. He receives two offers: (*a*) $1,000 down and a note which calls for monthly payments of $150 for 2 years and (*b*) $1,500 down and $250 per month for 1 year. Find the present value of each offer if the money is worth $j_{12} = 12\%$.

8.67   Brenda Owen wants to accumulate $25,000 in 4 years as a down payment on a new house. Find the size of each deposit if she makes deposits at the end of each quarter into a fund that pays 12% per annum compounded quarterly.

8.68   Find the size of each deposit in Prob. 8.67 if Brenda Owen makes deposits at the end of each month into a fund that pays interest at $j_{12} = 12\%$.

8.69   A refrigerator selling for $950 may be purchased for $150 down and the balance in equal monthly payments over a 1-year period. Find the monthly payment if the interest is charged at 18% compounded monthly.

8.70   Mr. and Mrs. Scott need to borrow $8,000 for some home renovations. They want to repay the loan with monthly payments over 4 years. A finance company will charge the interest at $j_{12} = 21\%$. Find the (*a*) monthly payment and (*b*) total interest on the loan.

8.71   What would be the monthly savings on interest in Prob. 8.70 if the Scotts could borrow the money at $j_{12} = 18\%$.

8.72   To prepare for early retirement a businessman deposited $5,000 into a retirement savings plan each year for 20 years, starting on his 45th birthday. When he is 65, he wishes to withdraw 30 equal annual payments. If the interest is at 11% effective, find (*a*) the accumulated value of the deposits on his 64th birthday and (*b*) the size of each annual withdrawal.

8.73   A company wants to accumulate $150,000 by December 31, 19X8, to buy new equipment. The company plans to make 12 semiannual deposits starting December 31, 19X2. If interest is $10\frac{3}{4}\%$ compounded semiannually, what semiannual deposit is required?

8.74   If the company in Prob. 8.73 makes semiannual deposits of $5,000, how much money will it have by December 31, 19X8?

8.75   A television set is bought for $60 down and $60 a month for 12 months. If interest is charged at $j_{12} = 19\frac{1}{2}\%$, what is the cash price of the television set?

8.76   An insurance policy pays a death benefit of $30,000 in a lump sum or in equal amounts at the beginning of each 3 months for 10 years. What size would these quarterly payments be if $j_4 = 9\%$?

8.77 What will the monthly payment be on a $6,500 purchase with $800 down and the rest to be amortized over 4 years at $19\frac{1}{2}$% payable monthly.

8.78 What is the finance charge in Prob. 8.77?

8.79 A loan of $2,000 is to be repaid over 2 years with equal quarterly payments. Find the quarterly payment required if interest on the loan is (a) 10% compounded quarterly and (b) 20% compounded quarterly.

8.80 A car costing $8,589 is purchased by paying $589 down and then equal monthly payments for 3 years at 15% payable monthly. Find (a) the monthly payment, (b) the finance charge, (c) the outstanding principal at the end of 1 year, and (d) the distribution of the thirteenth payment between payment of interest and repayment of the principal.

8.81 Solve Prob. 8.80 with interest at 21% payable monthly.

8.82 Ted Anderson purchased a condominium and signed a mortgage contract for $40,000 to be paid in equal monthly payments over 20 years with interest at $16\frac{1}{2}$% compounded monthly. Find the monthly payment.

8.83 In Prob. 8.82, how much interest did Ted Anderson pay during each of the first 5 years?

8.84 If the mortgage loan in Prob. 8.82 can be refinanced after 5 years, without penalty, at 12% compounded monthly, how much would Ted Anderson save monthly on interest?

8.85 Dorothy Weis is repaying a loan with 60 monthly payments of $112 each. After making her twentieth payment, she wants to pay the loan in full. If interest on the loan is at $13\frac{1}{2}$% per annum payable monthly, find (a) the amount of the loan payoff and (b) the unearned finance charge.

8.86 Solve Prob. 8.85 with interest on the loan at 18% per annum payable monthly.

8.87 What is the true annual percentage rate of a 9% add-on loan paid over 1 year in monthly installments?

8.88 Jack can pay his tennis membership fee of $160 all at once or over 1 year at $15 per month. Find the annual percentage rate on the time-payment option.

8.89 What is the maximum rate you can afford to pay on a 29-year mortgage of $50,000, if you want to pay a maximum of (a) $555 per month, (b) $450 per month?

8.90 Elsa Brown took out an $8,000 second mortgage on her new house. If the mortgage is to be paid in monthly payments of $200 over 5 years, what is the annual percentage rate?

8.91 Find the annual deposit for accumulating

(a) $10,000 by equal annual deposits made at the end of each of the next 4 years into a fund earning interest at 10% effective

(b) $15,000 by equal annual deposits made at the end of each of the next 5 years into a fund earning interest at 13% effective

8.92 A couple is saving for a down payment on a new home. They want to accumulate $15,000 at the end of 5 years by making equal deposits at the end of each month into a fund earning interest at 9% compounded monthly.

(a) Find the monthly deposit required.

(b) How much will be in the fund just after the twenty-fourth deposit?

(c) How much interest will be accumulated during the first 2 years?

(d) How much of the increase in the fund at the time of the twenty-fifth deposit will be due to interest?

8.93 A company borrows $200,000, paying interest annually on this sum at $16\frac{1}{4}$%. A sinking fund with annual deposits earning interest at 9% compounded annually is established to repay the debt at the end of 10 years. Find (a) the annual expense of the debt and (b) the book value of the company's debt at the end of 5 years.

8.94 Should the company in Prob. 8.93 borrow $200,000 for 10 years at 18% compounded annually and amortize the debt by equal annual payments?

8.95 A company requires an additional 300,000 square feet of storage space. Alternative 1 is to build a 300,000–square foot building now, at a cost of $19 per square foot. Alternative 2 is to build a 200,000–square foot building now at a cost of $20 per square foot, and then add 100,000 square feet 2 years from now, at a cost of $24 per square foot. Which alternative is better, based on annual interest rate 12%?

8.96 Henry Kugler is considering investing in one of three apartment buildings. If he is willing to accept a minimum rate of return of 15% payable monthly, which, if any, of the three alternative apartment buildings should he accept?

	Cost	Net Monthly Return	Life (Years)	Residual Value
(a)	$105,000	$1,400	20	$60,000
(b)	130,000	1,750	15	30,000
(c)	155,000	2,050	25	50,000

8.97 A car can be purchased for $11,500. The same car can be leased for 3 years by making payments of $280 at the beginning of each month and can be purchased at the end of the lease for $5,750. Which alternative is preferable if money is worth (a) 18% compounded monthly, (b) $13\frac{1}{2}$% compounded monthly?

8.98 A food processing company has to make a decision whether or not to expand its production facilities. A feasibility study showed the following estimates:

Initial cost outlay	$80,000
Further outlay in 4 years	60,000
Residual value after 10 years	20,000
Net returns at the end of each year for 10 years	22,000

Find the net present value of the project and indicate whether the expansion should be undertaken if the desired rate of return on investment is 13%.

8.99 An investor is presented with two alternative projects. Alternative A requires an investment of $18,000 now, with expected returns of $15,000 in 3 years and $20,000 in 6 years. Alternative B requires an investment of $10,000 now and another $10,000 two years from now, with expected returns of $2,000 at the end of each half-year for 10 years. Which project is preferable if the required rate of return is 12% compounded semiannually?

Answers to Supplementary Problems

8.51   (*a*) 16.154281, (*b*) 82.228576, (*c*) 204.84498

8.52   (*a*) $19,771.19, (*b*) $26,323.10, (*c*) $35,281.96

8.53   (*a*) $10,432.36, (*b*) $3526.51, (*c*) $33,251.49

8.54 $6,996.42

8.55 $1,056.42

8.56   (*a*) $16,790.56, (*b*) $31,436.88

8.57 $7,262.39

8.58   (*a*) 155.20686, (*b*) 5.889232, (*c*) 11.246074

8.59   (*a*) $13,833.63, (*b*) $12,297.96, (*c*) $11,011.86

8.60   (*a*) $4,282.76, (*b*) $37,003.43, (*c*) $20,248.04

8.61 $20,584.49

8.62 $10,677.54

8.63 $15,926.42

8.64 $10,096.54

8.65 $5,000

8.66   (*a*) $4,186.51, (*b*) 4,313.77

8.67 $1,240.27

8.68 $408.35

8.69 $73.34

8.70   (*a*) $247.73, (*b*) $3,891.04

8.71 $12.73

8.72   (*a*) $321,014.16, (*b*) $36,924.52

8.73 $8,750.77

8.74 $85,706.79

8.75 $709.38

8.76 $1,120.12

8.77 $171.94

8.78 $2,553.12

8.79   (*a*) $278.94, (*b*) $309.45

8.80   (*a*) $277.33; (*b*) $1,983.88; (*c*) $5,719.48; (*d*) interest = $71.49, principal portion = $205.84

8.81   (*a*) $301.41; (*b*) $2,850.76; (*c*) $5,865.33; (*d*) interest = $102.64, principal portion = $198.77

8.82 $571.57

8.83 $6,579.49, $6,529.77, $6,471.16, $6,402.13, $6,320.79

8.84 $115.39

8.85   (*a*) $3,591.64, (*b*) $888.36

8.86   (*a*) $3,350.57, (*b*) $1,129.43

8.87   16.25%

8.88   22.25%

8.89   (*a*) 13%, (*b*) 10.25%

8.90   17.25%

8.91   (*a*) $2,154.71, (*b*) $2,314.72

8.92   (*a*) $198.88, (*b*) $5,208.36, (*c*) $435.24, (*d*) $39.06

8.93   (*a*) $45,664.02, (*b*) $121,217.15

8.94   Yes. Annual savings = $1,161.09

8.95   Alternative 1

8.96   (*c*)

8.97   (*a*) leasing, (*b*) buying

8.98 $8,470; expansion should be undertaken

8.99   Alternative B

Chapter 9

Stocks and Bonds

9.1 STOCKS AND DIVIDENDS

One way to invest money is to buy *stock* or *shares* in a corporation. A *shareholder* is a part owner of the corporation and receives part of the corporation's profits in the form of *dividends*. The price of the share, called *par value*, is set by the company when the stock is first sold to the public. When the stock is resold on the *stock market*, its price is determined by what the buyer is willing to pay and the seller is willing to accept. This value, called the *market value*, is published in the financial section of most major newspapers. Typical stock quotations are shown in Table 9-1.

Table 9-1 Stock Quotations

19XX High	19XX Low	Stock	Dividend in Dollars	Sales 100's	High	Low	Close	Net Change
$27\frac{7}{8}$	20	A	1.50	1,221	$24\frac{1}{2}$	$23\frac{5}{8}$	$24\frac{1}{2}$	$+\frac{7}{8}$
$16\frac{1}{4}$	8	B	.60	48	$9\frac{3}{4}$	$9\frac{5}{8}$	$9\frac{5}{8}$	$-\frac{1}{8}$
$119\frac{1}{4}$	$97\frac{1}{8}$	C	2	54	$110\frac{3}{8}$	$108\frac{1}{2}$	$108\frac{5}{8}$	$-\frac{3}{8}$
83	$62\frac{1}{4}$	D	pf 5.50	9	$64\frac{1}{4}$	$64\frac{1}{4}$	$64\frac{1}{4}$	$+\frac{1}{4}$
$22\frac{1}{8}$	$15\frac{1}{8}$	E	pf .78	1	$20\frac{3}{4}$	$20\frac{3}{4}$	$20\frac{3}{4}$	$-\frac{1}{4}$

High price for the year — Name of the company — Number of shares sold that day — Low price for the day — Difference between the closing prices of the day and the prior trading day

Low price for the year — Dividend for the year — High price for the day — Price for the last trade of the day

EXAMPLE 1

Referring to Table 9-1, find (*a*) the total dividend paid for the past year to an investor owning 300 shares of stock A, and (*b*) the price of 100 shares of stock B purchased at the high price for the day.

(*a*) Dividend per share of stock A: $1.50

   Total dividend: $300 \times \$1.50 = \$450$

(*b*) High price of a share of stock B: $\$9\frac{3}{4} = \$9.75$

   Price of 100 shares at the high price: $100 \times \$9.75 = \$975$

The two kinds of stock sold are *common* and *preferred*. The dividend on preferred stock is fixed when the stock is issued. Stock D in Table 9-1 is a preferred stock (see the abbreviation "pf") paying a dividend of 5.50% of the par value (usually $100). Dividends to preferred stockholders are paid before dividends are paid to common stockholders. Most preferred stock is *cumulative*. When a company declares

226

dividends in any given year, the holders of cumulative preferred stock will receive all dividends not declared in previous years plus the current year's dividend. On *noncumulative* preferred stock, declared dividends are paid only for the current year.

EXAMPLE 2

The ABC Corporation has issued 2,000 shares of $100 par value common stock and 500 shares of 8%, $100 par value preferred stock. If the company declared $12,000 in dividends for the year, what will be the dividend per share of common stock?

Dividend per share of preferred stock: $8\% \times \$100 = \$8$

Total dividend on preferred stock: $500 \times \$8 = \$4,000$

Total dividend on common stock: $\$12,000 - \$4,000 = \$8,000$

Dividend per share of common stock: $\dfrac{\$8,000}{2,000} = \$4$

EXAMPLE 3

Paul White owns 120 shares of a cumulative $7\frac{1}{4}\%$, $100 par value preferred stock. He has not received dividends for the previous 2 years. How much dividend will he receive this year if the company declares dividends?

Yearly dividend for each share: $7\frac{1}{4}\% \times \$100 = \$7.25$

Yearly dividend on 120 shares: $120 \times \$7.25 = \$870$

Total dividend for 3 years: $3 \times \$870 = \$2,610$

Shares are usually traded in groups of 100 shares, called *round lots*. An *odd lot* refers to fewer than 100 shares. An *odd-lot differential fee* of $\$\frac{1}{8}$ for each share traded is added to the price of stock being purchased and subtracted from the price being sold to arrive at the statement price, known as the *execution price*. A commission, based on the dollar value of the stocks traded, is paid to a stockbroker, who acts as an agent performing transactions between buyer and seller. Commission rates depend on the brokerage firm.

All stock sales and transfers made through registered exchanges are liable to a Federal Securities and Exchange Commission (SEC) charge (currently 1¢ per $500 or fraction of $500 of gross proceeds). Additional charges may include the payment of city and/or state transfer taxes. In our examples the SEC charge and taxes will be omitted.

EXAMPLE 4

An investor bought 60 shares of stock selling at $35\frac{1}{8}$. What was the broker's commission if the commission rate was 1.4%?

Execution price per share: $\$35\frac{1}{8} + \$\frac{1}{8} \text{ (odd lot)} = \$35.25$

Cost of shares: $60 \times \$35.25 = \$2,115$

Commission: $1.4\% \times \$2,115 = \$29.61$

EXAMPLE 5

Mrs. Smith sold 130 shares of stock selling at $12\frac{1}{4}$. Find the broker's commission if the commission rate was 1.6%.

Round lot (100 shares)

Execution price per share: $\$12.25$

Gross proceeds from stock: $100 \times 12.25 = \$1,225$

Odd lot $(130 - 100 = 30)$

Execution price per share: $\$12\frac{1}{4} - \$\frac{1}{8} \text{ (odd lot)} = \$12.125$

Gross proceeds from stock: $30 \times \$12.125 = \$363.75$

Total gross proceeds: $\$1,225 + \$363.75 = \$1,588.75$

Total commission: $1.6\% \times \$1,588.75 = \$25.42$

Several criteria may be used to evaluate investments in stocks. The *annual yield*, often expressed as a percent, is the ratio of the annual dividend per share to the price per share.

$$\text{Annual yield} = \frac{\text{annual dividend per share}}{\text{price per share}}$$

The *capital gain* is the net proceeds less the total cost.

$$\text{Capital gain} = \text{net proceeds} - \text{total cost}$$

The *total gain* is the sum of total dividends plus the capital gain.

$$\text{Total gain} = \text{total dividends} + \text{capital gain}$$

Investors usually base their decisions of whether to buy or sell stock on the *estimated total gain* for a specified period of time. This estimate ignores commission, SEC charges, and transfer taxes.

EXAMPLE 6

Find the rate of annual yield on a common stock if the semiannual dividend is $1.35 and the price per share is $18.

Annual dividend: $2 \times \$1.35 = \$2.70$

$$\text{Annual yield} = \frac{\text{annual dividend}}{\text{price per share}}$$

$$= \frac{\$2.70}{\$18} = 0.15 = 15\%$$

EXAMPLE 7

An investor bought a common stock at $22 per share. Her quarterly dividend was 45¢ a share. She sold the stock after 2 years at $37.50 per share. What is (*a*) the total gain per share and (*b*) the percent of total gain relative to cost?

(*a*)   Total dividends per share: 8 quarters $\times$ \$0.45/quarter = \$3.60

$$\text{Capital gain per share} = \text{net proceeds} - \text{total cost}$$
$$= \$37.50 - \$22 = \$15.50$$

$$\text{Total gain per share} = \text{total dividends} + \text{capital gain}$$
$$= \$3.60 + \$15.50 = \$19.10$$

(*b*) $$\text{Total gain percent} = \frac{\text{total gain}}{\text{total cost}} \times 100$$

$$= \frac{\$19.10}{\$22} \times 100 \cong 86.82\%$$

SOLVED PROBLEMS

9.1   Find the cost of 85 shares of stock B in Table 9-1 at the closing price of the day.

   SOLUTION

   Execution price per share: $\$9\frac{5}{8} + \$\frac{1}{8}$ (odd lot) = \$9.75
   Cost of shares: $85 \times \$9.75 = \$828.75$

9.2   Find the gross proceeds from the sale of 215 shares of stock A in Table 9-1 at the low price of the day.

SOLUTION

Round lot (groups of 100 shares)

Execution price per share:	$23.625
Gross proceeds from stock:	$200 \times \$23.625 = \$4,725$

Odd lot $(215 - 200 = 15)$

Execution price per share:	$\$23\frac{5}{8} - \$\frac{1}{8} = \$23.50$
Gross proceeds from stock:	$15 \times \$23.50 = \$352.50$
Total gross proceeds from sale:	$\$4,725 + \$352.50 = \$5,077.50$

9.3   Find the broker's commission on the purchase of 20 shares of stock C in Table 9-1 at the high price of the day, if the commission rate is 2.2%.

SOLUTION

Execution price per share:	$\$110\frac{3}{8} + \$\frac{1}{8} \text{ (odd lot)} = \$110.50$
Cost of shares:	$20 \times \$110.50 = \$2,210$
Commission:	$2.2\% \times \$2,210 = \$48.62$

9.4   Find the broker's commission in Prob. 9.3 if the transaction was a sale.

SOLUTION

Execution price per share:	$\$110\frac{3}{8} - \$\frac{1}{8} = \$110.25$
Proceeds from shares:	$20 \times \$110.25 = \$2,205$
Commission:	$2.2\% \times \$2,205 = \$48.51$

9.5   The Sherlock Corporation declares a dividend of $42,540 to its 5,000 shares of 5.5%, $100 par value preferred stock and its 8,000 shares of common stock. What is the dividend per share of (*a*) preferred stock and (*b*) common stock?

SOLUTION

(*a*)   Dividend per share of preferred stock: $5.5\% \times \$100 = \$5.50$

(*b*)   Since dividends are paid first to preferred stock, the amount available to common stock is calculated as follows:

$$\text{Dividend to common stock} = \text{total dividend} - \text{dividend to preferred stock}$$

Total dividend to preferred stock:	$5,000 \times \$5.50 = \$27,500$
Total dividend to common stock:	$\$42,540 - \$27,500 = \$15,040$
Dividend per share of common stock:	$\dfrac{\$15,040}{8,000} = \$1.88$

9.6   The Ruben Corporation declares dividends as follows from 19X3 to 19X6:

19X3	$11,000
19X4	$37,000
19X5	$8,000
19X6	$45,000

Its outstanding stock consists of 3,000 shares of 7%, $100 par value cumulative preferred stock and 5,000 shares of common stock. No dividends are in arrears as of the end of 19X2. What amount of dividends is paid to each class of stock each year and what are the total dividends for each class for the 4 years?

SOLUTION

The normal preferred dividend is

$$7\% \times \$100 \times 3{,}000 \text{ shares} = \$21{,}000$$

Dividends

Year	Total	Preferred Stock		Arrears	Common Stock
19X3	$ 11,000		$11,000	$10,000*	$ 0
19X4	37,000	$21,000 + $10,000 =	31,000**	0	6,000†
19X5	8,000		8,000	13,000‡	0
19X6	45,000	$21,000 + $13,000 =	34,000**	0	13,000§
Total	$101,000		$84,000		$19,000

*Since the normal preferred dividend is $21,000, then the amount in arrears at the end of 19X3 is $21,000 − $11,000 (the declared dividend). Note that this means that none of the 19X3 dividend is available to common stock.

**The normal preferred dividend is added to the amount in arrears to determine the dividend available to cumulative preferred stock.

†The amount of the 19X4 dividend available to common stock is the total 19X4 dividend less the amount applied to preferred stock:
$$\$37{,}000 - \$31{,}000 = \$6{,}000$$

‡$21,000 − $8,000 = $13,000 in arrears

§$45,000 − $34,000 = $13,000

9.7   Solve Prob. 9.6 if the preferred stock is noncumulative.

SOLUTION

Dividends

Year	Total	Preferred Stock	Common Stock
19X3	$ 11,000	$11,000	$ 0*
19X4	37,000	21,000**	16,000†
19X5	8,000	8,000	0*
19X6	45,000	21,000**	24,000†
Total	$101,000	$61,000	$40,000

*The normal preferred dividend is still $21,000, so none of the 19X3 dividend is available to common stock.

**Since the stock is noncumulative, only the normal preferred dividend amount is available to preferred stock.

†Total dividend − dividend to preferred stock = dividend to common stock.

9.8   Bundy Products, Inc. declares a dividend of $45,000 to its 2,000 shares of 8%, $100 par value preferred stock and its 6,000 shares of common stock. After each common share has received $2.50, preferred shareholders participate with the common shareholders in the distribution of the remaining dividend, in the ratio of shares in each class. Find the total dividend and the dividend per share for each class of stock.

SOLUTION

Normal preferred dividend:	$8\% \times \$100 \times 2{,}000$ shares $= \$16{,}000$	
Stated common dividend:	$\$2.50 \times 6{,}000$ shares $=$ 15,000	

Remainder to be distributed by ratio:

Total shareholders:	$2{,}000 + 6{,}000 = 8{,}000$	
Amount available:	$\$45{,}000 - (\$16{,}000 + \$15{,}000) = \$14{,}000$	
To preferred shareholders:	$\dfrac{2{,}000}{8{,}000} \times \$14{,}000 =$ 3,500	
To common shareholders:	$\dfrac{6{,}000}{8{,}000} \times \$14{,}000 =$ 10,500	

Class of Stock	Total Dividend	Dividend per Share
Preferred	$\$16{,}000 + \$3{,}500 = \$19{,}500$	$\dfrac{\$19{,}500}{2000} = \$9.75$
Common	$\$15{,}000 + \$10{,}500 = \$25{,}500$	$\dfrac{\$25{,}500}{6{,}000} = \$4.25$

9.9 Solve Prob. 9.8 assuming that the preferred stock is not participating in the distribution of the remaining dividends.

SOLUTION

Class of stock	Total Dividend	Dividend per Share
Preferred	$\$16{,}000$	$8\% \times \$100 = \$8.00$
Common	$\$45{,}000 - \$16{,}000 = \$29{,}000$	$\dfrac{\$29{,}000}{6{,}000} = \$4.83$

9.10 Determine the rate of annual yield for stock A in Table 9-1, if bought at the low price of the day.

SOLUTION

Annual dividend is $1.50 per share.

$$\text{Annual yield} = \text{annual dividend per share/price per share}$$
$$= \frac{\$1.50}{\$23.625} \cong 0.0635 = 6.35\%$$

9.11 Three years ago Jeff purchased 100 shares of stock D at $47\frac{1}{8}$ and sold it at the day's closing price, shown in Table 9-1. Assuming that dividends have been constant for the 3-year period, what is (a) the total gain and (b) the annual rate of gain based on cost?

SOLUTION

(a) Gain from dividends per share: $3\,\text{yr} \times \$5.50 = \$16.50$

$$\text{Capital gain per share} = \text{net proceeds} - \text{total cost}$$
$$= \$64\tfrac{1}{4} - \$47\tfrac{1}{8} = \$17\tfrac{1}{8} = \$17.125$$

$$\text{Total gain per share} = \text{total dividends} + \text{capital gain}$$
$$= \$16.50 + \$17.125 = \$33.625$$

Total gain on 100 shares: $100 \times \$33.625 = \$3{,}362.50$

(b) Annual gain on 100 shares: $3,362.50 ÷ 3 yr = $1,120.83

Cost of shares: $100 \times $47.125 = $4,712.50

Annual rate of gain: $1,120.83/$4,712.50 \cong 0.2378 = 23.78\%$

9.12 Two years ago, an investor bought 200 shares of stock E at $31\frac{1}{4}$ and sold it at the day's closing price, shown in Table 9-1. Calculate (a) the investor's total loss and (b) the annual rate of loss based on cost.

SOLUTION

(a) Gain from dividends per share: 2 yr $\times$ \$0.78 = \$1.56

$$\text{Capital loss per share} = \text{total cost} - \text{net proceeds}$$
$$= \$31\tfrac{1}{4} - \$20\tfrac{3}{4} = \$10\tfrac{2}{4} = \$10.50$$

$$\text{Total loss per share} = \text{capital loss} - \text{total dividends}$$
$$= \$10.50 - \$1.56 = \$8.94$$

Total loss on 200 shares: $200 \times \$8.94 = \$1,788$

(b) Annual loss on 200 shares: $\$1,788 \div 2 \text{ yr} = \$894$

Cost of 200 shares: $200 \times \$31.25 = \$6,250$

Annual rate of loss: $\$894/\$6,250 \cong 0.1430 = 14.30\%$

9.2 BONDS

A *bond* is a long-term contract between a borrower (usually a corporation or the government) and a lender (bondholder). The bondholder is a creditor and is paid interest on the *face value* or *par value* of the bond at a specified rate of interest, called *bond rate*. The interest is usually payable semiannually on the dates specified on the bond certificate. On the *redemption date* (or *maturity date*) the bondholder receives the par value of the bond.

Table 9-2 Bond Quotations

Bond			Current Yield	Vol.	High	Low	Close	Net Change
A	$9\frac{3}{8}$	s	95	9.3	16	$102\frac{3}{8}$	$100\frac{1}{8}$	$100\frac{1}{8}$	$+\frac{1}{8}$
B	$7\frac{1}{8}$	s	03	8.0	57	89	$88\frac{1}{2}$	89	$+\frac{5}{8}$
C	$12\frac{1}{2}$	s	84	11.0	14	$110\frac{1}{8}$	110	110	$-\frac{1}{8}$
D	$4\frac{3}{4}$	s	87	6.3	51	$74\frac{7}{8}$	$74\frac{5}{8}$	$74\frac{3}{4}$	$+\frac{7}{8}$
E	8.7	s	02	8.4	265	103	$102\frac{3}{4}$	103	$+\frac{1}{8}$

Name of bond

Interest paid semiannually

Annual return divided by the current price

High price for the day

Price for the last trade of the day

Bond interest rate per year

Year of maturity

Number of $1,000 bonds traded

Low price for the day

Difference between the closing prices of the day and those of the prior trading day

Bonds may be bought and sold in bond exchanges. Current market prices, called *market quotations*, of $100 par value bonds are published daily in the financial pages of major newspapers. Typical bond quotations are shown in Table 9-2.

EXAMPLE 8

Find the market price of one $1,000 bond A in Table 9-2 at the day's closing price.

Day's closing price quotation: $100\frac{1}{8} = \$100.125$

Market price of a $1,000 bond: $10 \times \$100.125 = \$1001.25$

EXAMPLE 9

Find the market price of four $1,000 bonds D in Table 9.2 at the previous day's closing price.

Previous day's closing price quotation: $\$74\frac{3}{4} - \$\frac{7}{8} = \$73\frac{7}{8} = \$73.875$

Market price of four $1,000 bonds: $4 \times 10 \times \$73.875 = \$2,955$

EXAMPLE 10

Find the market price of a $5,000 bond C in Table 9-2 at the day's low price.

Day's low price quotation: $110 = \$110$

Market price of a $5,000 bond: $5 \times 10 \times \$110 = \$5,500$

EXAMPLE 11

How much bond interest will be paid semiannually to an investor who owns six $1,000 bonds E in Table 9-2?

Semiannual interest on $1,000 bond E: $\dfrac{8.7\%}{2} \times \$1,000 = \$43.50$

Semiannual interest on six $1,000 bonds E: $6 \times \$43.50 = \$261$

The market prices of bonds change to reflect changes in the economy and in the current interest rates. A bond priced below its face value is selling at a *discount* and a bond priced above its face value is selling at a *premium*.

EXAMPLE 12

Find the premium on a $1,000 bond A in Table 9-2 at the day's high price.

Day's high price quotation: $102\frac{3}{8} = \$102.375$

Market price of a $1,000 bond: $10 \times \$102.375 = \$1,023.75$

Premium: $\$1,023.75 - \$1,000 = \$23.75$

EXAMPLE 13

Find the discount on a $2,000 bond B in Table 9-2 at the day's low price.

Day's low price quotation: $88\frac{1}{2} = \$88.50$

Market price of a $2,000 bond: $20 \times \$88.50 = \$1,770$

Discount: $\$2,000 - \$1,770 = \$230$

Bonds pay interest semiannually. For bonds purchased between interest dates, the purchaser pays the seller the interest earned (accrued) from the last bond interest payment date to the date of purchase. This so-called *accrued bond interest* is computed by the simple interest formula

$$I = P \times r \times t$$

where I = accrued bond interest
        P = face value of bonds purchased
        r = annual bond rate
        t = time from last interest payment date to date of purchase

Approximate time (each month = 30 days) and a 360-day year is used to determine time t.

Total purchase price of a bond purchased between bond interest dates is then the sum of the market price and the accrued bond interest. Any commission to the broker should also be added to the purchase price. Since these commissions are relatively small, they are ignored in this book.

EXAMPLE 14

A \$5,000, 8% bond paying interest on February 1 and August 1 is sold on April 8. Find the accrued bond interest.

Time from:

Feb. 1 to Apr. 1 = 2 × 30 =	60 days
Apr. 1 to Apr. 8	7 days
Feb. 1 to Apr. 8	67 days

Accrued bond interest:

$$I = Prt$$

$$= \$5,000 \times 0.08 \times \frac{67}{360} = \$74.44$$

EXAMPLE 15

On March 26, an investor bought eight \$1,000 bonds D at the day's closing price, shown in Table 9-2. Calculate the total purchase price if the interest dates are June 1 and December 1.

Day's closing price quotations: $74\frac{3}{4} = \$74.75$
Market price of eight \$1,000 bonds: $8 \times 10 \times \$74.75 = \$5,980$
Time from:

Dec. 1 to Mar. 1 = 3 × 30 =	90 days
Mar. 1 to Mar. 26	25 days
Dec. 1 to Mar. 26	115 days

Accrued bond interest:

$$I = Prt$$

$$= \$8,000 \times 0.0475 \times \frac{115}{360} = \$121.39$$

Total purchase price = market price + accrued interest
$$= \$5,980 + 121.39 = \$6,101.39$$

To measure the rate of return on an investment in bonds, we may calculate either the rate of *current yield* or the rate of *yield to maturity*. The formula for the rate of current yield is

$$\text{Rate of current yield} = \frac{\text{annual interest}}{\text{market price}}$$

The estimate for the rate of yield to maturity is based on the average annual interest divided by the average investment.

$$\text{Average annual interest} = \frac{\text{total interest} + \text{par value} - \text{purchase price}}{\text{number of years to maturity}}$$

$$\text{Average investment} = \frac{\text{purchase price} + \text{par value}}{2}$$

$$\text{Rate of yield to maturity} = \frac{\text{average annual interest}}{\text{average investment}}$$

EXAMPLE 16

A $1,000, 8% bond is quoted at 110 five years before maturity. Find the rate of current yield.

Annual interest: $8\% \times \$1,000 = \$80$
Market price: $10 \times \$110 = \$1,100$

$$\text{Rate of current yield} = \frac{\text{annual interest}}{\text{market price}}$$

$$= \frac{\$80}{\$1,100} \cong 0.0727 = 7.27\%$$

EXAMPLE 17

Estimate the rate of yield to maturity for the bond in Example 16.

$$\text{Average annual interest} = \frac{\text{total interest} + \text{par value} - \text{purchase price}}{\text{number of years to maturity}}$$

$$= \frac{(5 \text{ yr} \times \$80/\text{yr}) + \$1,000 - \$1,100}{5} = \$60$$

$$\text{Average investment} = \frac{\text{purchase price} + \text{par value}}{2}$$

$$= \frac{\$1,100 + \$1,000}{2} = \$1,050$$

$$\text{Rate of yield to maturity} = \frac{\text{average annual interest}}{\text{average investment}}$$

$$= \frac{\$60}{\$1,050} \cong 0.0571 = 5.71\%$$

SOLVED PROBLEMS

9.13 Find the market price of each $5,000 bond in Table 9-2 at the day's low price.

SOLUTION

Market price of a $5,000 bond:

$$A = 50 \times 100\tfrac{1}{8} = \$5,006.25$$
$$B = 50 \times 88\tfrac{1}{2} = \$4,425$$
$$C = 50 \times 110 = \$5,500$$
$$D = 50 \times 74\tfrac{5}{8} = \$3,731.25$$
$$E = 50 \times 102\tfrac{3}{4} = \$5,137.50$$

9.14 Find the semiannual bond interest payment on each $10,000 bond in Table 9-2.

SOLUTION

Bond interest payment on $10,000 bond:

$$A = \frac{0.09375}{2} \times \$10,000 = \$468.75$$

$$B = \frac{0.07125}{2} \times \$10,000 = \$356.25$$

$$C = \frac{0.125}{2} \times \$10,000 = \$625$$

$$D = \frac{0.0475}{2} \times \$10,000 = \$237.50$$

$$E = \frac{0.087}{2} \times \$10,000 = \$435$$

9.15 Find the premium or discount on each $2,000 bond in Table 9-2 at the day's closing price.

SOLUTION

Market price of bond A:	$20 \times 100\frac{1}{8} = \$2,002.50$
Premium on bond A:	$\$2,002.50 - \$2,000 = \$2.50$
Market price of bond B:	$20 \times 89 = \$1,780$
Discount on bond B:	$\$2,000 - \$1,780 = \$220$
Market price of bond C:	$20 \times 110 = \$2,200$
Premium on bond C:	$\$2,200 - \$2,000 = \$200$
Market price of bond D:	$20 \times 74\frac{3}{4} = \$1,495$
Discount on bond D:	$\$2,000 - \$1,475 = \$505$
Market price of bond E:	$20 \times 103 = \$2,060$
Premium on bond E:	$\$2,060 - \$2,000 = \$60$

9.16 Jessica Guiso bought three $1,000, $11\frac{1}{2}$% bonds on August 9 at market quotation $109\frac{1}{8}$. If the interest dates are March 1 and September 1, find the accrued bond interest and the total purchase price.

SOLUTION

Time from:		
	Mar. 1 to Aug. 1 $= 5 \times 30 = 150$ days	
	Aug. 1 to Aug. 9	8 days
	Mar. 1 to Aug. 9	158 days

Accrued bond interest:

$$I = Prt$$
$$= \$3,000 \times 0.115 \times \frac{158}{360} = \$151.42$$

Market price of three $1,000 bonds: $3 \times 10 \times \$109\frac{1}{8} = \$3,273.75$

$$\text{Total purchase price} = \text{market price} + \text{accrued interest}$$
$$= \$3,273.75 + \$151.42 = \$3,425.17$$

9.17 Find the total purchase price in Prob. 9.16 if the market quotation was $87\frac{7}{8}$.

SOLUTION

Accrued bond interest is the same, i.e., $151.42.

Market price: $3 \times 10 \times 87\frac{7}{8} = \$2,636.25$

$$\text{Total purchase price}_1 = \text{market price} + \text{accrued interest}$$
$$= \$2,636.25 + \$151.42 = \$2,787.67$$

9.18 Andrew owns two $1,000, $9\frac{1}{4}$% bonds paying interest on May 15 and November 15. What will be his proceeds from sale of the bonds on July 20 at market quotation $92\frac{1}{4}$?

SOLUTION

Market price:		$2 \times 10 \times 92\frac{1}{4} = \$1,845$
Time from:		
	May 15 to July 15 $= 2 \times 30 = 60$ days	
	July 15 to July 20	5 days
	May 15 to July 20	65 days

Accrued bond interest:

$$I = Prt$$

$$= \$2,000 \times 0.0925 \times \frac{65}{360} = \$33.40$$

$$\text{Proceeds} = \text{market price} + \text{accrued interest}$$
$$= \$1,845 + \$33.40 = \$1,878.40$$

9.19   How much would Andrew receive in Prob. 9.18 at market quotation $103\frac{1}{8}$?

SOLUTION

Accrued bond interest is the same, i.e., $33.40.

Market price: $2 \times 10 \times 103\frac{1}{8} = \$2,062.50$

$$\text{Proceeds} = \text{market price} + \text{accrued interest}$$
$$= \$2,062.50 + \$33.40 = \$2,095.90$$

9.20   Find the rate of current yield in Prob. 9.16.

SOLUTION

Annual interest on a $1,000 bond: $11\frac{1}{2}\% \times 1,000 = \$115$
Market price of a $1,000 bond: $10 \times 109\frac{1}{8} = \$1,091.25$

$$\text{Rate of current yield} = \frac{\text{annual interest}}{\text{market price}}$$

$$= \frac{\$115}{\$1091.25} = 0.1054 = 10.54\%$$

9.21   In Prob. 9.16, at what price would Jessica have to buy a $1,000 bond for the rate of current yield to be 12%?

SOLUTION

We rewrite the formula for current yield to solve for the market price:

$$\text{Current yield} = \frac{\text{annual interest}}{\text{market price}}$$
$$\text{Market price} = \frac{\text{annual interest}}{\text{current yield}}$$

The annual interest rate in Prob. 9.16 is 11.5%. The annual interest on a $1,000 bond is therefore

$$0.115 \times \$1,000 = \$115$$

By substituting the known values into the formula for market price, we get

$$\text{Market price} = \frac{\text{annual interest}}{\text{current yield}}$$
$$= \frac{\$115}{0.12} \cong \$958.33$$

For the current yield to be 12%, the price of a $1,000 bond in Prob. 9.16 would have to be $958.33.

9.22   What market price would give the buyer of a $1,000 bond B in Table 9-2 a 10.5% rate of current yield?

SOLUTION

Annual interest:

$$7\tfrac{1}{8}\% \times \$1,000 = \$71.25$$

$$\text{Market price} = \frac{\text{annual interest}}{\text{current yield}}$$

$$= \frac{\$71.25}{0.105} \cong \$678.57$$

9.23 Twelve years before maturity, a \$5,000, 9% bond is quoted at $93\tfrac{1}{2}$. Find the rate of current yield.

SOLUTION

Annual interest: $9\% \times \$5,000 = \$450$

Market price: $5 \times 10 \times 93\tfrac{1}{2} = \$4,675$

$$\text{Rate of current yield} = \frac{\text{annual interest}}{\text{market price}}$$

$$= \frac{\$450}{\$4,675} \cong 0.0963 = 9.63\%$$

9.24 Estimate the rate of yield to maturity for the bond in Prob. 9.23.

SOLUTION

$$\text{Average interest} = \frac{\text{total interest} + \text{par value} - \text{purchase price}}{\text{number of years to maturity}}$$

$$= \frac{(12 \text{ yr} \times \$450/\text{yr}) + \$5,000 - \$4,675}{12} \cong \$477.08$$

$$\text{Average investment} = \frac{\text{purchase price} + \text{par value}}{2}$$

$$= \frac{\$4,675 + \$5,000}{2} = \$4,837.50$$

$$\text{Rate of yield to maturity} = \frac{\text{average annual interest}}{\text{average investment}}$$

$$= \frac{\$477.08}{\$4,837.50} \cong 0.0986 = 9.86\%$$

9.25 Estimate the rate of yield to maturity for a \$2,000, 12% bond quoted at 107 eight and a half years before maturity.

SOLUTION

Annual interest: $12\% \times \$2,000 = \$240$

Market price: $2 \times 10 \times 107 = \$2,140$

$$\text{Average interest} = \frac{\text{total interest} + \text{par value} - \text{purchase price}}{\text{number of years to maturity}}$$

$$= \frac{(8.5 \text{ yr} \times \$240/\text{yr}) + \$2,000 - \$2,140}{8.5} \cong \$223.53$$

$$\text{Average investment} = \frac{\text{purchase price} + \text{par value}}{2}$$

$$= \frac{\$2,140 + \$2,000}{2} = \$2,070$$

$$\text{Rate of yield to maturity} = \frac{\text{average annual interest}}{\text{average investment}}$$

$$= \frac{\$223.53}{\$2,070} \cong 0.1080 = 10.80\%$$

9.26 Dan Thomas owns some $9\frac{1}{4}\%$ bonds from TTR, Inc. that are due in 5 years, 3 months. He is considering selling these and buying some Satco 11% bonds due in 17 years. If he can sell his TTR at $92\frac{1}{4}$ and buy Satco at $102\frac{7}{8}$, which bonds would give him a better rate of current yield?

SOLUTION

TTR $1,000 bond:

Annual interest: $9\frac{1}{4}\% \times \$1,000 = \$92.50$
Market price: $10 \times 92\frac{1}{4} = \$922.50$

$$\text{Rate of current yield} = \frac{\text{annual interest}}{\text{market price}}$$

$$= \frac{\$92.50}{\$922.50} \cong 0.1003 = 10.03\%$$

Satco $1,000 bond:

Annual interest: $11\% \times \$1,000 = \$110$
Market price: $10 \times 102\frac{7}{8} = \$1,028.75$

$$\text{Rate of current yield} = \frac{\text{annual interest}}{\text{market price}}$$

$$= \frac{\$110}{\$1,028.75} \cong 0.1069 = 10.69\%$$

The Satco bond gives a better rate of current yield.

9.27 In Prob. 9.26, which bond would give Dan Thomas a better rate of yield to maturity?

SOLUTION

TTR $1,000 bond:

$$\text{Average interest} = \frac{\text{total interest} + \text{par value} - \text{purchase price}}{\text{number of years to maturity}}$$

$$= \frac{(5.25 \text{ yr} \times \$92.50/\text{yr}) + \$1,000 - \$922.50}{5.25} \cong \$107.26$$

$$\text{Average investment} = \frac{\text{purchase price} + \text{par value}}{2}$$

$$= \frac{\$922.50 + \$1,000}{2} = \$961.25$$

$$\text{Rate of yield to maturity} = \frac{\text{average interest}}{\text{average investment}}$$

$$= \frac{\$107.26}{\$961.25} \cong 0.1116 = 11.16\%$$

Satco $1,000 bond:

$$\text{Average interest} = \frac{\text{total interest} + \text{par value} - \text{purchase price}}{\text{number of years to maturity}}$$

$$= \frac{(17 \text{ yr} \times \$110/\text{yr}) + \$1,000 - \$1,028.75}{17} \cong \$108.31$$

$$\text{Average investment} = \frac{\text{purchase price} + \text{par value}}{2}$$

$$= \frac{\$1,028.75 + \$1,000}{2} \cong \$1,014.38$$

$$\text{Rate of yield to maturity} = \frac{\text{average interest}}{\text{average investment}}$$

$$= \frac{\$108.31}{\$1,014.38} \cong 0.1068 = 10.68\%$$

The TTR bond gives a better rate of yield to maturity.

Supplementary Problems

9.28   Refer to Table 9-1 and find the total dividends on (*a*) 120 shares of stock A, (*b*) 200 shares of stock B, (*c*) 50 shares of stock C, (*d*) 90 shares of stock D, and (*e*) 250 shares of stock E.

9.29   Find the total purchase cost of the shares in Prob. 9.28 at the closing price of the day.

9.30   Find the total purchase cost of the shares in Prob. 9.28 at the previous day's closing price.

9.31   Find the gross proceeds from the sale of the shares in Prob. 9.28 at the high price of the day.

9.32   Find the gross proceeds from the sale of the shares in Prob. 9.28 at the closing price of the day.

9.33   Fairway Electronics issued 20,000 shares of $7\frac{1}{2}\%$, $100 par value preferred stock. Calculate the total amount of dividends to be paid at the end of the year on (*a*) 1,500 shares, (*b*) 200 shares, and (*c*) 380 shares.

9.34   For each of the following, calculate the amount of dividends payable on $100 par value cumulative preferred stock.

	Number of Shares	Dividend Rate (%)	Time Since Last Payment (Years)
(*a*)	50	5	3
(*b*)	3,000	7	2
(*c*)	80	8	4
(*d*)	150	$6\frac{1}{4}$	1

9.35   Natco, Inc. has outstanding 4,000 shares of $6\frac{1}{2}\%$, $100 par value cumulative preferred stock and 10,000 shares of common stock. The company declares dividends as follows from 19X3 to 19X6:

$$
\begin{array}{ll}
19X3 & \$20,000 \\
19X4 & \$45,000 \\
19X5 & \$25,000 \\
19X6 & \$87,000 \\
\end{array}
$$

No dividends are in arrears as of the end of 19X2. What amount of dividends is paid each year to (*a*) preferred and (*b*) common stock?

9.36   Assuming that the preferred stock is noncumulative, find the total dividends for the common stock in Prob. 9.35 for the 4 years.

9.37   Gemini, Inc. has outstanding 7,000 shares of 8%, $100 par value cumulative preferred stock and 20,000 shares of common stock. Dividends on the preferred stock are currently $45,000 in arrears. If a dividend of $184,000 is declared in the current year, find the dividend per share for (*a*) preferred stock and (*b*) common stock.

9.38 Delita Corporation declares a dividend of $72,750 to its 5,000 shares of $8\frac{1}{2}\%$, $50 par value non-cumulative participating preferred stock, and its 15,000 shares of common stock. After each common share has received a dividend of $1.10, the preferred stock participates with the common stock in the distribution of remaining dividend in the ratio of shares in each class. Calculate the dividend per share for (a) preferred and (b) common stock.

9.39 Calculate the dividend per share for each class of stock in Prob. 9.38 if the dividend declared is (a) $76,150, (b) $48,350.

9.40 Assuming that the preferred stock is cumulative participating preferred stock and $7,000 dividends are in arrears, calculate the dividend per share for (a) preferred and (b) common stock in Prob. 9.38.

9.41 Assuming that the preferred stock is cumulative nonparticipating preferred stock and $11,900 dividends are in arrears, calculate the dividend par value for (a) preferred and (b) common stock in Prob. 9.38.

9.42 Calculate the broker's commission at the commission rate of 1.8% on the purchase of (a) 80 shares at $17\frac{7}{8}$ (b) 100 shares at $21\frac{1}{4}$, (c) 280 shares at $31\frac{1}{8}$.

9.43 What is the broker's commission in Prob. 9.42 if the transactions were sales?

9.44 Find the total cost, including 2.1% commission, of a purchase of 320 shares of stock E in Table 9-1 at the day's closing price.

9.45 Find the net proceeds, after a commission of 1.7% has been paid, on the sale of 190 shares of stock B in Table 9-1 at the day's low price.

9.46 Find the total cost for each of the following purchases:

	Number of Shares	Price	Commission Rate (%)
(a)	220	$43\frac{1}{8}$	1.4
(b)	25	$108\frac{7}{8}$	1.8
(c)	320	$7\frac{1}{4}$	2.0

9.47 Find the net proceeds if the transactions in Prob. 9.46 were sales.

9.48 What is the investor's annual yield on common stocks with

(a) Cost per share of $17.25 and quarterly dividend of $0.55

(b) Cost per share of $45 and semiannual dividend of $2.12

(c) Cost per share of $105.75 and annual dividend of $6.80

9.49 Determine the rate of annual yield for each stock in Table 9-1, if bought at the closing price of the day.

9.50 Determine the rate of annual yield for each stock in Table 9-1, if bought at the closing price of the previous day.

9.51 Arlene purchased 200 shares of stock A in Table 9-1 four years ago at $12\frac{1}{8}$ and sold it at the day's high price. If dividends have been constant for the 4-year period, what is (a) her total gain and (b) the annual rate of gain based on cost.

9.52 Assuming that Arlene bought the stock in Prob. 9.51 at $33\frac{3}{4}$, what is (a) her total loss and (b) the annual rate of loss based on cost?

9.53 Find the market price of each $2,000 bond in Table 9-2 at the day's high price.

9.54 At what market price would the $1,000 bonds in Table 9-2 give an 11% rate of current yield?

9.55 At what market price would the $1,000 bonds in Table 9-2 give a $7\frac{1}{2}$% rate of current yield?

9.56 Find the total semiannual interest payable to the owner of two $1,000 bonds A and three $1,000 bonds E in Table 9-2.

9.57 Find the total semiannual interest payable to the investor who owns one $2,000 bond of each type listed in Table 9-2.

9.58 Calculate the premium for the following bonds:

	Face Value	Market Quotation
(a)	$1,000	$107\frac{1}{8}$
(b)	5,000	$101\frac{7}{8}$
(c)	500	$117\frac{1}{2}$

9.59 Calculate the discount for the following bonds:

	Face Value	Market Quotation
(a)	$ 2,000	$73\frac{3}{4}$
(b)	10,000	91
(c)	100,000	$87\frac{1}{4}$

9.60 Find the accrued bond interest on each of the following bond transactions:

	Par Value	Bond Interest Rate	Interest Dates	Date of Sale	Market Quotation	Number of Bonds
(a)	$1,000	$9\frac{1}{4}$%	June 15, Dec. 15	Oct. 26	$92\frac{1}{2}$	2
(b)	500	8%	Mar. 1, Sept. 1	Feb. 4	87	10
(c)	5,000	$10\frac{1}{2}$%	Feb. 15, Aug. 15	Apr. 21	101	1
(d)	2,000	12%	June 1, Dec. 1	May 12	$105\frac{7}{8}$	4

9.61 Find the total proceeds of the bond transactions in Prob. 9.60.

9.62 Find the rate of current yield for the bonds in Prob. 9.60.

9.63 Referring to Table 9-2, find the accrued bond interest on each of the following bond transactions:

	Bond	Par Value	Number of Bonds	Last Interest Date	Date of Sale
(a)	A	$1,000	3	Oct. 1	Jan. 5
(b)	B	1,000	2	Sept. 15	Dec. 20
(c)	C	500	6	Apr. 1	June 11
(d)	D	2,000	5	Nov. 15	Mar. 26
(e)	E	5,000	2	May 1	Aug. 29

9.64　Find the total purchase price of the bonds in Prob. 9.63 if purchased at the day's closing price.

9.65　Calculate the rate of current yield for the following bonds:

	Par Value	Bond Interest Rate	Market Quotation	Time to Maturity
(a)	$1,000	$11\frac{3}{4}\%$	$102\frac{3}{8}$	5 yr
(b)	500	$7\frac{1}{2}\%$	86	10 yr
(c)	2,000	12.9%	$112\frac{1}{4}$	8 yr, 6 mo
(d)	5,000	$8\frac{1}{4}\%$	$92\frac{1}{2}$	3 yr, 3 mo

9.66　Estimate the rate of yield to maturity for the bonds in Prob. 9.65.

Answers to Supplementary Problems

9.28　(a) $180, (b) $120, (c) $100, (d) $495, (e) $195

9.29　(a) $2,942.50, (b) $1,925, (c) $5,437.50, (d) $5,793.75, (e) $5,193.75

9.30　(a) $2,837.50, (b) $1,950, (c) $5,456.25, (d) $5,771.25, (e) $5,256.25

9.31　(a) $2,937.50, (b) $1,950, (c) $5,512.50, (d) $5,771.25, (e) $5,181.25

9.32　(a) $2,937.50, (b) $1,925, (c) $5,425, (d) $5,771.25, (e) $5,181.25

9.33　(a) $11,250, (b) $1,500, (c) $2,850

9.34　(a) $750, (b) $42,000, (c) $2,560, (d) $937.50

9.35　(a) 19X3: $20,000, 19X4: $32,000, 19X5: $25,000, 19X6: $27,000; (b) 19X3: 0, 19X4: $13,000, 19X5: 0, 19X6: $60,000

9.36　$80,000

9.37　(a) $14.43, (b) $4.15

9.38　(a) $6, (b) $2.85

9.39　(a) preferred: $6.17, common: $3.02; (b) preferred: $4.78, common: $1.63

9.40　(a) $7.05, (b) $2.50

9.41　(a) $6.63, (b) $2.64

9.42　(a) $25.92, (b) $38.25, (c) $157.05

9.43　(a) $25.56, (b) $38.25, (c) $156.69

9.44　$6,781.99

9.45 $1,786.60

9.46   (*a*) $9,622.86, (*b*) $2,774.05, (*c*) $2,368.95

9.47   (*a*) $9,352.21, (*b*) $2,669.81, (*c*) $2,271.15

9.48   (*a*) 12.75%, (*b*) 9.42%, (*c*) 6.43%

9.49   A: 6.12%, B: 6.23%, C: 1.84%, D: 8.56%, E: 3.76%

9.50   A: 6.35%, B: 6.15%, C: 1.83%, D: 8.59%, E: 3.71%

9.51   (*a*) $3,675, (*b*) 37.89%

9.52   (*a*) $650, (*b*) 2.41%

9.53   A: $2,047.50, B: $1,780, C: $2,202.50, D: $1,497.50, E: $2,060

9.54   A: $852.27, B: $647.73, C: $1,136.36, D: $431.82, E: $790.91

9.55   A: $1,250, B: $950, C: $1,666.67, D: $633.33, E: $1,160

9.56 $224.25

9.57 $424.50

9.58   (*a*) $71.25, (*b*) $93.75, (*c*) $87.50

9.59   (*a*) $525, (*b*) $900, (*c*) $12,750

9.60   (*a*) $67.32, (*b*) $170, (*c*) $96.25, (*d*) $429.33

9.61   (*a*) $1,917.32, (*b*) $4,520, (*c*) $5,146.25, (*d*) $8,899.33

9.62   (*a*) 10%, (*b*) 9.20%, (*c*) 10.40%, (*d*) 11.33%

9.63   (*a*) $73.44, (*b*) $37.60, (*c*) $72.92, (*d*) $172.85, (*e*) $285.17

9.64   (*a*) $3,077.19, (*b*) $1,817.60, (*c*) $3,372.92, (*d*) $7,647.85, (*e*) $10,585.17

9.65   (*a*) 11.48%, (*b*) 8.72%, (*c*) 11.49%, (*d*) 8.92%

9.66   (*a*) 11.14%, (*b*) 9.57%, (*c*) 10.80%, (*d*) 10.97%

Chapter 10

Buying

10.1 TRADE DISCOUNTS

When merchandise is offered for sale by manufacturers or wholesalers, a *list* or *catalog price* is set for each item. This is the suggested price to charge the ultimate consumer. Rather than printing separate catalogs for each class of potential purchasers (wholesalers, retailers, consumers), the seller gives intermediate or trade buyers (wholesalers, retailers) separate discount sheets that detail the discount (usually stated as a percent rate) offered to the "trade." Thus the *trade discount* is not a true discount but is an *adjustment of the price.*

$$\text{Discount} = \text{list price} \times \text{discount rate}$$

The *net cost price* is the price that the buyer pays for the item. The net cost price is the list price less any discount and may be computed by using the following formula:

$$\text{Net cost price} = \text{list price} - \overbrace{(\text{list price} \times \text{discount rate})}^{\text{Discount}}$$

EXAMPLE 1

A television with a list price of $450 is offered to wholesalers at a 20% trade discount. What is the cost to wholesalers?

$$\text{Net cost price} = \text{list price} - (\text{list price} \times \text{discount rate})$$
$$= \$450 - (\$450 \times 0.20) = \$450 - \$90 = \$360$$

The preceding formula may be restated as the list price multiplied by the *complement* of the discount rate. The complement of the discount rate is the difference between the discount rate and 100 percent.

$$\text{Net cost price} = \text{list price} \times \overbrace{(100\% - \text{discount rate})}^{\text{Complement of discount rate}}$$

EXAMPLE 2

Using the information given in Example 1, the price of the TV to wholesalers is

$$\text{Net cost price} = \text{list price} \times (100\% - \text{discount rate})$$
$$= \$450 \times (100\% - 20\%) = \$450 \times 0.80 = \$360$$

Transportation costs (if applicable) are not subject to trade discounts and would be added to the net cost price.

SOLVED PROBLEMS

10.1 What is the trade discount if (*a*) the list price is $220 and the discount rate is 15%, (*b*) the list price is $149.25 and the discount rate is $33\frac{1}{3}\%$, (*c*) the list price is $1,574 and the discount rate is 40%, (*d*) the list price is $49.98 and the discount rate is $7\frac{1}{4}\%$, and (*e*) the list price is $7,569 and the discount rate is $2\frac{3}{4}\%$?

SOLUTION

(*a*)
$$\text{Discount} = \text{list price} \times \text{discount rate}$$
$$= \$220 \times 0.15 = \$33$$

(b)
$$\text{Discount} = \text{list price} \times \text{discount rate}$$
$$= \$149.25 \times 0.33333 = \$49.75$$

(c)
$$\text{Discount} = \text{list price} \times \text{discount rate}$$
$$= \$1,574 \times 0.40 = \$629.60$$

(d)
$$\text{Discount} = \text{list price} \times \text{discount rate}$$
$$= \$49.98 \times 0.0725 = \$3.62$$

(e)
$$\text{Discount} = \text{list price} \times \text{discount rate}$$
$$= \$7,569 \times 0.0275 = \$208.15$$

10.2 A snowmobile lists for $9,875 with a trade discount of $25\frac{3}{4}\%$. If the delivery charge is $60, what is the net amount of the bill?

SOLUTION

$$\text{Net cost price} = \text{list price} \times (100\% - \text{discount rate})$$
$$= \$9,875 \times (100\% - 25.75\%) = \$9,875 \times 0.7425 = \$7,332.19$$

$$\text{Total cost} = \text{net price} + \text{additional costs}$$
$$= \$7,332.19 + \$60 = \$7,392.19$$

10.2 SINGLE EQUIVALENT DISCOUNT AND CHAIN DISCOUNTS

Rather than give various increasing single discounts to different classes of purchasers, some companies use *chain discounts*. These have the advantage of appearing to be greater than a single discount, as well as emphasizing to the buyer the fact that he or she receives more than one discount.

Either of two methods may be used to compute the net cost price when chain discounts are involved.

Method 1:

Determine the *single equivalent discount* and then compute the net cost price as shown in Example 2. To compute the equivalent discount, multiply the complements of the discount rates and subtract the result from 100%. For example, the single equivalent discount of a chain discount of 10% and 20% is computed as follows:

Step 1: $(100\% - 10\%) \times (100\% - 20\%) = 90\% \times 80\%$

Step 2: $0.90 \times 0.80 = 0.72 = 72\%$

Step 3:   Single equivalent discount $= 100\% - 72\% = 28\%$

Note that the single equivalent discount would permit us to compare different chain discounts.

EXAMPLE 3

A stereo is offered to wholesalers at a list price of $600, less discounts of 25% and 20%. What is the net cost price?

Single equivalent discount:

1. $(100\% - 25\%) \times (100\% - 20\%) = 75\% \times 80\%$

2. $0.75 \times 0.80 = 0.60 = 60\%$

3. $100\% - 60\% = 40\%$

$$\text{Net cost price} = \text{list price} - (\text{list price} \times \text{discount rate})$$
$$= \$600 - (\$600 \times 0.40) = \$600 - \$240 = \$360$$

Alternative method:

1. $600 \times 0.25 = \$150$ Price $\times$ first discount rate = first discount
2. $600 - \$150 = \$450$ Price $-$ first discount = discounted price
3. $450 \times 0.20 = \$90$ Discounted price $\times$ second discount rate = second discount
4. $450 - \$90 = \$360$ Discounted price $-$ second discount = net cost price

Method 2:

The net cost price can be computed directly by multiplying the list price by the complement of each discount in the series. It does not make any difference in what order the discounts are arranged.

EXAMPLE 4

Assume the same information as in Example 3 and calculate the net cost price by using method 2.

Complements of the discounts:

$$100\% - 25\% = 75\% = 0.75$$
$$100\% - 20\% = 80\% = 0.80$$

Net cost price = list price $\times$ complement of each discount
$$= \$600 \times 0.75 \times 0.80 = \$600 \times 0.60 = \$360$$

SOLVED PROBLEMS

10.3 Company A gives a 20% discount on all items purchased. Company B gives chain discounts of 15% and 10%. If J. Snyder bought $500 in supplies from company B, how much did he save by dealing with company B rather than with company A?

SOLUTION

Company A

Discount = list price $\times$ discount rate
$$= \$500 \times 0.20 = \$100$$

Company B

Single equivalent discount:

1. $(100\% - 15\%) \times (100\% - 10\%) = 85\% \times 90\%$
2. $0.85 \times 0.90 = 0.765 = 76.5\%$
3. $100\% - 76.5\% = 23.5\%$

Discount = list price $\times$ single equivalent discount rate
$$= \$500 \times 0.235 = \$117.50$$

Savings from dealing with company B:

$$\$117.50 - \$100 = \$17.50$$

Alternative solution:

Difference between the two discounts:

$$23.5\% - 20\% = 3.5\%$$

Savings: $\$500 \times 0.035 = \$17.50$

10.4 What is the total trade discount and the net cost price for (a) a list price of $750 and discounts of 10%, 5%, and 5%; (b) a list price of $1,795.80 and discounts of 20% and 15%; (c) a list price of $978 and discounts of $10\frac{1}{4}\%$, $5\frac{1}{4}\%$, and 2%?

SOLUTION

(a) Single equivalent discount:

    1. $(100\% - 10\%) \times (100\% - 5\%) \times (100\% - 5\%) = 90\% \times 95\% \times 95\%$

    2. $0.90 \times 0.95 \times 0.95 = 0.81225 = 81.225\%$

    3. $100\% - 81.225\% = 18.775\%$

$$\text{Total trade discount} = \text{list price} \times \text{single equivalent discount}$$
$$= \$750 \times 0.18775 = \$140.8125 \cong \$140.81$$

$$\text{Net cost price} = \text{list price} - \text{discount}$$
$$= \$750 - \$140.81 = \$609.19$$

(b) Single equivalent discount:

    1. $(100\% - 20\%) \times (100\% - 15\%) = 80\% \times 15\%$

    2. $0.80 \times 0.85 = 0.68 = 68\%$

    3. $100\% - 68\% = 32\%$

$$\text{Total trade discount} = \text{list price} \times \text{single equivalent discount}$$
$$= \$1{,}795.80 \times 0.32 = \$574.656 \cong \$574.66$$

$$\text{Net cost price} = \text{list price} - \text{discount}$$
$$= \$1{,}795.80 - \$574.66 = \$1{,}221.14$$

(c) Single equivalent discount:

    1. $(100\% - 10.25\%) \times (100\% \times 5.25\%) \times (100\% - 2\%) = 89.75\% \times 94.75\% \times 98\%$

    2. $0.8975 \times 0.9475 \times 0.98 \cong 0.83337 = 83.337\%$

    3. $100\% - 83.337\% = 16.663\%$

$$\text{Total trade discount} = \text{list price} \times \text{single equivalent discount}$$
$$= \$978 \times 0.16663 \cong \$162.96$$

$$\text{Net cost price} = \text{list price} - \text{discount}$$
$$= \$978 - \$162.96 = \$815.04$$

10.5   The list price of a shipment of computer software is \$1,957.94. The trade chain discount is 25% and 10%. Find the net price.

SOLUTION

Complements of the discounts:

$$100\% - 25\% = 75\% = 0.75$$
$$100\% - 10\% = 90\% = 0.90$$

$$\text{Net cost price} = \text{list price} \times \text{complement of each discount}$$
$$= \$1{,}957.94 \times 0.75 \times 0.90 = \$1{,}321.61$$

10.6   R. James ordered four digital watches which list at \$75 each, less discounts of 10% and 5%. What is the total cost if a \$6 shipping charge was added to the invoice?

SOLUTION

$$\text{Total list price} = \$75 \times 4 = \$300$$

Complements of discounts:

$$100\% - 10\% = 90\% = 0.90$$
$$100\% - 5\% = 95\% = 0.95$$

$$\text{Net price} = \text{list price} \times \text{complement of each discount}$$
$$= \$300 \times 0.90 \times 0.95 = \$256.50$$

$$\text{Total cost} = \text{net price} + \text{additional costs}$$
$$= \$256.50 + \$6 \text{ shipping} = \$262.50$$

10.7 GAP, Inc. offers discounts of 20%, 15%, and 5% on a dryer which lists for $595. Find (a) the total trade discount and (b) the net price.

SOLUTION

(a) Single equivalent discount:

1. $(100\% - 20\%) \times (100\% - 15\%) \times (100\% - 5\%) = 80\% \times 85\% \times 95\%$
2. $0.80 \times 0.85 \times 0.95 = 0.646 = 64.6\%$
3. $100\% - 64.6\% = 35.4\%$

$$\text{Discount} = \text{list price} \times \text{discount rate}$$
$$= \$595 \times 0.354 = \$210.63$$

(b)

$$\text{Net cost price} = \text{list price} - \text{discount}$$
$$= \$595 - \$210.63 = \$384.37$$

10.8 Company A offers barbells at a chain discount of 21%, 9%. Company B offers similar quality barbells at a chain discount of 20%, 8%, 2%. Company C offers a single $28\frac{1}{2}\%$ trade discount on its barbells. Which company offers the greatest discount?

SOLUTION

Company A single equivalent discount:

1. $(100\% - 21\%) \times (100\% - 9\%) = 79\% \times 91\%$
2. $0.79 \times 0.91 = 0.7189 = 71.89\%$
3. $100\% - 71.89\% = 28.11\%$

Company B single equivalent discount:

1. $(100\% - 20\%) \times (100\% - 8\%) \times (100\% - 2\%) = 80\% \times 92\% \times 98\%$
2. $0.80 \times 0.92 \times 0.98 = 0.72128 \cong 72.13\%$
3. $100\% - 72.13\% = 27.87\%$

Company C discount $= 28.5\%$. Therefore company C offers the greatest discount.

10.9 What single discount is equivalent to a chain discount of 23%, 10%, 5%?

SOLUTION

Single equivalent discount:

1. $(100\% - 23\%) \times (100\% - 10\%) \times (100\% - 5\%) = 77\% \times 90\% \times 95\%$
2. $0.77 \times 0.90 \times 0.95 = 0.65835 \cong 65.84\%$
3. $100\% - 65.84\% = 34.16\%$

10.3 CASH DISCOUNTS

Cash discounts are offered to encourage buyers to pay their bills quickly. Cash discounts are applied to bills paid within a specified period of time. Hence cash discounts tend to narrow the time gap between sale of items and payment for them.

Cash discounts are referred to as *terms* and may appear on a bill as, for example, 2/10 net 30 (2/10, n/30)

where   2 = the percent discount

10 = number of days within which the buyer must pay in order to qualify for the discount

net 30 = number of days within which payment must be made at the full price

EXAMPLE 5

An invoice of $300, dated March 6, has terms of 2/10, n/30. If payment is made by March 16, what is (*a*) the discount and (*b*) the net cost?

(*a*) $$\text{Discount} = \text{list price} \times \text{discount rate}$$
$$= \$300 \times 0.02 = \$6$$

(*b*) $$\text{Net price} = \text{list price} - \text{discount}$$
$$= \$300 - \$6 = \$294$$

If payment is made on March 17, the full $300 must be paid.

Some companies offer varied cash discounts, depending on when payment is made; for example, 2/10, 1/20, n/30. This means that the company offers a 2% discount if the buyer pays within 10 days and a 1% discount if the buyer pays after 10 days but within 20 days; the full price amount is due within 30 days.

EXAMPLE 6

Albee Co. received an invoice dated September 11 for $7,250 with terms of 2/10, 1/20, n/30. (*a*) On what day must payment be made for Albee Co. to receive the 2% discount and what amount is due on that day? (*b*) On what day must payment be made for Albee to receive the second discount and what amount is due on that date? (*c*) What is the last day for Albee to make payment without becoming delinquent and what amount is due on that day?

(*a*)   Due date for 2/10 discount:

Sept. 11   Invoice date

  + 10   Days in discount period

Sept. 21

$$\text{Net cost} = \text{list price} - (\text{list price} \times \text{discount rate})$$
$$= \$7,250 - (\$7,250 \times 0.02) = \$7,250 - \$145 = \$7,105$$

(*b*)   Due date for 1/20 discount:

Sept. 11   Invoice date

  + 20   Days in discount period

31

  − 30   Number of days in Sept.

Oct.   1

$$\text{Net cost} = \text{list price} - (\text{list price} \times \text{discount rate})$$
$$= \$7,250 - (\$7,250 \times 0.01) = \$7,250 - \$72.50 = \$7,177.50$$

(*c*)   Due date for n/30:

Sept. 11   Invoice date

  + 30   Days allowed for payment

41

  − 30   Number of days in Sept.

Oct. 11

No discount is given for payments made after 20 days, so the full $7,250 is due on October 11.

Although in most cases the cash discount period begins with the "invoice" or purchase date, the discount period may also begin either on the date of the *receipt of goods* (r.o.g.) or on the first date after the *end of the month* (e.o.m.).

The r.o.g. discount period is used primarily when a significant gap exists between the date of sale and the delivery date. It eliminates the problem of asking a buyer to pay for goods not yet received in order to get a discount.

The e.o.m. discount period is used primarily as a convenience by companies who use traditional end-of-month billing practices.

EXAMPLE 7

Rupp Co. placed an order on April 2 for parts which were delivered on April 15, with an invoice for $1,250 at terms of 5/20 r.o.g. (*a*) To receive the discount, by what date must Rupp Co. pay the bill? (*b*) Including the discount, what is the net price?

(*a*) Since the terms of the discount are r.o.g., the due date is calculated from the date on which Rupp Co. received the goods.

Due date for 5/20 r.o.g.:

$$
\begin{array}{rl}
\text{April 15} & \text{Date of receipt of goods} \\
+\,20 & \text{Days in discount period} \\
\hline
35 & \\
-\,30 & \text{Number of days in Apr.} \\
\hline
\text{May}\quad 5 &
\end{array}
$$

(*b*) Net cost = list price − (list price × discount rate)
= $1,250 − ($1,250 × 0.05) = $1,250 − $62.50 = $1,187.50

EXAMPLE 8

J&H Co. received an invoice for $900 dated May 8, with terms of 2/15 e.o.m. (*a*) By what date must J&H remit payment to take advantage of the discount? (*b*) How much is the discount and what is the net cost?

(*a*) Since the terms specify e.o.m., payment is due 15 days after the end of the month. Therefore, to take advantage of the discount, J&H would have to pay the bill by June 15.

(*b*)   Discount = list price × discount rate
= $900 × 0.02 = $18

Net cost = list price − discount
= $900 − $18 = $882

EXAMPLE 9

As is shown below, the last date on which a discount can be taken depends on whether the terms stipulate r.o.g., e.o.m., or invoice date.

Invoice Date	Goods Received	Terms	Last Day on Which Discount Can Be Taken
Inv. $500 Oct. 3	Oct. 8	2/10, n/30 r.o.g.	Oct. 18
Inv. $700 Oct. 3	Oct. 8	2/10, n/30 e.o.m.	Nov. 10
Inv. $850 Oct. 3	Oct. 8	2/10, n/30	Oct. 13*

*Calculated from invoice date.

SOLVED PROBLEMS

10.10 C. Rodriguez receives an invoice totaling $98.75. Terms are 3/10, n/30. If the discount is taken, what is the net amount to be paid?

SOLUTION

$$\text{Net cost} = \text{list price} - (\text{list price} \times \text{discount rate})$$
$$= \$98.75 - (\$98.75 \times 0.03) = \$98.75 - \$2.96 = \$95.79$$

10.11 Vane Co. receives an invoice which totals $189.75, including a shipping charge of $50. Terms are 3/10, n/60. If the invoice is paid within 9 days of receipt, what is the amount of the payment?

SOLUTION

$$\text{Total amount} - \text{shipping charge} = \text{amount for discounting}$$
$$\$189.75 - \$50 = \$139.75$$

$$\text{Net cost} = \text{list price} - (\text{list price} \times \text{discount rate})$$
$$= \$139.75 - (\$139.75 \times 0.03) = \$139.75 - \$4.19 = \$135.56$$

$$\text{Total cost} = \text{net cost} + \text{additional costs}$$
$$= \$135.56 + \$50 \text{ shipping cost} = \$185.56$$

10.12 B. Kane makes a partial payment of $150 on a bill totaling $373.18. Terms are 3/10, n/60. If payment is made within the discount period, what amount is *credited* to Kane's account?

SOLUTION

We know that

$$\text{Net cost} = \text{list price} \times \text{complement of discount}$$

The same mathematical relationship exists between a payment and the amount credited to an account. We may therefore write

$$\text{Payment} = \text{amount credited} \times \text{complement of discount}$$

Solving for the amount credited, we get

$$\frac{\text{Payment}}{\text{Complement of discount}} = \text{amount credited}$$
$$\frac{\$150}{(100\% - 3\%)} =$$
$$\frac{\$150}{97\%} =$$
$$\frac{\$150}{0.97} =$$
$$\$154.64 =$$

Because the discount is applied to the $150 payment, the amount credited to Kane's account is $4.64 more than the payment made.

10.13 The JAX store receives a shipment of sporting goods totaling $1,986.57 and returns $675 worth of those goods. Terms are $2\frac{1}{4}$/10, n/90. If the discount is taken, what is the amount of the payment?

SOLUTION

$$\text{Total bill} - \text{returned goods} = \text{goods retained}$$
$$\$1,986.57 - \$675 = \$1,311.57$$

$$\text{Net cost} = \text{list price} \times \text{complement of discount}$$
$$= \$1,311.57 \times (100\% - 2.25\%) = \$1,311.57 \times 97.75\% = \$1,282.06$$

10.14 Kelly Co. receives an invoice for \$781 for the purchase of a typewriter. Terms are $6\frac{1}{2}/10$, n/120. If Kelly Co. takes advantage of the discount, how much will it save?

SOLUTION

$$\text{Discount} = \text{list price} \times \text{discount rate}$$
$$= \$781 \times 0.065 = \$50.77$$

10.15 An invoice totals \$96.80, including a freight charge of \$6.50. Terms are 2/10, n/30. What is the net amount due if the invoice is paid 11 days after receipt?

SOLUTION

No discount applies since the bill is paid after the discount period of 10 days. Hence the full \$96.80 is due.

10.16 E. Johnson receives an invoice for the purchase of lumber amounting to \$6,559. Terms are $5\frac{1}{2}/10$, n/60. How much will E. Johnson save if she takes advantage of the discount?

SOLUTION

$$\text{Discount} = \text{list price} \times \text{discount rate}$$
$$= \$6,559 \times 0.055 = \$360.75$$

10.17 N. Pollack receives a shipment of merchandise totaling \$2,567.46, including a shipping charge of \$26. He returns \$251.27 worth of the merchandise. Terms are $2\frac{1}{4}/10$, n/120. If he takes advantage of the discount, what is the net amount payable?

SOLUTION

$$\text{Total amount} - \text{shipping charge} = \text{list cost of merchandise}$$
$$\$2,567.46 - \$26 = \$2,541.46$$

$$\text{List cost of merchandise} - \text{merchandise returned} = \text{amount for discount}$$
$$\$2,541.46 - \$251.27 = \$2,290.19$$

$$\text{Net cost of merchandise} = \text{list price} \times \text{complement of discount}$$
$$= \$2,290.19 \times (100\% - 2.25\%) = \$2,290.19 \times 97.75\% = \$2,238.66$$
$$\text{Total cost} = \text{net cost of merchandise} + \text{additional costs}$$
$$= \$2,238.66 + \$26 \text{ shipping cost} = \$2,264.66$$

10.18 An invoice dated January 15 offers terms of 3/15, n/30. To take advantage of the discount, by what date must the buyer pay the bill?

SOLUTION

Jan. 15   Invoice date
<u>+ 15</u>   Days in discount period
Jan. 30

10.19 Find the number of days between each of the following invoice dates and the respective payment dates. (Use 28 days for February.)

	Inventory Date	Payment Date
(a)	Jan. 25	May 21
(b)	July 12	Sept. 30
(c)	Aug. 14	Oct. 22
(d)	Sept. 15	Dec. 24
(e)	Dec. 27	Mar. 15

SOLUTION

(a)
31	Days in Jan.
− 25	Inventory date
6	Days left in Jan.
28	Days in Feb.
31	Days in Mar.
30	Days in Apr.
21	Payment date in May
116	Days between Jan. 25 and May 21

(b)
31	Days in July
− 12	Inventory date
19	Days left in July
31	Days in Aug.
30	Payment date in Sept.
80	Days between July 12 and Sept. 30

(c)
31	Days in Aug.
− 14	Inventory date
17	Days left in Aug.
30	Days in Sept.
22	Payment date in Oct.
69	Days between Aug. 14 and Oct. 22

(d)
30	Days in Sept.
− 15	Inventory date
15	Days left in Sept.
31	Days in Oct.
30	Days in Nov.
24	Payment date in Dec.
100	Days between Sept. 15 and Dec. 24

(e)
31	Days in Dec.
− 27	Inventory date
4	Days left in Dec.
31	Days in Jan.
28	Days in Feb.
15	Payment date in Mar.
78	Days between Dec. 27 and Mar. 15

10.20 For each of the following, what is the last date for payment if you want to take advantage of the discount? (Assume 29 days in February.)

	Inventory Date	Discount Period (Days)
(a)	June 18	10
(b)	July 20	20
(c)	Jan. 12	30
(d)	Dec. 15	90

SOLUTION

(a)

June 18	Invoice date
+ 10	Discount period
June 28	Last date for discount

(b)

July 20	Invoice date
+ 20	Discount period
40	
6 − 31	Days in July
Aug. 9	Last date for discount

(c)

Jan. 12	Invoice date
+ 30	Discount period
42	
− 31	Days in Jan.
Feb. 11	Last date for discount

(d)

Dec. 15	Invoice date
+ 90	Discount period
105	
− 31	Days in Dec.
74	
− 31	Days in Jan.
43	
− 29	Days in Feb.
Mar. 14	Last date for discount

10.21 An invoice for $859.78 dated August 10 offers terms of 2/10 r.o.g. The shipment of goods arrived on September 29 and the bill was paid on October 8. Find the amount due.

SOLUTION

We must first determine whether the bill was paid within the discount period. Since terms are r.o.g., we use the delivery date as the first day of the discount period.

Sept. 29	Delivery date
+ 10	Discount period
39	
− 30	Days in Sept.
Oct. 9	Last date for discount

Since the bill was paid within the discount period, the discount applies.

$$\text{Net cost} = \text{list price} \times \text{complement of discount}$$
$$= \$859.78 \times (100\% - 2\%) = \$859.78 \times 0.98 = \$842.58$$

10.22 Woody's Lumber Co. received an invoice dated July 25 for $6,980, with terms of 3/15, n/60 r.o.g. The merchandise was received on August 21. (*a*) What is the last date of payment under the discount period? (*b*) What amount is due on that date?

SOLUTION

(*a*)

$$
\begin{array}{rl}
\text{Aug. 21} & \text{Delivery date} \\
+15 & \text{Discount period} \\
\hline
36 & \\
-31 & \text{Days in Aug.} \\
\hline
\text{Sept. 5} & \text{Last date for discount}
\end{array}
$$

(*b*)

$$
\text{Net cost} = \text{list price} \times \text{complement of discount}
$$
$$
= \$6{,}980 \times (100\% - 3\%) = \$6{,}980 \times 0.97 = \$6{,}770.60
$$

10.23 If an invoice dated October 2 has terms of 3/10, n/30 e.o.m., find the last date for the discount.

SOLUTION

Since terms are e.o.m., the discount period begins after the end of the month (October 31). The last day of the discount is therefore November 10.

10.24 Kites, Inc. received an invoice dated July 5 for $986.14. Terms are 2/10, n/30 e.o.m. What amount must be remitted if the invoice is paid on August 8?

SOLUTION

Since terms are e.o.m., the discount period begins with the first day of the following month and ends 10 days later, on August 10. An invoice paid on August 8 qualifies for the discount, and the amount remitted is:

$$
\text{Net cost} = \text{list price} \times \text{complement of discount}
$$
$$
= \$986.14 \times (100\% - 2\%) = \$986.14 \times 0.98 = \$966.42
$$

10.25 Eccleston, Inc. received an invoice dated January 21 for merchandise delivered the following May 5. The invoice is for $986.57, with trade discounts of 15%, 10%, and 5% and terms of 2/30 r.o.g. If the bill is paid on June 6, what amount must be remitted?

SOLUTION

Since terms are r.o.g., the discount period begins on the date of delivery (May 5).

$$
\begin{array}{rl}
\text{May 5} & \text{Delivery date} \\
+30 & \text{Discount period} \\
\hline
35 & \\
-31 & \text{Days in May} \\
\hline
\text{June 4} & \text{Last date for discount}
\end{array}
$$

A bill paid on June 6 does not qualify for the discount, but does qualify for the trade discount. Therefore the amount to be remitted is:

$$
\text{Net cost} = \text{list price} \times \text{complement of each discount}
$$
$$
= \$986.57 \times (100\% - 15\%)(100\% - 10\%)(100\% - 5\%)
$$
$$
= \$986.57 \times 0.85 \times 0.90 \times 0.95 = \$986.57 \times 0.72675 = \$716.99
$$

10.26 Jones Co. received an invoice dated March 13 totaling $1,857.60, with terms of 2/10 e.o.m. A trade chain discount of 20%, 15% is allowed. What amount is due if the invoice is paid by April 20?

SOLUTION

Since terms are e.o.m., the discount period begins after the end of the month (March 31) and ends on April 10. No discount (cash) is allowed but trade discounts are.

$$\text{Net cost} = \text{list price} \times \text{complement of each discount}$$
$$= \$1,857.60 \times (100\% - 20\%) \times (100\% - 15\%)$$
$$= \$1,857.60 \times 0.80 \times 0.85 = \$1,857.60 \times 0.68 = \$1,263.17$$

10.27 Kim's Fabric Shop received an invoice dated April 8 for $675, with terms of 5/20 e.o.m. (a) What is the last date for the discount and (b) what amount is due on that date?

SOLUTION

(a)   The last date for the discount is May 20.

(b) $$\text{Net cost} = \text{list price} \times \text{complement of discount}$$
$$= \$675 \times (100\% - 5\%) = \$675 \times 0.95 = \$641.25$$

10.28 For each of the following, find the final discount date and the final net invoice date. (Assume February has 28 days.)

	Invoice Date	Terms	Delivery Date
(a)	Jan. 11	3/10, n/30 e.o.m.	Feb. 2
(b)	July 14	2/20, n/30 r.o.g.	Sept. 4
(c)	Oct. 4	2/10, n/60	Nov. 1

SOLUTION

(a)   Final discount date: Feb. 10
      Final invoice date:

$$\begin{array}{r} 30 \\ -28 \\ \hline \text{Mar. } 2 \end{array}$$ Payment period (begins Feb. 1)
                                   Days in Feb.

(b)   Final discount date:

$$\begin{array}{r} \text{Sept. } 4 \\ +20 \\ \hline \text{Sept. } 24 \end{array}$$ Delivery date
                                   Discount period

      Final invoice date:

$$\begin{array}{r} \text{Sept. } 4 \\ +30 \\ \hline 34 \\ -30 \\ \hline \text{Oct. } 4 \end{array}$$ Delivery date
                                   Payment period

                                   Days in Sept.

(c) Final discount date:

Oct.	4	Invoice date
	+ 10	Discount period
Oct.	14	

Final invoice date:

Oct.	4	Invoice date
	+ 60	Payment period
	64	
	− 31	Days in Oct.
	33	
	− 30	Days in Nov.
Dec.	3	

10.4 TRADE AND CASH DISCOUNTS

When both trade and cash discounts are offered, the cash discount is computed *after* the trade discount has been taken.

EXAMPLE 10

An invoice of $300 dated March 17, with a trade discount of 30% and terms of 2/10, n/30, was paid on March 20. (a) How much is the cash discount and (b) what was the amount of the payment?

(a)   Net price = list price × complement of trade discount
$$= \$300 \times (100\% - 30\%) = \$300 \times 0.70 = \$210$$

Cash discount = net price × cash discount rate
$$= \$210 \times 0.02 = \$4.20$$

(b)   Payment amount = net price − cash discount
$$= \$210 - \$4.20 = \$205.80$$

SOLVED PROBLEMS

10.29 On September 10, Ace Co. purchased merchandise listing at $896.45, with trade discounts of 10%, 5% and terms of 3/10, n/30. What is (a) the trade discount amount and (b) the amount due by September 20 if freight of $6.75 must be paid?

SOLUTION

(a) Single equivalent discount:

1. $(100\% - 10\%)(100\% - 5\%)$
2. $0.90 \times 0.95 = 0.855 = 85.5\%$
3. $100\% - 85.5\% = 14.5\%$

Trade discount = list price × single equivalent discount
$$= \$896.45 \times 0.145 = \$129.99$$

(b) September 20 is the last date for the cash discount.

Net price = list price − discount
$$= \$896.45 - \$129.99 = \$766.46$$

Amount after cash discount = net price × complement of cash discount
$$= \$766.46 (100\% - 3\%) = \$766.46 \times 0.97 = \$743.47$$

Amount due by Sept. 20 = cash discount price + additional costs
$$= \$743.47 + \$6.75 \text{ freight} = \$750.22$$

10.30 Johnson Ltd. offers trade discounts of 15%, 10%, 5%, with terms of 2/15, n/60. If the list price on an invoice is $1,569.70, what amount is due to the company if both discounts are taken?

SOLUTION

$$\text{Net price} = \text{list price} \times \text{complement of each trade discount}$$
$$= \$1,569.70 \times (100\% - 15\%)(100\% - 10\%)(100\% - 5\%)$$
$$= \$1,569.70 \times 0.85 \times 0.90 \times 0.95 = \$1,569.70 \times 0.72675 = \$1,140.78$$

$$\text{Amount due after cash discount} = \text{net price} \times \text{complement of cash discount}$$
$$= \$1,140.78 \times (100\% - 2\%) = \$1,140.78 \times 0.98 = \$1,117.96$$

10.31 The list price of an electronic typewriter is $5,698. The manufacturer offers a trade discount of 20%, 10% and terms of 2/10, n/60. What is the cost of the typewriter if both discounts are taken?

SOLUTION

$$\text{Net price} = \text{list price} \times \text{complement of each trade discount}$$
$$= \$5,698 \times (100\% - 20\%)(100\% - 10\%)$$
$$= \$5,698 \times 0.80 \times 0.90 = \$5,698 \times 0.72 = \$4,102.56$$

$$\text{Cost after cash discount} = \text{net price} \times \text{complement of cash discount}$$
$$= \$4,102.56 \times (100\% - 2\%) = \$4,102.56 \times 0.98 = \$4,020.51$$

10.32 An invoice dated October 2 totaled $597.81; $7.41 freight must be added to the invoice. The manufacturer offers trade discounts of 15%, 10% and terms of $1\frac{1}{2}/10$, n/30. If the retailer paid the invoice on October 14, how much did the retailer remit?

SOLUTION

$$\text{Net price} = \text{list price} \times \text{complement of each discount}$$
$$= \$597.81 \times (100\% - 15\%)(100\% - 10\%)$$
$$= \$597.81 \times 0.85 \times 0.90 = \$597.81 \times 0.765 = \$457.32$$

The last date for the cash discount is October 12. Since the retailer paid the bill after this date, the cash discount is not applied. The amount due is therefore:

$$\text{Total cost} = \text{net price} + \text{additional costs}$$
$$= \$457.32 + \$7.41 \text{ freight} = \$464.73$$

10.33 Jones Bros. purchased a wood stove listing at $674, less trade discounts of 25%, 15%, 10%. Terms are $1\frac{1}{2}/10$, n/30. If the invoice (dated August 23) is paid on September 1, what is the net amount due?

SOLUTION

$$\text{Net price} = \text{list price} \times \text{complement of each discount}$$
$$= \$674 \times (100\% - 25\%)(100\% - 15\%)(100\% - 10\%)$$
$$= \$674 \times 0.75 \times 0.85 \times 0.90 = \$674 \times 0.57375 = \$386.71$$

Aug. 23		Invoice date
+ 10		Discount period
33		
− 31		Days in Aug.
Sept. 2		Last date of cash discount

Since payment is remitted within the cash discount period, the cash discount applies.

$$\text{Amount due} = \text{net price} \times \text{complement of cash discount}$$
$$= \$386.71 \times (100\% - 1.5\%) = \$386.71 \times 0.985 = \$380.91$$

Supplementary Problems

10.34 What is the trade discount of each of the following: (*a*) list price of $540 and discount rate of 12%, (*b*) list price of $259.60 and discount rate of $22\frac{1}{2}$%, (*c*) list price of $1,565 and discount rate of 40%, (*d*) list price of $754.87 and discount rate of $33\frac{1}{3}$%, and (*e*) list price of $89.79 and discount rate of $2\frac{1}{4}$%?

10.35 What is the total trade discount when

    (*a*)   The list price is $640 and the discount rates are 10%, 5%, 2%

    (*b*)   The list price is $1,257.60 and the discount rates are 25%, 15%, 10%

    (*c*)   The list price is $757 and the discount rates are $10\frac{3}{4}$%, $5\frac{1}{4}$%, 2%.

10.36 A pair of shoes which lists for $42 is allowed a trade discount of 15%. Find the net price.

10.37 The list price of a shipment of books is $2,154.85. The trade discounts are 20% and 15%. Find the net price.

10.38 Gerard orders six portable typewriters at $295 each, less discounts of 10% and 2%. What is the total net price if a shipping charge of $15 is added to the invoice?

10.39 Grey, Inc. offers a chain discount of 15%, 10%, 2% on a washer which lists for $988.50. Find (*a*) the total discount and (*b*) the net price.

10.40 An automobile lists for $10,697 with a trade discount of $22\frac{1}{4}$%. If the delivery charge is $60, what is the net amount of the bill?

10.41 On October 4, Jensen Ltd. purchased merchandise listing at $746.29, with trade discounts of 20%, 15%, 10% and terms of 2/15, n/60. Freight of $5.45 had to be added to the invoice. Jensen returned $97.50 worth of merchandise on November 5. If Jensen paid the bill on October 18, what is the total amount Jensen Ltd. remitted?

10.42 Harmin Bros. offers a trade discount of 15%, 10%, 5% with terms of 3/10, n/30. If the list price on the invoice is $2,146, what amount is due if the discount is taken?

10.43 The list price of a car is $6,949.47. If the manufacturer offers a trade discount of 25%, 15% and terms of $2\frac{1}{4}$/15, n/90, what is the dealer's net cost if both discounts are taken?

10.44 An invoice dated November 3 totaled $4,968.41; $6.65 freight must be added to the invoice. The manufacturer offers trade discounts of 22%, 18%, 12% and terms of 2/15, n/60. If the retailer pays the invoice on November 20, how much should she remit?

10.45 Don, Inc. purchased a video recorder at $989, less a trade discount of 20%, 15%. Terms are $2\frac{1}{2}$/15, n/30. If the invoice (dated October 17) is paid on November 1, what is the net amount due?

10.46 Find the single equivalent discount rate of each of the following: (*a*) 15%, 5%; (*b*) 20%, 12%, 5%; and (*c*) 25%, 15%, 10%.

10.47 A video tape player which lists for $650 has trade discounts of 10%, 8%, 5%. What is the net price?

10.48 What is the net price of a pair of skis listed at $985, less 21%, 15%, and $10\frac{1}{4}$%?

10.49 What single discount is equivalent to 22%, 9%, 6%?

10.50 Krane offers trade discounts of 23% and 8%. Sulco offers trade discounts for 15%, 7%, and 2%. (*a*) Which discount is higher? (*b*) By how much?

10.51 Galky, Inc. receives an invoice totaling $109.65. Terms are 2/15, n/30. If the discount is taken, what is the net amount to be paid?

10.52 Gaff Co. receives an invoice which totals $256.79, including a shipping charge of $50. Terms are 2/10, n/30. If the invoice is paid within 9 days of receipt, what is the amount of the payment?

10.53 Johnson makes a partial payment of $120 on a bill totaling $561.50. Terms are 3/10, n/60. If payment is made within the discount period, what amount is credited to the account?

10.54 The JET store receives a shipment of sporting goods totaling $2,581.79 and returns $761.50 worth. Terms are $3\frac{1}{2}$%/10, n/60. If the discount is taken, find the amount remitted.

10.55 Roz Corp. receives an invoice of $948 for the purchase of a copying machine. Terms are $4\frac{1}{2}$/10, n/90. If the company takes advantage of the discount, how much will it save?

10.56 An invoice totals $156.47, including a freight charge of $10. Terms are $1\frac{1}{2}$/10, n/30. What is the net amount to be paid if the invoice is paid 11 days from receipt?

10.57 Krane receives an invoice for the purchase of building materials amounting to $7,451. Terms are 6/10, n/120. How much will he save if he takes advantage of the discount?

10.58 Rhoades receives a merchandise shipment totaling $1,496.71. There is a shipping charge of $26 included, and she returns $310.52 worth of merchandise. Terms are 3/10, n/30. If she takes the discount, what is the net amount payable?

10.59 An invoice dated March 21 has terms of 2/15, n/30. What is the last day of the discount period?

10.60 Calculate the number of days between the invoice date and the payment date for each of the following:

	Invoice Date	Payment Date
(a)	Feb. 15	Apr. 7
(b)	May 4	July 16
(c)	Sept. 14	Nov. 2
(d)	Nov. 5	Jan. 2
(e)	Mar. 28	June 6

10.61 What is the last day an invoice can be paid for each of the following?

	Invoice Date	Discount Time (Days)
(a)	Sept. 11	10
(b)	June 24	15
(c)	Nov. 5	20
(d)	Jan. 22	10
(e)	Apr. 12	30

10.62 If an invoice dated November 6 has terms of 2/10, n/30 e.o.m., find the last day of the discount.

10.63 GAP, Inc. receives an invoice dated March 7 in the amount of $567.14. Terms are 3/10, n/60 e.o.m. What amount must be remitted if the invoice is paid on April 9?

10.64 Jaks Co. receives an invoice dated June 22 for merchandise received on November 6. The gross price shown is $1,586.50, with trade discounts of 10%, 6%, and 3%. Terms are 30 r.o.g. If the company pays the bill on December 1, what is the net amount?

10.65 Johnson Co. receives an invoice dated April 5 which totals $1,056.25. Terms are 20 e.o.m., with trade discounts of 15% and 10%. What amount is due if the invoice is paid by May 17?

10.66 Given the information below, find the final discount date and the final net date. (Assume 28 days in February.)

	Invoice Date	Terms	Delivery Date
(a)	May 11	2/10, n/30 e.o.m.	June 8
(b)	Jan. 5	3/20, n/30 r.o.g.	Apr. 6
(c)	Oct. 7	5/10, n/60	Oct. 29

10.67 The total invoice is $961.45; the invoice date is August 8; the terms are 2/10, n/60 r.o.g.; delivery date is September 27; the invoice is paid on October 6. Find the amount due.

10.68 Rohnkes Hardware received an invoice totaling $7,656, dated June 25. Terms are 2/10, n/60 r.o.g. The merchandise was received on July 21. (a) What was the final date of payment under the discount period? (b) What was the amount paid on that date?

10.69 Determine the amount to be paid for each of the following different situations:

	Amount	Date of Purchase	Goods Received	Terms	Date of Payment Made
(a)	$600	Apr. 4	Apr. 11	2/10, n/30	Apr. 10
(b)	$700	May 1	May 14	2/10, n/30, r.o.g.	May 23
(c)	$800	June 6	June 12	2/10, 1/20, n/30	June 25
(d)	$900	July 20	July 24	2/10, n/30, e.o.m.	Aug. 9

Answers to Supplementary Problems

10.34 (a) $64.80, (b) $58.41, (c) $626, (d) $251.63, (e) $2.02

10.35 (a) $103.75, (b) $536.06, (c) $129.66

10.36 $35.70

10.37 $1,465.29

10.38 $1,576.14

10.39 (a) $247.42, (b) $741.08

10.40 $8,376.91

10.41 $453.04

10.42 $1,512.82

10.43 $4,327.60

10.44 $2,803.11

10.45 $655.71

10.46 (*a*) 19.25%, (*b*) 33.12%, (*c*) 42.67%

10.47 $511.29

10.48 $593.63

10.49 33.23%

10.50 (*a*) Krane's, (*b*) 6.63%

10.51 $107.46

10.52 $252.65

10.53 $123.71

10.54 $1,756.58

10.55 $42.66

10.56 $156.47

10.57 $447.06

10.58 $1,151.38

10.59 April 5

10.60 (*a*) 51, (*b*) 73, (*c*) 49, (*d*) 58, (*e*) 70

10.61 (*a*) Sept. 21, (*b*) July 9, (*c*) Nov. 25, (*d*) Feb. 1, (*e*) May 12

10.62 December 10

10.63 $550.13

10.64 $1,301.91

10.65 $808.03

10.66 (*a*) Discount date: June 10, Net date: June 30; (*b*) Discount date: Apr. 26, Net date: May 6; (*c*) Discount date: Oct. 17, Net date: Dec. 6

10.67 $942.22

10.68 (*a*) July 31, (*b*) $7,502.88

10.69 (*a*) $588, (*b*) $686, (*c*) $792, (*d*) $882

Chapter 11

Selling

11.1 MARKUP

In order to make a profit, each company must sell its products for more than the products cost the company to make or buy. The difference between a product's cost and selling price is referred to as *markup*.

EXAMPLE 1

A washing machine selling for $300 costs the seller $200. The markup is

$$\text{Selling price} - \text{post} = \text{markup}$$
$$\$300 - \$200 = \$100$$

SOLVED PROBLEMS

11.1 Find the markup if (*a*) cost is $15 and selling price is $27, (*b*) cost is $30 and selling price is $42.65, and (*c*) cost is $21.50 and selling price is $52.87.

SOLUTION

(*a*)
$$\text{Selling price} - \text{cost} = \text{markup}$$
$$\$27 - \$15 = \$12$$

(*b*)
$$\text{Selling price} - \text{cost} = \text{markup}$$
$$\$42.65 - \$30 = \$12.65$$

(*c*)
$$\text{Selling price} - \text{cost} = \text{markup}$$
$$\$52.87 - \$21.50 = 31.37$$

11.2 If Johnson Sporting Goods, Ltd. sells a tent for $89.99 and their cost is $52.40, what is the markup?

SOLUTION

$$\text{Selling price} - \text{cost} = \text{markup}$$
$$\$89.99 - \$52.40 = \$37.59$$

11.3 Reed Stereo purchased casette tapes for $2.95 each. If they sell them for $7.95, what is the markup?

SOLUTION

$$\text{Selling price} - \text{cost} = \text{markup}$$
$$\$7.95 - \$2.95 = \$5$$

11.4 What is the markup on an automobile that sells for $7,958 and costs the dealer $4,621.98?

SOLUTION

$$\text{Selling price} - \text{cost} = \text{markup}$$
$$\$7,958 - \$4,621.98 = \$3,336.02$$

11.5 Shim, Inc. decides to sell lawn chairs for $28.47. They paid $15.25 for each chair. What is the markup?

SOLUTION

$$\text{Selling price} - \text{cost} = \text{markup}$$
$$\$28.47 - \$15.25 = \$13.22$$

11.2 PERCENT MARKUP

Markup is generally expressed in terms of a percent.

$$\text{Percent} = \frac{\text{percentage}}{\text{base}} \times 100$$

where   percent   = markup percent

percentage = markup

base   = selling price or cost

By substitution, we have:

$$\% \text{ Markup} = \frac{\text{markup}}{\text{selling price or cost}} \times 100$$

11.3 SELLING PRICE AS THE BASE

EXAMPLE 2

A book selling for $8 cost the seller $6. What is the percent markup based on selling price?

$$\text{Markup} = \text{selling price} - \text{cost}$$
$$= \$8 - \$6 = 2$$

$$\% \text{ Markup} = \frac{\text{markup}}{\text{selling price}} \times 100$$

$$= \frac{\$2}{\$8} \times 100 = 25\%$$

We can use the percent markup to compute either the cost or the selling price.

EXAMPLE 3

A book selling for $8 has a markup of 25% of retail (i.e., selling price). What is the cost?

$$\% \text{ Markup} = \frac{\text{markup}}{\text{selling price}} \times 100$$

$$25\% = \frac{\text{markup}}{\$8} \times 100$$

$$\$8 \times 0.25 = \text{markup}$$
$$\$2 =$$

$$\text{Markup} = \text{selling price} - \text{cost}$$
$$\$2 = \$8 - \text{cost}$$
$$\$8 - \$2 = \text{cost}$$
$$\$6 =$$

EXAMPLE 4

A book has a markup of $2, which is 25% of the selling price. What is the selling price?

$$\% \text{ Markup} = \frac{\text{markup}}{\text{selling price}} \times 100$$

$$25\% = \frac{\$2}{\text{selling price}} \times 100$$

$$0.25 \times \text{Selling price} = \$2 = \frac{\$2}{0.25} = \$8$$

SOLVED PROBLEMS

11.6 Find the percent markup of retail (i.e., based on selling price) when (*a*) retail = \$23.40 and cost = \$17.20, (*b*) retail = \$46.41 and cost = \$21.25, and (*c*) retail = \$164.60 and cost = \$126.

SOLUTION

(*a*)
$$\text{Selling price} - \text{cost} = \text{markup}$$
$$\$23.40 - \$17.20 = \$6.20$$

$$\% \text{ Markup} = \frac{\text{markup}}{\text{selling price}} \times 100$$

$$= \frac{\$6.20}{\$23.40} \times 100 = 26.5\%$$

(*b*)
$$\text{Selling price} - \text{cost} = \text{markup}$$
$$\$46.41 - \$21.25 = \$25.16$$

$$\% \text{ Markup} = \frac{\text{markup}}{\text{selling price}} \times 100$$

$$= \frac{\$25.16}{\$46.41} \times 100 = 54.21\%$$

(*c*)
$$\text{Selling price} - \text{cost} = \text{markup}$$
$$\$164.60 - \$126 = \$38.60$$

$$\% \text{ Markup} = \frac{\text{markup}}{\text{selling price}} \times 100$$

$$= \frac{\$38.60}{\$126} \times 100 = 23.45\%$$

11.7 If the markup is \$7 on a pair of jeans which costs Jones Bros. \$18, what is the percent markup based on retail?

SOLUTION

$$\text{Selling price} - \text{cost} = \text{markup}$$
$$\text{Selling price} = \text{markup} + \text{cost}$$
$$= \$7 + \$18 = \$25$$

$$\% \text{ Markup} = \frac{\text{markup}}{\text{selling price}} \times 100$$

$$= \frac{\$7}{\$25} \times 100 = 28\%$$

11.8 Dancin' Shoes has a markup of \$7.59 on a pair of shoes they sell for \$19.25. Find (*a*) the cost and (*b*) the percent markup based on retail.

SOLUTION

(*a*)
$$\text{Selling price} - \text{cost} = \text{markup}$$
$$\text{Cost} = \text{selling price} - \text{markup}$$
$$= \$19.25 - \$7.59 = \$11.66$$

(b)
$$\% \text{ Markup} = \frac{\text{markup}}{\text{selling price}} \times 100$$
$$= \frac{\$7.59}{\$19.25} \times 100$$
$$= 39.43\%$$

11.9 If an item costs $0.79 and sells for $1.25, find (*a*) the markup and (*b*) percent markup based on retail.

SOLUTION

(a)
$$\text{Selling price} - \text{cost} = \text{markup}$$
$$\$1.25 \times \$0.79 = \$0.46$$

(b)
$$\% \text{ Markup} = \frac{\text{markup}}{\text{selling price}} \times 100$$
$$= \frac{\$0.46}{\$1.25} = 36.8\%$$

11.10 Nature's Way, a sporting goods store, buys snow shoes for $26.50 a pair and sells them for $79.27. What is (*a*) the markup and (*b*) the percent markup based on retail?

SOLUTION

(a)
$$\text{Markup} = \text{selling price} - \text{cost}$$
$$\$52.77 = \$79.27 - \$26.50$$

(b)
$$\% \text{ Markup} = \frac{\text{markup}}{\text{selling price}} \times 100$$
$$= \frac{\$52.77}{\$79.27} \times 100 = 66.57\%$$

11.4 COST AS THE BASE

When cost is used as the base for markup percent, it is sometimes referred to as "markon." It has the advantage of expressing clearly the fact that the price increase is directly added to the base (cost).

$$\% \text{ Markup} = \frac{\text{markup}}{\text{cost}} \times 100$$

EXAMPLE 5

A record album that sells for $6 costs $4. What is the percent markup based on cost?

$$\text{Selling price} - \text{cost} = \text{markup}$$
$$\$6 - \$4 = \$2$$

$$\% \text{ Markup} = \frac{\text{markup}}{\text{cost}} \times 100$$
$$= \frac{\$2}{\$4} \times 100 = 50\%$$

To calculate the cost from the percent markup and the selling price, we solve the above formula for cost as follows:

$$\% \text{ Markup} = \frac{\text{markup}}{\text{cost}} \times 100$$

Since markup = selling price − cost, by substitution we have

$$\% \text{ Markup} = \frac{\text{selling price} - \text{cost}}{\text{cost}} \times 100$$

$$\frac{\% \text{ Markup}}{100} = \frac{\text{selling price}}{\text{cost}} - 1$$

$$\frac{\% \text{ Markup}}{100} + 1 = \frac{\text{selling price}}{\text{cost}}$$

$$\text{Cost} = \frac{\text{selling price}}{(\% \text{ markup}/100) + 1}$$

Note that the denominator of this equation [(% Markup/100) + 1] is simply 1 plus the percent markup expressed as a decimal.

EXAMPLE 6

If an item selling for $72 has a 20% markup on cost, what is the cost?

$$\text{Cost} = \frac{\text{selling price}}{(\% \text{ markup}/100) + 1}$$

$$= \frac{\$72}{\dfrac{20\%}{100} + 1} = \frac{\$72}{0.20 + 1}$$

$$= \frac{\$72}{1.20} = \$60$$

To calculate selling price from cost and percent markup, we restate the formula

$$\text{Selling price} - \text{cost} = \text{markup}$$

as

$$\text{Selling price} = \text{cost} + \text{markup}$$

Since

$$\% \text{ markup} = \frac{\text{markup}}{\text{cost}} \times 100$$

then

$$\frac{\% \text{ Markup}}{100} \times \text{cost} = \text{markup}$$

By substitution we have

$$\text{Selling price} = \text{cost} + \left(\frac{\% \text{ markup}}{100} \times \text{cost} \right)$$

Note that % markup/100 is simply the percent expressed as a decimal.

EXAMPLE 7

If a sweater which costs $10 has a markup of 30% on cost, what is the selling price?

$$\text{Selling price} = \text{cost} + \left(\frac{\% \text{ markup}}{100} \times \text{cost} \right)$$

$$= \$10 + (0.30)(\$10) = \$10 + \$3 = \$13$$

Alternative solution:

If we let cost = 100%, then

$$\text{Selling price} = \text{cost} + \text{markup}$$

$$= 100\% + 30\% = 130\% \text{ of cost}$$

$$\text{Selling price} = 130\% \times \text{cost}$$

$$= 1.3 \times \$10 = \$13$$

SOLVED PROBLEMS

11.11　Jones Company purchases radios at \$150 each. Their markup based on cost is 25%. What is the selling price?

SOLUTION

$$\text{Selling price} = \text{cost} + \left(\frac{\% \text{ markup}}{100} + \text{cost}\right)$$

$$= \$150 + (0.25 \times \$150) = \$150 + \$37.50 = \$187.50$$

11.12　Calvin Jenks purchases designer jeans at \$17.95 a pair. The markup based on cost is 41%. What is the selling price?

SOLUTION

$$\text{Selling price} = \$17.95 + (0.41 \times 17.95) = \$17.95 + \$7.36 = \$25.31$$

11.13　Nail polish is sold by the manufacturer at \$2.50. The dealer's markup is 35% on retail. What is the selling price?

SOLUTION

$$\text{Cost} = \text{selling price} - \text{markup}$$
$$= 100\% - 35\%$$
$$= 65\% \text{ of retail}$$

$$\text{Cost} = 65\% \times \text{selling price}$$
$$\$2.50 = 65\% \times \text{selling price}$$
$$\frac{\$2.50}{0.65} = \text{selling price}$$
$$\$3.85 =$$

11.14　Hondor, Inc. purchased a microwave oven for \$295.71 and wants to mark up 40% on retail. What must the selling price be?

SOLUTION

$$\text{Cost} = \text{selling price} - \text{markup}$$
$$= 100\% - 40\% = 60\% \text{ of retail}$$

$$\text{Cost} = 60\% \times \text{selling price}$$
$$\$295.71 = 60\% \times \text{selling price}$$
$$\frac{\$295.71}{0.60} = \text{selling price}$$
$$\$492.85 =$$

11.15　A boutique buys handbags for \$19.28 and wants a markup of 56% on retail. Find the selling price.

SOLUTION

$$\text{Cost} = \text{selling price} - \text{markup}$$
$$= 100\% - 56\% = 44\% \text{ of retail}$$

$$\text{Cost} = 44\% \times \text{selling price}$$
$$\$19.28 = 44\% \times \text{selling price}$$
$$\frac{\$19.28}{0.44} = \text{selling price}$$
$$\$43.82 =$$

11.16 June's Boutique plans to sell an ascot for $9.59. Her markup on cost is 75%. What is her cost?

SOLUTION

$$\text{Cost} = \frac{\text{selling price}}{\frac{\%\ \text{markup}}{100} + 1}$$

$$= \frac{\$9.59}{\frac{75\%}{100} + 1} = \frac{\$9.59}{1.75} = \$5.48$$

Alternative solution:

$$\text{Selling price} = \text{cost} + \text{markup}$$
$$= 100\% + 75\% = 175\% \text{ of cost}$$

$$\text{Selling price} = 175\% \times \text{cost}$$
$$\$9.59 = 175\% \times \text{cost}$$
$$\frac{\$9.59}{1.75} = \text{cost}$$
$$\$5.48 =$$

11.17 Solco TV & Appliances sells television sets for $674. Their markup on cost is 92%. Find their cost.

SOLUTION

$$\text{Cost} = \frac{\text{selling price}}{\frac{\%\ \text{markup}}{100} + 1}$$

$$= \frac{\$674}{\frac{92\%}{100} + 1} = \frac{\$674}{0.92 + 1}$$

$$= \frac{\$674}{1.92} = \$351.04$$

11.18 Jones, Ltd. sells a recliner for $479.57. If their markup is 40% on retail, what is their cost?

SOLUTION

$$\text{Cost} = \text{selling price} - \text{markup}$$
$$= 100\% - 40\% = 60\% \text{ of retail}$$
$$\text{Cost} = 60\% \times \text{selling price}$$
$$= 0.60 \times \$479.57 = \$287.74$$

11.19 A retailer sells a pair of shoes for $52.79. If his markup is 67% of retail, what is his cost?

SOLUTION

$$\text{Cost} = \text{selling price} - \text{markup}$$
$$= 100\% - 67\% = 33\% \text{ of retail}$$
$$\text{Cost} = 33\% \times \text{selling price}$$
$$= 0.33 \times \$52.79 = \$17.42$$

11.20 A suit sells for $249.50 and carries a markup of 42% on retail. Find the cost of the suit.

SOLUTION

$$\text{Cost} = \text{selling price} - \text{markup}$$
$$= 100\% - 42\% = 58\% \text{ of retail}$$
$$\text{Cost} = 58\% \times \text{selling price}$$
$$= 0.58 \times \$249.50 = \$144.71$$

11.5 MARKUP CONVERSIONS

Conversions between percent markups based on retail and cost are often necessary in business. We can convert percent markup based on retail (selling price) to a cost base by using the following formula:

$$\% \text{ Markup on cost} = \frac{\% \text{ markup on retail}}{\text{complement of } \% \text{ markup on retail}} \times 100$$

Note that the denominator is the cost expressed in terms of percent of retail, i.e.,

$$\text{Cost} = \text{selling price} - \% \text{ markup on selling price}$$
$$= 100\% - \% \text{ markup on selling price}$$
$$= \text{complement of } \% \text{ markup on selling price}$$

EXAMPLE 8

What is the percent markup on cost if the markup on retail is 63%?

$$\% \text{ Markup on cost} = \frac{\% \text{ markup on retail}}{\text{complement of } \% \text{ markup on retail}} \times 100$$

$$= \frac{63\%}{(100\% - 63\%)} \times 100 = \frac{63\%}{37\%} \times 100 = 170.27\%$$

The percent markup on retail can be calculated from the markup on cost by using the following formula:

$$\% \text{ Markup on retail} = \frac{\% \text{ markup on cost}}{\text{selling price (stated as percent of cost)}} \times 100$$

EXAMPLE 9

What is the percent markup on retail if the markup on cost is 45%?

$$\text{Cost} + \text{markup} = \text{selling price}$$
$$100\% + 45\% =$$
$$145\% =$$

$$\% \text{ Markup on retail} = \frac{\% \text{ markup on cost}}{\text{selling price (as percent of cost)}} \times 100$$

$$= \frac{45\%}{145\%} \times 100 = 31\%$$

SOLVED PROBLEMS

11.21 What is the percent markup on cost if the percent markup on retail is 50%?

   SOLUTION

$$\% \text{ Markup on cost} = \frac{\% \text{ markup on retail}}{\text{complement of } \% \text{ markup on retail}} \times 100$$

$$= \frac{50\%}{100\% - 50\%} \times 100 = \frac{50\%}{50\%} \times 10 = 100\%$$

11.22 What is the percent markup on cost if the percent markup on retail is 64%?

SOLUTION

$$\% \text{ Markup on cost} = \frac{\% \text{ markup on retail}}{\text{complement of } \% \text{ markup on retail}} \times 100$$

$$= \frac{64\%}{(100\% - 64\%)} \times 100 = \frac{64\%}{36\%} \times 100 = 177.78\%$$

11.23 What is the percent markup on cost if the percent markup on retail is 37%?

SOLUTION

$$\% \text{ Markup on cost} = \frac{\% \text{ markup on retail}}{\text{complement of } \% \text{ markup on retail}} \times 100$$

$$= \frac{37\%}{(100\% - 37\%)} \times 100 = \frac{37\%}{63\%} \times 100 = 58.73\%$$

11.24 Find the percent markup on retail if the markup on cost is 125%.

SOLUTION

$$\text{Cost} + \text{markup} = \text{selling price}$$
$$100\% + 125\% =$$
$$225\% =$$

$$\% \text{ Markup on retail} = \frac{\% \text{ markup on cost}}{\text{selling price (as percent of cost)}} \times 100$$

$$= \frac{125\%}{225\%} \times 100 = 55.56\%$$

11.25 Find the percent markup on retail if percent markup on cost is 27%.

SOLUTION

$$\text{Cost} + \text{markup} = \text{selling price}$$
$$100\% + 27\% =$$
$$127\% =$$

$$\% \text{ Markup on retail} = \frac{\% \text{ markup on cost}}{\text{selling price (as percent of cost)}} \times 100$$

$$= \frac{27\%}{127\%} \times 100 = 21.26\%$$

11.6 INVENTORY

In a mercantile business, inventory is merchandise that is held for resale. As such, it will ordinarily be converted into cash in less than a year and is thus a current asset. In a manufacturing business, there will usually be inventories of raw materials and goods in process in addition to an inventory of finished goods.

Retail method is one approach to costing inventory. This method of periodic inventory costing is used mostly by department stores and is based on the relationship between merchandise available for sale and the retail price of the same merchandise. Retail inventory is determined by subtracting retail sales from the retail price of goods available for that period. This retail inventory is changed to cost by means of the ratio of cost to selling price.

EXAMPLE 10

	Cost	Retail
Merchandise inventory, Dec. 1	$25,000	$35,000
Purchases	42,200	61,000
Goods available for sale	$67,200	$96,000
Sales for Dec.		81,000
Merchandise inventory, Dec. 31		$15,000
Merchandise inventory, Dec. 31	$10,500*	

$$\text{Ratio: } \frac{\$67,200 \text{ cost}}{\$96,000 \text{ retail}} = 70\%$$

*$15,000 × 70% = $10,500

Two advantages of this system are:

1. It provides merchandise figures for interim statements.
2. It aids in disclosing inventory shortages.

SOLVED PROBLEMS

11.26 Find the estimated inventory cost on April 30 from the following data:

		Cost	Retail
Apr. 1	Merchandise inventory	$350,000	$420,000
Apr. 1–30	Net purchases	400,000	830,000
Apr. 1–30	Net sales	0	410,000

SOLUTION

	Cost	Retail
Merchandise inventory, Apr. 1	$350,000	$ 420,000
Plus: net purchases	400,000	830,000
Merchandise available for sale	$750,000	$1,250,000
Less: net sales		410,000
Merchandise Inventory @ Retail		$ 840,000

Cost ÷ retail = $750,000 ÷ $1,250,000 = 60%

0.6 × $840,000 = $504,000 est. inv. @ cost

11.27 Estimate the cost of inventory for GAP, Inc. using the following information.

	Cost	Retail
Merchandise inventory, Sept. 1	$240,000	$420,000
Purchases	124,000	210,000
Purchases returns & allowances	2,400	0
Sales	0	205,000
Sales returns	0	1,500

SOLUTION

	Cost	Retail
Merchandise inventory, Sept. 1	$240,000	$420,000
Plus: purchases	124,000	210,000
	$364,000	
Less: purchases returns & allowances	2,400	
Merchandise available for sale	$361,600	$630,000
Less: sales & sales returns		206,500
Merchandise inventory @ retail, Sept. 30		$423,500

$$\$361{,}600 \div \$630{,}000 = 0.57 = 57\%$$
$$0.57 \times \$423{,}500 = \$241{,}395 \text{ merchandise inv. @ cost}$$

11.28 Figure the inventory at retail and at cost on October 31 for Gibson, Inc. using the following information.

	Cost	Retail
Merchandise inventory, Oct. 1	$221,000	$450,000
Purchases	122,000	246,000
Transportation	1,000	0
Purchases returns	1,500	2,000
Markups	0	2,500
Markdowns	0	1,200
Sales	0	321,500

SOLUTION

	Cost	Retail
Merchandise inventory, Oct. 1	$221,000	$450,000
Plus: purchases	122,000	246,000
transportation	1,000	0
	$344,000	$696,000
Less: purchase returns	1,500	2,000
		$694,000
Plus: markups		2,500
Merchandise available for sale	$342,500	$696,500
Less: sales & markdowns		322,700
Merchandise inventory @ retail		$373,800

$$342{,}500 \div 696{,}500 = 49\%$$
$$0.49 \times 373{,}800 = \$183{,}162 \text{ merchandise inv. @ cost}$$

11.29 Determine by the retail method the estimated cost of the December 31 inventory.

	Cost	Retail
Dec. 1, inventory	$280,000	$400,000
Dec. 1–31 purchases	110,000	180,000
Merchandise available for sale	$390,000	$580,000
Sales for Dec.		340,000

SOLUTION

	Cost	Retail
Dec. 1, inventory	$280,000	$400,000
Dec. 1–31 purchases	110,000	180,000
Merchandise available for sale	$390,000	$580,000
Sales for month		340,000
Dec. 31 inventory @ retail		$240,000
Inventory @ estimated cost ($240,000 × 67%*)	$160,800	

*Cost ratio 67% ($390,000 ÷ $580,000)

11.30 Estimate the cost of inventory of May 31 by the retail method.

	Cost	Retail
May 1 merchandise	$18,000	$24,000
May 1 purchases	34,000	41,000
Sales for May		37,000

SOLUTION

	Cost	Retail
May 1 merchandise	$18,000	$24,000
May purchases	34,000	41,000
Merchandise available for sale	$52,000	$65,000
Sales for May		37,000
May 31 inventory @ retail		$28,000
May 31 inventory @ estimated cost ($28,000 × 80%*)	$22,400	

*Cost ratio 80% ($52,000 ÷ $65,000)

11.31 Based on the following data, determine the inventory cost at March 31 by the retail method.

	Cost	Retail
Inventory, Mar. 1	$39,700	$63,000
Purchases in Mar. (net)	24,000	31,600
Sales for Mar.		56,000

SOLUTION

	Cost	Retail
Inventory	$39,700	$63,000
Purchases in Mar.	24,000	31,600
Merchandise available for sale	$63,700	$94,600
Less: Sales		56,000
Inventory Mar. 31, @ retail		$38,600
Inventory Mar. 31, @ cost ($38,600 × 67%*)	$25,862	

*Cost ratio 67% ($63,700 ÷ $94,600)

Supplementary Problems

11.32 Find the markup when

   (a)   cost = $24 and selling price = $51

   (b)   selling price = $22.95 and cost = $10.50

   (c)   cost = $14.79 and selling price = $21.50

11.33 If Jones Bros. sells a microwave oven for $679 and their cost is $226.29, what is the markup?

11.34 Facials Ltd. purchased cold cream for $1.75 a jar. If they sell it for $4.50, what is the markup?

11.35 What is the markup on a ski suit that sells for $159.60 and costs the retailer $79.41?

11.36 GAP, Inc. sells picnic tables for $75 each. They paid $25.79. What is the markup?

11.37 Find (a) percent markup based on cost and (b) percent markup based on retail when

   (1)   Retail = $26.90 and cost = $15.60

   (2)   Retail = $36.50 and cost = $19.48

   (3)   Retail = $150 and cost = $96.45

11.38 If the markup on a pair of shoes is $9.50, and the shoes cost the retailer $15, what is the percent markup on cost?

11.39 Jones Bros. has a markup of $15.50 on a pair of designer jeans that sells for $31.97. Find (a) the cost, (b) the percent markup on cost, and (c) the percent markup on retail.

11.40 If an item costs $1.21 and we sell it for $3.17, what is the (a) markup, (b) percent markup on cost, and (c) percent markup on retail?

11.41 A stereo center buys a tape deck for $27.50 and sells it for $42.49. What is the (a) markup and (b) percent markup based on retail?

11.42 What is the percent markup on cost if the markup on retail is 65%?

11.43 Find the percent markup on cost if the markup on retail is 38%.

11.44 Percent markup on retail is 42%. What is the percent markup on cost?

11.45 Find the percent markup on retail if the markup on cost is 121%.

11.46 The percent markup on cost is 48%. What is the percent markup on retail?

11.47 GAP, Inc. purchased doghouses at $75 each. Their markup based on cost is 35%. What is the selling price?

11.48 Rinkle Electronics purchased videotapes at $10.97 each. The markup based on cost is 53%. Find the selling price.

11.49 Karol's Kandle Shop buys a candelabra for $19.59. Her markup is 67% on retail. What is the selling price?

11.50 Curly's Modern Kitchens purchases a dishwasher for $159.67 and wants a markup of 52% on retail. What must the selling price be?

11.51   Johnson Co. buys card tables for $25 and wants a markup of 48% on retail. Find the selling price.

11.52   Jan's Boutique sells handbags for $39.87 each. Her markup on cost is 70%. Find her cost.

11.53   Willie's TV Service sells color television sets for $957.69 each. The markup on cost is 87%. Find the cost.

11.54   GAP, Inc. sells a tea cart for $249. If their markup is 40% on retail, what is their cost?

11.55   A retailer sells a suit for $197.50. If the markup is 52% on retail, what is the cost?

11.56   An automobile sells for $7,595 and carries a markup of 67% on retail. What is the dealer's cost?

11.57   Given the following information, use the retail method to find the estimated inventory cost on May 31.

	Cost	Retail
Merchandise inventory, May 1	$200,000	$390,000
Net purchases, May 1–31	150,000	250,000
Sales, May 1–31	0	410,000

11.58   Using the retail method, estimate the cost of inventory for Jones, Ltd. from the following information:

	Cost	Retail
Merchandise inventory	$300,000	$475,000
Purchases	125,000	300,000
Purchases returns & allowances	1,500	0
Sales	0	325,000
Sales returns	0	850

Answers to Supplementary Problems

11.32   (a) $27, (b) $12.45, (c) $6.71

11.33 $452.71

11.34 $2.75

11.35 $80.19

11.36 $49.21

11.37   1(a) 72.44%, (b) 42%; 2(a) 87.37%, (b) 46.63%; 3(a) 55.52%, (b) 35.7%

11.38 $63\frac{1}{3}\%$

11.39   (a) $16.47, (b) 94.11%, (c) 48.48%

11.40   (a) $1.96, (b) 161.98%, (c) 61.83%

11.41   (a) $14.99, (b) 35.28%

11.42   185.71%

11.43   61.29%

11.44   72.41%

11.45   54.75%

11.46   32.43%

11.47 $101.25

11.48 $16.78

11.49 $59.36

11.50 $332.65

11.51 $48.08

11.52 $23.45

11.53 $512.13

11.54 $149.40

11.55 $94.80

11.56 $2,506.35

11.57 $126,500

11.58 $247,032.50

Chapter 12

Insurance

12.1 INTRODUCTION

Every business operation faces risk. A fire may destroy the plant, an employee's negligence may result in liability judgments, a poorly produced product may cause harm, or a theft may produce a large loss. Any of these events could result in bankruptcy. *Risk* refers to uncertainty, and business owners often buy insurance to offset possible losses should an unfavorable event occur.

In order to qualify for insurance, a risk must possess the following characteristics:

1. The loss must be measurable and predictable.
2. The risk must be spread out.
3. The insured must be able to show some financial loss would be suffered should the event occur.

Why would an insurance company agree to assume a $10,000 risk for a premium of only $100? The answer lies in the law of averages. The *law of averages*—or law of large numbers, as it is sometimes called—is a mathematical concept which states that over a period of time many types of losses are predictable. The law of averages may be stated as follows: The degree of predictability of loss varies directly with the number of cases. Insurance companies know, for example, that based upon actuarial (historical) data, about 5 out of every 1,000 homes will be damaged by fire each year. Which five, however, is impossible to predict. It is therefore a gamble for a homeowner *not* to insure his or her home, but it is not nearly as great a gamble for an insurance company to accept this type of risk.

Inherent in the law of averages, however, is the concept of randomness. Losses must occur only at random and must be independent of one another. For example, an insurance company generally will not insure too many buildings in any one given location because a major catastrophe in that location could cause the events to become dependent and result in an overly great number of claims. For this reason also, most basic policy forms exclude losses caused by acts of war or riot.

12.2 FIRE INSURANCE

Fire insurance offers financial protection against property damage that results from fire. If there is extended coverage, it would include damage from smoke or from measures taken to prevent the spread of fire (water damage).

The cost of the fire insurance premium depends upon the type of structure (wood or brick), its location, its contents, proximity to fire hydrants, the type of coverage, and the amount of the policy.

Annual premiums are based on cents per $100 of insurance. To determine the amount of the premium (1) find the number of times $100 is contained in the amount of insurance and (2) multiply that number by the premium rate.

EXAMPLE 1

The annual premium for $86,000 of fire insurance at 64¢ per $100 would be computed as follows:

$$\$86,000 \div \$100 = 860 \qquad \text{number of \$100's in \$86,000}$$
$$860 \times \$0.64 = \$550.40 \qquad \text{annual premium}$$

12.3   LONG-TERM INSURANCE

Insurance companies that want their customers to take out policies for more than a year may offer reduced premium rates.

Multiyear Table

Period (Years)	Rate
2	1.75 × annual rate (instead of 2 × annual rate)
3	2.6 × annual rate (instead of 3 × annual rate)
4	3.5 × annual rate (instead of 4 × annual rate)

Therefore, to determine the premium of any long-term policy, first find the annual premium as in Example 1 and then multiply the annual premium by the long-term rate.

EXAMPLE 2

An \$86,000, 2-year policy at a premium of 64¢ per \$100, would be computed as:

$$\$86,000 \div \$100 = 860$$
$$860 \times \$0.64 = \$550.40/\text{yr}$$
$$\$550.40 \times 1.75 = \$963.20 \quad \text{2-year premium}$$

12.4   SHORT-TERM INSURANCE

If an insurance company were to cancel a policy or if the insured were to drop the coverage, a short-term rate for less than 1 year would apply. The short-term rate is usually stated as a percent of the annual rate.

EXAMPLE 3

If a \$60,000 fire policy was bought at a premium of 72¢ per \$100 and was canceled by the company 4 months later (the short-term rate being 45%), the computation for the premium would be:

$$\$60,000 \div \$100 = 600$$
$$600 \times \$0.72 = \$432 \quad \text{annual premium}$$
$$\$432 \times 0.45 = \$194.40 \quad \text{short-term premium}$$

12.5   THE INDEMNITY PRINCIPLE

The *indemnity principle* states that one may not collect more than the actual loss should an insured-against loss occur. This is intended to make it impossible to profit from a loss (e.g., by overinsuring one's property). If coverage is adequate, an insurance company will pay the exact amount of the loss or *actual cash value*, which is generally the replacement cost of the property less depreciation. It is thus uneconomical to carry too much insurance. The indemnity principle, however, does not apply to life insurance or most forms of health insurance because no upper limit can be placed on the value of either one.

SOLVED PROBLEMS

12.1 Harriet Hooper purchased a $25,000 fire insurance policy. If the annual premium rate is 27¢ per $100, what is her annual premium?

SOLUTION

$$\frac{\$25,000}{\$100} \times \$0.27 = \$67.50$$

12.2 Find the annual premium on each of the following insurance policies: (*a*) $2,500 @ $0.59/$100, (*b*) $10,500 @ $0.69/$100, (*c*) $50,000 @ $27.50/$1,000, (*d*) $1,460 @ $24.20/$1,000, (*e*) $15,750 @ $29.49/$1,000.

SOLUTION

(*a*)
$$\frac{\$2,500}{\$100} \times \$0.59 = \$14.75$$

(*b*)
$$\frac{\$10,500}{\$100} \times \$0.69 = \$72.45$$

(*c*)
$$\frac{\$50,000}{1,000} \times \$27.50 = \$1,375$$

(*d*)
$$\frac{\$1,460}{\$1,000} \times \$24.20 = 35.33$$

(*e*)
$$\frac{\$15,750}{\$1,000} \times \$29.49 = \$464.47$$

12.3 Joe Blough purchased a 1-year fire insurance policy on October 15, 19X1, having a premium of $240. The insurance company canceled the policy on January 11, 19X2. How much did Blough receive as a refund?

SOLUTION

No. days coverage:

31	Days in Oct.	
− 15	Purchase date	
16	Days of coverage in Oct.	
30		Nov.
31		Dec.
11		Jan.
88		total

$$\$240 \times \frac{88}{365} = \$57.86 \quad \text{retained by company}$$

$$\$240 - \$57.86 = \$182.14 \quad \text{refund}$$

12.4 PAC, Inc. purchased a 1-year insurance policy from Federal Fire Insurance Co. on September 2, 19X1. The annual premium was $465. If the company canceled the policy on March 21, 19X2, how much refund did PAC receive? (Assume 28 days in February.)

SOLUTION

No. days coverage:	30	Days in Sept.
	− 2	Purchase date
	28	Days of coverage in Sept.
	31	Oct.
	30	Nov.
	31	Dec.
	31	Jan.
	28	Feb.
	21	Mar.
	200	total

$$\$465 \times \frac{200}{365} = \$254.79 \quad \text{retained by company}$$

$$\$465 - \$254.79 = \$210.21 \quad \text{refund}$$

12.5   Jonie Jonke has a fire insurance policy with a face value of $110,000. Her annual premium is 75¢ per $100 of coverage. If she cancels the policy after 260 days, what is her refund?

SOLUTION

$$\frac{\$110,000}{\$100} \times \$0.75 = \$825 \quad \text{annual premium}$$

$$\$825 \times \frac{260}{365} = \$587.67 \quad \text{retained by company}$$

$$\$825 - \$587.67 = \$237.33 \quad \text{refund}$$

12.6   Calvin Cronk paid $105 annual fire insurance premium. If his property is valued at $42,000, find the rate per $100.

SOLUTION

$$\$105 \div \frac{\$42,000}{\$100} = \$0.25 \text{ per } \$100$$

12.7   Jackie Jones purchased a $27,000 fire insurance policy at an annual premium rate of 75¢ per $100. Find the cost of the policy.

SOLUTION

$$\frac{\$27,000}{\$100} \times \$0.75 = \$202.50$$

12.6   THE COINSURANCE PRINCIPLE

The *coinsurance principle* has two basic purposes: (1) it prevents policyholders from underinsuring their property; and (2) it makes the insured bear a specified percent of the loss.

In fire insurance, for example, most losses are not total losses. Thus, in an attempt to save on premium costs, a person or company may insure property for less than its full value and still have bought sufficient insurance to cover the full amount of the loss. The typical insurance contract therefore includes a *coinsurance clause*, which states that the company is liable in the event of loss only in the proportion that the amount of insurance carried bears to the full amount required. The most common coinsurance is the "80% clause," which states that in the event of loss, the company shall be liable for no amount more than the amount of the insurance carried bears to 80% of the cash value of the property at the time of loss.

EXAMPLE 4

If a building has a value of $50,000, the owners would have to carry at least 80% of $50,000, or $40,000, in insurance or else bear a portion of any loss themselves. When the amount of the coverage is less than 80%, the company will pay the insured on a pro rata basis, based on the following:

$$\frac{\text{Amount carried}}{\text{Amount required}} \times \text{loss} = \text{amount recovered}$$

EXAMPLE 5

An owner carries $30,000 in insurance on a $50,000 building. On a loss of $10,000, how much can be collected on an 80% coinsurance policy?

$$\text{Amount required for 80\% coverage} = \$50,000 \times 80\% = \$40,000$$

$$\frac{\text{Amount carried}}{\text{Amount required}} \times \text{loss} = \text{amount recovered}$$

$$\frac{\$30,000}{\$40,000} \times \$10,000 = \$7,500$$

EXAMPLE 6

Suppose that the amount carried in Example 5 was $40,000. How much would the owner be able to collect from the insurance company?

$$\frac{\$40,000}{\$40,000} \times \$10,000 = \$10,000$$

EXAMPLE 7

Suppose that the amount carried in Example 5 was $50,000. How much would the owner collect?

$$\frac{\$50,000}{\$40,000} \times \$10,000 = \$12,500$$

Because the $12,500 is greater than the loss, the owner here is overinsured. Under the indemnity principle, only the actual amount of the loss may be collected. The owner would collect only $10,000.

In health and property insurance, the coinsurance principle is usually stated in the form of a *deductible*—a limited loss which must be borne by the insured before the insurance coverage starts.

SOLVED PROBLEMS

12.8   A business has a replacement cost estimated at $250,000 and it is insured for $190,000. A fire occurs, resulting in a loss of $65,000. Assuming there is an 80% coinsurance clause, how much would the insurance company pay?

SOLUTION

$$\frac{\text{Amount carried}}{\text{Amount required}} \times \text{loss} = \text{amount recovered}$$

$$\frac{\$190,000}{(80\%)(250,000)} \times \$65,000 = \$61,750$$

12.9   Johnson's Garage is valued at $925,000 and is insured for 70% of its value. A fire in the building causes a loss of $500,000. If there is a coinsurance clause of 80%, how much will the insurance company pay Johnson?

SOLUTION

$$\frac{\text{Amount carried}}{\text{Amount required}} \times \text{loss} = \text{amount recovered}$$

$$\frac{\$925{,}000 \times 0.7}{(80\%)(\$925{,}000)} \times \$500{,}000 = \$437{,}500$$

12.10 Yates Corp. has a replacement cost of $275,000. It is insured for $200,000 with an 80% coinsurance clause. If the fire loss is $250,000, how much will the insurance company pay?

SOLUTION

$$\frac{\text{Amount carried}}{\text{Amount required}} \times \text{loss} = \text{amount recovered}$$

$$\frac{\$200{,}000}{(80\%)(\$275{,}000)} \times \$250{,}000 = \$227{,}272.73$$

12.11 Bache, Inc. carries 70% insurance coverage on a warehouse valued at $450,000. If the fire loss is $240,000 and there is an 80% coinsurance clause, what will the insurance company pay?

SOLUTION

$$\frac{\text{Amount carried}}{\text{Amount required}} \times \text{loss} = \text{amount recovered}$$

$$\frac{\$450{,}000 \times 0.7}{(80\%)(\$450{,}000)} \times \$240{,}000 = \$210{,}000$$

12.12 A fire does damage to a structure in the amount of $33,000. The building is insured for $50,000 with a market value of $75,000. Find out how much the insurance company will pay (to the nearest dollar) if there is a 75% coinsurance clause.

SOLUTION

$$\frac{\text{Amount carried}}{\text{Amount required}} \times \text{loss} = \text{amount recovered}$$

$$\frac{\$50{,}000}{(75\%)(\$75{,}000)} \times \$33{,}000 = \$29{,}333$$

12.13 PBC Corp. had a fire which caused $98,000 worth of damage. The building was valued at $210,000 and insured for $140,000. With an 80% coinsurance clause (*a*) how much should the building have been insured for; and (*b*) how much did the insurance company pay (to the nearest dollar)?

SOLUTION

(*a*) $0.8 \times \$210{,}000 = \$168{,}000$

(*b*)
$$\frac{\text{Amount carried}}{\text{Amount required}} \times \text{loss} = \text{amount recovered}$$

$$\frac{\$140{,}000}{\$168{,}000} \times \$98{,}000 = \$81{,}667$$

12.14 Ajax Corp. carries insurance on its buildings with three companies: XYZ Co., $25,000; ABC Co., $35,000; and PDG Co., $45,000. Loss from a fire amounts to $68,000. Find how much each insurance company will have to pay (to the nearest dollar).

SOLUTION

$$\$25,000 + \$35,000 + \$45,000 = \$105,000 \quad \text{total coverage}$$

$$\frac{\$25,000}{\$105,000} \times \$68,000 = \$16,190 \quad \text{XYZ Co.}$$

$$\frac{\$35,000}{\$105,000} \times \$68,000 = \$22,667 \quad \text{ABC Co.}$$

$$\frac{\$45,000}{\$105,000} \times \$68,000 = \$29,143 \quad \text{PDQ Co.}$$

12.15 MASTCA, Inc. had a fire which resulted in a loss of $42,500. The following insurance was carried: company A, $20,000; company B, $37,000. Find the amount each insurance company must pay (to the nearest dollar).

SOLUTION

$$\$20,000 + \$37,000 = \$57,000 \quad \text{total coverage}$$

$$\frac{\$20,000}{\$57,000} \times \$42,500 = \$14,912 \quad \text{company A}$$

$$\frac{\$37,000}{\$57,000} \times \$42,500 = \$27,588 \quad \text{company B}$$

12.7   PROPERTY INSURANCE

Property insurance refers to protection against loss of or damage to property. It includes fire, marine, liability, and casualty insurance. Premium rates are generally based upon dollars per $1,000 of coverage. Factors to be considered in determining the rate are location of property, length of time of coverage, and the nature of the note.

EXAMPLE 8

Assume that a company charges $6.25 per $1,000 of coverage. The cost of property insurance based upon $50,000 protection against loss would be computed as follows:

$$\$50,000 \div \$1,000 = 50 \text{ units}$$
$$50 \text{ units} \times \$6.25 = \$312.50$$

SOLVED PROBLEMS

12.16 John Johnson paid an annual insurance premium of $57.75 at the rate of $8 per $1,000. Find the amount of insurance.

SOLUTION

$$\$57.75 \div \$8 = 7.22 \quad \text{units of } \$1,000$$
$$7.22 \times \$1,000 = \$7,220 \quad \text{face value}$$

12.17 The annual insurance premium is $249.50 on $10,000 of insurance. What is the premium rate per $1,000?

SOLUTION

$$\$10,000 \div \$1,000 = 10 \text{ units}$$
$$\$249.50 \div 10 = \$24.95 \text{ per } \$1,000$$

12.18 Merchandise inventory was insured on June 1 for 1 year for $11,000 at $7 per $1,000, and the insured canceled the policy on December 1. Find the amount of the premium refunded if the short-rate penalty was 15% of the annual premium.

SOLUTION

$$\frac{\$11,000}{\$1,000} \times \$7 = \$77 \quad \text{annual premium}$$

$$\$77 \times \tfrac{1}{2}\,\text{yr} = \$38.50 \quad \text{unused premium}$$

$$\$38.50 - (\$77 \times 0.15) = \$26.95 \quad \text{refund}$$

12.19 A house and contents is insured by company A for $35,000 and by company B for $28,000. A loss of $8,500 occurs. If each company has to pay a proportionate amount of this loss, how much does each company pay?

SOLUTION

$$\$35,000 + \$28,000 = \$63,000 \quad \text{total coverage}$$

$$\frac{\$35,000}{\$63,000} \times \$8,500 = \$4,722.22 \quad \text{company A}$$

$$\frac{\$28,000}{\$63,000} \times \$8,500 = \$3,777.78 \quad \text{company B}$$

12.20 GAP, Inc. carries insurance on its property with three companies. Following an explosion, there was property damage of $98,000. Ajax Company carried $150,000; Morris Insurance carried $175,000; and Acme Insurance carried $100,000. Determine the amount of insurance paid by each company.

SOLUTION

$$\$150,000 + \$175,000 + \$100,000 = \$425,000 \quad \text{total coverage}$$

$$\frac{\$150,000}{\$425,000} \times \$98,000 = \$34,588.24 \quad \text{Ajax}$$

$$\frac{\$175,000}{\$425,000} \times \$98,000 = \$40,352.94 \quad \text{Morris}$$

$$\frac{\$100,000}{\$425,000} \times \$98,000 = \$23,058.82 \quad \text{Acme}$$

12.21 Jensen Books Co. incurred a $25,000 loss from water damage on its inventory, which was valued at $65,000. They were insured for $40,000. To the nearest dollar, find the amount recovered from the insurance company.

SOLUTION

$$\frac{\$40,000}{\$65,000} \times \$25,000 = \$15,385$$

12.22 Kelly Corp. pays an annual insurance premium of $159.80 at the rate of $10 per $1,000. What is the amount of the insurance coverage?

SOLUTION

$$\$159.80 \div \$10 = \$15.98 \quad \text{per } \$1,000$$

$$\$15.98 \times \$1,000 = \$15,980 \quad \text{face value}$$

12.8 AUTOMOBILE INSURANCE

Liability means legal responsibility. Anyone who drives or owns a car may be held liable, in the event of an accident, for property damage, medical bills, and for pain and suffering of other people involved, even if the accident is someone else's fault. Several types of insurance are therefore available to car owners.

Bodily injury provides insurance coverage in the event that someone is injured by the owner's auto. A fraction is used to determine the extent of the coverage.

EXAMPLE 9

An automobile insurance policy reads 50/100/10. Each of the three numbers represents a sum of money in thousands of dollars. The 50 means that the insurance company will pay up to $50,000 for injury to one person. The 100 means the company will pay up to a total of $100,000 for injuries to all people involved in the one accident. The 10 means the company will pay up to $10,000 maximum for damage to property.

Collision insurance is designed to protect the car owner against the high costs of repairing any damage to his or her vehicle. The rate charged for the insurance depends upon: (1) driver classification (age, etc.); (2) car size; (3) car age; and (4) deductible clause. A deductible clause of $200 means that the driver must pay the first $200 of the loss. The insurance company will pay the remainder, up to the face value of the policy or value of the car.

EXAMPLE 10

Damages of $950 occurred to Bob's car. If his insurance policy contains a $150-deductible clause, how much will the insurance company pay?

$$\$950 - \$150 \text{ deductible} = \$800$$

Comprehensive insurance protects the car owner from all other possible losses to his or her car (fire, theft, storm, vandalism, etc.).

SOLVED PROBLEMS

12.23 The court awarded Nancy $28,000 for personal injuries received in an auto accident. The insured's policy reads 20/50/5. How much of the court award will the insurance company pay?

SOLUTION

The coverage for one person in an accident is $20,000. Therefore, only $20,000 will be paid by the insurance company. The insured will have to pay the remaining $8,000.

12.24 After an accident, Billy was awarded $14,000 and his son, $9,000. What will the insurance company pay on a 10/20/5 policy?

SOLUTION

The insurance company will cover only $10,000 of Billy's award, since this is the maximum stated on the policy for any one person. The son will collect the $9,000 award in full from the insurance company because (1) the two amounts together (Billy's $10,000 + son's $9,000) do not exceed the $20,000 maximum for all people injured and (2) the award is below the $10,000 limit for one person.

12.25 On a liability policy of 10/20/5, how much will an insurance company pay for body-damage awards of $13,000 and $8,000 for one accident?

SOLUTION

The insurance company will pay $10,000 of the $13,000 award and the full amount of the $8,000 award. (See explanation to Prob. 11.24.)

12.26 Tom damages his car to the extent of $1,600. His policy has a $200 deductible clause. (*a*) What amount will his insurance company pay? (*b*) How much will Tom have to pay?

SOLUTION

(*a*)

$1,600   damages
− 200   deductible
$1,400   insurance company

(*b*) The $200 deductible is the liability of the owner.

12.27 Mary has a 10/20/5 liability policy. She was in an accident in which several people in the other car were injured. A woman was awarded $12,000; her husband, $10,000; their child, $3,000. The damage to their car was set by the court at $2,000. How much will Mary's insurance company pay?

SOLUTION

Since no one person can collect more than $10,000, the woman will receive only $10,000 from Mary's insurance company. The remaining $2,000 is Mary's liability.

The husband and child together were awarded a total of $13,000. The insurance company will pay only $10,000 of the $13,000 since the policy specifies a maximum of $20,000 for all persons injured in a single accident and $10,000 must be paid to the woman. Mary is liable for the additional $3,000 for the husband and child, bringing her personal liability to $5,000 for the accident.

The insurance company will pay the property damage of $2,000 in full because it is less than the $5,000 maximum stated in the policy.

12.28 Frank carries 10/20/5 liability and is at fault in a two-car accident. Damage to the cars is estimated at $1,000 each. Frank's hospital bill totals $600. The court awards the other driver $14,000 and the two passengers $5,000 each. (*a*) How much will the insurance cover? (*b*) How much is Frank's liability?

SOLUTION

(*a*) The insurance company will pay the following:

$10,000   to the other driver (maximum per person)
10,000   total to both passengers ($5,000 each)
 1,000   to other car (not Frank's own since he is at fault)
$21,000   total

(*b*) Frank is liable for:

$4,000   to other driver
  600   to hospital
1,000   damage to his car
$5,600   total

12.29 A driver has a 10/20/5 liability policy, for which the annual premium is $200. The driver wishes to raise the coverage to 20/40/10. The new premium will be 125% of the current premium. How much will the new premium be?

SOLUTION

$$125\% \times \$200 = \$250 \quad \text{premium for the new policy}$$

12.9 LIFE INSURANCE

Many different types of life insurance are available.

A *term* life insurance policy, known as pure insurance, is issued for a specified, limited time, such as 1 year, 5 years, 10 years, or term to age 65. If the insured person dies during the term, the face value of the policy is paid to the beneficiary. However, once the insured period is over, the protection ends and the insured receives nothing.

A *straight* life insurance policy combines life insurance with a savings plan. A fixed payment is made each year until the insured dies. At that time, the value of the contract is paid to the beneficiary. Straight life insurance accumulates cash value, which may be borrowed during the life of the policy or cashed in for retirement benefits.

A *limited payment* policy is similar to straight life insurance, except that payments are made for a specified number of years rather than for the entire life of the insured. Although premium payments cease at the specified maturity date, the policy remains in force until the death of the insured.

An *endowment policy* also has a specified maturity date. It differs from other policies in that the death of the insured is not required for payoff. At the maturity date, the value of the policy is remitted to the insured, if still surviving, otherwise to the beneficiary.

The rates given in Table 12-1 will be used to solve the problems in this chapter.

Table 12-1   Annual Premium Rates per $1,000*

Age at Time of Purchase	10-Year Term	Straight Life	20-Year Limited Payment	20-Year Endowment
20	$ 8.64	$17.26	$27.50	$48.28
21	8.86	17.64	27.98	48.35
22	9.07	18.03	28.48	48.43
23	9.29	18.43	28.98	48.51
24	9.51	18.86	29.51	48.60
25	9.73	19.30	30.05	48.69
30	10.93	21.87	33.02	49.34
35	12.67	25.15	36.54	50.40
40	15.07	29.39	40.80	52.12
45	18.13	34.88	45.95	54.74
50		42.05	42.38	58.78
55		51.53	60.74	65.02
60		64.26	42.04	74.59

*These rates apply to males. For females, use 3 years younger actual age.

From: Maryann Doe and Michael Warlum, *Business Mathematics: A Positive Approach*, Scott, Foresman & Co., Glenview, Ill., 1982, p. 443. Reprinted by permission.

EXAMPLE 11

Betty Star is 33 years old and buys a 20-year endowment policy of $60,000. What is her annual premium?

For women, we must subtract 3 years from the actual age in order to use the table. From the table, we find that a 20-year endowment policy for someone aged 30 has an annual premium rate of $49.34/per $1,000. Therefore:

$$\$49.34 \times \frac{\$60,000}{\$1,000} = \$2,960.40 \quad \text{annual premium}$$

SOLVED PROBLEMS

12.30 What is Joel Grey's annual premium on a 20-year limited payment policy of $20,000 if he is age 50?

SOLUTION

$$\text{Premium rate (from Table 12-1)} = \$42.38/\$1,000$$

$$\$42.38 \times \frac{\$20,000}{\$1,000} = \$847.60$$

12.31 Marcy Cella purchased a $28,000, 20-year endowment policy at age 33. What is her annual premium?

SOLUTION

$$\text{Age} = 33 - 3 = 30$$

$$\text{Premium rate} = \$49.34/\$1,000$$

$$\$49.34 \times \frac{\$28,000}{\$1,000} = \$1,381.52$$

12.32 If John Jay contracts for a $75,000, 10-year term life insurance policy at age 40, what is his annual premium?

SOLUTION

$$\$15.07 \times \frac{\$75,000}{\$1,000} = \$1,130.25$$

12.33 How much will it cost GAP, Inc. in annual premiums for 10-year term policies to insure the following employees? (*a*) Allan Micjac, age 30, for $15,000; (*b*) Janet Linsk, age 24, for $10,000; (*c*) Sylvester Obern, age 35, for $25,000; (*d*) Margaret Svedt, age 28, for $20,000; and (*e*) Marty Ilsip, age 30, for $30,000.

SOLUTION

(*a*)
$$\$10.93 \times \frac{\$15,000}{\$1,000} = \$163.95$$

(*b*)
$$\$8.86 \times \frac{\$10,000}{\$1,000} = \$88.60$$

(*c*)
$$\$12.67 \times \frac{\$25,000}{\$1,000} = \$316.75$$

(*d*)
$$\$9.73 \times \frac{\$20,000}{\$1,000} = \$194.60$$

(*e*)
$$\$10.93 \times \frac{\$30,000}{\$1,000} = \$327.90$$

12.34 John Johnson, age 45, wants to purchase a straight life insurance policy with a face value of $40,000. What will his annual premium be?

SOLUTION

$$\$34.88 \times \frac{\$40,000}{\$1,000} = \$1,395.20$$

12.35 Barbara Kopp (age 25) and Kenneth Klinger (age 30) are partners in a business venture. They decide to take out $45,000, 10-year term insurance policies, declaring each other as beneficiaries. What is the total combined premium?

SOLUTION

$$\$9.07 \times \frac{\$45,000}{\$1,000} = \$408.15$$

$$\$10.93 \times \frac{\$45,000}{\$1,000} = \$491.85$$

$$\$491.85 + \$408.15 = \$900 \quad \text{total}$$

12.36 Jack Durnley, age 40, is trying to decide which life insurance policy he should take out. Find the annual premium on a $40,000 policy under (*a*) straight life, (*b*) 20-limited payment, (*c*) 20-year endowment.

SOLUTION

(*a*)
$$\$29.39 \times \frac{\$40,000}{\$1,000} = \$1,175.60$$

(*b*)
$$\$40.80 \times \frac{\$40,000}{\$1,000} = \$1,632$$

(*c*)
$$\$52.12 \times \frac{\$40,000}{1,000} = \$2,084.80$$

12.37 If you are a 33-year-old female, and you take out a straight life insurance policy of $50,000, how much will you pay each year?

SOLUTION

$$\$21.87 \times \frac{\$50,000}{\$1,000} = \$1,093.50$$

Supplementary Problems

12.38 Larry Lawson purchased a $50,000 fire insurance policy. If the annual premium rate is 46¢ per $100, what is his annual premium?

12.39 Find the annual premium on each of the following fire insurance policies:

(*a*)　$30,000 @ $0.40/$100　　　　(*d*)　$1,580 @ $25.50/$1,000

(*b*)　$12,750 @ $0.75/$100　　　　(*e*)　$20,700 @ $27.80/$1,000

(*c*)　$75,000 @ $35/$1,000

12.40 Lou Halpern purchased a 1-year fire insurance policy on April 15, 19X1, having a premium of $375. The insurance company canceled the policy on October 10, 19X1. How much did Halpern receive as a refund?

12.41 GAP, Inc. purchased a 1-year insurance policy from Glenco Fire Insurance Company on October 1, 19X1. The annual premium was $525. If the company canceled the policy on December 21, 19X1, how much refund did GAP receive?

12.42 Anne Jones has a fire insurance policy with a face value of $150,000. Her annual premium is 95¢ per $100. If she cancels the policy after 300 days, what is her refund?

12.43 Charles Rietz paid $225 annual fire insurance premium. If his property is valued at $80,000, find the rate per $100.

12.44 Kathy Price purchased a $36,000 fire insurance policy at an annual premium rate of 85¢ per $100. Find the cost of the policy.

12.45 A business has a replacement cost estimated at $175,000 and is insured for $125,000. A fire occurs, resulting in a loss of $55,000. Assuming there is an 80% coinsurance clause, how much would the insurance company pay?

12.46 Kelly's Garage is valued at $525,000 and is insured for 75% of its value. After a fire, a loss of $250,000 is found. If there is a coinsurance clause of 80%, how much will the insurance company pay Kelly?

12.47 Yoko, Inc. has a replacement cost of $250,000. It is insured for $200,000, with an 80% coinsurance clause. If the fire loss is $175,000, how much will the insurance company pay?

12.48 SOTH Corp. carries 75% insurance coverage on a warehouse valued at $500,000. If the fire loss is $210,000 and there is an 80% coinsurance clause, what will the insurance company pay?

12.49 A fire damages a building in the amount of $45,000. The building is insured for $60,000, with a market value of $110,000. How much will the insurance company pay if there is a 75% coinsurance clause?

12.50 Jaco Corp. had a fire which did $100,000 damage to a building valued at $250,000 and insured for $150,000. With an 80% coinsurance clause

(a) How much should the building be insured for?

(b) How much did the insurance company pay?

12.51 Acme Corp. carries insurance on its buildings with three companies: XYZ Co., $35,000; ABC Co., $45,000; and PDQ Co., $55,000. Loss from a fire results in $78,500 damage. Find how much each insurance company will pay.

12.52 GAP, Inc. had a fire at its plant, resulting in a $54,000 loss. The following insurance was carried: company A, $25,000; company B, $40,000. How much must each company pay?

12.53 Minnie Morse paid an annual insurance premium of $79.86 at the rate of $9 per $1,000. Find the amount of insurance.

12.54 The annual insurance premium is $467.50 on $15,000 of insurance. What is the premium rate per $1,000?

12.55 Merchandise was insured on March 1 for 1 year for $13,000 at $7.50 per thousand, and the insured canceled the policy on August 1. Find the amount of the premium refunded if the short-rate penalty was 10% of the annual premium.

12.56 A house and contents is insured by company A for $32,000 and by company B for $25,000. A loss of $7,850 occurs. If each company has to pay a proportionate amount of the loss, how much does each company pay?

12.57 Stratton carries insurance on its property with three companies. Following an explosion, there was property damage of $75,000. Ajax Co. carried $125,000; Morris Insurance carried $50,000; and Acme Insurance carried $35,000. Determine the amount of insurance paid by each company.

12.58 The Municipal Library incurred a $42,000 loss from water damage to its books, which were valued at $135,000. The library was insured for $50,000. Find the amount recovered from the insurance company.

12.59   Rolf Corp. pays an annual insurance premium of $249.60 at the rate of $12 per $1,000. What is the amount of the insurance coverage?

12.60   What is Marcus Meehan's annual premium on a 20-limited payment life insurance policy of $40,000 if his age is 45? (Use Table 12-1.)

12.61   Peggy Zimmerman purchased $30,000 of life insurance. Find her annual premium if she is 43 years old and the policy is a 20-year endowment policy.

12.62   If Jay Jones contracts for a $50,000, 10-year term life insurance policy at age 35, what is his annual premium?

12.63   How much will it cost Toys, Ltd. in annual premiums to insure the following employees with 10-year term insurance?

   (*a*)   Joyce Jackson, age 25, $15,000

   (*b*)   John Jones, age 30, $10,000

   (*c*)   Carol King, age 27, $25,000

   (*d*)   Robert Reed, age 45, $20,000

12.64   Robert Reeves, age 40, wants to purchase a straight life insurance policy with a face value of $75,000. What will his annual premium be?

12.65   Roberta Loop (age 33) and Mark Dredd (age 35) are business partners. They decide to take out $30,000, 10-year term insurance policies, declaring each other as beneficiaries. What is the total combined premium?

12.66   Calvin Krebs, age 35, can't decide which life insurance policy he should take. Find the annual premium on a $40,000 policy under

   (*a*)   Straight life

   (*b*)   20-pay life

   (*c*)   20-year endowment

12.67   If you are a 28-year-old female, and you take out a straight life insurance policy of $40,000, how much will you pay each year?

Answers to Supplementary Problems

12.38 $230

12.39   (*a*) $120, (*b*) $95.63, (*c*) $2,625, (*d*) $40.29, (*e*) $575.46

12.40 $192.12

12.41 $407.05

12.42 $253.77

12.43 $0.28/$100

12.44 $306

12.45 $49,107.14

12.46 $234,375

12.47 $175,000

12.48 $196,875

12.49 $32,727.27

12.50   (*a*) $200,000, (*b*) $75,000

12.51   XYZ Co.: $20,351.85, ABC Co.: $26,166.66, PDQ Co.: $31,981.48

12.52   company A: $20,769.23, company B: $33,230.77

12.53 $8,873

12.54 $31.17

12.55 $46.88

12.56   company A: $4,407.02, company B: $3,442.98

12.57   Ajax Co.: $44,642.86, Morris: $17,857.14, Acme: $12,500

12.58 $15,555.56

12.59 $20,800

12.60 $1,838

12.61 $1,563.60

12.62 $633.50

12.63   (*a*) $136.05, (*b*) $109.30, (*c*) $237.75, (*d*) $362.60

12.64 $2,204.25

12.65 $708

12.66   (*a*) $1,006, (*b*) $1,461.60, (*c*) $2,016

12.67 $772

Appendix

Averages

A.1 INTRODUCTION

Averages are frequently discussed in our everyday lives, as well as in business; example, batting averages, average temperature, the average person, average inventory, average cost, average income, etc. An average is a means of presenting a group of numbers in summary form. The three most common averages used are the mean, the median, and the mode.

A.2 MEAN

The mean is the most popular of the three averages and is computed by adding all the numerical figures in a list and dividing by the number of figures in the list. The equation used to compute the mean is

$$M = \frac{S}{N}$$

where M = mean
S = sum of the figures in the list
N = number of figures in the list

Its major advantage is that it takes every value into account. However, when the data contain extreme values, the mean tends to give misleading results.

EXAMPLE 1

What is the mean weekly salary of the following group of employees?

Salary	Number of Employees	Total Amount Earned
$190	2	$ 380
200	1	200
210	2	420
220	4	880
230	2	460
240	1	240
250	1	250
	13	$2,830

The total amount earned by the 13 employees is $2,830 per week. The mean weekly salary is computed as follows:

$$S = \$2,830 \quad \text{and} \quad N = 13$$

$$M = S/N = \$2,830/13 = \$217.70 \text{ (rounded)}$$

SOLVED PROBLEMS

A.1 Find the mean of 57, 196, 461, and 359.

SOLUTION

$$S = 57 + 196 + 461 + 359 = 1,073$$

$$N = 4$$

$$M = S/N = 1,073/4 = 268.25$$

A.2   Joan's Boutique had sales of $156,757 this year. Last year, sales totaled $197,451. Find the mean monthly decrease in sales for this year.

SOLUTION

$$\text{Sales decrease} = \$197{,}451 - \$156{,}757 = \$40{,}694 \text{ for the year}$$

$$S = \$40{,}694$$
$$N = 12 \text{ months}$$
$$M = S/N = \$40{,}694/12 \text{ months} = \$3{,}391.17/\text{mo}$$

A.3   Find the mean of (a) 1,467 and 1,529; (b) 47, 34, 41, and 52; (c) 265, 215, 220, 159, and 198; (d) 7, 14, 8, and 15; (e) 29, 20, 24, 35, 21, and 45.

SOLUTION

(a)
$$S = 1{,}467 + 1{,}529 = 2{,}996 \qquad N = 2$$
$$M = S/N = 2{,}996/2 = 1{,}498$$

(b)
$$S = 47 + 34 + 41 + 52 = 174 \qquad N = 4$$
$$M = S/N = 174/4 = 43.5$$

(c)
$$S = 265 + 215 + 220 + 159 + 198 = 1{,}057 \qquad N = 5$$
$$M = S/N = 1{,}057/5 = 211.4$$

(d)
$$S = 7 + 14 + 8 + 15 = 44 \qquad N = 4$$
$$M = S/N = 44/4 = 11$$

(e)
$$S = 29 + 20 + 24 + 35 + 21 + 45 = 174 \qquad N = 6$$
$$M = S/N = 174/6 = 29$$

A.4   When Fran filled her car with gasoline, the odometer registered 28,562 miles. The next time she filled up, the odometer read 29,250 miles and the car required 14 gallons of gasoline. How many miles did she average on a gallon of gasoline?

SOLUTION

$$\text{Miles traveled} = 29{,}250 - 28{,}562 = 688 \qquad \text{Gallons used} = 14$$
$$S = 688 \text{ mi} \qquad\qquad N = 14 \text{ gal}$$
$$M = S/N = 688 \text{ mi}/14 \text{ gal} = 49.15 \text{ mi/gal}$$

A.5   Find Bentwood's mean daily production of chairs if the number produced in three 6-day work weeks was 51, 42, and 49, respectively.

SOLUTION

$$S = 51 + 42 + 49 = 142 \text{ chairs} \qquad N = 6 \text{ days/wk} \times 3 \text{ wk} = 18 \text{ days}$$
$$M = S/N = 142 \text{ chairs}/18 \text{ days} = 7.89 \text{ chairs/day}$$

A.6   What is the average daily mileage if a delivery truck records 150 miles on Thursday, 125 miles on Friday, and 110 miles on Saturday?

SOLUTION

$$S = 150 \text{ mi} + 125 \text{ mi} + 110 \text{ mi} = 385 \text{ mi} \qquad N = 3 \text{ days}$$
$$M = S/N = 385 \text{ mi}/3 \text{ days} = 128.34 \text{ mi/day}$$

A.7   Jack's Junk Shop is open 7 days a week. If he sold $27,561 in merchandise in the month of October, what was his take per day?

SOLUTION

$$S = \$27,561 \qquad N = 31 \text{ days in Oct.}$$

$$M = S/N = \$27,561/31 \text{ days} = \$889.07/\text{day}$$

A.8   Jackson's Grocery Store had the following monthly sales: Jan., $20,561; Feb., $18,468; Mar., $21,581; Apr., $24,650; May, $25,250; June, $25,798. Find the mean monthly sales.

SOLUTION

$$S = \$20.561 + \$18.468 + \$21,581 + \$24,650 + \$25,250 + \$25,798 = \$136,308$$

$$N = 6 \text{ mo}$$

$$M = S/N = \$136,308/6 \text{ mo} = \$22,718/\text{mo}$$

A.9   A vacuum cleaner salesperson made four calls on Wednesday. Two people were not at home, one was not interested, and one bought a vacuum cleaner for $459.60. Find the salesperson's mean sales for the day.

SOLUTION

$$S = \$459.60 \qquad N = 4 \text{ calls}$$

$$M = S/N = \$459.60/4 = \$114.90$$

A.10   Fred Terris is a traveling salesperson. He logged the following trips in a 5-day week: Mon., 35 miles; Tues., 76 miles; Wed., 125 miles; Thurs., 97 miles; Fri., 51 miles. What was his mean mileage per day?

SOLUTION

$$S = 35 + 76 + 125 + 97 + 51 = 384 \text{ mi} \qquad N = 5 \text{ days}$$

$$M = S/N = 384 \text{ mi}/5 \text{ days} = 76.8 \text{ mi}/\text{day}$$

A.3   MEDIAN

Did you ever notice the sign on a highway that says, "Keep off the median"? The median separates the highway into two equal parts. In statistics, the median serves the same purpose. It is the numerical value that separates a group of numbers in half. In order to find the median, the list of numbers must be placed in ascending or descending order of value. When the list has an *odd* number of figures, the median is the number in the middle of the list. To find it in a long list of figures, we use the formula

$$M = \frac{N+1}{2}$$

where M represents the median and N represents the number of figures in the list.

EXAMPLE 2

Based on the data presented in Example 1, the median salary is computed as follows:

$$M = \frac{N+1}{2} = \frac{13+1}{2} = 7$$

The seventh person's salary in the list is therefore the median. Counting down from the top of the salary list in Example 1, we see that the seventh person earns $220. The median value is therefore $220.

When there is an even number of figures in a list, the median will fall midway between the middle two figures and its value must be estimated.

EXAMPLE 3

Find the median of $180, $140, $170, $150.

$$M = \frac{N+1}{2} = \frac{4+1}{2} = 2.5$$

The median falls between the second and third numbers in the list, which must be arranged in sequential value. To find the median value, add the middle two numbers and divide by 2.

$$
\begin{array}{l}
\$140 \\
\$150 \\
\$170 \\
\$180
\end{array}
\quad\longleftarrow \text{Median} = \frac{\$150 + \$170}{2} = \$160
$$

The advantage of the median is that it is easy to compute and not affected by extremes. However, it tends to give misleading results if the data are composed of two distinct groups, one high in value and the other low. In this case the median might fall in either the high-value or the low-value group, rather than *between* the two groups, where an average should be.

EXAMPLE 4

Salary	Number of Employees	Total Amount Earned
$120	1	$ 120
125	2	250
130	1	130
400	1	400
410	1	410
420	1	420
	7	$1730

$$M = \frac{N+1}{2} = \frac{7+1}{2} = 4$$

The fourth person in the list earns a salary of $130. However, the median value of $130 is *not* a true indication of the average since it is not the middle value between the two groups of numbers. In contrast, the mean would be

$$M = S/N = \$1,730/7 = \$247$$

Because of the nature of the data, the mean gives the more accurate average in this case.

SOLVED PROBLEMS

A.11 Find the median for the following weekly net sales: $215.75; $320.33; $510.25; $221.64; $329.40.

SOLUTION

$$M = \frac{N+1}{2} = \frac{5+1}{2} = 3$$

$$
\begin{array}{l}
\$215.75 \\
\$221.64 \\
\$320.33 \longleftarrow \text{Median} \\
\$329.40 \\
\$510.25
\end{array}
$$

A.12 Find the median for the following test grades: 98; 76; 85; 74.

SOLUTION

$$M = \frac{N+1}{2} = \frac{4+1}{2} = 2.5$$

74

76 ⟵ ——————— Median $= \frac{76+85}{2} = \frac{161}{2} = 80.5$

85

98

A.13 There are 10 employees in the Horvath Co. Their hourly rates are $7.60, $7.20, $6.70, $6.50, $6.40, $6.20, $6.20, $6.20, $5.90, and $5.60. Find the median hourly rate.

SOLUTION

$$M = \frac{N+1}{2} = \frac{10+1}{2} = 5.5$$

$7.60

$7.20

$6.70

$6.50

$6.40

⟵ ———————Median $= \frac{\$6.40+6.20}{2} = \frac{\$12.60}{2} = \$6.30$

$6.20

$6.20

$6.20

$5.90

$5.60

A.14 Find the median salary for the following payroll: $6,500; $7,200; $7,500; $6,700; $6,200; $6,000.

SOLUTION

$$M = \frac{N+1}{2} = \frac{6+1}{2} = 3.5$$

$7,500

$7,200

$6,700

$6,500 ⟵ ——————— Median $= \frac{\$6,700+\$6,500}{2} = \frac{\$13,200}{2} = \$6,600$

$6,200

$6,000

A.15 Find the median attendance for the following schools: school A, 200,000; school B, 94,000; school C, 120,000; school D, 127,000; school E, 193,500.

SOLUTION

$$M = \frac{N+1}{2} = \frac{5+1}{2} = 3$$

94,000

120,000

127,000 ⟵——————— Median

193,500

200,000

A.16 Murray's Market delivery truck recorded the following mileage in a 5-day week: Monday, 81 miles; Tuesday, 137 miles; Wednesday, 95 miles; Thursday, 121 miles; Friday, 82 miles. What is the median mileage?

SOLUTION

$$M = \frac{N+1}{2} = \frac{5+1}{2} = 3$$

81
82
95 ←——————— Median
121
137

A.17 Josie Brown works as a bookkeeper for Scanlan Enterprises. Monthly sales figures for the last 8 months were: $14,569, $14,400, $13,995, $14,768, $12,560, $12,888, $13,550, and $11,000. Find the median.

SOLUTION

$$M = \frac{N+1}{2} = \frac{8+1}{2} = 4.5$$

$11,000
$12,560
$12,888
$13,550
$13,995   ←——— Median $= \frac{\$13,550 + \$13,995}{2} = \frac{\$27,545}{2} = \$13,772.50$
$14,400
$14,569
$14,768

A.18 The monthly payrolls for Gilbey's Corp. are as follows:

Jan.	$9,456	May	$9,680	Sept.	$10,450
Feb.	$8,279	June	$10,420	Oct.	$9,620
Mar.	$8,798	July	$11,200	Nov.	$8,480
Apr.	$7,143	Aug.	$10,590	Dec.	$8,225

Find the median.

SOLUTION

$$M = \frac{N+1}{2} = \frac{12+1}{2} = 6.5$$

$7,143
$8,225
$8,279
$8,480
$8,798
$9,456
$9,620   ←——— Median $= \frac{\$9,620 + \$9,456}{2} = \frac{\$19,076}{2} = \$9,538$
$9,680
$10,420
$10,450
$10,590
$11,200

A.19 Find the median for each of the following:

	(a)	(b)	(c)
	75	46	89
	58	12	91
	37	89	9
	72	40	88
	45	35	10
	18	14	92
	53	89	88
	45	38	90
	15	22	93
	32	59	95
		54	90
			11

SOLUTION

(a) $M = \dfrac{N+1}{2}$

$= \dfrac{10+1}{2}$

$= 5.5$

15
18
32
37
45
$\longleftarrow$ Median $= \dfrac{45+45}{2}$
45       $= 90/2$
53       $= 45$
58
72
75

(b) $M = \dfrac{N+1}{2}$

$= \dfrac{11+1}{2}$

$= 6$

12
14
22
35
38
40 $\longleftarrow$ Median
46
54
59
89
89

(c) $M = \dfrac{N-1}{2}1$

$= \dfrac{12+1}{2}$

$= 6.5$

9
10
11
88
88
89
$\longleftarrow$ Median $= \dfrac{89+90}{2}$
90       $= 179/2$
90       $= 89.5$
91
92
93
95

A.20 Piper Co. has 22 employees. Their hourly rates are:

$8.00	$6.50	$6.00
$7.50	$6.30	$5.90
$7.50	$6.20	$5.90
$7.20	$6.20	$5.80
$6.50	$6.10	$5.60
$6.50	$6.10	$5.50
$6.50	$6.10	$5.50
		$5.40

Find the median hourly rate.

SOLUTION

$$M = \frac{N+1}{2} = \frac{22+1}{2} = 11.5$$

The median value lies between the eleventh and twelfth hourly rates. The eleventh rate is $6.20. The twelfth rate is $6.10.

$$\text{Median salary} = \frac{\$6.20 + \$6.10}{2} = \frac{\$12.30}{2} = \$6.15$$

A.4 MODE

The mode is the number that occurs most frequently in a list of figures. There are no calculations for finding the mode. Just look over the data to find the number that appears most often.

EXAMPLE 5

Based upon the information in Example 1, the model salary would be $220 because this salary occurs most frequently.

For statistical purposes, the mode need not be numerical. For example, if a poll were taken of men in the state of Connecticut and disclosed that most favor blue-green over any other color combination, then blue-green would be the modal combination for men in Connecticut.

Of the three averages presented, the mode is the simplest to find and is not affected by extreme values. Its disadvantage is that it provides the least statistically accurate answer.

SOLVED PROBLEMS

A.21   Find the mode of the following group of examination grades.

86	95	85
95	85	87
74	86	94
57	69	85

SOLUTION

There are three grades of 85.

A.22   What is the mode of the following payroll?

$4,700	$5,800	$5,600
$5,600	$4,700	$4,700
$6,500	$5,000	$5,100

SOLUTION

There are three salaries of $4,700.

A.23   Find the mode for the following hourly wages at Greystone Co.:

$1.20	$1.62	$2.72	$2.27
$2.12	$1.74	$2.21	$2.04
$2.11	$1.85	$1.82	$3.14
$2.15	$1.93	$1.81	$1.86
$2.04	$2.03	$2.01	$1.77

SOLUTION

There are two hourly wages of $2.04.

A.24 What is your mode in an economics class if you receive the following grades: 85, 92, 73, 63, 84, 98, 73, 78?

SOLUTION

There are two grades of 73.

A.25 XYZ Corporation had the following monthly sales:

Jan.	$28,562
Feb.	$25,480
Mar.	$25,470
Apr.	$28,562
May	$29,452

Find the mode.

SOLUTION

There are two months with sales of $28,562.

A.26 Find the mode age of the following groups of students:

(a)	(b)	(c)
16	29	41
17	28	40
18	31	40
17	32	42
18	31	43
16	30	42
17	27	42
18		
18		

SOLUTION

(a) There are four ages of 18.

(b) There are two ages of 31.

(c) There are three ages of 42.

A.27 Jerri Lynn works as an account clerk for Bendicks Co. Monthly sales figures for the year were: $12,800; $12,450; $12,050; $11,750; $12,450; $10,000; $10,500; $10,100; $11,500; $12,450; $11,250; $10,000. Find (a) the mean, (b) the median, (c) the mode.

SOLUTION

(a)
$$M = S/N$$
$$= \$137,300/12 = \$11,441.67$$

(b)
$$M = \frac{N+1}{2}$$
$$= \frac{12+1}{2} = 6.5$$

$12,800

$12,450

$12,450

$12,450

$12,050

$11,750

$11,500   ←————————————— Median $= \dfrac{\$11,750 + \$11,500}{2} = \dfrac{\$23,250}{2} = \$11,625$

$11,250

$10,500

$10,100

$10,000

$10,000

(c)   There are three figures of $12,450.

A.28   Find the (a) mean, (b) median, and (c) mode for the following hourly wages:

$3.35	$3.90	$4.25
$3.40	$4.00	$4.50
$3.45	$4.00	$4.25
$3.35	$4.25	$4.75

SOLUTION

(a)
$$M = S/N$$
$$= \$47.42/12 = \$3.95$$

(b)
$$M = \frac{N+1}{2}$$
$$= \frac{12+1}{2} = 6.5$$

$3.35

$3.35

$3.40

$3.45

$3.90

$4.00

$4.00   ←————————————— Median $= \dfrac{\$4 + \$4}{2} = \$4$

$4.25

$4.25

$4.25

$4.50

$4.75

(c)   There are three figures at $4.25.

A.29   Find the (a) mean, (b) median, and (c) mode of the following group of business math grades: 87; 89; 94; 98; 69; 73; 87; 79; 84; 87.

SOLUTION

(*a*)
$$M = S/N$$
$$= 847/10 = 84.7$$

(*b*)
$$M = \frac{N+1}{2}$$
$$= \frac{10+1}{2} = 5.5$$

69
73
79
84
87 ⟵──────── Median = $\frac{87+87}{2}$ = 87
87
87
89
94
98

(*c*)   There are three grades of 87.

A.30   The ages of students in a business math class are as follows: 16; 17; 18; 17; 29; 18; 17; 24; 21; 17. Find the (*a*) mean, (*b*) median, and (*c*) mode.

SOLUTION

(*a*)
$$M = S/N$$
$$= 194/10 = 19.4$$

(*b*)
$$M = \frac{N+1}{2}$$
$$= \frac{10+1}{2} = 5.5$$

16
17
17
17
17
18 ⟵──────── Median = $\frac{17+18}{2} = \frac{35}{2}$ = 17.5
18
21
24
29

(*c*)   There are four ages at 17.

Supplementary Problems

A.31   Find the mean of 98, 147, 521, 256, and 412.

A.32   Janet's Junk Shop had sales of $255,560 this year. Last year they were $290,420. Find the mean monthly decrease in sales this year.

A.33   Find the mean of

    (*a*)   1,569 and 1,968   (*d*)   9, 41, 6, and 51

    (*b*)   36, 43, 14, and 25   (*e*)   92, 50, 42, 53, 12, and 54

    (*c*)   562, 512, 120, 951, and 891

A.34   When Frank filled his car with gasoline, the odometer read 24,563. The next time he filled up, the car required 11 gallons. If the odometer read 24,802, how many miles did he average on a gallon of gasoline?

A.35   Find the mean average daily production of doghouses if the number produced in three 6-day weeks was 18, 24, and 29, respectively.

A.36   What is the average daily mileage if a delivery truck records the following mileage in a 5-day period? Monday, 120 miles; Tuesday, 125 miles; Wednesday, 115 miles; Thursday, 121 miles; Friday, 125 miles.

A.37   Jackson's Boutique is open 7 days a week. If it sold $17, 429 in merchandise for the month of November, what was its mean sales per day?

A.38   Ken's Grocery Mart had the following monthly sales: January, $15,420; February, $14,980; March, $15,260; April, $17,291; May, $17,989; June, $21,457. Find the mean monthly sales.

A.39   An encyclopedia salesperson made calls last Tuesday. One person was not home, one person was not interested, and three persons purchased sets of encyclopedias at $349.27 each. Find his mean average sales for the day.

A.40   Connie Collins is a traveling salesperson. If she logged the following trips in a 5-day week, what was her mean average mileage per day? Monday, 51 miles; Tuesday, 48 miles; Wednesday, 57 miles; Thursday, 69 miles; Friday, 73 miles.

A.41   Find the median for the following weekly net sales: $569.28; $421.42; $496.43; $397.86; 437.41.

A.42   Find the median for the following test grades: 75; 68; 99; 100; 66; 82.

A.43   Howell Co. has 10 employees whose hourly rates are: $7.00; $6.95; $6.95; $6.50; $6.50; $6.25; $6.15; $6.15; $6.15; $6.00. Find the median hourly rate.

A.44   Find the median salary on the following payroll: $7,250; $6,800; $7,500; $6,800; $7,000; $6,850.

A.45   Find the median attendance for the following schools: school A, 256,000; school B, 149,000; school C, 180,500; school D, 126,429; school E, 212,568.

A.46   Joe Brown's delivery truck recorded the following mileage in a 6-day week: Monday, 82 miles; Tuesday, 115 miles; Wednesday, 129 miles; Thursday, 98 miles; Friday, 63 miles; Saturday, 126 miles. Find the median mileage.

A.47   Monthly sales figures of Scott's Market for the last 8 months were: $12,461; $12,249; $13,586; $14,629; $12,506; $15,468; $14,250; $12,369. Find the median monthly sales.

A.48 The monthly payrolls for Gilbert's Agency are:

Jan.	$8,560	May	$ 9,500	Sept.	$9,680
Feb.	$7,979	June	$ 8,998	Oct.	$8,540
Mar.	$8,640	July	$10,460	Nov.	$7,850
Apr.	$7,868	Aug.	$10,525	Dec.	$7,960

Find the median.

A.49 Find the medians for the following groups of numbers.

(a)	68	(b)	46	(c)	26
	46		59		39
	53		73		29
	96		54		42
	42		69		53
	58		47		29
	73		59		27
	91				29

A.50 Potts Co. has 16 employees at the following hourly rates:

$9.00	$7.40	$8.28
$8.75	$7.50	$8.15
$9.00	$7.95	$8.15
$8.85	$7.50	$8.10
$9.20	$7.50	$7.95
		$8.00

Find the median hourly rate.

A.51 Find the mode of the following group of examination grades: 87; 96; 75; 58; 96; 86; 87; 60; 86; 88; 95; 86.

A.52 Find the mode of the following payroll: $4,800; $5,700; $6,600; $5,900; $4,800; $5,100; $3,700; $4,800; $5,200.

A.53 Find the mode of the following hourly wages at ZERO, Inc.: $3.35; $3.40; $3.80; $4.60; $3.90; $4.50; $3.90; $4.50; $3.90; $4.50; $4.25; $4.50; $4.75; $4.50; $3.80; $3.75; $4.95; $4.85.

A.54 Find your mode in a business math class if you receive the following grades: 86; 93; 74; 64; 85; 99; 74; 79.

A.55 Find the mode for the following monthly sales for ABC Co.: January, $27,265; February, $25,480; March, $25,840; April, $27,265; May, $26,480.

A.56 Find the mode age of each of the following groups of students:

(a)	17	(b)	30	(c)	42
	18		29		41
	19		32		41
	18		33		43
	19		32		44
	17		31		43
	18		28		43
	19				
	19				

A.57   John Block works as an account clerk for XYA Co. Monthly sales figures for the year were: $12,900; $12,550; $12,150; $11,850; $12,550; $10,100; $10,600; $10,200; $11,600; $12,550; $11,350; $10,100. Find the (*a*) mean, (*b*) median, and (*c*) mode.

A.58   Find the (*a*) mean, (*b*) median, and (*c*) mode for the following hourly wages: $3.40; $3.45; $3.50; $3.40; $3.95; $4.05; $4.05; $4.30; $4.30; $4.55; $4.30; $4.80.

A.59   Find the (*a*) mean, (*b*) median, and (*c*) mode for the following group of statistics grades: 88; 90; 95; 99; 70; 74; 88; 80; 85; 88.

A.60   The ages of students in an economics class are as follows: 17; 18; 19; 18; 29; 19; 18; 24; 22; 18. Find the (*a*) mean, (*b*) median, and (*c*) mode.

Answers to Supplementary Problems

A.31   286.8

A.32 $2,905

A.33   (*a*) 1,768.5, (*b*) 29.5, (*c*) 607.2, (*d*) 26.75, (*e*) 50.5

A.34   21.73

A.35   3.94

A.36   121.2

A.37 $580.97

A.38 $17,066.17

A.39 $209.56

A.40   59.6

A.41 $437.41

A.42   78.5

A.43 $6.38

A.44 $6,925

A.45   180,500

A.46   106.5

A.47 $13,046

A.48 $8,645

A.49 (*a*) 63, (*b*) 59, (*c*) 29

A.50 $8.13

A.51 86

A.52 $4,800

A.53 $4.50

A.54 74

A.55 $27,265

A.56 (*a*) 19, (*b*) 32, (*c*) 43

A.57 (*a*) $11,541.67, (*b*) $11,725, (*c*) $12,550

A.58 (*a*) $4, (*b*) $4.05, (*c*) $4.30

A.59 (*a*) 85.7, (*b*) 88, (*c*) 88

A.60 (*a*) 20.2, (*b*) 18.5, (*c*) 18

Index